THE DEFIANT LIFE OF
Vera Figner

THE DEFIANT
LIFE OF
Vera Figner

SURVIVING THE RUSSIAN REVOLUTION

LYNNE ANN HARTNETT

INDIANA UNIVERSITY PRESS

Bloomington & Indianapolis

This book is a publication of
Indiana University Press
Office of Scholarly Publishing
Herman B Wells Library 350
1320 East 10th Street
Bloomington, Indiana 47405 USA

iupress.indiana.edu

Telephone   800-842-6796
Fax   812-855-7931

♾ The paper used in this publication meets
the minimum requirements of the American National Standard for Information
Sciences—Permanence of Paper for Printed
Library Materials, ANSI Z39.48–1992.

Manufactured in the United States of
America

Library of Congress Cataloging-in-
Publication Data

Hartnett, Lynne Ann, author.
    The defiant life of Vera Figner : surviving
the Russian revolution / Lynne Ann
Hartnett.
        pages ; cm
    Includes bibliographical references and
index.
    ISBN 978-0-253-01284-5 (cl : alk. paper)—
ISBN 978-0-253-01394-1 (eb) 1. Figner, Vera,
1852–1942. 2. Women revolutionaries—
Russia—Biography. 3. Women socialists—
Russia—Biography. 4. Women socialists—
Soviet Union—Biography. I. Title.
    HX313.8.F54H37 2014
    335'.83092—dc23
    [B]

                                    2013046385

1 2 3 4 5 19 18 17 16 15 14

For Paul, Brendan, Ryan, and Camryn

CONTENTS

10

An Old Revolutionary in a New Revolution

11

Revolutionary Survivor

ACKNOWLEDGMENTS

For the last several years, my husband and children have grown accustomed to a familiar refrain in our house: the sound of my voice uttering the words "as soon as my book is done." So now, as this book goes to press, it appears that I will be painting the rooms, organizing the closets, and filling the photo albums that have awaited my attention for far too long. I have postponed all of these tasks, some more gleefully than others, and spent my days and many late nights with a rather exacting, impatient Russian woman. For more years than I care to admit, Vera Figner has demanded a great deal of my attention. As I tried to balance Vera's claim upon my time with my other professional and personal responsibilities, I realized what she understood more than a century ago; that is, few things in life that are truly worthwhile and rewarding are ever done alone.

I suspect that most people who write only casually don't realize the extent to which writing is a collaborative process. Although I physically wrote this manuscript stowed away in isolation in my office, the foundations of its strongest elements were born and/or nurtured with friends, students, and colleagues at various conference presentations, around seminar tables, over lunch, in colleagues' offices, and in the hallway of the St. Augustine Center at Villanova University. I have had the wonderful fortune to benefit from the guidance, insight, and direction of a great many people. Although any shortcomings of the book are mine alone, the manuscript's strengths certainly resulted in no small measure from the productive, affirming, collective endeavors that define my professional life.

Two of the men who proved instrumental in the development of this project passed away before it was completed. Raymond McNally was always an inspiration and a delight. He introduced me to Vera and indulged my developing fascination with this woman. In spite of the daunting prospects associated with writing a biography, he was a tireless champion of the project and of my historical career. I learned many things from Ray McNally but perhaps the most important lesson that he taught me was that historical scholarship should be fun. The second scholar in whose debt I will always remain is Richard Stites. He provided me with invaluable guidance and advice as I delved into Vera's life, assured me that the world did indeed need a critical biography of Vera Figner, and convinced me that I should be the one to write it.

Roberta Manning brought a keen eye to the manuscript in its early stages, and her insights have stayed with me. She proved a staunch ally and a source of inspiration. Carol Petillo taught me invaluable lessons about the methodology of historical life narratives and gender analysis. Her delight as the book took shape was infectious and sustained me when progress temporarily stalled.

It has been my tremendous good fortune to find myself at Villanova University. Here I have discovered colleagues and friends who demonstrate the highest level of scholarship and collegiality. Adele Lindenmeyr has been the greatest mentor that I could ever imagine. Her knowledge of Russian history and her parallel journey in biography have helped me tremendously. Adele has been tireless in her support of my scholarship and my academic career; I treasure her insight and her friendship more than I can say. Through his example Paul Steege consistently reminds me of the hallmarks of great scholarship and stellar writing. His attention to detail, as well as his astute theoretical insights, have been invaluable. The ongoing conversations about history, teaching, research, and scholarship that I have shared with Adele, Paul, Judith Giesberg, Craig Bailey, Marc Gallicchio, Catherine Kerrison, Tim McCall, and Paul Rosier have enriched my biography and sweetened the journey immensely.

I owe a great debt to the anonymous readers secured by Indiana University Press; their comments guided my revisions and redirected me in several critical areas. I am most grateful for the precise, clever comments made by Ann Hibner Koblitz. She devoted a great deal of time to reading the manuscript, and I reaped extraordinary insights from her scholarly generosity. I have admired the work of Barbara Clements since my first days in graduate school, so it was a tremendous honor that she read my work. Her comments about and suggestions for my manuscript reinforced my admiration for her and confirmed that my respect for her work was well deserved.

I always will be tremendously grateful to Janet Rabinowitch for the encouragement and patience that she showed to me, and for the tireless devotion that she demonstrated toward the publication of this project. When Janet announced her retirement, I was disheartened that she wouldn't be there when

Vera finally went to press. However, Janet left Vera and me in the wonderful hands of Raina Polivka, Darja Malcolm-Clarke, Peter Froehlich, and Jill R. Hughes, whose individual talents and wonderful attention collectively guided the last stages of the publishing process. I also would like to thank Jehanne Gheith and Louise McReynolds for offering professional guidance when it was needed the most. Thanks are similarly due to Tim Wessel, who read several chapters of the manuscript in its final stages of production. His smart comments and prompts to remember the readers who are not Russian historians kept me well grounded and inspired me to enhance the narrative.

I would be remiss if I didn't thank Christine Filiberti, Jutta Seibert, Barbara Joyce, Olga Foltz, Marina Dobronovkaia, Lawrence Clifford, Stephanie Lisle, Dana Isley, Kyle Robinson, Alexandra Webster, and Jacqueline Beatty. All rendered great assistance at various stages of the research and writing process. My gratitude similarly extends to the librarians and archivists at the State Archives of the Russian Federation, the Russian State Archive of Literature and Art, the Russian State Historical Archive, the Lenin Library, the International Institute of Social History, the Hoover Institution Archives, Falvey Library, and the New York Public Library. I am also grateful for the Villanova University History Faculty Research Fund and the Lepage Research Fund that allowed me to take several last-minute trips to archives in order to gain access to crucial collections.

I could not have finished this book without the invaluable help provided me by my family and friends. Pat Wessel, Kaitlyn Wessel, Evan Wessel, and Mary Kay Meeks-Hank invariably gave of themselves to lend a hand in countless, unexpected ways and provided last minute child care at critical moments. You are my village and I am eternally grateful.

My parents did not live to see the publication of this book. Though endowed with great talents, my mom never had the opportunity to realize her professional potential. Patricia McGarry channeled everything into her children. This book is just one of many manifestations of her tireless dedication and inspiration. My father, Thomas F. McGarry, always called Vera the Russian Molly Pitcher. While the analogy is questionable, his interest and pride in my project delighted me and inspired me to return to Vera after several years away from her.

Living with me over this past decade has entailed living with Vera Figner as well. Thus, all of my children have lived with the specter of Vera since they were born. Brendan, Ryan, and Camryn embraced this challenge and often

saw it as an opportunity. They answered my all too frequent absences and distractions with support and love. Their attitude and pride sustained me.

My greatest debt is to my husband, Paul Hartnett. Paul has been at my side
and has been my inspiration for more than twenty-five years. His patience with
my scholarly endeavors is endless and his emotional support unfailing. Paul
avidly read this manuscript at many of its stages. Realizing that I had several
people who would offer constructive criticism, Paul decided (purposefully,
I suspect) to render me only praise. His confidence in me and in this project
allowed me to return to Vera and gave me the self-confidence to see her biography through to its completion. In spite of the logistic difficulties involved
in balancing our jobs, our children, our dogs, our home, and this book, Paul
remained my perpetual champion, always willing to give me support, understanding, and love. There is no greater gift.

INTRODUCTION

Vera Figner was supposed to die in 1884. A tsarist court declared it; Vera herself expected and even welcomed it. Although she would have been only the second woman in more than a century to die on the scaffold by decree of the Russian state, her notoriety and prominence within the terrorist group the People's Will was such that few people expected leniency for the condemned criminal. If the sentence decreed by an imperial military tribunal in October 1884 had stood, newspapers across Europe would have noted Vera Figner's execution and most likely recounted the dramatic and seemingly tragic turns that the notoriously beautiful young woman's life had taken in the previous decades. Journalists would have found it hard to resist regaling their readers with the details of this beguiling revolutionary's life, as it poetically seemed to symbolize the fervor, promise, idealism, and desperation of a generation of Russian radicals. In childhood Figner seemed destined for a life of privilege as a member of the Imperial Russian nobility. But amid the turbulent decade in which she came of age, Vera exchanged privilege for political radicalism; abandoned legal, professional aspirations for a life in the revolutionary underground; and foreswore marital ties for a desperate plot to assassinate the Russian tsar. She certainly was not alone in her beliefs, her dedication, or her willingness to die for her cause, but she was exceptional for the seamless manner in which her life and commitment personified her age of political radicals and exemplified the ideals to which her generation aspired. In the late 1870s and early 1880s, Vera Nikolaevna Figner was at the center of a movement and a series of events that transformed the political landscape in Russia and ultimately changed the empire of the tsars irrevocably.

If she had died in 1884, Vera Figner's life would be significant for what it conveys about Russian noblewomen who came of age in the twilight of the era of serfdom and for what it indicates about those among them who pursued education as a means of intellectual and moral autonomy and a path to economic

independence. Even if it had ended when she was thirty-two, Vera's life would
have historical importance for the insight it provides into the motivation that
drove such a significant number of young, privileged Russians to embrace terrorism as a solution to the country's ills. As a leader of the revolutionary organization the People's Will, Vera Figner helped to change the course of Russian history through the 1881 assassination of the most powerful man in the
country, the Tsar Liberator, Alexander II.

Yet Vera Figner did not die in 1884. After Alexander III, the son and heir of
the man she helped to murder, commuted her death sentence to life in prison
at hard labor, her life continued, as did her revolutionary influence. Although
the tsarist state resolved to bury her alive in Shlisselburg Fortress, a notorious prison known as the Russian Bastille, Vera's two decades of incarceration became an essential element of her revolutionary identity and infused the
subsequent narrative of revolution both before and after 1917. Vera survived
Shlisselburg; in fact, she lived for almost six decades after her death sentence
was declared and survived the regime that she had sought to topple.

After her release from Shlisselburg, Vera Figner wrote voluminously about
her life. As an introspective and prolific chronicler of her revolutionary experiences, her life writings provide a window into situations and experiences
usually shrouded in silence and offer details about events normally defined by
conjecture and supposition. With her homeland wracked by upheaval, revolution, and civil war, Vera's story of political idealism; reckless, radical commitment; and years of sacrifice and suffering took on monumental proportions. By studying both her life and her retelling of it, we can access an often
unexplored side to the Russian Revolution and uncover the ways that revolutionary lives and legacies were manipulated to construct foundational myths
for the Russian revolutionary movement and the Socialist state that came into
being in October 1917. By analyzing the construction of Vera Figner, the revolutionary legend, we gain insight into how revolutionary narrative was gendered and how notions of femininity and feminine virtue were reconstructed
in a revolutionary milieu to form a leitmotif for appropriate revolutionary behavior that carried through 1917.

Although she was in her sixties and in fragile health when the Bolshevik
Revolution occurred, Vera survived the dislocations of the subsequent period.
She survived devastating food shortages, civil war, and Stalin's Great Purges,
in which the Communist leader executed and exiled millions of Soviet citi-

zens for mostly imagined political crimes. In spite of chronic illness, Vera remained socially active for the first two decades of Soviet rule until old age and
health concerns made a public existence impossible. As a prolific writer, humanitarian, and advocate for cultural and educational initiatives, Vera Figner's life is significant for what it illustrates about the opportunities for and
limits of social and cultural initiatives on the part of non-Communist Soviet
citizens in the early Soviet period. As a veritable icon of the revolution, Vera
became a living symbol whose perseverance, survival, and self-constructed
life narrative of sacrifice defined revolutionary heroism and martyrdom for a
generation and became a model of appropriate revolutionary behavior for the
new Soviet woman.

More than a half century after her death, this former terrorist's name continues to evoke memories of daring, self-sacrifice, and often dubiously violent
actions. Yet despite her notoriety and her involvement in so many historically
significant events, until the present study there has never been a scholarly biography of Figner. During the Soviet period, the myth of Vera Figner in its
broadest contours was more useful to Marxist-Leninist doctrine than the reality of this remarkable woman's existence and political outlook. Thus, although almost all Russian citizens are aware of this revolutionary icon, few if
any have a grasp of the woman behind the legend or a historical understanding of the circumstances that determined the contours and significance of the
legend itself. This book seeks to right that situation.

Sources for this study include a wealth of archival documents in Moscow,
St. Petersburg, Amsterdam, and the United States; revolutionary periodicals;
press reports; memoir literature; and secondary works on a variety of subjects
related to Vera Figner's life and revolutionary career. Not surprisingly, Vera's
own recollections of her life loom large. With seven volumes of published
autobiographical writings, she attempted to craft the final historical version
of her life. Undoubtedly, she would be displeased that an American historian
was deconstructing her version of events. But an essential part of her biography is the manner in which she attempted to write her own definitive life account. Never admitting the uncertainties that came from memory lapses or
the doubts that derived after long introspection, Vera described her entire life
story until the Bolshevik Revolution of 1917 as a coherent and logical narrative
in which her social consciousness once aroused came to dictate every significant choice and action. But this was far from the case. In fact, I argue that the

manner in which she told the story of her life conveys as much about her position as a Russian revolutionary woman of her generation as do her specific
actions and associations.

While Vera crafted her memoirs, perhaps unwittingly, according to some
literary standards of the time,[1] she also went to great lengths to justify her radicalism as she wrote under the long shadow of the Bolsheviks.[2] Many of the
details she conveys are as much trope as truth. To a certain extent this tendency is an almost inevitable function of autobiographical writing. But given
the political violence she advocated and abetted, especially given the ultimate
inefficacy of the People's Will, her natural impetus to explain and justify is
all the more pronounced and potentially misleading. While one might expect
that Vera's account of her childhood would be devoid of a political agenda,
its similarity to the remembrances of other radicals' early years demonstrates
the extent to which the Russian revolutionary narrative was born in its authors' conception of their childhoods. Although the biography and recollections of Vera's younger brother Nikolai does indeed corroborate some of the
most pertinent details of the Figner family and household, many of the anecdotes and personalities Vera describes in reference to her childhood must be
viewed with a good measure of skepticism. Thus, her description of her family
and youth is more instructive as an analytical tool for uncovering this generation of revolutionaries' feelings toward privilege and patriarchy in Imperial
Russia than it is for the concrete details it conveys.

Scholars of Russian women owe a tremendous debt to some of the pioneers in the field. Without the efforts of Barbara Alpern Engel, Richard Stites,
Barbara Clements, Ann Hibner Koblitz, Jay Bergman, Christine Faure, Amy
Knight, Christine Johanson, Margaret Maxwell, Elena Pavliuchenko, and
Sheila Rowbotham, this book would certainly be less informed. It was, after
all, these scholars who reminded their readers that women were indeed involved in the Russian revolutionary movement and actually influenced its
contours and dynamics. In spite of the efforts made by individual radicals,
like Vera Figner, to convince the world that having crossed the threshold and
joined the revolutionary movement, gender ceased to be a factor, the careful
and perceptive work of historians, especially those noted above, demonstrated
that the revolution both before and after 1917 had very definite gendered di-
mensions.

Publishing this biography in a post–September 11 world puts the violent
activities in which Vera Figner engaged in a new perspective. With the dis-

tance of more than a century, it is possible for the modern reader to justify and understand the use of violence and murder by the People's Will. One can be swept away by the high price that Vera's generation paid in prison and on the scaffold for their political ideals. But there are significant parallels between these nineteenth-century terrorists and their twenty-first-century counter-parts, and these similarities demand attention. Vera Figner and the other members of *Narodnaia Volia* (The People's Will) were radical zealots whose un-wavering dedication to the liberation of their homeland, as they defined it, made bloodshed and death immaterial. Subsequently, a detailed analysis of this group and its members has strategic significance for a modern world try-ing to understand and confront the threat emanating from violent extremists.

Although this infamous revolutionary's life has been called the history of the People's Will organization,[3] I do not pretend that the present study is an exhaustive examination of this terrorist group. I am interested in presenting the history of the People's Will through the experiences of Vera Figner. While I concede that Vera's career as a terrorist was essential, her revolutionary ex-perience and significance transcend this period of her life. Her involvement in the People's Will may have been the bloodiest and most dramatic of her radical endeavors, but it was just one brief example of a lifelong revolutionary exis-tence. Born into one category of nobility, Vera Nikolaevna Figner died at the age of eighty-nine as a representative of another, even more exclusive caste. Through her tireless dedication to revolutionary ideals, her willingness to sacrifice her life in their service, and the published celebration of her revolu-tionary commitment and sacrifice at a moment when the nascent Soviet state sought to create and commemorate a new category of radical heroes, proph-ets, and saints, Vera Nikolaevna Figner, although never a Communist, joined the ranks of a new type of nobility: a purposefully constructed revolutionary nobility whose fortunes ebbed and flowed along with the political vagaries of the Soviet state.

NOTE ON TRANSLITERATION

Throughout this book I have used the Library of Congress system of translit-eration. However, for common first names, I use the more conventional spell-ing, with which English-speaking audiences are more familiar. For example, I reference Alexander instead of the transliterated Aleksandr and Lidia in-stead of Lidiia.

THE DEFIANT LIFE OF

Vera Figner

1

IN THE TWILIGHT OF A FADING AGE

ON A LATE WINTER MORNING IN 1861, in sleepy villages, provincial towns, and bustling cities throughout the vast Russian Empire, somber-faced Russian Orthodox priests, conscious of the import of the moment, read an official proclamation penned in the imperial capital. After two centuries of legalized serfdom[1]—for all intents and purposes an institution that was indistinct from slavery—priests informed their congregations that the autocratic regime of Alexander II decreed the Russian serfs emancipated from their noble overlords. Although the details of the abolition of serfdom and the caveats contained within the decree made "freedom" a bitter pill to swallow,[2] Russia entered a new age that morning. The new age that dawned, though, differed markedly from what the manifesto's authors had hoped or expected. Fearful of a new round of intensified uprisings and rebellions against this legislated, unrelenting system of inequality and oppression, those who crafted the Emancipation Manifesto hoped that the abolition of serfdom would settle underlying social, economic, and political tensions in the land of the tsars. Yet in many respects the terms of emancipation ushered in a new period of destabilization and revolutionary activity that would culminate not in periodic localized rebellions but in a revolution that would ultimately destroy the imperial regime itself.

Almost eight hundred miles to the southeast of the gilded, pastel-hued palaces in which the emperor and his ministers delineated the terms of emancipation, a noble family found themselves on the precipice of this new age.

None of its members had a hand in writing the Emancipation Manifesto, but the lives of everyone in the Figner household stood poised to change irreversibly once the dictates of the document were implemented. The decree that abolished serfdom in Russia was determined in formal governmental meeting rooms in sumptuous St. Petersburg mansions, but it was intended to alter centuries of tradition in the provinces and reconfigure life for both serfs and their noble owners in the Russian countryside. Thus, as the priests announced the end of serfdom in Russia, the Figner family found themselves on the front lines of the state-directed transformation of rural life that would bring both brief hope and unmitigated disappointment to millions.

In comparison to their slave-owning counterparts in the United States, the Figner family owned a substantial amount of land. Both Nikolai Alexandrovich Figner and his wife, Ekaterina Khristoforovna Kuprianova, had been born into the Russian nobility and inherited lands in a number of provinces in the empire. To these holdings, Nikolai added considerable acreage in the same village as the Kuprianovs' estate when he took advantage of plummeting land prices after the abolition of serfdom was announced.[3] Thus, as the terms of the emancipation were implemented, Nikolai and Ekaterina owned more than 500 *desiatinas* (1,350 acres) of land in the district of Tetiushi alone.[4] Even though the family inherited acreage in other provinces as well, it must be recognized that this level of landowning was not impressive in the circles of the Russian nobility. Given the expanse of the Russian Empire and the often contentious soil and climate, which presented seemingly infinite agricultural challenges, Russian nobles amassed lands on a grandiose scale. Consequently, the Figners belonged to only the middle level of serf owners.[5] Many memoirists lament the financial straits of the nobles at the socioeconomic level of the Figners. But as Peter Kolchin points out, those occupying the median rung of landowning wealth in pre-emancipation Russia earned between 3,000 and 20,000 rubles annually from their land, "far from trifling sums when a typical peasant family of eight got by on 75 to 100 rubles a year."[6]

In many ways the Figner family was typical of the late Imperial Russian nobility. Although the Figners benefited from the privileges of their class, unlike the leading magnates in St. Petersburg, the opulence that defined the lives of nobles in the imperial capital eluded them.[7] They lived comfortable lives but not luxurious ones. Servants tended to their needs within their home, but only by the handful, as opposed to the dozens or even hundreds who indulged the wealthiest Russian nobles' every whim.[8] While the grandees of Russian society spent the majority of their time in either St. Petersburg or Moscow, only temporarily retiring to one of their many provincial estates for brief respites each summer, the Figners' lives were firmly rooted on their estate in the midst of the rolling hills of the Tetiushi district (*uezd*) in the province (*guberniia*) of Kazan.[9] There Nikolai and his wife, Ekaterina, raised their family of four daughters and two sons in a comfortable two-story home surrounded by gardens, meadows, streams, and the huts and fields of the serfs whom they owned.

Unlike some of their more affluent neighbors who soaked up the social scene in the provincial capital of Kazan, a relatively large city with a population almost thirty times larger than that of the Figners' local district capital of Tetiushi,[10] the Figners lived rather secluded, socially constricted lives, except for Nikolai, who traveled in his various civil service posts. Fate would eventually carry the Figner children not only to the distant reaches of the Russian Empire but also to the far corners of Europe; however, as children they lived essentially as "country bumpkins" without access to the cultural pleasures and social delights afforded their wealthier noble counterparts.

Sheltered from the tumult besieging Russia as Alexander II succeeded Nicholas I to the throne and Russia's humiliating defeat in the Crimean War dictated the need for immediate and drastic modernization and reform, the Figner children did not grasp the monumental historical significance of the abolition of serfdom;[11] rather they understood this watershed moment in purely personal terms. When the Emancipation Manifesto was announced, the oldest of the Figner children, a little girl named Vera Nikolaevna, was only eight years old.[12] Decades after the abolition of serfdom as Vera wrote several volumes of memoirs, she recalled that the decree that freed more than 23 million privately owned serfs was personally noteworthy for the moderating change it had seemed to effect in her strict, authoritarian, even despotic father.[13] In her words, the emancipation of the serfs amounted to a "moral revolution" in her father.[14] In addition, cherished servants, whom Vera thought of as permanent fixtures in her home, quickly left to establish their own lives, giving evidence that their years of service were rooted not in tender loyalty and mutual benefit but merely in the dictated system of serfdom. But as she grew and discovered the world beyond her family's estate, Vera's mounting disgust with the seemingly endless impoverishment and powerlessness of the Russian peasants, which emancipation did little to rectify, led her to view the conditions of the Russian peasantry as just one manifestation of a woefully corrupt and illegitimate political and social system. Her disillusionment with the regime and the institutions that bequeathed certain material and social advantages to her and her family in her youth, along with a measure of guilt for her family's complicity in this system, ultimately led Vera Nikolaevna Figner down a long, winding road from her noble estate and the privileges of her station to the radical underground and the mortal challenges posed by a vengeful tsarist prison system.

But in 1861 the bare, foreboding solitary cells of the empire's most notorious political prisons did not intrude on Vera's wildest imagination. Instead, according to her own testimony, the future revolutionary lived a bucolic existence cavorting with her five younger siblings.[15] On the day when millions of serfs learned of the emancipation decree, Vera lived with her parents, Nikolai and Ekaterina, and her siblings Lidia, Peter, Eugenia, and Nikolai on her mother's family estate, Khristoforovka.[16] According to Vera, Khristoforovka was an ideal gentry estate.[17] The house itself was a sprawling wooden structure, its left side, from which a porch extended, rising to two stories while the remainder of the house rose to a mezzanine level. Around the back of the house stood several towering trees that offered the family shade during the warm summer months. Beyond the tree line a simple wooden fence separated the manor house from the fields. A "beautiful old garden" and a grove of fruit trees surrounded the house. Past the immediate gardens, there was a park, where the Figner children ran free and collected mushrooms, nuts, and berries.[18] In the warmer months the siblings took long walks, fished, and swam in the estate's ponds and streams.

Vera's description of her carefree days on her family's estate conforms to a pattern adopted by most gentry memoirists, in which young nobles' provincial childhoods are romanticized for the degree of freedom and proximity to nature that their estates afforded.[19] Given the dislocation and upheaval that characterized Vera's life in the intervening years between her early days at Khristoforovka and the period when she recalled them in writing, it is understandable that she would have even more cause to recall this time in such an idealized fashion. But it must also be recognized that there was some justification for Vera's romanticism. Khristoforovka, where the Figners lived from 1858 to 1862, was located in an area dotted with forests and countless valleys intersected by rivers, including the Volga, and their tributaries. Natural beauty abounded. Rolling hills traversed farmlands and meadows that were laden with beautiful flora native to the area.[20]

Although the soil was rich and the climate continental in Vera's native district, in the nineteenth century agricultural production remained low. In this regard Tetiushi was typical of most Russian agricultural regions; neither the agricultural nor industrial revolution transformed lives here. Instead, the peasants in Tetiushi uezd farmed, as did most of the agricultural laborers in the Russian Empire, as their ancestors did before them. Even after the former serfs were emancipated, change and innovation were slow to come, farming methods remained rudimentary, and yields were consistently lower than the climate and soil might have allowed.

As children Vera and her siblings did not think about the agricultural yields of their family's lands or the surrounding fields. Their material comfort was a privilege that was not analyzed and its basis never questioned. The Figner children looked at the land that encircled their estate not as a source of income but as a natural playground to be enjoyed, and they basked in the relative freedom afforded by its wide-open spaces. This was the children's domain. With the exception of their peasant nanny, who trailed after the children to keep them out of harm's way, once the youngsters ventured outside the four walls of their home, no adults materialized to chastise, deride, or reprimand. Instead the Figner girls and boys enjoyed the warm sunshine, gentle breezes, license, and abandon that could be found on the seemingly endless acres of their familial lands.

But if the grounds of the estate beckoned Vera and her siblings with their promise of liberty and proximity to natural delights, the house itself signaled decorum, order, and artificial propriety. Like most children of their class, Vera and her brothers and sisters dressed formally on a daily basis, used impeccable table manners, and followed the old adage that the youngest members of a proper household should be seen and not heard.[21] Ensuring that order reigned were the exacting expectations of Nikolai A. Figner. Vera's father was not an anomaly in this regard. Countless memoirists from the Russian gentry describe the strict, authoritarian behavior of their fathers that instilled terror and fear in their progeny.[22] For her part, Vera remembered her father as a "stern, hot-tempered, and despotic" man whom she feared above all else.[23] Like most Russian fathers of the age, Nikolai Figner dominated his wife, his children, and his servants and serfs. Although a harsh word or belittling glance usually sufficed, extraordinary examples of defiance or simple outbursts of independent thinking or behavior often necessitated corporal punishment. As Vera relates, her father's "stick or belt always lay in wait in his office."[24]

In this respect both Khristoforovka and Nikiforovo, the neighboring estate to which the family moved in 1862,[25] functioned as a microcosm of the strict imperial state. Just as the tsarist autocracy utilized fear and repression to maintain a staunchly inequitable political and social order, Nikolai Figner's despotism invariably reminded his underlings, including his wife, of their subordinate place in the household. As Michel Foucault argues, the ability to punish and to exercise control over a body is a function of power and an exercise in sovereignty.[26] Thus, in the Figner home, as in other homes of the Russian gentry, each disapproving scowl, reprimand, slap, or beating that emanated from the male head of the household reaffirmed gender, class, and generational hierarchies. Such severity, as long as it did not verge into sadism, was expected as a legitimate tool that maintained order and censured outbursts of independence and nonconformity in both the home and society. As Barbara Alpern Engel contends, "By fostering discipline and respect for authority on the personal level, the patriarchal family prepared people for social discipline and respect for state authority."[27]

Just as there appears a uniformity among memoirists in describing the harsh discipline and authoritarian behavior of noble fathers, there is a trend among many of these same authors that celebrates the tempering of their fathers' moods and household despotism after the emancipation of the serfs. Although the consistency with which disillusioned and radicalized members of the Russian gentry describe the ferocity of their fathers before the abolition of serfdom and their ensuing moderation after the reforms in part results from an intentional literary device designed to indict the political and social system of the era, there is as much truth in their assertions as trope. To be sure, "the traditional social order survived the impact of reforms and the demographic effects of economic change, especially in the rural parts of the empire."[28] Yet the early 1860s were a period when the overarching results of the Abolition of Serfdom and the ensuing Great Reforms were not yet determined.[29] Although the political, social, and cultural hierarchies of the pre-emancipation period survived the era primarily intact, thus driving the ensuing revolutionary movement, the immediate post-emancipation years "led to the emergence of a more vital, diverse, and assertive civil society" that was independent of the autocratic state and held the promise of further liberalization.[30] In general the 1860s were a period marked by hope, expectations, and optimism.[31] The intoxication of this hope discredited rigidity, invited social critiques, and helps to explain the "moral revolution" that Vera witnessed in her father as he became, in her words, more liberal and restrained.[32]

Nikolai A. Figner's growing liberalism was not simply the impressionistic assumption of his young daughter. In the wake of the emancipation of the serfs, Vera's father left the forestry service to become a peace arbitrator or peace mediator. This position was created by the state to help ease the Russian peasants' transition from bondage to freedom while maintaining order in the countryside and loyalty to the autocratic state. Peace mediators were critical linchpins in the reforms that followed the abolition of serfdom. As Roxanne Easley relates, "The institution of peace arbitrator had a hand in nearly every aspect of the reform . . . [as it was designed to] be the main administrative, judicial, and notarial institution in the countryside after emancipation."[33] Although the position was a lucrative and prestigious one, with peace arbitrators earning approximately fifteen hundred rubles a year and answering directly to the Imperial Senate, by and large it attracted sincere individuals who jumped at the chance to help "remold Russia on modern and democratic ideals."[34]

Yet the job was a challenging one. "In a peculiar mix of election and appointment, provincial governors chose the arbitrators from lists of local landowners qualified in terms of age, landholding, and education, prepared by the district noble assemblies."[35] But if the mediators discharged their obligations faithfully and honestly, they ran the risk of incurring the ire of their fellow landowners, who only stood to lose from the betterment of their former serfs, and the resentment of the peasants, who viewed the office as a tool of their continued exploitation. Vera remembers her father being committed to the peasants' best interests while he held the position, often doing battle with those who attempted to exploit their uneducated compatriots.[36] The extent to which Nikolai Figner advocated for the local peasantry is largely immaterial. What is significant is that Vera viewed her father's position as a peace mediator as indicative of his growing liberal penchant and understood his role as encapsulating the principles of selfless public service and contentious advocacy on behalf of the Russian masses.

As discussion swirled in educated circles about how society needed to change to accommodate the millions of newly freed Russian peasants, some insisted that gender and family relations needed to be reformulated as well. The inequitable hierarchy between men and their wives was dramatically apparent in the Figner household. Ekaterina Figner had been born to noble parents who arranged her marriage to Nikolai Figner after less than a handful of meetings between the pair.[37] Only eighteen years old when she married and only minimally educated, Ekaterina was understandably deferent and even intimidated by her husband, who was fifteen years her senior. Vera's younger brother Nikolai Nikolaevich Figner pointedly described his mother as a "weak-willed woman whose individuality was robbed by her husband."[38] Given their age difference and the traditional views about marriage and the subordinate role of women, the elder Nikolai easily dominated his wife, who answered her husband's verbal and occasional physical abuse of their children with silence.

As a woman well into middle age grappling with the challenge of crafting her life for a literary public, Vera sought to make sense of the silence with which her mother greeted the volatile tirades and the sometimes ferocious punishments meted out by her domineering father. When directly confronting the issue, Vera forgives her mother for never rising to her or her siblings' defense. Exoneration ensues thanks to Vera's decision to interpret her mother's silence as a painful choice that Ekaterina made in order to maintain peace in the household. Vera asserts, "We understood without words that her silence was a condemnation, and we always agreed with her."[39]

Yet her mother's silent acquiescence was not the manifestation of innate moral strength; rather it epitomized her subordinate position in both her own household and Imperial Russian society. In adulthood Vera negotiated power, independence, and control for herself within the revolutionary milieu by operating according to the premise that men and women were equal in this progressive underground sector.[40] While the extent to which gender equality actually existed in the revolutionary movement will be examined in subsequent chapters, the assertion that Ekaterina Figner claimed power for herself through her "silent condemnation" is simply not supportable. Even as Nikolai Alexandrovich became increasingly enchanted with developing liberal conceptions in the reform period, he did not reconsider gender norms and relations within his family, only the methods with which he maintained them. Although his stick and belt may have been used with less frequency, he remained in control. Empowered by society and custom to speak on behalf of the other members of his family, Nikolai's voice remained the definitive one in the Figner home until his death in 1870.

Vera's attempt to cast her mother as a silent collaborator is reflective of the license she takes in her autobiographical writings. All memoirists make conscious decisions about how to frame their lives in print; they decide what to

include, what to exclude, what to emphasize, and how to render random, isolated events and experiences as part of a logical historical narrative. As they
read their present lives into the memories of their pasts, they write their past
to affirm the present. As an autobiographer, Vera seeks to identify and condemn the oppression that existed in Imperial Russia; at the same time, she attempts to celebrate the latent strength and power of the oppressed. Both tendencies are designed to justify her radicalism and revolutionary career. Thus,
it serves Vera's purpose to describe her mother as a woman whose will, intellect, and moral courage were constrained by the patriarchal order but not
extinguished by it. By doing so she can tout the subsequent resurrection of
Ekaterina's faculties and moral strength once the source of oppression was
removed. In this regard Nikolai A. Figner functions as both a stand-in for
the autocratic state and as an entity distinct from it whose power and privilege within the home remains unmitigated even as other elements of the political order are reformed. Consider Vera's description of the intellectual and
moral development of her mother. While she contends that the liberalization
of the 1860s and the period of the Great Reforms allowed Ekaterina's intellect
to blossom, Vera maintains that her mother's true emancipation did not occur until the 1870s and 1880s when she "began to manage the fate of her children and her friends."[41] Although Vera never explicitly connects this development to her father's death in 1870, it is clear that it was only when Ekaterina
was fully free of her husband's constrictive influence that her moral strength
and power bloomed and she began to express her sympathy with the advocates of radical change, a fact that her eldest daughter interprets as evidence
of her enlightened development.

As an adult Vera remembered her deceased mother as a wonderful woman
who was a continual source of "joy and consolation" for each of her children.[42]
But as a mother to her younger children, Ekaterina was cold and distant as
were many women of her class. Although a Russian noblewoman was expected
to oversee her children's caretakers,[43] she was not counted among them. Dis-
charging most of the daily responsibility for her children to those in her employ, Ekaterina rarely made time for her daughters and sons, whose interaction
with their parents was confined to mealtimes and formal encounters. During the first ten years of her life, Vera recalls that her mother was primarily a
source of "cold and loveless authority."[44]

In the Figner home, as in the households of many of their fellow Russian
nobles, Vera's parents relinquished primary childrearing duties in their chil-

dren's early years to their *niania,* or nanny, Natalia Makarevna.[45] Niania had served Vera's family for three generations. Originally a serf who was enlisted as a playmate for Vera's grandfather, this kind, simple peasant reared Ekaterina Figner, her brother and sisters, and all six of Ekaterina and Nikolai's children. For Vera, Niania was a constant source of affection in whose room the Figner children could "find solace, pour out [their] grief and insults and find caresses and comfort."[46] With Niania there was no need to stand on ceremony or curb their childish impulses. In her presence Vera and her siblings were able to indulge the feelings that they were forced to deny in their parents' presence.

Vera and her siblings spent the majority of their time as young children with Niania. Like most Russian nannies, Natalia Makarevna would "wake, wash, and dress the children in the morning and . . . supervise their play during the day. In the summer this meant taking them on walks around the estate and teaching them such things as how to gather berries and mushrooms."[47] From Niania, Vera gained insight into elements of Russian peasant culture, reveled in the delights of Russian fairy tales and folklore, and romanticized what she thought was the essence of the simple peasant masses.[48] Just as her father served as a psychological stand-in for the tsarist state, Vera engaged in the transference of her affection for and appreciation of Niania to the Russian peasantry at large. But though Natalia Makarevna understood peasant ways and communicated old Russian culture to her charges, her decades in a gentry home erased the cruelest realities of peasant life. Thus, her life allowed no real insight into the hardships and burdens of the Russian masses, and Vera remained ignorant to the actual condition of the vast majority of the Russian people.

Although nianias were clearly socially inferior to their gentry employers, or owners before emancipation, they were given significant autonomy and license. Even members of the gentry who were highly conscious of social and cultural hierarchies typically thought of their nianias as members of the family.[49] Yet there were differences in terms of the privileges and license that these pseudo family members enjoyed. These distinctions were obviously rooted in class, but they were also embedded in gender as were all interpersonal and social relationships in Imperial Russia.

In a gentry household a noble birthright brought access to the material wealth of a family. Yet other benefits of both nobility and wealth were either bestowed or withheld on a gendered basis. Only the adult noblemen of the house enjoyed all the vestiges of their entitled position. That is, these men obviously shared in the material inheritance of their family as did their female counterparts, but unlike their female family members, only the boys could look forward to educational opportunities and professional fulfillment. Similarly, although the younger generation of boys within a noble home knew that their voice was immaterial compared to that of their father, they invariably realized that one day they would inherit the full power and privilege of the patriarchal system that would bring them full authority within their homes and a voice in the public sphere.

But these young male nobles' sisters enjoyed no assurances. Although educational opportunities for Russian girls, especially of noble birth, improved in the 1860s, these gains were tenuous. In addition, outside of the most radical of circles, the idea that men and women were equal and that women should enjoy an equitable share of authority in their homes with their husbands or an independent voice outside of their homes was outrageous. Thus, even when the state and reformers emphasized girls' education, it was designed to produce dutiful, moral, graceful creatures who would conform to their husbands' expectations, meet their spouses' needs, and uphold the political and social status quo. The pedagogical thinking of the time operated according to the premise that "women are lower creatures appointed by nature to be dependent on others . . . it is their role to serve[,] not command, they need to submit to their husband and work only to fulfill their familial obligation."[50] In this way young Russian noble girls were groomed to render *silent* obedience. Clearly, despite never having had the benefits of formal education, Ekaterina Figner learned her lesson well as she lowered her gaze, bit her lip, and remained silent while her husband disciplined, berated, and even struck their children.

Yet the unmarried, elderly peasant nanny Natalia Makarevna, who had no education, no husband, and no pretensions toward ladylike behavior, enjoyed a greater license to express her ideas and opinions, albeit privately, in spite of, or perhaps because of, her lower social station. Given her peasant origins, Niania was not held to the same standards as the family for whom she cared. Her unorthodox, even crass, behavior charmed her charges, who viewed her uncultured demeanor as indicative of her freedom from traditional social constraints. Unmarried, completely dependent upon the good graces of the Figner family, and well past her sexual prime, Niania was completely innocuous. Without any semblance of political, economic, or sexual power, she was nonthreatening. Consequently, her powerlessness allowed for a vestige of private independent expression. Yet the extent to which she negotiated verbal autonomy should not be overly inflated. There is no indication that Natalia Makarevna ever directly challenged or confronted Nikolai A. Figner. While Vera remembers finding comfort and sympathy in the arms of her nurse after being disciplined by the father, Niania's solace could be found only behind closed doors. She made no attempt to interfere in her employer's decisions or alter his behavior; she merely soothed the wounded sensibilities of her young charges who experienced his temper and wrath. This was more license than that enjoyed by Ekaterina, who greeted her husband's disciplinary rage not with regretful solace but with silent acceptance and thus tacit affirmation of the class, generational, and gender hierarchies in play.

If class boundaries and expectations influenced how the adult women in the Figner household reacted to Nikolai's expressive exercise of power and sovereignty, gender was a critical factor in determining the extent to which subversive challenges to the socioeconomic hierarchy on the Figner estate were permitted. That is, Nikolai's social prerogatives were reinforced by the privileges accrued through his manhood. Yet his wife's social position was undercut rather than buttressed by her gender. Whereas Natalia Makarevna did not dare rebuke Nikolai personally or directly, she did not feel a similar compunction against challenging his wife. Because Ekaterina was a woman, the authority that her class bestowed upon her proved fluid and contingent enough to defy. Consequently, Vera recalls boisterous battles of wills between her mother and Niania becoming so heated that the beloved nanny would announce that she was abandoning the family.[51] While these invariably proved to be empty threats, given her financial dependence upon the Figners, the fact that this peasant woman felt entitled to levy them in a power struggle with the noblewoman of the house shows the extent to which social hierarchies were influenced and sometimes mitigated by dynamics of gender.

In spite of her noble pedigree, because Ekaterina was born a girl, her education was limited to basic lessons in French and the piano in her parents' home.[52] This minimal education was typical. In 1856 only "one-tenth of one percent of the female population attended primary school" in Russia, whereas 1.3 percent of their male counterparts enjoyed an elementary education.[53] With state service and the professions the exclusive domain of men, neither parents nor governmental authorities saw the purpose in investing in the intellectual development of women. As Ekaterina's eldest daughter came of age, there was a new urgency toward improved educational opportunities that accompanied discussions about reform. Although this discussion would affect

Vera's inclination toward a university education, she had been born too soon to enjoy a serious revolution in the quality of her primary or secondary education. Instead, governesses came to the Figner home to instruct Vera and her sister Lidia in French, dance, and piano much as they had her mother. Intellectual development was irrelevant; what mattered was the cultivation of the requisite social graces needed to secure a respectable husband.

In describing herself as a child, Vera paints a picture of a young girl running away from artifice, superficiality, and selfishness and toward a radical calling that demands asceticism, sacrifice, and devotion. In an essay culled from the autobiographical writings of Vera Figner, her revolutionary contemporaries, and their Bolshevik successors, Hilda Hoogenboom argues that in their memoirs Vera's generation of female radicals consciously constructed an impression that was intended to "dissociate themselves from their gender in order to be taken seriously."[54] Thus, they focus on their intellectual pursuits and secluded lives "in an attempt to limit their association with society and its implications of feminine excess."[55] Yet Vera goes even further than Hoogenboom suggests. While she certainly writes about her affinity for reading and her aversion to dolls, she describes her intellectual and social development as being *purposely* cultivated and influenced by her strength of will. That is, she admits to a *natural* inclination toward gold trinkets, fashionable dresses, and the vanity of her youth in order to highlight how influential authors, the example of certain individuals, and her own determination vanquished the superficial and shallow elements of her life.[56] Vera purposely presents a paradoxical image of herself in order to manifest the role that choice and will played in her intellectual and revolutionary development. Just as she describes her mother in terms that synthesize the seemingly contradictory elements of her personality and behavior to allow for her individual flowering and emancipation, Vera portrays opposing aspects of her character to highlight the moral superiority of the path she followed.

Like all children of the Russian nobility, Vera was raised in an environment that defined legitimacy and derived identity through service.[57] In one way or another, every man in her family rendered service to the tsarist state. Although she asserts that she paid no attention to the plaintive appeals and heated demands voiced by desperate peasant voices in her father's study, the frequency and intensity of the encounters between her father, the peace mediator, and the freed serfs who sought his intercession served as a constant reminder for Vera of the urgent need for and value of civic and state service.

The service performed by men like her father was predicated upon its public nature. Conversely, the service rendered by Russian noblewomen was inherently private and contained within the narrow boundaries of the home. Since feminine service lacked a public component, it was thus devalued.

In their analyses of gender, representation, and language in the French Revolution, both Lynn Hunt and Joan Landes have brilliantly described republicans' feminization of the aristocracy of the Old Regime in France.[58] This universal feminization and thus belittlement of nobility does not apply to the Russian context, primarily because the notion of the gentry's public or state service was so well entrenched in society. Rather than castigate this service because of its connection to autocracy, Russian radicals found the notion of public service sufficiently commendable to appropriate for themselves as they redefined its focus and ultimate objective. Although Russian revolutionaries do not openly differentiate between the men and women of the Russian nobility, as in France there existed a distinct, palpable disdain for women of the gentry. Karl Marx's argument about the worthlessness of domestic service is instructive in this regard. In the 1850s he contended that since domestic servants "did not create wealth themselves but lived off surplus wealth enjoyed by the bourgeoisie . . . [they belonged to] a separate, parasitic category of labor."[59] Marx's focus was domestic service, but it was not the service part of the occupation that bothered him; rather it was the domestic element. Because this type of service took place within the home, it was deemed unproductive and thus without intrinsic value. Marx and his fellow Socialists could excuse those toiling in bourgeois households, because this labor ensued from the inherently exploitative condition of capitalism. But their female bourgeois employers, with no claim to any form of labor beyond the requisite attention to their own vanity, became emblematic of the parasitic nature of both the autocracy and the nobility.

More than a half century after Marx's discussion of the empty productive quality of domestic service, Alexandra Kollontai decried the existence of "idle women [among a rejuvenated bourgeoisie] who did not engage in wage labor," but instead chose to languish in the "domestic bondage" of bourgeois marriage.[60] For Kollontai, these women were best described as "doll-parasites" and represented a critical threat to the Russian Revolution. Bereft of the public duties of their male counterparts and detached from the system of wage labor, Russian noblewomen could become the personification of the exploitative, selfish nature of an unjust system.

In her early years Vera Figner seemed destined to live as one of these women. From her youth, she captivated those around her with her dark complexion; big brown eyes; dark, smooth, often upswept hair; and equally appealing character. She remembers always being cognizant of the power of her appearance.[61] Unlike many of the female radicals of her generation and the nihilists who came of age in the 1860s, Vera never tried to downplay her looks. She continually enjoyed the attention that her good looks afforded, and she jealously guarded her beauty throughout her long life. Yet she claims that she decided relatively early on that her attractive appearance needed to be complemented with a depth that eluded typical "noble-dolls."

In her first volume of memoirs, which appeared the same year as the Alexandra Kollontai article referenced above, Vera relates a story that depicts her determination to run away from what she conceived as the parasitic existence that her class and gender held in store for her. She remembers hearing two relatives discussing her and her sister Lidia when they were children. While these older relatives acknowledged that Vera was more beautiful than her younger sister, they said that Vera's beauty masked a shallowness of character. In their estimation Vera was like a "beautiful doll that was hollow inside."[62] Being born a woman of the privileged class in Imperial Russia brought material benefits and comforts but no purpose. For some women these privileges could feel dehumanizing, because they often came at the price of self-sufficiency, autonomous thought, and social value. In Russia in the 1860s, nihilists, a group of social critics who called for the dismantling of the existing social structure and cultural norms, including the patriarchal family, argued that "women should be treated as people, not as empty-headed, decorative dolls."[63] But the path through which one's socially meaningless life could gain public purpose was narrow and blocked to all but the most determined and resourceful female souls. Limited by the legal restraints that tied Russian women first to their fathers and then to their husbands, and denied the opportunity to seriously engage and develop their intellect, the answer to the question of how to achieve a meaningful life was not readily apparent.

After several years of lessons directed by a number of live-in governesses, some more vapid than others, Vera Figner was ready to embark on the next chapter of her academic development. In 1863 she left the sheltered existence of her family's estate of Nikiforovo for the equally isolated Rodionovskii Institute for Noble Girls in the city of Kazan. Although this institute was located in a bustling provincial capital, Vera and her fellow classmates lived essentially as "cultural castaways,"[64] detached from contemporary social issues and secure from distractions behind Rodionovskii's walls. In her memoirs Figner is unsentimental in her descriptions of the school where she spent her early teenage years. She describes neither fear nor insecurity as she notes her first prolonged foray away from the cosseted atmosphere of the Figner family and their estates. Instead she boasts that she entered the institute as a member of the VI class instead of the VII class, in which her age should have placed her.[65] In fact, she contends that her last governess, a recent institute graduate herself, had imparted so much to her that she could have started the institute in the V class, but her tender age of eleven precluded this. Yet according to the reminiscences of Sofia Khvoshchinskaia, an institute alumna and successful author, the VI division was reserved for girls with little aptitude when they arrived,[66] and thus Vera's placement within it did not warrant any self-congratulatory boasting.

Nevertheless, Vera extols her academic virtues upon her arrival at the Rodionovskii Institute in order to intimate to her readers that she was naturally intelligent and to distinguish herself from the vast majority of her classmates. While she clearly was an intelligent woman, at the tender age of eleven there was little that differentiated her from the other girls at the school. Her pre-institute academic preparation mirrored that of the other young ladies who entered Rodionovskii Institute. Not privy to a varied social scene or diverse cultural experiences, Vera was just as unsophisticated, if not more so, than the majority of her classmates. In addition, the political proclivities and social awareness that she found at home were replicated on noble estates throughout the country. Although she goes to great lengths to chart the political awareness and escalating progressive penchants of her father, mother, and her beloved uncle Peter Kuprianov during the turbulent decade of the 1860s, their behavior and literary patterns were consistent with many of their provincial noble counterparts.

As she chronicles her childhood experiences in order to define the influences that impelled her to devote her life to the revolutionary cause, Vera describes her parents' and uncle's affinity for some of the leading liberal theorists and writers of the day. Vera's father and her uncle Peter had subscriptions to Nikolai Chernyshevskii's *The Contemporary*.[67] In both *The Contemporary* and his famous novel *What Is to Be Done?*—which functioned as a veritable devotional tract for the radicals of the 1860s[68]—Chernyshevskii urged his readers to embrace the principles of "moral and social emancipation,"[69] and to apply these ideals in their "devotion to the people."[70] Extolling the virtues that both men and women could gain from education, economic independence, and social activism, Chernyshevskii provided a new generation of critically thinking Russians with a concrete model of an effective and worthwhile existence. In addition, Peter Kuprianov also enjoyed Dmitrii Pisarev's *Russkoe Slovo,* which was considered even more radical than the journal edited by Chernyshevskii. But this was nothing unusual. These journals were found in the studies of noble homes throughout the empire. Thus, the discussions that Vera overheard in her home about utilitarianism, the need to be socially active, and the injustice born of the autocratic state were not exceptional. In 1863, when Vera Nikolaevna Figner entered Rodionovskii, she was typical and unexceptional; there was nothing that indicated that her life would diverge in any meaningful way from the lives of the scores of other young provincial noble ladies with whom she would share the next six years.

Located in the provincial capital of Kazan, the Rodionovskii Institute for Noble Girls was established in 1841.[71] For decades it remained the only middle/secondary educational institution for women in the region and was one of only eight in the entire province.[72] A bustling city with over 130,000 inhabitants in the second half of the nineteenth century, Kazan played an important role in the cultural and economic life of the Middle and Lower Volga regions. As the provincial capital, Kazan was a center of Russian government, culture, and religion, and in the nineteenth century it was one of only six cities in Russia to host a university.

But according to Vera, none of the richness of the locale permeated the monastery-like setting of Rodionovskii.[73] School officials secluded their pupils from the rest of the world and actively worked to filter all outside influences from their students' experience. Rather than foster the critical intellectual development of its pupils, Rodionovskii, like other institutes for Russian noble girls, focused on developing charming young women who would be pleasing wives to their husbands and loyal subjects to the tsar. Independent thinking and creativity were anathema and potentially dangerous. Women were not considered to be autonomous individuals with a public role to fulfill; they were merely supporting cogs in the machine of the Russian social order whose presence and influence were limited to the home. Thus, the training of Russian girls was tailored to their expected function, and institutes churned out what the pedagogue and writer Elizaveta Vodovozova termed "mannequins, or in any case weak, helpless, useless, defenseless creatures."[74]

By the late nineteenth century, "the *institutka* became a veritable synonym for the lightheaded and ultra naive female."[75] Thus, at a time when few Russian women received any type of education, many of those who were educated were derided for their mindless behavior. Although the government began to redress the country's educational deficiencies in the 1860s, change came slowly. Alexander II's administration implemented some of the most substantial educational reforms during the 1850s and 1860s at the noteworthy Smolny Institute in St. Petersburg with notable effect.[76] But when Vera entered the Rodionovskii Institute, such reforms had only recently begun to travel the eight hundred miles from Smolny to Kazan. So even though Rodionovskii began to offer courses in the sciences, the school's commitment to scientific instruction was not sufficient to warrant the purchase of either textbooks or microscopes. These courses continued to be considered supplementary to the institute's primary preoccupation with teaching feminine skills such as drawing and penmanship.[77]

Consequently, Vera recalls that while her years in the institute instilled in her a sense of "deportment, camaraderie and discipline . . . in the sense of scientific studies and especially intellectual development," her Rodionovskii education gave her "very little and even delayed [her] spiritual growth."[78] The derision that Vera applies to her institute education is consistent with the complaints leveled by other memoirists of the age.[79] While memoirists lament the Spartan environment and pedagogical failings of the institutes, it is the artificial isolation these schools created that was the source of the greatest opprobrium.[80] At the very moment when Imperial Russian society seemed to emerge from its long intellectual and social apathy, the preteen and adolescent sons and daughters of the Russian nobility found themselves cut off from this emerging energy. Especially precocious students may have resented the unnatural isolation they experienced as they lived it, but most students ultimately realized their social naïveté only when they finished their education or returned home for brief school vacations. It was then that these young people understood the extent to which their educational institutions denied them access to the social foment that swirled in the 1860s. The trend toward the liberalization of censorship that was apparent in the early years of Alexander II's reign was not reflected in the secondary schools run by the state. Unable to control the rising political passions and critiques in Russian society at large, the state, aided by its educational institutions, sought to isolate its young people from this turmoil and thus render the generation that would come of age in the 1860s and 1870s allies instead of antagonists.

For the most part, students in Russian institutes and gymnasia returned to their homes and visited with their families for only a few weeks every year. Although the time spent outside of their educational institutions was limited, it was significant, especially for those who returned to liberal surroundings. The institutes may have sharply limited access to potentially contentious reading materials, but their students often found these books and journals on the shelves of their families' libraries during their summer sojourns at home. With every new provocative book or critical essay read, the deficiencies of their education became apparent and the unnatural seclusion they suffered behind institute or gymnasium walls became glaringly obvious and a source of resentment.

Over time, students, like Vera, conceptualized themselves as being oppositionally situated vis-à-vis their schools, and they increasingly disparaged the values imparted by these educational institutions. For example, Vera recalls returning from one summer vacation with a new book secured at home. Since the institute frowned upon independent reading, Vera needed to find a way to read surreptitiously. The glow from the candles and lamps in the icon corner in her dormitory room provided the means that she sought. As she read by this gentle light, she was able to quickly hide her book and pretend to be deep in prayer when a school official walked through the dormitory on a nightly surveillance check. Assuming the guise of a devout Christian in order to read her forbidden book—which was no more serious or threatening than a light English novel—Vera writes, "I used the religiosity of this little shrew" and plunged into reading.[81]

Although she was raised in the Russian Orthodox faith, Vera describes herself as leaning toward materialism and feeling essentially indifferent to the Church and its institutions from an early age.[82] Recalling her efforts to read on her own while away at school, she establishes a potent dichotomy between both her intellectual aspirations and her school's attempts to extinguish them, and the religious devotion cultivated by the institute and her disinclination toward it. While it is unlikely that Vera had as little respect for religion and its practices as her comment above indicates, her decision to read a novel in the sacred space of the icon corner points to a level of disengagement that is palpable. In addition, her success in fooling the school official charged with the bed checks creates an association between religion and gullibility for Vera that she intentionally conveys to her readers.

Vera Figner spent six years at the Rodionovskii Institute. By her own recollection, she did well in school and especially shined in history, geography, and literature.[83] Though dissatisfied with the standard of education that Rodionovskii offered, she excelled in her studies. In fact, when she completed the Rodionovskii Institute in 1869, she received the coveted Gold Ribbon—the award for highest overall academic achievement.

It must be noted that despite Vera's published denigration of her education at the Rodionovskii Institute, she took pride in the Gold Ribbon. Although she accords this prize no special significance in her memoirs—other than to say she had coveted it since her arrival in 1863—it is one of the few facts of her early life to which she repeatedly alludes in later years. For instance, in 1922 the Museum of the Revolution published a brief brochure that celebrated Vera's seventieth birthday. There are almost no details about her childhood or adolescence in this brochure; however, along with such fundamental information as the date and place of her birth is mentioned her receipt of the Rodionovskii Institute's Gold Ribbon.[84] As a prominent member of the museum's organizing committee, Vera collaborated on the details of the brochure, and thus the inclusion of this fact indicates that she still viewed this accomplishment as notable more than fifty years later. Vera similarly mentioned her Gold Ribbon in her application for membership to the State Academy of Artistic Science in 1926.[85] Despite her rich publishing career—by that time she had published thousands of pages of writings—and her contributions to the revolutionary process, her Gold Ribbon was significant enough to include in her application to this official academic union.

Thus, Vera left the Rodionovskii Institute as its premier graduate in 1869. But as she stood on the precipice of adulthood, her home life and education during the preceding years indicated what she wanted to run away from but not what she wanted to run toward. Vera felt ill suited for traditional feminine pursuits; she scorned the life of a provincial noblewoman, which in her mind "was confined to a narrow framework of petty interests."[86] Most Russian women willingly embraced these normative roles and many found personal satisfaction in them, but Vera viewed such a life as primarily marked by silence and public uselessness. Yet for a woman in Imperial Russia, even a member of the Russian nobility and a winner of a coveted Gold Ribbon, there had almost never been any viable alternatives to lives defined through familial relationships, private obligations, and political anonymity. In 1869, however, Vera Figner emerged from the Rodionovskii Institute at a unique historical moment as a new age dawned and new, though daunting, possibilities for intelligent young Russian women appeared on the horizon.

2

AGE OF CONSCIOUSNESS

SITTING ALONE IN AN ISOLATED POLICE interrogation room a short carriage drive from her cell in the Peter and Paul Fortress, a thirty-one-year-old Vera Figner thought about her life. As she took pen to paper to explain to gendarmes, government officials, herself, and (she hoped) posterity, how she, a woman born to the Imperial Russian nobility, faced a likely death sentence for a series of violent political crimes, Vera sought continuity. In chronicling her revolutionary activities, she asserts that her illegal radical activity during the previous few years "had its own history," because it was rooted in "logical links with [her] previous life."[1] Rather than viewing her revolutionary career as an abrupt rupture with a privileged past, she saw it as the understandable consequence of her own personal history and that of her country.

Vera Figner's path to revolutionary notoriety was not predestined; instead it was dictated by coincidence, circumstance, and choice. In both the confession that she wrote over a period of weeks in 1883 and the autobiographical accounts she penned over more than a decade in the twentieth century, Vera attempts to guide those who want to understand her life and radical career. For Vera, every step she took along the way toward the unforgiving prison cell whose cold, damp walls became the boundaries of her solitary universe for two decades was a conscious one; every choice she made was determined by a moral purpose and strength of will. Yet much of what impelled Vera Figner into the revolutionary underground and the annals of Russian history was timing. Being born in the twilight of the age of serfdom, and reaching the age of consciousness in a period filled with political and social reform, upheaval, and uncertainty, Vera found both exciting opportunities and insurmountable hurdles. How she interpreted and managed each of these at different historical moments invariably influenced her subsequent options and choices and ultimately determined her place in history.

As part of the Russian nobility, the Figner family enjoyed privileges not extended to their less affluent neighbors in the villages surrounding Khristoforovka and Nikiforovo. But the perquisites that they derived from their social position were not guaranteed and continued only at the pleasure of the autocracy; such was the nature of the political system. This discretionary system of privilege was intended to ensure the tsar of a dependable cadre of supporters within society. Yet even those whose loyalty never wavered were not completely secure and could find themselves and their material fortunes at the mercy of the capricious whims of the autocratic state.

In spite of Nikolai and Ekaterina Figner's developing sense of liberalism in the period of the Great Reforms, they were loyal subjects to the tsar, as were the members of their extended family. Yet events that took place in 1863 and 1864 more than one thousand miles from Nikiforovo illustrated for the Figner family that one's loyalty did not guarantee one's security in the empire of the tsars. Sensitive to the fact that relatively minor protests could swiftly degenerate into full-blown rebellions against a system rooted in inequality and repression, the imperial state reacted forcefully and pervasively to any discernible challenge to its authority. Government retribution was designed both to punish the guilty and to warn potential provocateurs against future incendiary action. Thus, the retaliatory nets that the autocracy cast were wide and often swept up individuals and groups whose only crime was that of association and those whose culpability rested exclusively in their ethnic or religious identity.

Such was the case in the wake of the Polish uprisings against Russian rule in the middle of the nineteenth century. Inspired by Alexander II's apparent commitment to reform in Russia and some modest reforms the tsar's government implemented in Poland, disparate groups and individuals in the kingdom of Poland pressed for more substantial improvements in the beleaguered country's subordinate position vis-à-vis Russia. As the Russian administration in Poland adopted an increasingly hard line in reaction to these challenges, the demands mutated into a full-blown uprising in January 1863 that was not finally subdued until the fall of 1864. In an effort to punish the rebels and send a message to other disenchanted groups, Alexander II's government reacted forcefully against both the insurgents and seemingly uninvolved Polish elites throughout the empire.

Approximately one year before the Polish rebellions, Ekaterina Figner's younger sister Elizaveta Khristoforovna married Mecheslav Feditsianovich Golovin, a noble of Polish descent. Although he was living in Kazan and working in the forestry service as his brother-in-law Nikolai had done before him, his family owned a substantial amount of property in Poland.[2] The Golovin family's Polish landholdings and Mecheslav's Polish heritage were sufficient cause to bring the retributive arm of the Russian state down on this unsuspecting couple in the wake of the Polish uprising. In an effort to send a message to ethnic groups whose nationalist aspirations threatened the viability of the multinational empire, Russian gendarmes arrested not only the uprising's provocateurs and participants but also many uninvolved members of the Polish gentry throughout the empire, including Mecheslav Golovin. Although the government soon released Vera's beleaguered uncle from prison, Golovin lost his service position and he and his young wife were relocated to an interior part of Russia.[3]

Sitting in the police department's interrogation room, Vera recalled this distant event and gave it great weight in her attempt to explain her revolutionary career. Aside from the inherent injustice implicit in members of an innocent family being incarcerated, this event demonstrated the capricious power of the government in an autocratic state. Guilt and innocence seemed immaterial even to the allegedly reform-minded government of Alexander II, and the long arm of the tsar's political police appeared powerful and arbitrary.[4] Having recently fallen prey to the latest incarnation of this political police apparatus, the persecution of her innocent relatives two decades earlier loomed large. Charged with silencing the political and social aspirations of the tsar's subjects, the very existence of a special political police force reinforced the absence of popular sovereignty in Imperial Russia. As Vera reached adulthood and experienced her own personal obstacles erected by the Russian government, the memory of the misfortune suffered by her aunt and uncle in the 1860s seemed to confirm her nascent ideas about the political oppression and legal injustice that ruled Russia and gave her developing notions weight through the benefit of a concrete example.

The Golovin family saga shook a young Vera's faith, but at the time it did not squelch her youthful enthusiasm or hopes for the future. Knowing little of the world beyond her estate, local village, and the Rodionovskii Institute, she did not have sufficient knowledge or the breadth of experience to put this event into its broader context or to understand it as indicative of the unrelenting oppression that was at the essence of the Russian political system. That would come later. But the exile of her young aunt and uncle, which fused personal grief and political oppression, remained in Vera's memory ready to spring to the fore when other experiences recalled the injustice and fear associated with the Golovins' persecution.

With the rich political and social messages prevalent in mid-nineteenth-century Russian literature and literary criticism, these occasions were quite common. In any society or culture, the literature produced provides invaluable insights about the intellectual tenor of the time. But in Russia in the 1850s and 1860s, the connection between literary and political movements was especially pronounced. Despite continued censorship, during this period opportunities existed for Russian writers to express ideas that ran counter to those espoused by the state. Authors and editors might suffer harsh consequences for their politically heretical assertions, but their punishments only accentuated their influence and that of their writings among literate society. In a country bereft of political freedom and basic civil rights, literary productions became *the* avenue for the politicization of the populace. It was through the pages of these so-called thick journals that a public sphere developed. In these periodicals and the discussions they prompted among a literate populace, the emerging "public sphere's development was measured by the state of the confrontation between government and press."[5] A century after a similar process in France revolutionized politics in that country, the intellectual exchange between Russian authors and readers politicized a growing number of impressionable young Russians and ultimately forced the tsarist autocracy to confront criticism, the prospect of reform, and modernity.

Prompted by Vissarion Belinsky, the influential editor of both *The Contemporary* and *Notes of the Fatherland,* who called on Russian authors to write works that conveyed a social and political message, Russian writers from this period invariably cloaked critical commentary beneath the veneer of literature and literary criticism. A hungry literary public consequently read these works as much for social and political guidance as for their aesthetic value. As a result, mid-nineteenth-century Russian literature serves as an unusually useful barometer in that it not only reflects its own contemporary historical moment but also serves as a compass that leads to new ideological and social developments, as young radicals drew inspiration and found guidelines for subsequent social and political activity from the significant literary works of the day.

Like so many other radicals who ultimately recall their lives in published autobiographies, Vera cites the influence exerted by authors like Dmitrii Pisarev, Nikolai Dobroliubov, and Nikolai Chernyshevskii on her developing revolutionary consciousness. From Pisarev's exaltation of science and socially useful activity, to Dobroliubov's call to members of Russia's privileged class to engage in social activism, to Chernyshevskii's model of emancipated womanhood in the veritable devotional tract *What Is to Be Done?* Vera, like so many of her contemporaries, found inspiration in literature.[6] While the reality that surrounded her in the provinces offered no opportunities for self-expression, literary models illuminated an alternate route that allowed for individuality, independence, and a public role. But it was not only the concrete examples offered up by these authors that roused young Russians from their passivity. Inundated in their formal schooling with ideas and paradigms designed to serve the interests of the prevailing political and social order, these readers were shocked by the disparate reality offered in the pages of the thick journals they read. This dissonance became enlightening and potentially radicalizing in and of itself, as the very process of reading these unofficial and unsanctioned writings conditioned criticism and censured uncritical acceptance of morally unacceptable norms. Thus, while traditional education like the one Vera received in the institute reinforced the subordinate role that her gender and class seemed to ordain for her, alternative models lurked in the lines of the politically and socially contentious literature that flourished with the easing of censorship.

These writings laid the foundations for Vera's future radical endeavors, but they did not provoke them. Instead they cultivated her evolving ideas about justice and morality and informed her determination to be a productive member of society. Her moral outlook was similarly influenced by conventional writings as well, including the collection of writings that could be considered the epitome of traditional tracts. In her effort to trace the roots of her social conscience and political commitment, Vera not only enumerates the influence exerted by the typical progressive and nihilist authors of the age, but also details the significant impact that the Gospels had on her political activism and moral outlook.

Nikolai and Ekaterina Figner raised their children in the Russian Orthodox faith. Years after Ekaterina's death, her eldest daughter lovingly details her memories of her mother's religious devotion. As a girl, Vera relished watching her mother unobserved as she knelt deep in prayer. Serene, earnest, and devout, Ekaterina's faith and the visible manifestations of it had an almost hypnotic effect on the young Vera as she witnessed her mother's belief in and dedication to something greater than herself.[7] Yet for Vera, what she ultimately mimicked was not the object of her mother's devotion but the intensity of the devotion itself. While Vera cast much of the doctrine aside, she saw the beauty in many of the moral lessons contained within the Gospels and continued to feel their influence throughout her life.

The Figner children grew up during a time when other secular creeds exerted a ferocious moral influence and vigorously competed for their attention. The Figner girls especially showed little proclivity toward religion and the Orthodox Church in spite of the religiosity of their mother. While these New Testament writings that Vera found influential did not abet her religiosity, the selfless humanity and sacrifice of Jesus Christ inspired her in her secular pursuits.[8] Along with the popular novel *One in the Field Is Not a Warrior* by Friedrich Spielhagen, Vera credits the Gospels with "laying the foundation of the spiritual tenor of [her] life."[9] In general, these writings aroused in Vera a commitment to devote herself toward a higher social goal. Rather than viewing the Gospels as ideologically distinct from the progressive and nihilist writings of the mid-nineteenth century, she saw them as parts of a larger literary tradition that endeavored to enlighten its readership about issues of justice, morality, and how one should live one's life.[10] Reading these texts and essays critically, she extracted elements from each of them and crafted her own moral consciousness and code of ethics.

In the 1860s, given the political climate and her stage in life, Vera's ethical code objectively examined did not portend an irreparable rupture with the government. Instead, her developing ideas about sacrifice and devotion to the public good conformed to the mood of the times and the progressive sensibilities of the liberal nobility during the period of the Great Reforms. What would make her ideas potentially radical was the fact that she consciously tried to put them into effect and that she was a woman. With no sanctioned place or function for Russian women in the public sphere, aside from the fictional ones penned by members of the intelligentsia, girls like Vera who imagined and eventually sought such social roles showed an independence of mind and even insolence in their willingness to confront conventional norms. Their reaction to the subsequent opposition to their plans depended on the individual woman and eventually determined her fate.

As Vera left the Rodionovskii Institute after she completed her term of study, these notions of altruism and social utility swirled through her mind. As a seventeen-year-old daughter of the Russian nobility and an institute graduate, there was little expected of Vera beyond finding a husband and establishing her own family in the provinces. But the intellectual exchange that developed in the months leading up to emancipation and flourished in the ensuing years between literary society (both in Western Europe and the imperial capital) and provincial readers brought novel notions to the countryside and to Nikiforovo. One such idea that spoke to the younger generation of relatively educated Russians was nihilism. First articulated by Dmitrii Pisarev, nihilism stressed the need for a new class of people who would reject sentimentality and devote themselves to science. Nihilist ideals were especially attractive to young Russian women, because they sanctioned a public role for them. Nihilism "promised [women] social and intellectual equality, and the eventual chance of useful, meaningful work. It made them dream of something more serious than balls, marriage, and a dull existence as solely a wife and mother."[11] Central to these gendered imaginings was the prospect of a medical education.

Obtaining a medical degree fused nihilist notions about the importance of science and the need to find meaningful work with a social purpose. As the hellacious death toll in the Crimean War affirmed the need for more trained medical practitioners in the empire, opportunities for medical study were consciously cultivated. The demand was so great that the government even permitted *women* to study medicine (although they were not permitted to obtain a medical degree) at the St. Petersburg Medical-Surgical Academy. Welcomed by a growing retinue of progressive professors, a number of scientifically and socially minded Russian women took advantage of this opportunity and relished the intellectual fulfillment and professional promise it afforded.[12] Yet this period of intellectual emancipation was only temporary, as the tsarist government demonstrated the potency it accorded women's education and independence. After a series of student protests and uprisings in the early 1860s, the state reacted by closing the doors of the empire's universities "to all but regularly-enrolled students, in the hope that 'subversive' elements could be more easily controlled."[13] Given women's de jure unofficial status at the university, they soon found themselves cast out of lab and library and deprived of their professional aspirations. While it could be argued that women's enforced exodus from universities was the consequence of their earlier failure to gain admission on an equal footing and not explicit gender discrimination, the subsequent 1864 order that purposely ousted women from the St. Petersburg Medical-Surgical Academy was gender specific.[14]

Even as the state embraced educational reforms in the early reign of Alexander II, the official commitment to education for women remained tenuous at best. When improved educational opportunities for women coincided with the government's wider agenda, it saw fit to provide occasions for its female youth to attend school and classes, even at the post-secondary level. However, as soon as social disquiet and criticism of the government became amplified, the state discontinued its sanction of nonconventional opportunities for women, obviously connecting political radicalism with unorthodox gender roles.

After Russian universities and the St. Petersburg Medical-Surgical Academy closed their doors to women in the early 1860s,[15] feminists and liberals continued to agitate for a woman's right to receive a higher education in Russia. As this long battle got under way, a handful of determined women refused to wait for the imperial government to sanction their career aspirations. Driven to action by rumors that the University of Zurich was willing to "admit foreign women without entrance examinations or *gimnazium* certificates,"[16] Russian women cast out of classrooms in their homeland boarded trains for Switzerland. The first woman to gain admittance to the Swiss university was Maria Kniazhnina; yet despite her pioneering achievement, Kniazhnina never completed her course of study and thus remains a relatively unheralded name in the fight for women's educational opportunities.[17] Instead, it was her compatriot Nadezhda Suslova who broke the gender barrier by becoming the first woman to receive her medical degree from the Swiss university in 1867.[18]

Reading about Suslova's achievement in the periodical *Delo*, Vera saw a possibility. Imbued with the giddy excitement of youth as her life stretched ahead of her, she yearned to do something significant with her life. Under the influence of the synthesized literary suggestions about contributing to the public good and the commitment to service that she had learned from the practical example of several of her male relatives, she was inspired to emulate Suslova and ultimately make a contribution to society. Vera describes finishing the institute and being overwhelmed by a "joyous sensation of freedom" that height-

ened a vague pervasive feeling of gratitude.[19] Imbued with the heady potential
of these feelings, the prospect of an anonymous private life lived in a state of
dependence on a man while she endured long days "saddled with children and
cooking" was appalling to her.[20] Medical studies offered a potential way out
of the drudgery for which she seemed destined. Although the medical profes-
sion in Russia was "far less prestigious than elsewhere in Europe,"[21] medicine
enabled "its practitioners to combine the desire to serve society with the near
mystical faith in science so characteristic of the 1860s."[22] In fact, a medical career offered a unique opportunity for Vera and other women of her generation. For although they believed that they would be able to "battle illness,
poverty, and ignorance" in their work as physicians and thus conform with
prevailing progressive ideas about working on behalf of the larger society,[23] a
degree and career in medicine would also allow them to vanquish their own
economic incapacity and overcome the limitations of a previously superficial
education. Medical studies thus lured young Russian women with the prospect of empowerment, economic emancipation, and enlightenment.

Yet a nineteenth-century woman with a medical degree in hand was radical.
Girls who deigned to dream of their own emancipation and fulfillment demonstrated an audacity that was both unusual and unsettling for the time, because it directly challenged the patriarchal hierarchy of state and society. Thus,
as these aspiring medical students approached their fathers for the necessary
permission to obtain a passport and enroll in the University of Zurich, many
balked at such an unconventional future for their daughters. Even those fathers who fancied themselves as being progressive or liberal were apt to chafe
at the notion of their daughters following a path that diverged so greatly from
tradition. Nikolai A. Figner was among these. When Vera asked her father for
permission to pursue a medical degree, he categorically refused.[24]

In spite of the periodical subscriptions that brought articles celebrating
the need for improved educational opportunities for women to his attention,
Nikolai A. Figner had no desire to see his eldest daughter follow such an unconventional path in life. Apprehensive about the streak of independence that
Vera's medical aspirations seemed to portend, he resolved to set his daughter
back on the proper path. To that end, Vera asserts that her father decided to
tempt her with diversions of a more worldly variety.

When Vera asked her father's permission to study medicine abroad, she
was a seventeen-year-old naïve girl from the provinces. Heretofore completely
sheltered from both the pleasures and pain of a world beyond her family, es-

tate, and school, but with a self-professed penchant for material concerns, it would not be far-fetched to conclude that the theater, balls, and young men of the provincial capital might distract Vera from the more altruistic and arduous goal of becoming a medical practitioner. Thus, in December 1869 Nikolai and Ekaterina sent their eldest daughter to the city of Kazan, where the family of her father's friend and colleague, the nobleman Viktor Fedorovich Filippov, hosted the young institute graduate as she made her debut on the provincial capital's social scene.

The winter social season proved to be an exciting whirlwind for Vera. She discovered the delights of the provincial capital in a way that had been impossible while she attended the Rodionovskii Institute. The Filippov home was "one of the best and biggest" houses in the city, and the family proved to be wonderfully gracious hosts.[25] During the weeks that she stayed with the Filippovs, Vera attended the theater, danced the night away at a bevy of balls, and met the man she would marry.

Vera did not have to look very far in Kazan to discover romance. In addition to having one of the finest houses in town, the Filippovs also had an intelligent young son, who had recently graduated from the University of Kazan and became Vera's constant companion. By all accounts, Alexei V. Filippov was enchanted with the dark-haired, olive-skinned beauty from Tetiushi and quickly fell hopelessly in love.[26] Although there is no concrete analogous evidence to indicate Vera's feelings for Alexei, one can presume that the first genuine romantic relationship of her life was a heady one for the teenager. Alexei was besotted and seemed willing to do whatever he could to please his paramour. The attentions of this relatively worldly, wealthy university graduate who was on his way to an advanced law degree must have been intoxicating to this seventeen-year-old country girl. Alighting at a series of successive balls on the arm of this well-connected, amorous young nobleman infused Vera with confidence and added to the delight she experienced in Kazan that winter.

When the time came for Vera to return to Nikiforovo, Alexei arranged for a new post for himself in Tetiushi so that distance would not stand in the way of the couple's budding relationship.[27] Over the next several months, Vera and Alexei grew closer as they spent hours reading together, talking, and sharing their ideas about the world and society.[28] This match was certainly approved of if not explicitly engineered by their respective families. Thus, when Alexei asked Vera's father for his eldest daughter's hand in marriage, Nikolai not only consented but most likely rejoiced as well. On October 18, 1870, less than ten months after they first met, the young couple joined their lives and their families together as they wed in the little church in Vera's native village of Nikiforovo.[29]

During the ten months of her courtship with Alexei, Vera remained committed to the idea of pursuing a medical degree. Rather than impeding her professional aspirations, her romance aided her designs. In addition to the companionship and potential love that her relationship with Alexei afforded, marriage to him held the prospect of emancipation from her father and thus the opportunity to begin her medical education. When Vera became Alexei's wife in the Nikiforovo village church, her father lost control of her fate. According to custom and law, Vera's husband became legally responsible for her and supplanted her father as the defining authority in her life. Nikolai's refusal to allow Vera to enroll in a medical program in Zurich was suddenly immaterial; the only permission she needed to secure now was that of her husband.

Alexei proved much more pliant than his father-in-law. Not only did he quickly consent to his young wife's plans, but he also agreed to abandon his career and accompany her to Switzerland so as not to be separated from her.[30] With her unabated resolve and the requisite legal permission secured, Vera began to amass the funds and skills she needed to make her goal a reality.

While it is doubtful that Vera engineered a relationship with the smitten Alexei in order to effect her emancipation from her father, it was certainly an added benefit. Yet within weeks of her marriage, the necessity of such emancipation eroded. Soon after he watched his eldest daughter became a married woman, Nikolai Alexandrovich Figner passed away at the age of fifty-three.

In his perceptive monograph *Battle for Childhood,* Andrew Wachtel contends that "in Russian gentry autobiography the death of a close relative is often described in detail, and it often plays a major structural role."[31] While many elements of Vera's memoirs conform to the tropes recognized and detailed by Wachtel, her description of her father's death is not one of them. In every autobiographical version of her life, she merely cites her father's death as an incident that occurred within the context of other events. The treatment she gives her father's passing in her memoirs is typical: "Several weeks after [I was married] my father died, and then my mother with her two youngest daughters moved to Kazan, where my brothers—Peter and Nikolai—were studying at the gymnasium, and my sister Lidia was finishing the institute."[32] In this part of her autobiography, a volume that numbers several hundred pages, Vera does not accord her father's death a page, a paragraph, or even a full sentence, merely a single phrase. Although she never expresses any real fondness for her father in her writings, his death was surely not as negligible in her psyche as she presents it in her memoirs.

Throughout her published autobiographical writings, Vera displays uneasiness with the purely personal elements of her life. Most of her writings are designed to tout her political agenda and revolutionary career. Personal, private elements are used merely to reinforce the public role she played. Vera utilized her father and her relationship with him toward such an end. In her imagination and life narrative, he functioned as a symbol for both the despotic regime of the tsars and the liberalizing tendencies of post-emancipation Russia. Throughout her childhood and adolescence, Vera feared her father, yet not enough that she followed the traditional path that he envisioned or that custom ordained for her. Thus, their relationship and Vera's understanding of it was fraught with ambiguity. Still essentially a child when Nikolai died and only recently returned home from six years in boarding school, she did not have time to work out the complexities of her feelings for her father in her own mind before his death. Instead, her relationship with him was destined to remain mired in confusion and ambiguity. Thus, in Vera's conception and autobiographical account, Nikolai Figner remains both a villain and a potential hero: a figure to be resented while his sympathies were to be cultivated. In Vera's effort to create a neat and tidy exposition of her life experiences and the political motivations that defined them, she ultimately chose to all but ignore her father's death.

The period of time surrounding Vera's marriage and her father's death were difficult for Vera to discuss, but not just because they were personal. They also illustrate her vulnerability, subordinate position, and dependence on the good graces of the men in her life. When she walked into the Nikiforovo village church on October 18, she entered as the civil and legal dependent of one man and walked out legally dependent on another. As she aged and wove her way through the surprising turns of fate, she found herself an emancipated and independent woman; as such, her formerly subordinate position unnerved her. Rather than make excuses for her relationship with Alexei Filippov, Vera essentially minimizes it. In none of her autobiographical indulgences does she ever mention love, passion, or even companionship with respect to her husband. He serves primarily as a subordinate player who allows the plot of her life to take certain turns; he is a secondary figure, relegated to the background of his soon to be famous wife's life.

Vera Figner was not a cold, unaffected person. On the contrary, in her childhood, adolescence, and early adulthood, she greatly enjoyed and relished life. She loved parties, socializing with friends, a good joke, and a healthy dose of mischief. Her friends recall her as a woman who exuded warmth, tenderness, and merriment. Unlike many of the radicals of her generation and some of the most famous characters found in Russian literature from the time, Vera was not an ascetic. While she was certainly serious and determined to achieve her professional ends, in her first few decades of life she did not see the need to deny herself the pleasures of life. Yet when she found it necessary to examine her life and present it in literary form, traces of vulnerability and frivolity are nearly expunged from her self-designed record. Purposely crafting a political missive, personal details are curtly described with seemingly unmitigated stoicism. Thus, the feelings that Vera wrestled with soon after her marriage and her father's death are concealed from the prying eyes of the reading public and certainly from the probing curiosity of the government prosecutors who read her 1883 confession. She fails to disclose whether she spent the winter of 1870–1871 weighed down by complicated feelings of grief about her recently deceased father or basking in the tender delights of life as a young newlywed planning for the future. Yet certainly she was and did both simultaneously.

As the new year of 1871 dawned, Vera found herself in a state of life that was much different from that of the previous year. She was a young married woman whose fate suddenly seemed within her control, thanks to the accommodating attitude of her husband. Together, she and Alexei began the necessary arrangements in order to move to Switzerland and enroll in the University of Zurich as soon as possible.

Having convinced her husband to abandon his law career and study medicine with her in Switzerland, Vera became a diligent pupil as Alexei tutored her in German, geometry, and algebra in order to maximize her chances of success in Zurich.[33] With her father gone, Vera felt the unmitigated support and sympathy of her family and friends for her medical aspirations. Sustained by this support and their dream of turning their manor house into a hospital for local peasants, the young Filippov couple squirreled away every extra kopeck, sold some personal items, and tried to overcome the deficiencies of Vera's institute education.

After several months engaged in these daily activities, in the fall of 1871 Vera temporarily relocated to the provincial capital of Kazan. Rumors reached Nikiforovo that implied a tightening of restrictions on Russian women who attempted to travel to the University of Zurich for a medical degree; thus, Vera decided to try to attend lectures in medicine at the University of Kazan.[34] With her sister Lidia, who had recently completed her course of study at Rodionovskii, Vera alighted into the classroom of Peter F. Lesgaft. This was decisive for the Figner girls, because Lesgaft was not just sympathetic to the cause of furthering women's higher educational opportunities; he was also an outspoken proponent of their benefits.[35] As a result, he welcomed the Figner sisters into his lecture hall and went out of his way to make their experience rewarding.

Professor Lesgaft had begun teaching anatomy at the University of Kazan in 1868 and quickly became one of the most popular professors on the faculty.[36] As Vera walked into his anatomy lab for the first time, her romantic imaginings of scientific education confronted its stark reality as the pungent odor from a human dissection in progress permeated the room.[37] Fighting the nausea that came over her, Vera was nonetheless delighted. The aroma was like a chrism that baptized her into the world of science. With an intensity that could not be captured through the independent study she conducted at home, science extended its grip upon her and she became its devotee.

For the first time, Vera experienced a rigorous scientific education, and her dream of becoming a doctor seemed within grasp. But circumstances soon showed the folly of such confidence. Mimicking the unjust repression suffered by her uncle and aunt several years before, the celebrated Professor Lesgaft fell victim to the despotic whims of the imperial government. Just months after Vera and Lidia fell under his spell, the authorities charged him with having a pernicious influence on the student body and fired him from his university post.[38]

Vera was devastated. She had escaped the controlling grasp of her father only to discover that another entity controlled her in a more pervasive way than Nikolai Figner ever had. Marriage had brought liberation from her father, but it seemed that no mechanism existed to engineer her personal emancipation from governmental despotism in tsarist Russia. Recent events demonstrated that Vera's private domestic life could be negotiated to enable a certain personal autonomy (as long as her husband continued to be malleable), but this was ultimately immaterial, because the tsar and the autocratic repression effected by his government still exercised ultimate control over her public, social existence. Born into a life of material privilege, Vera increasingly saw that her privileges were few and tenuous. As the situations with both her uncle Mecheslav Golovin and Professor Lesgaft had demonstrated, opportunities and privileges in Imperial Russia could suddenly vanish without provocation or warning. Thus, Peter Lesgaft's termination increased Vera's urgency in getting to Zurich and securing entrance into its university.

Possible disaster loomed when a spate of articles began to discuss the reaction against the prevalence of so many Russian girls in Zurich. Rumors circulated that the University of Zurich Council might implement measures to curb this flow. Time suddenly seemed to be of the essence. Although the young Filippovs had planned to enroll in the Swiss university in the fall of 1872, the buzz about impending restrictions hastened their departure. Fully supportive of her daughter Vera's plan to study medicine in Zurich, Ekaterina Figner decided to send Lidia to Zurich along with her sister and her husband so that she could enroll at the university as well.[39] While marriage brought emancipation for Vera, widowhood enabled her mother's liberation. Free from the constrictions imposed by her recently deceased husband, there was nothing to curb Ekaterina's sympathies or assistance, and she provided her two oldest daughters with the emotional support and money that "opened the doors of the university to [them]."[40]

Her experience at the University of Kazan demonstrated to Vera that even should the imperial government develop opportunities for women to study at the university level, they could be in continual jeopardy. Thus, in the late spring of 1872, Vera left her home province for the first time. Accompanied by Alexei and Lidia, she traveled by boat up the Volga, then by train to the capital, where she and her small entourage boarded a railcar for Zurich. As their train left St. Petersburg behind, Vera knew that her life was about to irrevocably change. With every mile the locomotive put between its occupants and the land of the tsars, she came closer to realizing the academic and professional objectives she had devised over the previous few years. Possibilities abounded and Vera was energized. As she left Russia in 1872, she was correct in surmising that great life changes awaited her in Switzerland, but she soon discovered that not every opportunity was easily claimed. Thinking she could enjoy all the freedom and autonomy that Zurich had to offer, Vera soon found out that she was not as liberated as she thought when she discovered that the arms of the tsarist government were long indeed.

3

PIONEERS DIVERTED

LIKE MOST EUROPEAN CITIES OF ITS size in the late nineteenth century, Zurich bustled with activity. With the majestic, snow-kissed Alps that hugged the clear, pale-green waters of Lake Zurich towering in the background, merchants, artisans, financiers, and industrial workers darted off to work each weekday morning along the well-groomed streets of this cosmopolitan city.[1] On the weekends, families strolled along the quays bordering the Limmat River to any number of Zurich's public squares and lush green parks. Here they would often cross paths with the poets and artists who traveled to Zurich to indulge their creativity amid the breathtaking scenery and political freedom that the Swiss canton offered. In the second half of the nineteenth century, Zurich was a center of finance, industry, art, and culture. But it was also a center of learning. With its colleges of theology, arts, jurisprudence, and medicine, the University of Zurich attracted students from across Switzerland and Europe. In the streets that surrounded the university, students babbled to one another in most of the languages of Europe. While this polyglotism surely characterized the corridors and courtyards at any number of the major universities on the Continent, Zurich was unique in that many of the student voices that rose above the clamor of the horse-drawn streetcars trotting by the college belonged to women. As the first university in Europe to admit women on the same basis as men, the University of Zurich exerted a magnetic pull on young women who were anxious to expand their minds and professional opportunities. Between the winter of 1864–1865 and the summer of 1872, "a total of 203 women were enrolled as auditors or students" at the University of Zurich; of these "there were 23 English, 10 Swiss, 10 Germans, 6 Austrians, 6 Americans and 148 Russians,"[2] including two provincial noblewomen from the province of Kazan.

A light, persistent rain muted Zurich's natural beauty as Vera; her husband, Alexei; and her sister Lidia alighted from their long journey. As they weaved their way through the streets from the newly constructed Hauptbahnhof railroad station to their hotel on the Limmatquai in the historic part of the city, the contrasts with Mother Russia were great. Churches in the Romanesque style replaced the colorful cupolas that adorned Russian Orthodox churches, and fashionable shops that serviced the rising financial and industrial elites surpassed the standard retail fare in the group's native Kazan. The well-groomed streets, distinctive Swiss architecture, and the sounds of the German language made it clear to the newly arrived trio just how far from home they had ventured. But as they left the narrow streets of historic Zurich and neared the university and its polytechnic institute, Vera, Alexei, and Lidia entered a "corner of Russia" in the shadow of the Alps.[3]

Here the dozens of newly arrived female medical students mingled with young Russian men who came to Zurich to take advantage of the stellar reputation of the city's university. For a generation of Russians enraptured by the promise of science, Zurich beckoned both with its university's college of medicine and the neighboring Federal Polytechnic Institute, which offered some of the best scientific instruction on the Continent while at the same time having relatively lax entrance requirements.[4] Vera was beside herself with anticipation when she arrived in Zurich with her husband and sister. As she walked up the broad steps that led to the polytechnic's main building to seek permission to join the ranks of other pioneering women in the college of medicine, her twentieth birthday was a few weeks away. But at this moment she felt that she was being reborn and baptized into the world of science.

Religious imagery pervades the section of Vera's autobiographical writings that deal with her early days at the University of Zurich as she recounts medicine as a veritably holy mission to which she consecrates herself. Actively recalling the religious imagery of Mary, the Mother of Jesus, standing at the peak of a cathedral and extending her arms to the world, Vera recasts Suslova in the Madonna role and interjects herself as her disciple: "Golden threads stretched out from Suslova to me, and then continued further, into the village, to its inhabitants and from there further still—to people in general, to my country and to humanity."[5] Imbued with the scientific fanaticism of the age and the hopeful prejudice of youth, Vera invested scientific disciplines, especially medicine, with fantastic powers that could cure the world—or at least localized parts of it—of its most egregious physical ills. Transferring notions of sacrality from traditional religiosity to the modern veneration of science, the university generation of the 1860s and 1870s viewed the study and practice of science with sanctified reverence and saw their efforts to secure an education and vanquish ignorance, poverty, and illness as a modern crusade. Consciously envisioning themselves as "new people," like the character of Yevgeny Bazarov in Ivan Turgenev's *Fathers and Sons,* these students of science invested their field of inquiry with miraculous reformative powers that lay at the essence of modernity. Thus, as Vera approached the Federal Polytechnic Institute's newly designed main building, she remembers dramatically that she "entered the temple of science and was canonized its servant."[6]

In a manner typical of those newly converted to any creed, Vera ferociously dedicated herself to science and the study of medicine. After having waited to enter the University of Zurich's hallowed lecture halls for over two years by the time she arrived, she was quickly overwhelmed as she sat bewildered in classes in zoology, mineralogy, and anatomy as esteemed professors rapidly led students through the intellectual minefield of science in a tongue she struggled to understand. Though demoralized, she persevered. Determined to fulfill her self-designed goal, and desperate not to disappoint herself or her supportive relatives back home, she committed herself to her studies to the exclusion of anything else.[7]

Given her myopic focus on her studies, initially Vera and her husband took little notice of the extracurricular activities of the sizable Russian émigré community in Zurich and stayed mainly to themselves.[8] In spite of the flurry of activity on the streets in the Oberstrass suburb of the city, where they and most of their compatriots lived, the Filippovs eschewed these distractions and concentrated on their studies and their mutual goals—at least originally. But Vera's sister Lidia was a different story. Although she arrived in Switzerland with her sister and brother-in-law, Lidia soon liberated herself from them. Eighteen years old, attractive, romantically unattached, and with a lively, engaging personality, Lidia quickly formed social relationships beyond her familial ties. In her anatomy class Lidia met a Russian woman named Varvara Ivanovna Aleksandrova and through her became friends with a group of Rus-

sian female students who had preceded the Figner sisters to Zurich.[9] Linked
by a commonality of purpose and sentiment, this group of women quickly ce-
mented their bonds of friendship by becoming roommates. In Zurich only a
short time, Lidia exercised her independence and moved out of the quarters
she shared with Vera and Alexei and into her own apartment with her new
friends.

It was at this point that the trajectory of the two Figner sisters' lives temporarily diverged. Vera and Alexei continued to live in matrimonial peace, if
not bliss. Their union distinguished them from many of the other young students at the university, and their social network reflected their more conventional personal lifestyle. In the spring and summer of 1872, the two were preoccupied with their studies and with Alexei's growing influence among the
more moderate members of the Russian colony.[10] Meanwhile, Lidia became
exposed to the more progressive element of the émigré community. As a result, the younger Figner sister increasingly became just as interested in the
sociopolitical theories circulating in the Swiss university town as she was in
the scientific ideas emanating from lecture podiums.

In the early 1870s Zurich welcomed not only university students from abroad
but many of their politically disenchanted compatriots as well. Taking advantage of the liberal nature of the Swiss political environment, many radical
theorists descended upon Zurich in the wake of the Paris Commune's dramatic demise in 1871 while a number of Russian revolutionaries found asylum
from tsarist prisons in this Alpine state. Soon theorists and activists mingled
with the young students pursuing higher education and found many of the
Russian students especially receptive to their unconventional ideas.

The young Russians who enrolled in the University of Zurich and the city's
polytechnic experienced an education that rivaled any of their classroom lessons just by living in Zurich. The federal constitution of Switzerland granted
its citizens civil and political rights and significant freedoms to all who lived
within its borders. Thus, the Russian students who heretofore knew primarily
censorship and government repression found themselves able to peacefully
assemble and discuss the potentially endless array of literature to which they
now had access. Thirsty for the political tracts they were denied at home, some
of the first Russian students who came to Zurich, along with Russian political émigrés, established a Russian library in the city.[11] Filled with books on
the "history of revolution and the workers' movement," political journals, and

even German Social Democratic newspapers,[12] the Russian library allowed Russian expatriates to discover and engage the fundamental aspects of liberal democracy, Socialism, Social Democracy, and anarchism for a nominal fee. As Vera notes, in the literature the Russian students encountered at the library, "everything was new and unexpected, as was everything in this new country. Here we came to know freedom of speech and assembly and saw the higher cultural level of the people."[13]

The radical ideas that they discovered with their subscriptions to the library especially resonated with the young Russian women in Zurich. They had not left Russia in order to develop a revolutionary consciousness. Imbued with poignant ideas about social utility and personal emancipation that emanated from literary figures in the 1860s, these women were desperate to be socially useful and autonomous individuals, yet they had been actively denied the means to achieve their goals in their homeland. By virtue of their sex, the Russian government deemed them unworthy and incapable of realizing these aspirations. To be fair, this misogynistic attitude was not confined to the tsarist autocracy or the patriarchal system in Russia. After all, Simone de Beauvoir writes about a similar battle in post–World War II France that was waged by women who endeavored to repudiate their "condition of vassalage" and to cease "to be parasites" by attaining economic freedom through employment and personal independence through serious intellectual engagement.[14] But it was in the tsar's empire during this particular historical moment that the forces of female ambition and government intransigence collided most directly and forcefully. What allowed these Russian women's frustrations to slowly mature and ripen into political opposition to the tsarist state was the alternate opportunity and political model that Zurich afforded, the intellectual access provided by the Russian library, and the ability to participate publicly for the first time in civil society.

In a process reminiscent of that described by Jürgen Habermas in reference to the effect of reading rooms, coffeehouses, and libraries in eighteenth-century France, the Russian library in Zurich allowed "a political consciousness [to develop] in the public sphere of civil society."[15] This consciousness was not inherently revolutionary. As a prominent member of the library notes, the Russian library was not consciously designed to "engage in revolutionary work, only in enlightenment."[16] Yet enlightenment is powerful and potentially revolutionary depending on its context, since it "thus requires a rupture with obligatory thought patterns inherited from the past and the duty of all to think for themselves."[17] Freed from the intellectual intervention of Russian censors, readers in Zurich's Russian library employed their critical faculties to come to their own conclusions about a host of different topics. The dissonance between what they previously had learned about politics, society, and economic relations and the arguments contained in these newly discovered tracts about the inherent injustice of such political and social systems challenged their fundamental assumptions about themselves and their country and forced them to rethink their personal goals. In addition to providing access to an independent literary sphere, the Russian library was also a living example of a developing civil society, as its members collected funds to help striking workers and Russian émigrés and sponsored assorted lectures and debates.[18] Subsequently, though perhaps not by original design, in the words of Vera, the "library functioned as a silent school of propaganda."[19]

Introduced to the library by her circle of friends, Lidia was the first Figner sister to discover the intellectual and sociopolitical stimulation this organization provided. Stirred by what she found there, Lidia's political interests quickly extended beyond the Russian library. Soon after Lidia left her sister's apartment, her engagement with and interest in political issues and Socialist theories prompted her and her friends to form their own Socialist study group called the "Fritschi" after Frau Fritschi, their landlady in Zurich.[20] Young, energetic, and idealistic, this group of young women embraced Socialist questions that they examined with moral vigor. Despite the intellectual and social satisfaction that she found with her fellow Fritschi members, Lidia never invited her married sister to join the study circle. Chronicling this slight in her memoirs, Vera explains, "I was not involved with the Fritschi at its inception. I wasn't invited to attend the meetings because the members did not like my husband who looked down on their activities. They assumed that I felt similarly and I was too proud to correct them."[21]

Given the rapidity with which Lidia Figner moved out of her sister and brother-in-law's apartment after the group's arrival in Zurich, one can assume that tension between the in-laws was long-standing; rather than cause a rupture, the politicized energy in the Russian colony merely brought what may have been essentially latent, manageable frustrations to the surface. The extent of any direct confrontations between Lidia and Alexei is unclear, but Lidia Figner's disgust with her brother-in-law is evident from a letter she wrote soon after her arrival in Zurich. In the letter she rails against her sister's husband and unceremoniously curses him for his "intolerable moralistic outbursts."[22]

In the early days of their marriage, it is clear that Vera exercised considerable influence over her husband; she not only convinced him to allow her to enroll in the University of Zurich but also engineered his attendance. Thus the Filippov marriage seemed to illustrate the modern rethinking of marriage that was typical of nihilists and radicals in the aftermath of the Great Reforms.[23] Yet once in Zurich, a more traditional gender hierarchy within their marriage seemed to prevail. Vera's alienation from the colony's radical elements was in keeping with her husband's sentiments. Thus, far from acting as Alexei's Svengali, Vera's behavior conformed to the long-standing articles of Russia's family law that stated a wife's responsibility to "submit to [povinovat'sia] her husband as head of the household and to love, respect, and render him unlimited obedience [neogranichennoe poslushanie]."[24]

Alexei Filippov was not a reactionary. Even the Biographical-Bibliographic Dictionary of Revolutionary Figures published in the Soviet Union in 1931 deems him a man of "moderate political opinions."[25] In Mikhail P. Sazhin's recollections of his time in Zurich, he includes Alexei Filippov as one of a group of ardent followers of the populist and Socialist theorist Peter Lavrov who defended his positions most vociferously.[26] Yet Filippov was traditional enough to attempt to keep his young wife isolated from the radical ruckus. This ultimately became a problem for the trio from Kazan, as Alexei's paternalistic treatment of Vera, and, it seems, her sister, put him at odds with Lidia and ultimately with his wife as well.

Vera Figner wrote voluminously about her life. But the attention that she gives to her marriage is minimal. While this stems partly from the fact that Russian women revolutionaries tend to highlight their political activities at the expense of their personal lives in their autobiographical writings,[27] it more specifically derives from Vera's discomfort with a period of time when she was the legal and, worse yet, the moral subordinate of her husband. As a young institute graduate, she yearned for economic and moral autonomy. A medical career seemed a realistic path to such independence, and her marriage was critical to its realization. Yet while marriage brought emancipation from her father, it did not abet Vera's full autonomy, as she became beholden to her husband and subject to his authority. In Zurich Vera's marital dependence set her apart from many of her female compatriots, including her sister and the other

Fritschi members. Their successful achievement of the independence that she craved was a continual reminder of what she lacked and hampered any potential for marital bliss between the Filippovs.

Alexei's paternalistic protection of his young wife had ample opportunity to find expression throughout the fall of 1872, when ideological debates and radical energy abounded. Within the Russian colony in Zurich in 1872, one found just as much ideological enmity as political consensus, especially after two of the most important radical Russian theorists of the day, Mikhail Bakunin and Peter Lavrov, arrived in town. Both men were proponents of populism, a form of agrarian Socialism that glorified the Russian masses, yet there were significant differences between the two. While both believed that the privileged, educated youth of Russia needed to put themselves at the disposal of the Russian people (the *narod*), Bakunin advocated provoking an uprising or revolution among the masses as quickly as possible. Lavrov, on the other hand, espoused patience and urged populists to pave the way for revolution by educating the masses but allowing the Russian people to take the reins of revolution for themselves. In spite of their mutual focus on the Russian masses, the theoretical controversy over tactics eroded any affinity between these two populist theorists and their respective followers, and the Lavrists and Bakuninists soon found themselves on opposite sides of a heated polemical debate. Personal loyalties were tested, and sometimes ties of friendship severed as young politically energized Russians aligned behind one of these two men. Yet the ability to engage such issues freely was a heady experience for the men and women who hitherto had been silenced by political repression.

A new opportunity for political passions to become inflamed presented itself in the fall of 1872 when Sergei Nechaev, one of the most controversial figures in the Russian revolutionary movement, was arrested in Zurich and extradited to Russia to stand trial. Although Nechaev's duplicitous murder of the revolutionary student Ivan Ivanov repulsed many members of the Russian colony, others supported him, choosing to believe his version of events, which labeled Ivanov a secret agent of the police and thus Nechaev's murder of the student as a justifiable revolutionary act. Despite the diverse personal feelings about Nechaev, the Swiss government's cooperation in the arrest and ultimate extradition of the notorious revolutionary raised intense debate and inflamed political passions in Zurich. Even after Nechaev was back in the Russian empire awaiting trial, the atmosphere remained volatile in the Russian colony.

Alexei's efforts to shield his wife from this energized political climate aroused her ire and heightened her desire to emancipate herself from her husband's control. As Vera saw it, "in everything he stood in my way and like the Great Wall of China separated me from people with whom I agreed."[28] But even if she had wanted to free herself from her relationship and sever her ties with her husband, securing a divorce would have been a daunting prospect.

Until 1917 marriage remained a religious matter in Russia and its dissolution required the approval of the church. As Gregory Freeze notes, "In contrast to most of contemporary Europe, where the state gradually usurped control over [marriage], the Russian church successfully retained jurisdiction until the end of the *ancien regime* and made the exercise of this authority one of its major preoccupations."[29] Subsequently, divorces were granted only under exceptional circumstances. In order for the Orthodox Church to grant a divorce, the couple had to go through a long, arduous, and expensive process in which they proved adultery, sexual incapacity (as distinct from infertility, which was not a justifiable cause for divorce), or the long-term desertion of one spouse. Even though Church policy liberalized slightly in the second half of the nineteenth century, by 1900 the divorce rate in Russia was still "several times lower than in most other European countries," with only one thousand divorces granted annually.[30] Thus, it would have been counterintuitive for Vera to assume that she and her husband's difference of opinion would be sufficient cause to end their marriage.

Even though Vera did not pursue a divorce at this time, she did explore opportunities for self-expression beyond the classroom. By the end of 1872 she joined the Russian library and attended a series of social-political meetings designed exclusively for Russian women in Zurich. Consequently, despite Alexei's best efforts to prevent it, she entered the public fray of debate, became politicized, and disengaged "from [her] solitary life" in Zurich.[31]

Vera found the courage to engage in political opportunities through her friendship with Sofia Bardina, a young Russian agronomy student and a member of the Fritschi circle whom she met in her mineralogy class. Bardina was a strong personality whose political convictions were far more sophisticated than Vera's at the time. From their first meeting, she challenged Vera's assumptions about her and her family's place in the socioeconomic-political order of Russia and urged Vera to renounce the material privileges that her nobility afforded.[32] Bardina's allegations troubled Vera, but she was not yet inclined to accept them; nevertheless, she grew close to Bardina and came to rely on her political tutelage. Thus, in spite of her discomfort, she accepted Bardina's invitation to attend a meeting of the so-called All-Women's Union.

Consciously designed as a venue in which women could learn to articulate themselves logically without being intimidated by men, this group was not radical. Beyond providing a venue where women would gain the experience of and confidence in exercising their critical reason in a public space, however, the All-Women's Union had limited significance. Without a clear political agenda, but infused with the varied ideologies and passionate spirits of its attendees, the union soon dissolved in a storm of commotion and argument after only the first few meetings. Yet for Vera it marked a turning point, because it represented her autonomous decision to fuse her scientific education with a sociopolitical one.

Even after the demise of the All-Women's Union, Vera maintained a social relationship with Bardina that ultimately proved momentous. As Vera remembers it, one night the two were spending time in Bardina's apartment when suddenly Lidia and the other members of the Fritschi walked in.[33] Aware that a meeting of a group to which she did not belong was about to start, Vera rose to leave. But as she tells her readers decades later, "Bardina gently stopped me and from that moment on I did not miss a meeting."[34] Whether Vera's inauguration into the Fritschi was as nonchalant and coincidental as she describes it is doubtful. But what is significant is that no matter how much this event was fictionalized for her reading public, Vera deems Bardina, rather than her own sister, as the party responsible for her inclusion in the Fritschi group.

Inevitably, part of the reason for this lies in the tensions fomented by Vera's marriage to Alexei Filippov. But one can also surmise that tension between the two sisters existed independent of Alexei's influence. Throughout their lives, the two girls spent an inordinate amount of time together. Secluded on their family estate as children, the sisters were only seventeen months apart in age and thus shared meals, a bedroom, lessons, playtime, and the limited attention of their mother. In their preteen years both girls attended the same boarding school and then in late adolescence traveled together to Zurich. Although a spirited and fun-loving woman, Vera was also opinionated and self-righteous and had a domineering personality. One could easily see how she could be a younger sibling's Achilles heel. In many ways Lidia always struggled to keep up with her older sister as teachers and relatives inadvertently and explicitly established a sense of competition between the two. Even the manner in which Vera recalled her ultimate departure for Western Europe in 1872 cast

Lidia in a subordinate role, as her mother "decided to send Lidia as well."[35] Thus, it would not be surprising if, irrespective of her disapproval of Vera's husband, Lidia wanted a place of her own and a group to which she belonged and contributed without her sister. But as the fall semester gave way to a new year, although she did not precipitate it, Lidia was thrown together with her older sister yet again in a quasi-Socialist sorority known as the Fritschi circle.

The group of young women who joined together in the Fritschi was extraordinary. These women combined academic diligence with a commitment to the study of Socialism that was unrivaled in Zurich. Living together in a few rooms let from Frau Fritschi, a spirit of solidarity and mutual aid pervaded the group. Although several members of the Fritschi, especially the three Subbotina sisters, Maria, Eugenia, and Nadezhda, were quite well off financially and able to rent more luxurious accommodations,[36] they instead chose to live in the cramped and relatively unkempt flat with the other members of their student-Socialist society.[37] Here the young women lived according to the egalitarian notions they studied as they pooled funds and resources for the benefit of the whole. These material sacrifices fostered a sense of asceticism like that celebrated by Chernyshevskii in *What Is to Be Done?* and to which the nihilists and political radicals of their generation aspired. As Peter Kropotkin noted, the Russian women students in Zurich as a whole lived on very little: "Tea and bread, some milk, and a thin slice of meat cooked over a spirit lamp, amidst animated discussions of the latest news from the Socialist world or the last book read,—that was their regular fare. Those who had more money than was needed for such a mode of living gave it for the common cause."[38] Rather than bemoan their material deprivation, the women of the Fritschi celebrated it, because it fostered "purity of motives, rigorous asceticism, and complete self-sacrifice."[39]

The women who belonged to the Fritschi were not seasoned radicals. They were young girls who only recently had begun to live independent lives free from the restrictions imposed by strict parents, cloistered girls' institutes, and the repressive Romanov autocracy. Although a latecomer to the group, Vera was one of the oldest members when she joined at the advanced age of twenty! But despite their previous inexperience in the public sphere and with seemingly endless radical theories emanating from every corner of Europe, they found ample opportunities to test their burgeoning political ideals in Zurich. As they discussed Socialist theory, worked for the printing press that churned out Lavrov's populist journal *Vpered!*, and participated in the Russian library, the girls' political maturity grew. As it did, theory gave way to active involvement. Ironically, the focus of their collective action was the organization that had done so much to foment their political awareness: the Russian library.

Founded in 1870, the Russian library in Zurich distinguished between two groups of its members: the founders and the general members.[40] Increasingly, the members (which included the Fritschi) resented the fact that, unlike the prerogatives enjoyed by the founders that allowed them to effectively manage the collection and direction of the library, they were denied any control over the acquisition of new materials or the overall direction that the library would take. After their protestations about the inherent injustice of this situation passed unnoticed, a group of Russian students, led by the Fritschi, announced that they were withdrawing from the existing library and establishing their own library along more equitable lines. Among the protesters who officially registered their intentions and agenda in a letter to Peter Lavrov were seven members of the Fritschi, including Sofia Bardina, Lidia Figner, and Vera Filippova.[41] Less than one month after they withdrew from the original Russian library, these headstrong women opened a new one.[42] In a small two-story house (purchased largely through funds donated by the Subbotina sisters and their mother), the new Russian library had a large reading room and small kitchen on the first floor and rooms on the second, into which several Fritschi members relocated.[43] Reflective of the equity and justice they viewed as essential to Socialism, the new Russian library made no distinction between members, and the kitchen was open to all the library's readers.[44]

In the early months of 1873, Vera was attending Fritschi meetings and publicly taking a visible political stand in the Russian colony. How this affected her home life is unknown. The tension or lack thereof in the Filippov home during the winter and spring of 1873 remains a mystery. Was Vera disgusted with her personal life and revolted by her husband as she tacitly endured a situation to which there seemed to be no resolution? Did the couple's relationship become increasingly and openly combative over Vera's recent display of autonomy? Did both spouses want to abandon the other but saw no way to do so? Or was there more peace in the home than Vera's memoirs insinuate? Perhaps it was merely in hindsight that Vera viewed her husband's behavior as constrictive, or maybe she simply chose to portray Alexei in this light to validate her own behavior. Each scenario is possible as are subtle variations on each. But no matter the state of the personal relationship of Vera and Alexei Filippov during the early part of 1873, external considerations forced the couple to decide the fate of their marriage sooner than they expected when the Imperial Russian government issued a *ukaz* (decree) in May 1873.

News of the government's ukaz traveled quickly through Zurich. There was hardly a flat or rooming house in the city that was not preoccupied with the news. Although it concerned only one group of students attending the university and the polytechnic, the decree became the talk of the town. The native Swiss population buzzed with the news as the international collection of students analyzed every point addressed in the ukaz. Within weeks, newspapers around the world printed translations of the decree and analyzed its significance. The ukaz inflamed passions around the globe. But, naturally, nowhere did the news have more significance than in Zurich's Russian colony.

As students and émigrés read the decree, more than one hundred Russian women attending the University of Zurich and the Federal Polytechnic Institute realized that their government deemed it time to end their Zurich sojourn and reassert its control over their lives and their futures. The language contained within the decree is so pointed that it is worth quoting at length. Exclusively referencing its female subjects in Zurich, the Russian government alleged the following:

> Very unfavorable reports have reached the Government relative to the conduct of these young women. At the time when their number began to increase, the leaders of the Russian emigration made Zurich the centre of their revolutionary propaganda, and they spared no efforts to draw the students into it. Under their influence all serious study gave place to a fruitless political agitation . . . The young women who have thus been dragged into politics are entirely under the influence of the leaders of the emigration, and have become their obedient instruments . . . Others allow themselves to be deluded by the communistic theories of free love and under the protection of a fictitious marriage, act in utter forgetfulness of all the fundamental principles of morality and decorum . . . Such immorality cannot be allowed by the Government to pass unnoticed. It must not be forgotten that these women will, sooner or later, come back to Russia there to become wives, mothers, and teachers, and it is the duty of the Russian Government to prevent them as far as possible, from corrupting the youth of the country . . . In order to put an end to this abnormal state of things, it is hereby announced to all the Russian women who attend the lectures at the University and the Polytechnic School of Zurich, that such of them as shall continue to attend the above lectures after the 1st of January, 1874, will not be admitted on their return to Russia to any examination, educational establishment, or appointment of any kind under the control of the Government.[45]

Another element of the decree was so scandalous that several foreign newspapers edited it from their coverage of the ukaz. It stated that "these girls have fallen so deep that they are making a special study of that branch of obstetrics which in all countries is punished by criminal law and despised by honest people."[46] In addition to indicting their female subjects in Zurich with charges of political agitation and sexual promiscuity, the imperial government of Alexander II insinuated that the women medical students were most interested in learning how to perform abortions so that they could exercise their notions of "free love" with more impunity.[47]

Within one short decree the government of Alexander II maligned the moral character of its female subjects studying in Zurich, accused them of being the witless lackeys of male revolutionaries, and denied them the chance of fulfilling their professional goals in their native land should they decide to continue their studies in Switzerland. The government crafted their accusations against the Russian women in terms that contemporary audiences would understand and, it hoped, in a manner with which they would sympathize. Given the opinion of many within Western Europe that Alexander II's Russia was an uncivilized exercise in political despotism, the imperial government could not simply blame the increasing political activism of the female students. While unnerving to many conservative elements, given the political repression in Russia, such finger pointing would not have been sufficient to elicit wide-scale support. Thus, the imperial regime had to inextricably connect their denunciations of political radicalism to charges that were much more dangerous, scandalous, and familiar; to notions with which every upstanding citizen and burgher could empathize. That is, they tied women's political activism to scathing indictments of sexual impropriety. In doing so they recalled radical models of "new people" like those outlined by writers such as Nikolai Chernyshevskii and defined the essential characteristics of a woman who violated the mores of feminine virtue. Consequently, an immoral woman was characterized as a woman who was at once sexualized and politicized, as overt sexuality and political radicalism became intimately connected as primary indicators of a wicked deviation of feminine nature.

Russian men were just as active in the radical political milieu in Zurich as their female compatriots, yet their government did not recall them. Had Alexander II's regime attempted to exercise control over their male subjects abroad as they did the women students, vigorous protests would have ensued in reaction to such an egregious violation of the men's personal sovereignty. But the paternalistic reprimand of the Russian women studying in Zurich was less likely to raise objections. Treating these women like errant children, the government's recall was framed not in political terms, but in moral ones, giving evidence that women were not considered to be morally autonomous creatures but were instead viewed as lesser beings who needed supervision and regular admonishment.

The governmental decree called upon well-established notions of women's roles as both mothers and educators of the next generation in order to make the threat that these women supposedly posed as pernicious as possible. To allow these young medical students to continue their present course in Zurich, the decree insinuated, would not only consign them to lives bereft of virtue but would ultimately allow them to spread their depravity to subsequent generations. The decree therefore charged that these same women were pliant and stupid enough to be easily corrupted, but once they were, they could spread their diabolical perversity with impunity within the haven of the home and to unsuspecting pupils in the Russian Empire. But judging from the apparent logic of the decree, it seems as if in the summer of 1873 there was still time for these Russian women students and Russia's future generations. In spite of the government's assertion that these women were already engaged in immoral political and sexual acts, the decree alleged that the timely cessation of the students' stay in Zurich would enable their redemption.

In many ways the government's ukaz engaged an ongoing debate about the Russian women students in Zurich and, more generally, about women students living and studying on their own apart from patriarchal families. For many in Europe the idea of a young woman living independent of male influence was scandalous. So-called respectable European society was outraged by such a concept but even more so by the idea of these independent young women working alongside male students in the indelicate world of science and medicine. Necessarily privy to the human form in classes like biology and anatomy, female medical students seemed to defy traditional norms of feminine behavior and social decorum. But the presence of so many women students of one nationality ultimately focused much of the social indignation upon the Russian women attending the University of Zurich.

Depending on one's perspective, the Russian women students were either pioneering trailblazers who came to Zurich to claim an education on behalf of all women or an immoral invasion from the east. While advocates for women's rights joyously watched as new opportunities unfolded for female students in Zurich, detractors sought to besmirch the girls and close the university's doors to all women. Complaints circulated about the Russian female students' lack of preparation, their manner of dress, and their unconventional behavior.[48] As one contemporary report noted, within Zurich itself the complaints revolved around essentially petty issues. "Some excitement has been lately caused in Zurich by the foolish conduct of a few of the young Russian lady students. The accusations against them have never amounted to anything very serious, being limited to fast dressing, smoking, and loud conversation."[49] For the non-Russian community, what offended them was not the Russian women students' growing affinity for radical politics but the unfeminine and visible manner in which they lived their lives. As Joan Landes contends, the French revolutionary period bequeathed definite notions about virtue and gender to the modern world.[50] While what defined political virtue was specific to an individual country and thus dependent upon particular characteristics, such as a region's form of government, the virtue of gender was universal; public virtue was masculine and private virtue was feminine.[51] Should women transgress the boundaries of gender, enter the public sphere, and seek to "act like men," they abdicated their claim to respectability and proved themselves devoid of virtue.

Once the Russian ukaz circulated, the debate about the morality of the Russian women reverberated through Zurich and the international press. Papers from New York to New Zealand covered the incendiary ultimatum issued by the tsar's government and weighed in on the topic. Some were swayed by the allegations contained within the decree. For example, the editors of the *Boston Medical Surgical Journal* noted on July 10, 1873, "We are sorry to hear that the female students at Zurich, of whom we have had such glowing accounts, are too immoral even for Russia, who has recalled her daughters to be redeemed by home influences."[52]

There were undoubtedly those in Zurich who rejoiced that the Russian female presence at the university would be dwindling in the wake of the tsarist ukaz. But others, both within the canton and from across the globe, expressed their sympathy for the women whose dreams were now being denied. Despite the tsarist government's efforts to ground its denunciations of the women students in moral terms, most informed observers realized that the ukaz was rooted in the Russian state's political concerns. In a letter to the editors of the journal quoted above, an unknown source at the University of Zurich claimed, "It is not on account of immorality that the Russian government forbids attendance upon the lectures at Zurich, but on account of the revolutionary and socialistic tendencies of some of the female students."[53] For some the decree spoke just as much to the Russian government's despotism as it did to the morality of its female subjects in Switzerland. Consequently, even those who agreed that "the Russian women students often behave in a manner discreditable to their sex" condemned "the arbitrary conduct of the Russian government in the matter."[54]

The level of interest that the ukaz generated around the word demonstrates the significance of the battle being waged between the women students and their government. Women's rights advocates informed their supporters that the developing situation in Zurich was not just a local concern. An article in the English women's newspaper the *Women's Journal* railed that the "blow which the Russian government has struck must therefore be felt outside the circle of those at which it was aimed."[55] But, ironically, as voices rose in support around the globe, the women most directly affected by the decree were silent.

Immediately after learning of the imperial ukaz, the Russian women students in Zurich convened a general meeting. As Vera remembers it, most of the women wanted to issue a vociferous protest against the charges contained in the decree and defend their characters and motives, but a more conservative group refused to take part in such a protest. In fact, this second group of women, which included a number who were imminently close to receiving their degrees, pledged to issue a public retort should other women proceed with their idea of a printed protest. With no prospect of a united response, the women directly affected by their government's unjust decree were silent and allowed others to speak on their behalf.[56]

In the weeks that followed, the Russian women who were enrolled in the university and polytechnic planned what to do next. A small number of them decided to remain in Zurich and try to complete their studies before the end of the year. Some returned to Russia to continue their scientific education in the newly formed (as of 1872) Women's Medical Courses in St. Petersburg. Established through a private endowment, the tsarist regime sanctioned these courses in large part as an effort to "stem the flow of women abroad."[57] Although the level of instruction in these courses was laudable, it was not the same as what the women had found in Zurich. In addition, the Russian women who attended the Women's Medical Courses found that their level of independence was tempered in a way that their Zurich counterparts' was not. Not only did the St. Petersburg students need to "observe Lent and religious holidays," but they were also "forbidden to smoke, to applaud professors," and they were prohibited from walking "in the main corridors of the Academy" (where the men studied).[58] These restrictions thus dissuaded most of the Zurich veterans from enrolling in the St. Petersburg courses. Taking advantage of the Russian government's shortsightedness in mentioning only the University of Zurich in its May decree, many of the affected women hoped to prevail upon the good graces of university administrations in other European capitals (like Bern, Geneva, and Paris) and secure admission.

The women of the Fritschi were among this latter group. But before they left Zurich, they went on an excursion to the lakeside town of Neuchâtel, Switzerland. As the friends gathered in Neuchâtel's neighboring picturesque village of Liutri, they realized that their lives were about to irrevocably change. Yet the impending changes were not limited to venue. Although most planned to continue their studies for the moment, more dramatic goals loomed on the horizon. Whether it was the natural outgrowth of their Socialist studies and public activism in Zurich or precipitated by the Russian government's most recent demonstration of repression targeting the Russian women of Zurich, or most assuredly the combination of the two, the members of the Fritschi transformed themselves from a Socialist study group into a yet unnamed revolutionary organization whose members resolved to dedicate their lives to the radical cause. But as she departed Zurich for Neuchâtel, Vera Figner knew nothing about this transformation. Still unsure of Vera's level of commitment, the Fritschi initially did not apprise their married friend of their revolutionary agenda. Unlike her inclusion in the study circle months earlier, though, this time it was not Sofia Bardina who prompted Vera's more formal involvement, but Lidia Figner, who initiated her sister as a full-fledged member of the newly formed radical organization.

According to Vera, soon after the group's arrival in Liutri, her sister asked "if I had decided to devote my efforts to revolutionary affairs? She asked if I would sever my ties to my husband if circumstances necessitated it? If I would abandon my medical career and throw aside science [in order to devote myself to the cause]?"[59] After answering enthusiastically to each of her sister's questions in the affirmative and voicing her agreement with the group's revolutionary platform (which was copied almost verbatim from the rules of the Swiss section of the International Workingmen's Association, or the First International)' Vera joined her sister Lidia and her radical colleagues as a fully committed member of the group.[60]

At the end of their Liutri sojourn, the members of the organization returned to Zurich for the remainder of the summer as they decided what to do next. Although Vera and her friends committed themselves to political radicalism, they were not yet ready to abandon their university studies. After the governmental decree, "the majority of [Russian women] who remained abroad enrolled in the medical faculty of Bern University, which, by the summer of 1874, had admitted thirty-four Russian women."[61] Included among them were Vera Figner and several other Fritschi members. Initially, a second group of Fritschi members that included Lidia Figner traveled to Paris in an effort to enroll in the university there. Facing administrative delays and high costs, these women persevered and enrolled in the Sorbonne until the Russian government once again engineered their expulsion, at which point they relocated to Geneva. Soon they were joined by a few of their Fritschi colleagues who had previously enrolled in Bern University.[62] By 1874 the only two members of the Fritschi circle who remained in Bern were Dora Aptekman and Vera Figner.

Although not ordered to by their government, men joined the Russian exodus from Zurich as well. Before the imperial decree, there had been approximately 150 Russian students enrolled in the University of Zurich and the polytechnic; in the fall semester, after the ukaz was promulgated, less than 10 remained enrolled.[63] Among the men who left Zurich was Alexei Filippov. But he did not join his wife in Bern. Instead, after withdrawing from the University of Zurich along with his wife and sister-in-law in August 1873, he went home to Kazan.[64]

In spite of the miles that separated Vera and her husband, they remained married and connected. The couple continued to correspond and Alexei provided for Vera financially.[65] Vera still considered herself a married woman and introduced herself as such to new friends and acquaintances. But with her husband more than a thousand miles to the east, Vera now experienced a level of functional independence and a sense of autonomy that she had never known before.

Regardless of the large numbers of Russian students who transferred from Zurich to Bern, the Russian colony could not be recreated. A city with less than half the population of Zurich, Bern could not duplicate the radical energy of its fellow university town. Neither the leading revolutionary figures nor their presses followed the students to Bern. In the words of Vera Figner, "the path to revolution remained in Zurich from which we were banned."[66] If the balance between a preoccupation with academic degrees and a focus on Socialist activism tipped in favor of political activism in Zurich, in Bern scholastic enterprises prevailed. Thus, the year that the Figner sisters spent in Zurich was shown to be a unique historical moment when impressionable, idealistic students merged with seasoned political theorists and activists to create a vibrant radical environment that fueled the revolutionary sentiments of all of those involved. Giving evidence to this is the reality that of the ninety-three Russian women studying medicine in Zurich from 1871 until 1873, forty-three were subsequently arrested, twenty-seven of these for "relatively serious activities."[67]

In the winter of 1873–1874, no other European city seemed capable of reproducing the radical incubator that was found in Zurich. With their revolutionary sensibilities irreversibly aroused, some Russian students suddenly found the academic pursuits that they had previously longed for banal. Eager to put their socialist ideals to the test on behalf of their native land, advanced degrees seemed a self-indulgent, pointless distraction. Thus beginning in 1874 a steady stream of Russian students abandoned Western Europe for a life in the revolutionary underground in their homeland. Among these were most of the members of the Fritschi, including one Figner sister: Lidia.

Having relocated to Geneva with a number of her fellow Fritschi members, Lidia Figner's radical energies grew. Committed to applying their socialist ideals to the realities of Russian life, the Geneva Fritschi began to collaborate with a group of young radical men from the Caucasus. Together, this now co-ed revolutionary organization began to plot their return to Russia and their course of action. The Fritschi women brought to the group a radical morality that stressed asceticism, self-sacrifice, and even a suggestion for a commitment to celibacy. While the group's men were impressed with the women's moral vigor—though decidedly less so with the idea of celibacy, which they quickly rejected—they urged that more focus was needed on practical issues, including the method of struggle they were to employ.[68] Subsequently the newly formed organization fused ideals and practicality in a way that Vera admired.[69]

Before this group, deemed the Pan-Russian Social Revolutionary Organization, formalized their ties, they sought permission from the two Fritschi members who remained in Bern. Highly sensitive to issues of revolutionary solidarity and desperate to avoid authoritarian methods, the Geneva Fritschi would not commit to their new male comrades until Vera and her Bern roommate, Dora Aptekman, expressly consented to the collaboration. Both women agreed without hesitation, but neither demonstrated any desire to join the group.[70]

It was obvious at this point to Vera and Dora that their Fritschi colleagues were moving ahead with their plans to become more actively involved in political issues in their homeland. Although they approved of and admired their friends' intentions and commitment, neither Vera nor Dora were inclined to join them in their quest at the moment. Both women dove into their medical studies with gusto, desperate to achieve their doctoral degrees. Even when the girls in Geneva summoned Vera to leave Bern for a political project in Serbia, she quickly refused, allowing another one of the Fritschi to go in her place.[71] For Vera, the lure of science was too tempting, the dream of a medical degree in her name too intoxicating. Even after her sister and friends left Switzerland and returned to Russia in 1874 to begin their careers propagandizing workers, Vera refused to exchange her medical books for radical leaflets and days spent in factories. Science exerted a pull that she chose not to resist.[72]

In the early months of 1875, Vera met a man who would become a lifelong friend. She wrote of Nikolai Morozov that it was impossible not to love him, and his own writings detail his immediate enchantment with the dark-eyed beauty. Of her initial impressions of Morozov, Vera notes, "He was twenty years old, I was twenty-two, but I felt much, much older than him; with the tender feelings of a sister or a mother I was spiritually attracted to his personality.[73] For his part, Morozov writes, "[Vera] made a deep impression on me from the start . . . I almost fell in love with her."[74] He continues, "In the person of Vera I first became acquainted with a new higher type of woman and I realized this immediately. Her big, brown shining eyes thoughtfully watching when we talked about philosophical and social questions. Her remarks showed her elegance and grace."[75]

Nikolai Morozov and Vera were kindred spirits in many ways. Both aroused to work for the betterment of the Russian masses, they saw science as their vehicle to do so. But as Nikolai and Vera were discussing how and when to help the Russian peasantry and working class in a boardinghouse in Bern, the majority of the Fritschi were living in industrial centers in Russia, working in factories, and attempting to indoctrinate their uneducated, poverty stricken co-workers in the tenets of Socialism as part of their self-formed Pan-Russian Social Revolutionary Organization, soon deemed the Moscow Organization. Nikolai Morozov informs his readers that although Vera was torn between her sense of radical solidarity with her friends and her personal scientific pursuits, for almost the first year of their acquaintance she chose the latter. Morozov contends, "She couldn't resolve to accompany her friends to Russia and engage in propaganda though she wanted to very much."[76] Vera had several plausible reasons why she should remain in Bern for the time being. Prominent among these was her reasoning that if the Russian women students abandoned their studies, they would do irreparable harm to the cause of women's education.[77] But the truth is that she just did not want to leave. She liked her studies and her life in Bern, and she was not ready to sacrifice herself for her friends, her husband, or the Russian masses, at least not yet.

Telling herself she was just as committed to the socialist struggle as her friends who were spreading propaganda to Russian workers, Vera remained in Bern and bided her time. Here she studied medicine, socialized with radically inclined Russians, and contributed to the cause financially. The Fritschi members were not the only young Russians to return to their country to fully embrace radical pursuits. Students and émigrés left Switzerland on a regular basis. Many found themselves without the funds to secure the means of travel. At this point Vera often stepped in.

During the time that she lived in Switzerland, Vera had material means. Through the support of both her husband and her mother, Ekaterina, she was secure financially. She alleges that with the rest of the Fritschi circle back in Russia, in order to make the most of her money she pared down her lifestyle in Bern and slowly gave her excess funds away to her more financially compromised friends and acquaintances,[78] and even to students and émigrés whom she had never met.[79] Because of this, she asserts that she quickly developed a reputation among the many Russians in Western Europe as someone to whom those in economic need could turn.[80]

Like Vera, Nikolai Morozov relished his education and longed for a life as a scientist. But a few months after he made Vera's acquaintance, he decided to join his fate to that of the radicals who preceded him to the Russian underground. As he recalls in his memoirs, he decided that he could not live a life of intellectual privilege and personal safety when others struggled, suffered, and even died for the cause of the Russian masses. "How could I quietly work in my laboratory when persecution and prosecution enveloped them . . . It was awfully difficult for me to abandon my childhood dream of becoming a scholar but it was necessary."[81]

It pained Vera to see yet another friend leave for the fate that she sensed should be hers, but she made no move to join him. Claiming that she was "still undecided" about the future course of her life, she resolved to stay in Bern and gave Morozov one hundred rubles to pay for his trip home.[82] As she saw Morozov and their mutual friend Nikolai Sablin off on their journey, she stood on the railroad station platform waving her red scarf until the train was out of sight.[83] Then she returned to her flat and her life as a student.

Over the course of 1875, Vera Figner was fooling herself. She considered herself a committed radical, but she was essentially living as a philanthropist. To a certain extent, her actions were barely more radical than those of her mother, who had organized a fund-raising drive on behalf of the Russian women students in Zurich just a few years earlier.[84] Ekaterina's acquaintances were certainly less politically deviant than Vera's friends, but both mother and daughter focused on rendering financial and emotional aid to the causes they believed in rather than compromising themselves directly. Living in Switzerland, associating with revolutionary students and émigrés, subsidizing radical dreams, and even attending Bakuninist and Marxist congresses demonstrated Vera's radical affinities but presented no real personal danger. In fact, despite her allegations to the contrary, the years she spent in Bern were some of the most fulfilling of her life.

In the volume of her autobiographical writing that Vera Figner devotes to her years as a student in Switzerland, there is a palpable difference between her description of her time in Zurich and that of the period she spent in Bern. Her description of her years in Zurich reads like a conversion story. With a serious tone that charts her socialist awakening and developing commitment, Vera's account of the months that she spent at the University of Zurich places all distractions behind her incipient radicalism. But the chapters detailing her experience in Bern feel lighter; political danger and utopian dreams retreat while friendships, social ties—albeit it with revolutionary figures—and intellectual vigor take center stage. Although she alleges that her sense of inner turmoil over her inability to commit to the revolutionary cause while her sister and Zurich friends embraced their radical mission brought her physical and emotional distress in the two years that she spent in Bern, one should be leery of her protestations.

In Bern, Vera enjoyed a vast social network of her own making with whom she was free to associate without the constrictions imposed by a protective husband. She was making steady progress in her studies, gaining ground on her medical degree, and relishing the freedom of deciding her fate. Even after the news arrived that her sister Lidia and the other members of the Moscow Organization had been arrested and were imprisoned in the House of Preliminary Detention awaiting trial, Vera maintained her commitment to her studies and made no arrangements to return to Russia—at least, that is, not until Mark Natanson walked into her flat in November 1875.

Over the previous few years, while Vera studied medicine and discovered Socialism, Mark Natanson had built an impressive radical resume. He belonged to several radical student organizations and had been arrested several times.[85] In 1875 he was free, but most of his former radical colleagues were still incarcerated or exiled. Remaining hopeful that a social revolution would succeed in Russia, Natanson attempted to recruit a new generation of political activists in Moscow, Kiev, Odessa, Kharkov, London, Paris, and various cities in Switzerland, including Bern.[86]

Vera was just two semesters away from completing her courses for her medical degree when Natanson materialized in her doorway.[87] He had sought out Vera and Dora Aptekman because of their close connection with the imprisoned members of the Moscow Organization. Playing on their feelings of solidarity and radical responsibility, he painted a dire picture of the state of radical forces back home in Russia. He described the incarcerated former Fritschi members as just the latest in a long line of arrests by the tsar's gendarmes.[88] The revolutionary ranks had been depleted and reinforcements were critically needed. Would Vera and Dora replace their imprisoned friends on the front line of the struggle?

Months before Natanson's visit, Vera and Nikolai Morozov had discussed Vera's intention to remain in Bern. While Morozov told Vera that he understood her motivation for staying in Switzerland, he contended that she would be unable to remain in Switzerland pursuing her dream when the news came that "our friends all sit in Russian prisons or die slow painful deaths in Siberian exile."[89] In November 1875 he was proven right.

Mark Natanson played on Vera's and Dora's emotions. Although he made no headway with Aptekman, Vera was open to his ideas. When Natanson reminded the women that their friends were calling them from behind prison walls, Vera was ashamed of her selfishness.[90] More than two years earlier, she had pledged to her sister, her friends, and herself that she "would abandon [her] medical career and throw aside science [in order to devote herself to the cause]" when circumstances necessitated it.[91] Now, in the fall of 1875, it seemed time to fulfill her pledge.

In describing this moment in her literary account of her years in Switzerland, Vera resurrects her conversion tale as she describes her renewed active commitment as part of a religious crusade. Consecrated by the sacrifice of her scientific dreams and medical career, she recalls the passage in the Gospel of Luke that says, "No one who places their hands on the plow and looks back is reliable for the Lord God," in order to describe her mission and dedication.[92] That November, as she prepared to leave Switzerland and her medical degree to answer Mark Natanson's appeal, Vera recalled that she "placed [her] hands on the plow" and did not look back.[93] Her days of uncertainty and vacillation were behind her. From this point on, she writes, "social interests always took precedence over the personal."[94]

Within weeks of her meeting with Mark Natanson, Vera abandoned the dream she had relentlessly pursued for the past five years. As fall gave way to another Alpine winter, she said good-bye to Dora Aptekman, the university, and Switzerland. This time, instead of pressing money into the hands of departing friends and bidding them adieu from a railway platform, Vera stepped from the platform herself and onto a train headed to St. Petersburg. Her Swiss sojourn was ended. Three years earlier she had disembarked from her train in Zurich with her husband and her sister full of hope and enthusiasm for a satisfying medical career. But in the fall of 1875, estranged from her husband, who had returned to his legal career in Kazan, and cut off from her sister, who sat in a prison cell awaiting trial, Vera boarded the train that would take her back to Russia alone, unsure of what she would find back home and uncertain if she would fulfill the grandiose task that she, her friends, and the revolutionary community set before her.

4

TOWN AND COUNTRY

AS SHE SAT IN A RAILROAD CAR crossing the capitals, farmlands, and villages of the northeastern edges of Europe, Vera tried to stave off an unrelenting chill. Over the previous three years, her body had become acclimated to the more temperate climate in Switzerland; now the lap robes she slung over her legs as the train chugged along through Poland and the Baltic region provided little defense against the cold arctic air, and her discomfort grew with each passing mile. But it was not only the weather that she found disconcerting on this train trip east in late November 1875; she had grown used to much more than just the climate in Western Europe. Since arriving in Zurich in 1872, Vera had grown accustomed to pursuing her own goals, publicly speaking her mind, and experimenting with radical new political ideas. In Switzerland she did so openly and with impunity, and this changed her significantly. Having discovered socialist theory, she embraced its teaching and identified herself as a proponent of its principles as they applied to Russia. Now, as she sat amid anonymous fellow travelers on her way back to Russia, this diminutive, well-dressed, apparently demure young woman seemed to be the antithesis of the unconventional, allegedly promiscuous radicals and nihilists pilloried by the government and the conservative press. But Vera's looks belied her intentions. She was no longer the idealist who dreamed of living a legal, publicly acknowledged existence tending to the ills of those less fortunate than her. Three years removed from an earlier train trip west, she now returned to her native land, a committed populist, resolved to confront the injustice she witnessed not just by ameliorating its consequences but also by conspiring to eradicate its root causes. Switzerland did not make Vera Figner a doctor; it transformed her into a radical.

In spite of her acknowledged commitment to the revolutionary agenda of the Fritschi group, Vera successfully dodged applying her radical ideals in her homeland for several years. Although she admits that her reluctance to fully commit caused her great shame and spiritual turmoil as other women, including her younger sister, proved their mettle by abandoning professional goals and jeopardizing their personal aspirations for a sociopolitical cause, Vera refused to relinquish her dream of becoming a medical doctor. Despite her belief that revolutionary propaganda and agitation were needed to transform Russia, she did not want to have to be the one to conduct them. She did not want to leave Switzerland. She did not want to give up her chance to become a physician. But when Mark Natanson pointedly called upon her to replace her friends and comrades who faced uncertain futures in prison and exile because of their political beliefs, Vera realized that her refusal would be tantamount to an admission of vanity, hypocrisy, weakness, and selfishness. At that moment she knew that "my answer would speak to my moral character. I was not needed in the future, I was needed now."[1]

Much had changed in the years that Vera spent in Switzerland. Soon after she moved west, so did her family, although admittedly not as far. With Vera and Lidia in Switzerland, Ekaterina Figner moved the rest of her brood to the imperial capital of St. Petersburg so that her younger children could take advantage of educational opportunities there.[2] So when Vera left Western Europe, she returned not to her beloved Tetiushi but to the political and cultural heart of the tsarist empire.

Vera's journey home was exhausting. She was full of anxiety about the future that awaited her, and the long train ride eastward took a toll. The multiday journey through sparsely populated areas of Eastern Europe seemed to confirm that with her departure from Switzerland she had left European civilization. On her native soil, the endless swatch of brambles, birches, and firs visible through the train car window spoke to anxious assumptions about the backwardness of the land to which she returned. Since she was relatively unfamiliar with St. Petersburg, this was not so much a homecoming for Vera as it was a relocation, the results of which were anything but determined. As her train car approached the grand city on the Neva, however, she could not help but be dazzled by the power and brilliance of the imperial capital claimed from the sea more than a century before. In the words of one nineteenth-century traveler, as one approached the city by train, "St. Petersburg seems like an oasis in the desert."[3] For much of the preceding three years, as Vera and other budding radicals living in Western Europe pilloried its autocratic repression and the social and economic inequality it promoted, the tsarist government seemed little more than a theoretical construct. But walking along the Nevskii Prospect, past gilded palaces; dramatic domed cathedrals; and charming, picturesque canals, the power of the government she declared herself ready to confront was in full display.

The Figner family lived on Sadovaia Ulitsa just a block off Nevskii, on the backside of the Gostinyi Dvor marketplace. As Vera approached the home that she had never known, she found its rooms darkened and its occupants absent.[4] Admitted by servants who were as much strangers to her as she was to them,[5] she waited for her unsuspecting family members to return from an evening at the theater.[6] With no letter or telegram to forewarn them, Ekaterina and her children were shocked to see their long-absent relative standing before them in their St. Petersburg home and quickly besieged Vera with questions.

Recalling the scene years later, Vera describes her mother's calm reaction to the jarring news that her eldest child had quit medical school to begin a life dedicated to political propaganda as being indicative of Ekaterina's highly developed sensibilities and confident belief in her children's abilities to chart their own courses in life.[7] Yet this explanation defies credibility. Just a few months before, all of the Figner children had promised to become respected professionals and productive members of Russian society. Now both daughters whose medical education Ekaterina helped to fund, and in which she showed considerable interest, had withdrawn from the university and professed their intentions to contest the political and economic injustice in Russia. Lidia's radical career was short-lived, as she was quickly arrested. Now with one daughter waiting in a prison cell to be tried for a crime against the state, another stood before Ekaterina and announced that she was poised to emulate her imprisoned sister.

Although Vera interprets her mother's stoic acceptance as an indication of her sympathetic attitude, Ekaterina's quiet resolve illustrates the extent to which she was conditioned for self-abnegation. The Figner matriarch certainly exhibited politically liberal tendencies, and like many liberally inclined members of Russian society at the time, she emotionally sympathized with more radical figures and agendas. But these were her children. Lidia's imprisonment in a prison fortress illustrated the unhappy fate that awaited Russian radicals. While Ekaterina could not have been pleased with Vera's decision, she denied her feelings as she had done so many times in her adult life. Whether it was in answer to her husband berating her children or her children embracing a dangerous life course, Ekaterina's response was unspoken and internalized. Trained to sacrifice her own wants and needs in a manner befitting the ideals of femininity, Ekaterina Figner choked down her fears and wished her eldest child Godspeed. Yet within the next several weeks, Ekaterina's internalized disquiet became evident. Following a tradition long popular among the country's elite, she left Russia with her two youngest daughters, Eugenia and Olga, and journeyed to Western Europe in an effort to soothe her nerves and reclaim some emotional solace.[8]

Even in Switzerland, though, Ekaterina and her daughters could not escape the lure that revolutionary politics exerted on the youth of the day. According to Vera, even her youngest sister, Olga, then only thirteen, jumped at the chance to interact with this illicit world when Vera entrusted her with six hundred rubles and asked her to relay it to a small radical group.[9] Dangerous, exciting, and filled with men and women who seemed to forsake their own welfare for the cause of social justice, the revolutionary milieu enticed and attracted even liberally inclined young people. During the winter and spring of 1876, while they lived in Switzerland, the Figner women socialized with many of the same men and women with whom Vera and Lidia had interacted months before. As a result, Vera contends that her sisters and mother became more sympathetic to the revolutionary cause.[10] This assertion is consistent with Eugenia Figner's decision to enter the revolutionary fold in the months after this trip. While her Swiss sojourn may not have been solely or even primarily responsible for Eugenia's choice, it certainly did nothing to dissuade her from this path. Thus, if Ekaterina Figner went to Western Europe to assuage her grief over her two eldest daughters' radical aspirations and fate, the relief that ensued was only temporary, since soon after their return Eugenia joined Vera in the revolutionary underground.

St. Petersburg was a locus of radical activity in the 1860s and early 1870s, but by 1875 it had ceased to be so. Thus, as her mother and sisters left for Switzerland, Vera left the capital for Moscow. There she found a ragtag assortment of budding radicals. One could not properly define those who assembled in

Moscow that winter as an organization. They shared neither a common history nor a uniformity of revolutionary designs. At this point one would be hard-pressed to claim that there was any formal revolutionary movement in Russia. Most young radicals would have declared themselves populists, but populism was a nebulous ideology comprised of "odds and ends of socialism and anarchism of all sorts, held together only by a sense of obligation to 'the people' and hatred of the tsarist regime."[11] While most of the so-called Russian radicals and populists active in 1875 yearned to bring about a socioeconomic revolution through close cooperation with the masses, very few had a concrete tactical agenda to transform their aspirations into reality. Thus, forging a spiritual connection among a group of people united merely by a vague political philosophy and a sense of obligation to "substitute for the members of various circles who had recently been arrested" was exceedingly difficult.[12]

Vera loathed the weeks that she spent in Moscow. When she abandoned her dream of becoming a doctor and returned to Russia, she did so under the assumption that she would work among the Russian masses she so idealized. She also assumed that she would fill the role of a secular missionary tending to the needs of the politically and economically downtrodden while preaching to this population about the necessity of rebellion. But in Moscow she had no contact with the "people" (the *narod*). Instead she spent her time encoding and decoding conspiratorial correspondence between imprisoned comrades. On icy winter evenings in the back alleys of Moscow, she exchanged money for letters with a seedy assortment of gendarmes and noncommissioned officers willing to trade access to political prisoners for rubles.[13] Disillusioned by the absence of an intense, soulful relationship with other radical youth and frustrated by this tedious work, in the midst of her first foray into the Russian revolutionary underground Vera claims that she felt on the verge of suicide.[14]

She shared her grief with Anton Taksis, an experienced radical whom she befriended in Moscow. She lamented to him that in Moscow she was just "a small cog in a wheel" over which she had no control.[15] Although Taksis sympathized with his new friend, he also urged her to cast away her romantic ideas about radical enterprises. He told Vera that life in the village was "uglier and simpler than she imagined and that a revolutionary's work was difficult and long."[16] But if she could endure the hard work, poor conditions, and disappointments that were the inevitable consequences of political and social activity in the village, Taksis said, she should follow her heart, leave Moscow, and "go to the people."[17]

After only weeks in Moscow, Vera made arrangements to do just that. Turning her back-alley midnight duties over to other young activists, she left Moscow. Given her medical training, she decided that medicine would be her path
to the people, and she began to search for a position as a medical assistant
(*fel'dsher*) in the countryside. Yet this was more difficult than one might expect. Although her studies in Switzerland more than qualified her for such a
post, she had to hide her education abroad because of the presumed link between women's foreign education and political radicalism. The arrest of her
sister and so many of the other Fritschi members in 1875 only affirmed this
reputed correlation. But enrolling in a fel'dsher program simply to secure the
needed documentation for such a position would have been a waste of time
for Vera.

The solution materialized in the falsified documents provided her through
a colleague's relative, the Moscow physician Dr. Dmitrii M. Glagolev. On February 7, 1876, Dr. Glagolev certified in writing that "in the course of six months
under my immediate supervision [Vera Nikolaevna Filippova] studied the art
of medical assistance . . . with appropriate effort and devotion."[18] This blatant
falsification was not without risks for its author. By fabricating Vera's domestic medical training, Dr. Glagolev easily could have exposed himself not only
to considerable professional risks but to criminal charges as well. Since he was
not a revolutionary himself, Glagolev's complicity raises the question of why
he would knowingly lie for Vera.

Yet the doctor's efforts on Vera's behalf are illustrative of the sympathetic
attitude toward and tacit approval of the revolutionary ventures of Russia's
youth on the part of the intellectual and professional elite in Russia. Because
of the cessation of reforms in the aftermath of student and nationalist uprisings in the early 1860s and Dmitrii Karakozov's 1866 attempt to assassinate
Tsar Alexander II,[19] as well as the "arrests and long detention of hundreds of
ineffectual propagandists," the government lost "the respect of the educated
class."[20] While the majority of these intellectuals and professionals would
not dream of directly confronting the tsarist regime, they appreciated the efforts of those who did. For the remainder of the 1870s and the early 1880s, this
sympathetic attitude of liberal society emboldened their more radical compatriots. Without the reactive censure of public opinion to constrict their activities, Russian revolutionaries felt justified, because the expressed sympathy
and even the silence of these moderate intellectuals seemed to reaffirm the
wisdom and morality of radical actions. Just as Vera interpreted her mother's

silence in the face of her father's despotism as condemnation, so she and her fellow revolutionaries rightly viewed liberal society's silence as an indictment of Alexander II's autocracy.

Once Vera secured Dr. Glagolev's certification, she traveled to Yaroslavl to see a relative of a Zurich friend who worked at the Yaroslavl Provincial County Hospital.[21] Taking the aspiring fel'dsher under his wing, the physician, whom Vera identifies as simply Dr. Pirozhkov, arranged for her to accompany various doctors on their rounds from February through April. Although she did not learn anything new in this internship of sorts, it gave her the documented domestic experience she needed to sit for her fel'dsher exam. On April 24, 1876, the chief of staff of Yaroslavl's Provincial County Hospital certified that over the "last three months and under the daily supervision of doctors," Vera had demonstrated "the practical knowledge necessary for fel'dshers."[22] With this documentation in hand, she took and effortlessly passed the medical assistant examination.[23]

At this point, for the first time since she had returned from Switzerland, Vera went home to Tetiushi. With her mother and sisters in Western Europe, her brothers in St. Petersburg, and her beloved Niania, who had died while Vera was in Zurich, gone for good, the Figner patrimonial estate of Nikiforovo held little interest for Vera. Thus, she settled into a room in the house that she used to call home on her uncle Peter's estate of Khristoforovka. There she spent warm days and entertaining evenings with her cherished aunts and uncles. In the midst of this lovely sojourn, however, she tore herself away and traveled to the provincial capital of Kazan in order to see her husband for the first time in almost three years in order to determine the conditions necessary to obtain a divorce.

By the time the estranged couple met in the summer of 1876, much had changed in their lives. After their time together in Zurich, Vera had committed herself to radicalism while Alexei became a respected local government official and legal member of the community. It was thus essential, and only fair to Alexei, that Vera divorce him before she officially began life in the radical underground. Even if he retained romantic feelings for his wife, his professional life and position within the government precluded a marital reconciliation. His active support of Peter Lavrov and his variant of populism while he was enrolled in the University of Zurich only reinforced the pragmatic wisdom of severing his relationship with Vera. With a revolutionary for a wife and a questionable political past in Western Europe, it would only be a matter of time before Alexei's reputation would be questioned and his position compromised. Thus, in spite of the negative consequences associated with obtaining a divorce, he decided that the dissolution of his marriage would be the lesser of two evils.

Adultery, sexual incapacity, abandonment, and penal exile were the choices that the Filippovs faced. Obviously neither spouse was yet subjected to penal exile, and given Alexei's continued financial support of his wife even after he returned to Russia, a case could not be made for abandonment. Thus, the only two possible grounds for divorce involved the couple's intimate affairs. Even if neither adultery nor sexual incapacity plagued their marriage, which they almost certainly did not, Vera and Alexei could do as other Russian couples faced with a severely restrictive divorce law did both before and after them. As Gregory Freeze notes, even given the vice grip that the Holy Synod held on marriage and divorce, divorces could be easily attained "if both partners desired it, for they could easily collude, manufacture the requisite evidence, and arrange a prompt dissolution of their union."[24] Given the fact that witnesses were required to attest to a case of adultery, and that the Church and state prohibited the guilty spouse from remarrying even after the divorce was finalized, adultery was rarely the cause chosen by those couples looking for a credible reason for their divorce. Although adultery certainly existed and aggrieved partners vocally attested to its occurrence, if the year 1890 can be considered representative—and there is no reason why it should not be—barely more than 20 percent of divorces were granted on the grounds of adultery.[25] To a certain extent sexual incapacity was easier to manufacture and document. Although a physical examination was needed to verify sexual incapacity, the medical community balked at the Church's restrictive definition that defined the condition as anatomical impotence; instead physicians preferred a looser interpretation of sexual incapacity that was not limited to a technical impotence but included infertility.[26] Thus, someone with the social and professional contacts of Alexei Filippov could easily find a cooperative physician to provide the documentation needed to support a case for "sexual incapacity."

By the fall of 1876, Alexei and Vera filed the necessary paperwork seeking the dissolution of their marriage on the grounds of sexual incapacity.[27] Of course, this claim was not without negative consequences for Alexei. With both his masculinity and sexuality questioned, Vera's formerly besotted husband surely became the butt of ridicule and tongue-in-cheek remarks like the one leveled by his once fellow Lavrist Vladimir Smirnov, who declared,

"I think he is very incapable indeed."[28] But the Filippov divorce suited both partners, since it allowed Vera to continue with her radical plans and Alexei to maintain his professional reputation unscathed by any lingering association with the soon-to-be revolutionary. Thus, even after Vera was arrested in 1883, when questioned about his relations with his ex-wife, Alexei could truthfully attest that "after 1876 I knew about her only what I read in the newspapers."[29]

With her divorce all but final, Vera returned to St. Petersburg in August. There she met Alexandra Ivanovna Kornilova, a fellow radical and a woman who would become her lifelong friend. Unable or unwilling to find a position as a medical assistant, for the time being Vera maintained her legal existence and with Kornilova (and Kornilova's sizable family fortune) raised money for political prisoners and collected scores of books to send to their friends in prison.[30] In the company of a kindred spirit and engaged in the sort of "respectable" philanthropic work that occupied her in Switzerland, Vera discovered the peace that had escaped her the winter before in Moscow.

As summer faded into autumn, both the Figner home and St. Petersburg sprang back to life. Ekaterina, Eugenia, and Olga Figner returned from Switzerland while populists and radicals of various persuasions poured into the city.[31] Many of the young people who came to the capital that autumn were survivors of the mass arrests of the "go to the people" movement of 1874. Inspired by the populist mantra that privileged Russians needed to put themselves at the disposal of the masses, thousands of young educated Russians had poured into the countryside during the summer of 1874 only to encounter a suspicious populace and police repression. Hundreds within this "go to the people" movement were arrested and imprisoned. While they languished in prison awaiting trial, scores of their colleagues remained free and committed to the populist cause despite the risk. These survivors, along with other youth who were outraged by the arrest and imprisonment of the idealistic populists, gradually found one another in the capital and began to meet in small, informal groups to plot their next steps.[32] As a result of their discussions, a formal political organization named Land and Freedom (*Zemlia i Volia*) was born in St. Petersburg in the autumn of 1876.

Although Land and Freedom was constituted in the capital that fall, the group's roots could be traced back to the Emancipation Manifesto of 1861. Technically, serfs had been freed by the decree, but the details of their alleged freedom ensured that Russian peasants remained mired in poverty and backwardness. Land and Freedom sought to right the wrongs of the Emancipation Manifesto. The group's objectives included the transfer of all land to those who worked it, the division of the Russian Empire according to local desires, the extension of political freedom to all classes, and the establishment of some form of self-government for the masses.[33] These objectives were not piecemeal reforms; the realization of such demands would have entailed a complete political and social revolution in Russia. In the opinion of Land and Freedom, the Russian intelligentsia were critical to the triumph of this revolution.[34] Convinced that such action was inevitable, the members of the nascent party as well as unaffiliated populists assumed that they could provide the spark to ignite the dormant socialist tendencies of the Russian masses through agitation by words and deeds.[35]

Learning from the lessons of the recent past, the members of Land and Freedom resolved not to repeat the mistakes made by the Moscow Organization, to which Lidia Figner and other Fritschi members belonged. Although the *narodniki*, as the populists were called, still planned on living and working among the people, the fate of the aforementioned group had demonstrated the futility of efforts by members of the intelligentsia to blend imperceptibly with uneducated, poverty-stricken workers. Unable to mask the manifestations of a privileged upbringing, the Moscow Organization immediately aroused the suspicion of workers and officials alike and fell prey to arrest after only weeks of activity. Thus, the members of Land and Freedom decided that they would not attempt to mask their background or education. Instead, they would use their intellect and skills to defend the people and secure their trust. Working as teachers, medical providers, and district clerks, the populists would settle in the countryside and attempt to further the peasantry's interests while simultaneously developing their "spirit of self-respect and protest."[36]

As the leaders of Land and Freedom outlined the group's platform and the responsibilities and charges of its members, other populists were made uncomfortable by the formal concrete ties envisioned by those directing the organization. Vera Figner was among this latter group. Although she and some of her close colleagues shared "the same ideas [as the organized narodniki, they] . . . wanted to retain the type of organization that prevailed during the first half of the decade."[37] They clung to the idealistic notion that they could engage in social and political work in the village as a "community of friends, rather than a party."[38] Recalling the independence that she enjoyed as a member of the Fritschi in Switzerland, Vera balked at the notion that she might be constrained or compelled by formal obligations. Her brief stint in Moscow the previous winter had reaffirmed her need to maintain some sense of autonomy in the radical milieu. Although Vera conjures up the ghost of Nechaev in her effort to explain her reticence to join the formal Land and Freedom organization, her real reasons were rooted in a reluctance to be duty-bound to perform tasks that she found repugnant. Among her circle of friends in the imperial capital, she found a handful of other radicals who shared her views. Consequently, Vera, Alexander Ivanchin-Pisarev, Iuri Bogdanovich, Maria Leshern, Nikolai Drago, Alexandra Kornilova, and Eugenia Figner formed an informal group of "separatists" that shared the program of *Zemlia i Volia* but was a fully autonomous circle.[39]

All of the members of Vera's separatist group were eager to leave the capital for productive work among the peasantry in the countryside. Yet despite the dire physical conditions in many provincial areas, local officials seemed disinclined to arrange positions for these young people from St. Petersburg. As she wrote letters of applications to various *zemstvo* boards and awaited their response,[40] Vera took part in what she later described to police as her first revolutionary act.[41]

On December 6, 1876, Vera and Eugenia Figner took a sixteen-year-old worker named Iakov Potapov to lunch and then walked with him to the Cathedral of Our Lady of Kazan on Nevskii Prospect. When they arrived, a memorial service for Russian volunteers killed in the recent Balkan uprising was nearing completion. As the sounds of the service drifted beyond the cathedral's semicircular colonnades and filled the air on the adjacent square, the Figner sisters and their young charge were joined by about two hundred others: members of Land and Freedom, workers, sympathetic friends, and curious onlookers. When the service ended and the mourners recessed, the political activists in the square sprang into action. With a captive audience spilling out of the cathedral, Georgii V. Plekhanov, a teenage populist who was to become one of the founders of Russia's first Marxist organization, jumped up and delivered a passionate speech in which he indicted the Russian government "for rotting the country's best sons in prison."[42] As Plekhanov finished speaking, other Land and Freedom members hoisted up the young worker Potapov, who unfurled a large red banner emblazoned with the phrase *Zemlia i Volia*. At that moment a whistle blew and police descended upon the crowd.[43]

As Potapov was seized, Vera and Eugenia jumped into a passing cab in order to avoid arrest.[44] Although they and other members of "the high command of the revolutionary organization fled, some of their hot-headed followers re-sisted arrest."[45] Confusion reigned. By the time the dust settled, thirty-two people, who were at most only tangentially involved in the demonstration, were in police custody.[46]

The distaste aroused by the manner in which the Land and Freedom leader-ship scurried away, avoiding arrest while allowing mostly innocent specta-tors and casual supporters to be captured, was quickly replaced by a stronger sense of rancor toward Alexander II's government when it prosecuted those in custody without mercy.[47] Although this overly zealous retribution ultimately worked against the government, it became the state's established method of dealing with its radical sons and daughters. For the remainder of the decade, the tsarist regime proved to be a slow learner. Seeking to use fear to dissuade Russia's youth from radical propaganda and agitation, the government inad-vertently created a generation of political martyrs whose entrance onto the public stage excited both young imaginations and liberal compassion.

The first young martyrs created by state prosecution took the stage in Feb-ruary 1877 at the so-called Trial of the Fifty. During the trial, which took place over several weeks in February and March, fifty young propagandists, includ-ing eleven members of the former Fritschi circle, had their days in court.[48] If the government had tried to find a more sympathetic group of defendants, it would have been hard-pressed to do so. Although the court charged the defen-dants with "having formed an illegal association that aimed to overthrow the existing order and with dissemination of printed matter inciting [the masses] to revolt,"[49] the public saw the accused as martyrs for the people. For many of those who followed the trial, the presence of the young female defendants who gave up wealth and educational opportunities to work in factories was especially moving.[50] Poets wrote verses in honor of the girls, while a number of Russian subjects pledged money to tend to their needs.[51] Spectators at the trial compared the women to the early Christians as "teachers of love, equality and fraternity."[52] For many, these women were saints. Adding to their aura of self-sacrifice was the fact that most of the accused did not try to defend them-selves and freely admitted their guilt. In doing so they exploited the chance given to them to speak in court as an opportunity for political propaganda and condemned Alexander II's regime.

Other Russian radicals took full advantage of the drama unfolding in the courtroom. While the defendants' speeches were not reprinted in the government-sanctioned newspaper, populist presses rushed to print the emotional testimony given by the editors' friends and colleagues. The defendants' speeches prompted a palpable reaction among society. Especially stirring were the alleged words of Vera's friend and former radical muse Sofia Bardina. The story of how in a calm, steady voice the former agronomy student took full responsibility for her actions and castigated the repressive policies of the Russian government was retold countless times by righteous allies and an inspired public.[53] As the press reported, Bardina told the court, "Persecute us, you have physical force on your side, sirs; but moral force, and the force of historical progress, the force of ideas is on our side, and ideas, alas, cannot be pierced by bayonets."[54]

If the government retained any sympathy after Bardina's words were reprinted, it was lost when the Russian Senate pronounced sentence. Originally, the defendants were sentenced to five to ten years of hard labor for their few months of propagandizing workers. For many in Russian society, the severity of the pronounced punishment was a travesty. Sergei Kravchinskii summed up the population's general feeling about these and similar sentences when he wrote, "Years of hard labor were inflicted for two to three speeches made in private to a handful of working men or for a single book read or lent. Thus what is freely done in every country in Europe was punished among us like murder."[55] So many Russians expressed their outrage at the apparent injustice of the trial's outcome that the court reduced the sentences of the convicted. Although all the defendants' punishments were diminished, the newly convicted women enjoyed the greatest alteration in sentences. Their sentences were universally changed from hard labor to simply exile or settlement in Siberia.[56] But this reduction failed to satisfy the mounting disgust pervading society. Thus its attempts to use fear to dissuade Russia's youth from a revolutionary path through this retributive exercise cost the government many potential allies that could have been used to counteract the growing radicalism in the country.

In addition, the publicity surrounding the trials and the harsh sentences imposed served to impel young people toward rather than away from political radicalism. "Many a young man or woman who ordinarily would not dream of engaging in strenuous and dangerous propaganda work was now dazzled by the prospect of 'starring' in a spectacle which the whole country followed."[57] For budding revolutionaries, the Trial of the Fifty reaffirmed their commitment and reinforced the positive aspect of political martyrdom.

Among those most impelled to emulate the alleged martyrdom of the defendants prosecuted in the Trial of the Fifty was Vera Figner. Of her friends sentenced to varying terms of exile in Siberia, Vera writes, they "motivated others to follow in the footsteps of the condemned."[58] Many times in her autobiographical writings, she notes that to live a life devoted to others while being persecuted and even martyred for a higher cause is the noblest existence to which a person could aspire.[59] This aspiration informed Vera's adult life after she returned to Russia from Switzerland. How she would realize this goal was still uncertain in 1877. But as the revolutionary movement of the 1870s progressed and became increasingly public and dramatic, Vera's potential opportunities clarified. She became determined not only to walk onto the stage of the revolutionary passion play that the Trial of the Fifty inaugurated but also to attract the spotlight.

After evading arrest in the December demonstration at the Cathedral of Our Lady of Kazan, Vera's political martyrdom still loomed ahead of her. In the weeks that followed Land and Freedom's public debut at the demonstration, she and Eugenia assumed they were under police surveillance and decided to move out of their mother's home and into their own apartment on Nevskii Prospect.[60] There, Vera continued her efforts to find a medical position in the countryside, albeit without success. Frustrated, she traveled to Moscow in her quest, but her luck proved no better. As she prepared to return to St. Petersburg, she decided to pay a visit to some of her friends who had been incarcerated in Moscow prisons before she left for the capital. Assuming that officials would not authorize these meetings, Vera took advantage of the still lax security measures in place at Russian political prisons and approached her incarcerated friends surreptitiously.[61] Although no harm befell her on her first prison visit, on her second gendarmes arrested the stealthy visitor and held her in Moscow's Butyrka prison.[62]

Determined not to compromise the friends with whom she had been staying, for several days Vera refused to give her name or place of residence and remained imprisoned in Butyrka. Describing this initial incarceration decades later, she goes out of her way to paint a portrait designed to inspire her readers with an appreciation for what she endured. Her literary depiction accentuates her noble background and privileged lifestyle to make the juxtaposition with the deprivation she experienced in the Butyrka prison all the more pronounced. Thus she describes the elegant black dress and delicate rose-dotted hat that she wore as incongruous with the dirty, bug-infested fortress.[63] Insinuating that her punishment was more intense than that of less privileged inmates, Vera's brief stay in Butyrka serves as the first chapter in what would become a lifelong martyrdom parable.

Despite her efforts to describe the deprivation of prison, Vera's account points to a peculiarity in the Russian penal system of the mid-1870s. As Adam Ulam describes, a relatively lenient attitude from the administration and quite comfortable conditions for the inmates defined the experience of political prisoners in the mid-1870s.[64] Vera's reminiscences inadvertently support this. She claims that when she realized that she was without a change of collar and cuffs and had no face powder to freshen her appearance in prison, she asked the guard on duty to fetch her some. While guards in a later period would have dismissed this request out of turn, the battle between the state and the revolutionaries had not yet reached its later dire proportions. Thus, although the guard maintained that he would not be able to obtain the items needed for her toilette, he arranged for a teacup, tea, and sugar for the "young lady."[65]

After several days in Butyrka, Vera finally disclosed her identity and officials contacted Ekaterina to collect her daughter. Given her relationship with the secretary of the Kazan Circuit Court, her estranged husband, Alexei Filippov, officials remanded Vera to her mother's custody on the condition that she reside with Ekaterina in the capital.[66] Consequently, the Figner women returned to St. Petersburg posthaste and Vera remained in the capital for several months.

Meanwhile, in the spring of 1877, a few dozen members of Land and Freedom and a group of "separatists" left the capital for provincial towns in Saratov, Samara, Astrakhan, Tambov, and the vicinity along the lower Don River, an area in Russia that had been referred to as the Don Cossack Region.[67] The aspiring propagandists chose these sites carefully, hoping that histories of uprisings and agrarian difficulties in these provinces, along with their sizable population of religious dissidents, would allow their agitational message to find fertile soil.[68] Although they had no job prospects on the horizon, separatists Alexander Ivanchin-Pisarev, Iuri Bogdanovich, Maria Leshern, Alexander Solovev, and a worker by the name of Griaznov left St. Petersburg to see what they could turn up in the countryside.[69] The Figner sisters did not immediately join their comrades. We can assume that Vera was nervous about her mother's liability after her conditional release from Butyrka. But before the other separatists left, they made plans for the Figner girls to meet them in Samara at a later date.[70]

As she remained in the imperial capital with nothing serious to occupy her time, Vera grew restless. In spite of, or perhaps because of, the stay in prison with which the government had rewarded her last visit to an incarcerated friend, Vera and her friend Alexandra Kornilova went to visit Nikolai Morozov, who was then imprisoned in the House of Preliminary Detention awaiting trial. Recuperating from a serious illness, Morozov was resting when he heard Vera's familiar contralto voice exclaim, "Hello Nikolai!"[71] Already "secretly in love," with Vera, Morozov delighted in his friend's "courage and selflessness."[72] This time Vera escaped the gendarmes' attention. But for Morozov the visit was monumental, as his infatuation with the budding radical grew only more intense.

Vera finally left the capital for Samara province in August 1877. There she met her friends from St. Petersburg and a "whole group of bright, honest people ready to help."[73] Almost immediately she started to network in order to find a position as a fel'dsher.[74] She finally met success in October when through mutual friends she was introduced to Dr. Nikolai Popov. Ironically, this was not the first encounter between the two; both had studied anatomy under Professor Peter Lesgaft in Kazan, and Popov had instantly recognized Vera. When she asked her former classmate for help in finding a job as a medical assistant, he quickly secured her a fel'dsher position in the village of Studentsy.[75]

Over the next three months, Vera "diligently fulfilled her responsibilities" in the village.[76] Her efforts were exhausting. In addition to rendering medical care in the enormous village of Studentsy, for eighteen days every month she traveled between the twelve villages that comprised her territory.[77] Desperate for some type of medical care, a constant stream of peasants came to her for help. The overworked fel'dsher recalls that it was not unusual for thirty to forty peasants to be standing outside her hut, waiting their turn to be seen by the young medical provider.[78]

Vera had never seen such a level of filth and deprivation as she saw in Studentsy, and she realized that the predicament facing the Russian masses was worse than she expected. Her work began to feel pointless: the medications she dispensed were just stopgap measures, and the ailments she treated were only symptoms of the more serious, permanent illness of poverty. She had hoped to address the underlying problem of economic oppression by propagandizing her patients, but with the villagers engaged in a daily struggle to survive, the idea of talking to them about resistance and protest seemed pointless and bizarre.

The daily grind and seeming futility of her job dismantled the enthusias-
tic romanticism with which Vera came to the people. Her experiences in Studentsy shocked her into seeing how little she knew about the Russian masses
before she started to live among them. Although she spent her formative years
living in the Russian countryside, in the autumn of 1877 she realized that "at
twenty-five years old, I stood before [the people] as a child, confronting some
kind of bizarre, unheard of subject."[79] Working in Studentsy without the com-
forting support of family and friends, Vera came "face to face with village life"
for the first time in her life.[80]

Although she found no time to engage in propaganda in Studentsy, Vera's
very presence in the village in an era of rejuvenated populism made her suspect in the eyes of the police. Officials in the Third Department suggested that
local gendarmes arrest Vera as early as December 20, 1877,[81] but for the time
being, she remained free.[82] Then on January 10, 1878, Alexander Solovev appeared on her doorstep to inform her that several members of their circle had
been compromised and that she needed to leave Studentsy without delay.[83]
Wanting to see how serious the situation was before she permanently abandoned her job, Vera asked Dr. Popov for his permission to go to the provincial
capital for a few days.[84] With her zemstvo boss's consent, late in the evening
on January 10, she and Solovev left for the city of Samara. That night the pair
reunited with Ivanchin-Pisarev and Bogdanovich. Although at first Vera dismissed her friends' concern about the danger of imminent arrest, she finally
relented.[85] Informing Popov that there was a family emergency at home, she
resigned her position and left Studentsy for good.[86]

Within a few weeks Vera and her friends were back in St. Petersburg just
as a new round of political energy gripped the city. Over the preceding two
months, the "Trial of the 193" had captivated the attention of St. Petersburg
society. The tsar's subjects of virtually every political ilk closely followed the
reports emanating from the courtroom where 193 young Russians, most from
privileged backgrounds, were on trial for revolutionary agitation against the
imperial state. Most of those accused were participants in the 1874 "go to the
people" movement. For more than three years they had languished in the St.
Petersburg House of Preliminary Detention awaiting trial. Dozens of the men
and women originally imprisoned in this case lost either their minds or their
lives in the interim, but the 193 who survived the ordeal of imprisonment and
were not prematurely released by the government finally learned their fate on
January 23, 1878, when the infamous trial came to a close.

Although dozens of the defendants were condemned and sentenced to prison, hard labor, or banishment, most of the accused were acquitted.[87] For many of these newly freed souls, their months and years in prison only intensified their radical sentiments, and within days of their release they joined new revolutionary circles in the capital. As a result the St. Petersburg apartments of known radicals were filled from morning until night as new comrades continually issued forth to plan their future political activity.[88] Yet before any of the acquitted could make definite plans, one of their comrades, who was not a defendant in the Trial of the 193, initiated a desperate and violent new phase in the radical contest with the state.

Early in the morning on January 24, 1878, Vera Zasulich, a young gentry woman who had long moved in radical circles without great distinction, entered the office of General Fyodor Trepov, the governor-general of St. Petersburg. Zasulich had gained admittance along with several other subjects who had come to present the general with petitions. But as Trepov approached Zasulich, she drew a pistol from under her shawl and shot him at point-blank range. In the ensuing bedlam, Zasulich offered no resistance and was quickly arrested. When asked why she shot the general, the would-be assassin replied that she did it to avenge Trepov's persecution of a political prisoner.[89] Although her shot failed to permanently fell Trepov, Zasulich's endeavor brought about consequences she never anticipated. As Sergei Kravchinskii notes, Zasulich's action gave political violence "a most powerful impulse. It illuminated it with its divine aureole and gave it the sanction of sacrifice and public opinion."[90] It would be another year and a half before a sizable number of Russian revolutionaries embraced terrorism as the most expedient method to realize their goals. However, the publicity surrounding the Zasulich assassination attempt immediately fueled the radical fires in Russia. This fervor only intensified two months later when a jury acquitted Zasulich. Given the fact that she freely admitted her guilt, her acquittal was an occasion for renewed revolutionary celebration, as it illustrated the extent to which Russian society endorsed insurgency against the tsarist state.[91]

Yet at the same time, Zasulich's violent response to Trepov's brutality exposed fissures in the Russian revolutionary community. Although some populists sought to continue their work in the countryside, others, emboldened by the publicity regarding Zasulich's attack on Trepov, believed that henceforth activists needed to focus on urban areas and consider additional acts of political violence. Vera Figner was among the former. She still felt the full power of the "evangelical impulse that urged [populists] into the countryside."[92] With the enthusiasm of a recent convert, her aspirations to work among the people could not be tempered by "rational restraints."[93] Thus, in March 1878, despite the radical energy in the capital, Vera departed for the provinces accompanied by her fellow separatists Bogdanovich, Solovev, Ivanchin-Pisarev, and the recently freed Nikolai Morozov.

Although Morozov was one who believed that revolutionaries needed to concentrate on urban centers, he accompanied Vera to the countryside, because he yearned to be near her. Morozov writes, "I felt such love and adoration for Vera . . . I put myself at her disposal."[94] Even though he did not know if his romantic feelings were reciprocated, Morozov went against his better judgment and his radical loyalties just so he could delight in the company of his beloved. But according to Morozov, he was not alone in his feeling; both Solovev and Bogdanovich were in love with Vera as well.[95] Ivanchin-Pisarev seems to have been the only man in the group who went to the provinces because he believed in the efficacy of work among the peasantry. But even he was not immune to Vera's charms. Recalling this period years later, Ivanchin-Pisarev notes that in the company of this "educated, sharp-witted, extremely impressionable and responsive comrade," the hours melted away.[96]

After they failed to find positions in Tambov, the quintet journeyed on to Saratov.[97] With a sympathetic population, a long-standing tradition as a center of radical activity, and an enviable location along both a major rail line and the Volga River, "the leftist movement in Saratov was the broadest of any in all the Volga cities."[98] While Vera focused on finding productive work in Saratov, Nikolai Morozov was distracted by his romantic feelings for his comrade. Unable to tolerate the tension of living in such close proximity to Vera without knowing if a romantic relationship with her was possible, several weeks after they arrived in town, Nikolai bared his feelings in a long, heartfelt letter to the object of his affection.[99]

Vera's response illustrates the depth of her conviction to the revolutionary cause. Responding to her friend by letter, she declared with "the melancholy of a selfless soul" (in the opinion of the rejected Morozov) that her radical priorities left no room in her life for love.[100] Although she simply may have been trying to soften the blow of her rejection, her vow to deny herself a personal life so as not to be distracted from her political commitments speaks to a characteristic of her generation of revolutionary women. Unlike their male comrades, women radicals never believed they could have it all. They assumed that their devotion to the cause needed to consume all of their attention and passion. Thus, most of these women remained unmarried and childless; wed only to the revolutionary movement, their maternal feelings were reserved solely for their comrades and the Russian masses facing continual need.[101] Because her response was so consistent with the prevailing attitude of revolutionary women, when Vera invoked her radical dedication as the reason why she could not begin a romantic involvement with Morozov, her friend accepted the veracity of her response without question.

With his relationship with Vera finally defined, Morozov left Saratov for St. Petersburg. In his opinion, revolutionary efforts needed to be redirected from propaganda in the villages to a direct struggle with the government in an effort to secure political freedom. But for the time being Vera could entertain no possibility beyond working in the countryside. Her patience paid off. By mid-summer, Ivanchin-Pisarev, Solovev, and Bogdanovich found jobs as district clerks, and Vera secured work as a fel'dsher in the village of Viazmin, in Petrovsk uezd.[102]

Vera officially began her position in Viazmin on July 1, 1878.[103] Almost immediately, Eugenia Figner joined her sister. Over the next ten months, the sisters worked together "with one mind and spirit."[104] Eugenia, who had studied to be a medical assistant, made an invaluable contribution to her older sister. Tending to as many patients "as a district physician along with several junior surgeons see in a city hospital over an entire year,"[105] the two women dispensed medications and tended to the sick from five o'clock in the morning until nightfall.[106]

No matter how dedicated the revolutionaries who went to the villages in the 1870s were, their experience in the countryside was difficult. Working exceedingly long hours amid an often suspicious population, life in the country for the radical intelligentsia was frustrating, tedious, and lonely.[107] Osip V. Aptekman, the committed populist leader and cousin of Vera's old roommate Dora Aptekman, described his activity working among the Russian peasantry in the 1870s as follows: "with a noticeable feeling of weariness I worked among the people, with the bitter consciousness that one in the field is not a warrior."[108]

Besieged with patients, the sisters nonetheless decided to expand their responsibilities and opened a school in Viazmin. They were amazed at how desperate the educational situation in Petrovsk district was. In spite of the increased emphasis on education in the post-emancipation era, there was no school in the three districts that surrounded Viazmin. Wanting to improve more than just the physical health of the people they served, the women decided that Eugenia would teach whatever peasants were interested free of charge. As soon as she announced that she was opening a school where the students would not have to purchase pens, paper, or books, twenty-five boys and girls immediately enrolled.[109]

For months the sisters fell into an exhausting but satisfying pattern. During the day, Vera treated the sick while Eugenia taught the uneducated. Then at ten or eleven o'clock at night, the two women would visit peasants' homes. With their neighbors and relatives crowded into the hosts' hut, Vera and Eugenia read progressive articles and poems, talked to those present about their relationship to landowners and the authorities, and listened to their patients' and pupils' "problems, hopes, and joys."[110] The next day, at the crack of dawn, their work began anew. Without the luxuries and comforts that they had grown used to over the years, the Figner girls discovered "a bewitching charm to their lives during this time."[111] A less desperate village than Studentsy,[112] Viazmin did not present Vera with the same sense of despondency as her earlier assignment. Instead of feeling that she was merely tending to the hopeless, she and her sister felt needed in their new post. They had the sense that for the first time they were not "superfluous."[113]

Six years after her stint in Viazmin, Vera argued that although she was in the village with fully revolutionary intentions, had she lived and worked as she did in Petrovsk in any other country, she would have been considered a useful member of society.[114] In Alexander II's Russia, however, her promotion of the peasants' interest brought her under an ever mounting level of scrutiny and suspicion. Eventually realizing the allies they had in Vera and Eugenia, the peasants started to invite them to village and district meetings to be their advocates against the pressure, extortion, and demands of government officials and powerful landowners. As their presence at such gatherings became more common, the fel'dsher and the teacher increasingly aroused the ire of local elites. As Vera recalls, her and her sister's support of peasant interests and their very presence in the village "threatened traditional exploitative appetites."[115] Subsequently, there were repeated efforts to drive the Figners away from the peasants and out of Viazmin.

Regardless of falling under increasing scrutiny, Vera and Eugenia stayed in Viazmin through the winter and early spring of 1879. Officials closed the school that the two had founded on the pretense that they taught that God did not exist and that there was no justification for the autocracy, but Vera retained her position as the village fel'dsher. Having found work that she loved and a population that needed her, she resolved to remain in the village as long as possible. But after her old friend and separatist comrade Alexander Solovev fired five shots at Tsar Alexander II on April 2, Vera's position became untenable. Even though the emperor walked away unharmed, Solovev's failed assassination attempt unleashed a new, more violent stage in the battle between Russian revolutionaries and the state in which Vera was irrevocably swept up.

When the news of Solovev's crime reached Viazmin, it came as no surprise to Vera. Weeks before his assassination attempt, Solovev had confided his plans to her. After giving all that he had to the countryside, he told her that as long as political repression and arbitrary autocratic rule remained, their plans to improve the lives of the Russian masses were doomed to failure. In order to facilitate their work, Solovev argued, "the death of the emperor can be a turning point. The atmosphere will clear, . . . and the intelligentsia will receive access to broad and fruitful activity among the people."[116] Impressed with his courage and self-sacrifice and swayed by his arguments, Vera wished her friend luck and bid him adieu.

As she watched him depart, Vera must have realized that her time in Viazmin was nearing its end. Even if Solovev's plans did not go awry, the turning point that the would-be assassin imagined would not be immediate. In the short term, one had to expect arrests on a massive scale. But Solovev's failure created a state of emergency for the radical milieu. As gendarmes scoured the cities and the countryside for anyone who may have been remotely involved with Solovev's plot, Russia's propagandists and radicals had to decide how to respond in the face of this onslaught.

Vera's decision entailed leaving Viazmin and entering a new phase in her revolutionary career. Telling her zemstvo supervisors that she had to abandon her job because her mother was ill, she left the Petrovsk uezd on April 29, 1879.[117] The next day police investigators arrived in the village to question her in connection with the Solovev case, only to find her already gone.[118]

When Vera left her job and home of ten months, she did not plan on abandoning her work among the people forever. She was still committed to social and political activity among the Russian masses but knew that the narodniki had to adopt measures to protect themselves. Since its inception several years before, Land and Freedom had sanctioned violent attacks against the state as a method of self-defense for embattled radicals. In its founding charter the group acknowledged the potential need to engage in "the systematic anni-

hilation of the most dangerous and important elements in the government"
who might hinder the populists' work among the masses.[119] With the escalating police repression that ensued in the wake of Solovev's assassination attempt, influential revolutionary figures, including Vera Figner, believed that
the time for a direct confrontation with the state had arrived.

Meeting with her fellow separatists in the provincial capital in the weeks
after the latest attempt on Alexander II's life, Vera announced that she was
going to join the larger organization of Land and Freedom and would support those factions in the group that supported the assassination of the tsar.[120]
Naïvely, Vera expected that she and her fellow revolutionaries could violently
target the government, exact certain political concessions, and then return
to peaceful activity among the people. She believed that the revolutionaries
could remain essentially propagandists and peaceful altruists while temporarily engaged in terrorism as a means of self-defense. The next four years illustrated the naïveté of such a plan. The battle that ensued between the state
and the revolutionaries left dozens dead and hundreds imprisoned. By the
time the confrontation between the populists and the government ended,
Vera Figner and her comrades were no longer simply revolutionaries. They
were terrorists.

Vera Figner in her school days.
*Slavic and Baltic Division, New York Public Library,
Astor, Lennox & Tilden Foundations.*

Vera Figner in the 1870s.

*Slavic and Baltic Division, New York Public Library,
Astor, Lennox & Tilden Foundations.*

Vera Figner in the People's Will.

Slavic and Baltic Division, New York Public Library,
Astor, Lennox & Tilden Foundations.

View of Shlisselburg Fortress.

*Slavic and Baltic Division, New York Public Library,
Astor, Lennox & Tilden Foundations.*

Vera Figner after her release from Shlisselburg Fortress.

Boris I. Nicolaevsky Collection, Hoover Institute Archives,
Stanford University.

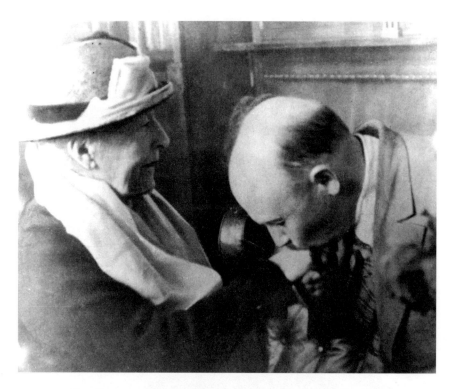

Vera Figner and Nikolai Bukharin at the offices of *Izvestiia*, 1935.
International Institute of Social History, Amsterdam.

5

THE TSAR'S DEATH SENTENCE

MORE THAN ANY RULER IN RECENT Russian history, Alexander II believed that his relationship with his subjects was predicated on feelings of love. He was, after all, the Tsar Liberator, who accomplished what no other Romanov had dared to risk when in 1861 he freed millions of Russian peasants from the bonds of serfdom. Over the subsequent decade, Alexander II complemented the emancipation by instituting a series of educational, military, governmental, and judicial reforms. Though none of his reforms diminished his autocratic authority, Alexander II was convinced that in granting these and a measure of free discourse, he would engender harmony between educated society and the monarchy,[1] thereby ensuring the longevity of the autocracy. The unsuccessful attempt on the life of the tsar made by Dmitrii Karakozov in 1866 only reinforced this scenario of love between the ruler and the ruled as the people demonstrated their affection for the autocrat through the wrath they directed at the would-be regicide. But a little more than a decade later, continued repression, a succession of disappointing reforms, and a series of political trials of Russia's educated youth eroded the patience of society, and the curtain lowered on Alexander II's scenario of love. No pretense of mutual affection remained. "Love had turned into its antithesis, bitter rage, indulgent to violent revolutionary acts."[2] Thus, as a generation of radicals abandoned peaceful agitation in the countryside to bear arms against their government, they found society strangely receptive to their propaganda by deed, a reaction that only reinforced their perception of the morality and justice of their violent agenda.

Vera Figner did not leave medical school in 1875 with a bomb in her hand. Her transformation from a young woman with predominantly liberal views and eager to work as a physician among the people to a woman who actively supported the political murder of the autocrat was gradual. It was predicated on experience, frustration, hopelessness, egotistical urgency, and, perhaps most importantly, the apparent sanction of fellow radicals and liberal society. Vera was not a rogue figure. While she consistently displayed an independent streak within all of the groups and subgroups to which she belonged or with which she was affiliated, she essentially embraced the youthful fashion of her friends and the time, whether it was pursuing a medical decree, exploring Socialist theory, working as a populist in the village, or resorting to political violence. As the incidence of terrorism increased in Russia and the bulk of educated society outside government circles failed (or refused) to openly indict such violence, budding radicals, including Vera, interpreted the silence of society as public affirmation of the inherent morality of violent methods. Thus, young revolutionaries viewed terrorism directed against the Russian state as a righteous battle that was both necessary and efficient.[3]

Alexander Solovev's assassination attempt against Alexander II did not introduce a previously unfathomable specter of violence into the confrontation between revolutionary idealists and the government. Land and Freedom approved of violence against state officials as a weapon of self-defense, and Vera Zasulich's attempt on the life of General Trepov demonstrated the potential of propaganda by deed. But Solovev's attempted assassination invariably raised the stakes involved in the use of political violence by refining the target of the revolutionaries' wrath to the emperor himself.

During the late 1870s, regicide experienced a renaissance throughout Europe. Assassins targeted Germany's Wilhelm I, Spain's Alfonso XII, and Italy's King Umberto in 1878 alone.[4] Thus, as Vera Figner contends, the idea of assassinating Alexander II "hung in the air" even before Alexander Solovev's attempt.[5] But after the botched April 2 attack and the intensified pursuit of Russian radicals that ensued, the notion of tsaricide acquired renewed vigor. Equating the Third Department's attempts to round up anyone even remotely connected to Solovev as just the latest chapter in a long history of governmental persecution, the revolutionaries donned the mantle of the aggrieved party and retaliated. Their decision to utilize violence did not represent "the suspension or absence of moral standards";[6] rather, from their point of view, the revolutionaries understood their turn toward violence as a supremely moral decision that was both selfless and righteous.

In an article assessing the relationship between morality and political violence, William Ascher explores the psychology that allows otherwise peaceful citizens to support intergroup violence. Although his study does not consider the case of nineteenth-century Russia and the revolutionary terrorism that ensued in the land of the tsars, his conclusions are consistent with Russian conditions. Ascher argues that to proponents of terrorism, "there are four criteria for the legitimate use of violence: the existence of grave injustice, the exhaustion of nonviolent means, the restraint of violence to proportionality to the gravity of the injustices, and the high likelihood that the violence will indeed eliminate the injustices."[7] All of these factors played into the decision of Russian revolutionaries to employ terrorism in 1879. The men and women who would condemn the tsar to death believed that their actions held the greatest prospect for initiating change in their country. They felt frustrated in their efforts to use nonviolent means in the preceding years and were convinced that peaceful methods were doomed to fail. In their minds, they were too few, the problem was too great, and police persecution was too intense for success to arise through conventional means.[8] As one convicted terrorist confessed at his trial, "I never would have become a terrorist if the very conditions of Russian life hadn't compelled me to it."[9] Viewing Alexander II as the literal embodiment of oppressive despotism, the formerly peaceful radicals who adopted primarily violent means in the spring and summer of 1879 not only held the tsar ultimately responsible for the complete disenfranchisement of the Russian masses, but they also condemned him for the lives lost and the minds ruined through the regular imprisonment and exile of Russia's radical youth.[10]

The exponents of political violence had yearned to connect with the Russian masses in the hopes that they could unleash a revolutionary maelstrom in the countryside. Not surprisingly, Alexander II's government aspired to prevent this. Rather than concede that the state's actions were rooted in self-preservation, Russian radicals looked at the Third Department's efforts to arrest agitators as the unjust persecution of righteousness and its defenders. Describing the escalating arrests as part of a concerted governmental effort to obstruct the altruistic objectives of a group of privileged youth seeking to work on behalf of a people too mired in disease, filth, and poverty to defend themselves, the revolutionaries absolved themselves from any culpability. In describing the local reaction to gendarmes' attempts to question and possibly arrest her in the wake of Solovev's assassination attempt, Vera indulges in this literary self-absolution. While acknowledging that the police arrived because of her connection with the would-be assassin, she relates the alleged response of locals in order to infer that the true underlying cause of her potential arrest—and one can presume hundreds of others—was not her advocacy of violence, but her support of peasant interests. Thus, Vera describes the supposed collective indictment voiced by an unspecified group of poor villagers: that the defenders of the defenseless were under attack "because they stood up for the peasants."[11] For the nascent terrorists, directed violence against the state in general and the tsar in particular therefore became "a means to destroy the obstacles that separated revolutionaries from the masses."[12]

In the spring of 1879, when Vera abandoned her post as fel'dsher in Viazmin, she settled briefly in Tambov with her sister Eugenia and a handful of radical colleagues.[13] Although these young populists relished one another's company, revolutionary harmony did not prevail. Instead the Russian radical community was torn apart by discussions about resources and objectives. While many activists felt that a continued revolutionary presence in the countryside was ineffectual and advocated for a more immediate, dramatic, and violent route, others believed that terrorism would sound the death knell for radical aspirations and socialist dreams. Solovev's plot to assassinate the tsar and an inflammatory article by Nikolai Morozov titled "Regarding Political Murder" brought the controversy to a head.[14] Eager to settle internal divisions, a general meeting of Land and Freedom was scheduled for the end of June.[15]

Preparing for what they thought would be an inevitable rupture within Land and Freedom at the upcoming meeting in Voronezh, eleven revolutionaries who espoused political violence met secretly in the neighboring town of Lipetsk a few days before the general Land and Freedom conference.[16] Led by such dynamic figures as Alexander Mikhailov and Andrei Zheliabov, the group decided that, given the political repression that existed in Russia, no sustained activity on behalf of the people was possible. Instead they believed it was necessary to engage the government with force until the state conceded general freedoms that would allow political and social questions to be discussed and resolved.[17] In complete agreement that the revolutionary movement needed to concentrate on political issues, the group constituted themselves as the "Executive Committee" and developed a strict code of rules and ethics by which they would abide.[18] Although conspiratorial needs dictated the necessity of a relatively limited membership, the group aspired to recruit additional men and women for the committee; among the potential recruits were Vera Figner, Anna Iakimova, Alexander Presniakov, and Sofia Ivanova.[19] With their course of action clear, the Lipetsk conference attendees set off for Voronezh resolved to either convince their friends and comrades to join them in their battle or abandon Land and Freedom themselves.[20]

Vera attended the Voronezh meeting at the invitation of Mikhail Popov.[21] Those assembled at the conference wasted little time before tackling the pressing question of whether to support propaganda or political violence. Although he later asserted that he expected to fail in his efforts, the populist and future Marxist Georgii Plekhanov raised the issue of terrorism and tried to convince his colleagues to foreswear terrorism as a dangerous and ultimately ineffectual method.[22] Plekhanov argued that political terror would not provoke fundamental reform in the Russian political and social system; instead, he contended, it would do no more than change the number of roman numerals after Alexander's name.[23] But the majority of those assembled disagreed. Based on their experiences in the countryside, most of the populists in attendance believed that political freedom was essential to their activities and that the only way such freedom could be achieved was through an armed struggle with the government. Disheartened by the reaction of his fellow narodniki, and unwilling to sanction the use of political terror, Plekhanov dramatically withdrew from Land and Freedom. Unwilling to sever additional ties or make the rupture within the organization complete, the group essentially decided to do nothing. Thus, those in attendance left the organization's statutes untouched and agreed that an armed political struggle with the government was in keeping with the section of the group's program that dealt with the disorganization of the state.[24] In an effort to preserve solidarity within Land and Freedom, for the time being, the aspiring terrorists were satisfied when the propagandists conceded that their violently inclined counterparts could "continue the work of Solovev" with some measure of independence.[25]

At the close of the Voronezh conference, many of the populists, including Vera, left the provinces for St. Petersburg. Still in danger of being arrested for her association with Solovev, Vera began life in the revolutionary underground under an assumed name and a forged passport. Instead of returning to the Figner home on Sadovaia Ulitsa, she moved into a shared apartment with fellow revolutionary Alexander Kviatkovskii in the Lesnoi section of the city.[26] The relationship between Vera and Alexander was completely platonic, and their living arrangement was characteristic of the methods of operation employed by revolutionaries. Realizing that women living outside of tradi-tional patriarchal settings were automatically suspect because of their "uncon-ventional" lifestyle, the revolutionary leadership paired young women with male members of the group. These pairs would then pose as normal married couples whose lifestyle seemingly conformed to social expectations and thus aroused no suspicion on the part of curious neighbors.

Back in St. Petersburg, the narodniki's proponents of political violence real-ized that the Voronezh conference "did not eliminate dissension, it only stifled it."[27] As each faction attempted to organize its activities, a divisive debate over resources and control of the group's periodical, *Zemlia i Volia*, erupted. Al-though no one wanted to dismantle the group, tension brewed and a rupture seemed inevitable.

The state's execution of five populists on August 10 and 11 brought the ten-sion to a head.[28] Determined to avenge these deaths without delay,[29] the pro-ponents of terrorism severed their formal ties with their peaceful counter-parts and Land and Freedom dissolved on August 15, 1879.[30] In its place arose two separate organizations. The members of the Black Repartition (*Chernyi Peredel*) continued the old populist route of engaging in propaganda and cul-tural activity among the peasants,[31] but those who charted the new course of political violence declared war against the government. Because this group of radicals alleged to "want what the people wanted and existed only to fulfill their will,"[32] they adopted the name "People's Will," or *Narodnaia Volia*.

The birth of the People's Will took place in Vera Figner's and Alexander Kviatkovskii's apartment, which had become the de facto headquarters of the militant populists over the summer.[33] Although she had not attended the Lipetsk conference as had most members of the self-constituted Execu-tive Committee of the People's Will, when her comrades invited her to join the party leadership, Vera gladly accepted.[34] In doing so, she became one of seven women among the twenty-two-member committee. In this respect the People's Will was exceptional for its relative gender equity. Its members had been reared in the progressive 1860s and had assimilated notions of women's practical emancipation into their radical conceptions. Yet in spite of the wom-en's presence on the Executive Committee, as will be shown later in this chap-ter, notions about the gendered division of labor, even in the revolutionary movement, proved durable.

While posterity calls them terrorists, the members of the People's Will (the *narodovol'tsy*) deemed themselves Socialist-Populists. Their ends, they alleged, were the same as those of Land and Freedom; it was only their methods that differed.[35] In their minds, their quest was just. Assassination was merely the necessary means to depose a government they judged illegitimate by virtue of its oppressive and autocratic rule.

In the third issue of the new party's publication, *Narodnaia Volia*, the Executive Committee detailed its objectives. Its long-term goal was the reestablishment of Russian society along Socialist foundations so that "liberty, equality, fraternity, a state of general well being and the complete development of the individual" could flourish.[36] But more immediately, these revolutionaries aspired to "remove oppression from the people and bring about a political revolution that [would] transfer authority to the Russian masses."[37] Acknowledging the "significance and influence of the central state authority in all aspects of the Russian people's lives,"[38] the social, political, and economic subjugation of the masses dictated that "all the party's forces be directed towards an active struggle with the government without delay."[39] Thus on August 26, 1879, the Executive Committee of the People's Will condemned Tsar Alexander II to death.[40]

For the members of the People's Will, assassinating the tsar was not a means to an end but a means to a means to an end. The group's members were not delusional. They realized that the endemic problems plaguing Russia preceded Alexander II, yet it was their hope that these troubles would not survive the present tsar. Using the tool of violence and the weapon of fear, the members of the People's Will claimed their right to interfere in politics in a state bereft of political rights. In doing so, in the words of Claudia Verhoeven, they utilized terrorism in a "paradigmatic way" to become "modern political subject[s]" by acting in "a historically meaningful manner."[41] Political murder at the highest echelons of state power would either allow the revolutionaries to wrest dramatic reforms and concessions from the government or, failing that, would provoke a rebellion among the long-suffering, complacent masses by spectacularly demonstrating the state's ultimate vulnerability and weakness in the face of righteous, heroic self-sacrifice.

Tsaricide was not unknown in autocratic Russia. Since the early seventeenth century, aristocrats and palace insiders had not infrequently intervened in the "divine" right enjoyed by the Godunov, Shuiskii, and Romanov dynasties in order to exercise their prerogatives and affect the course and personnel of the autocracy. In fact, in the generations that preceded that of the People's Will, two separate coups d'état left former rulers dead as they placed new sovereigns on the throne. But these earlier palace revolutions merely changed the person of the autocrat and left the system of autocracy itself unmolested. Unlike the palace revolutions of 1762 and 1801,[42] the revolutionaries of 1879 resolved to dismantle the institutions that protected privilege, fomented repression, and squelched the will of the people. Even if the murder of Alexander II did not frighten his successor into abolishing the vestiges of government oppression, the revolutionaries believed that the publicity that would result from an assassination would allow for the dissemination of their Socialist-Populist message not only on a national scale but on an international one as well.

The twenty-two men and women who comprised the first Executive Committee of the People's Will envisioned their fight against the tsarist leviathan as a war. To that end the group's members devoted themselves entirely to the quest. The statutes of the Executive Committee stipulated that its members "forget all ties of kinship, personal sympathies, love, and friendship, devote all of their mental and emotional strength and give their lives if necessary to revolutionary work."[43] Just as in any military conflict, casualties were inevitable and the members of the People's Will prepared themselves for battle and death. As Nikolai Morozov contends, Russian terrorists of the 1870s and 1880s accepted "both the risk of death and the obligation of murder."[44] For the most part, rather than dissuading the narodovol'tsy, the danger inherent in their task inspired them. So, too, did their chosen means. Unlike other failed assassins, the People's Will resolved to employ dynamite as a weapon instead of relying on the more conventional revolver or the classical dagger.

For a generation enamored with science and the discernible emblems of progress, the development of dynamite and nitroglycerine-based explosive devices in the 1860s and 1870s spoke to the potency science conveyed to its adherents not only in the lab but also on the streets and, by extension, in the political arena. As the condemned Russian terrorist Mikhail Frolenko notes, the prospect of using a bomb against the tsar transformed the planned assassination of Alexander II from "an ordinary murder" into an event so spectacular that it "expressed a new stage in the revolutionary movement."[45] One of the members of the People's Will was the railway engineer turned explosives expert Nikolai Kibalchich. Since the inception of the People's Will, Kibalchich had spent hours developing bombs and handheld explosive devices for his comrades to employ against the tsar. Kibalchich worked to create devices whose impact would be concentrated and precise; to that end his "bombs were carefully designed to have a destructive radius of only about a meter."[46] While this design mitigated the potential for collateral damage, it also required that the bomb thrower be in close proximity to his or her victim, thus "minimizing any possibility of escape for the assassin."[47] In this way the terrorist's death would serve as a final penance, transforming him or her from an assassin into a martyr for a sacred secular cause.

As soon as the Executive Committee sentenced the tsar to death, its members sprang into action. The group's declaration of war against the tsarist government demanded the utmost secrecy and conspiratorial techniques. As a security precaution, the party abandoned its apartment in the Lesnoi section of the capital and Vera and Kviatkovskii moved across town to an apartment on Leshtukov Alley.[48] Having relinquished its press to its Black Repartition counterparts, the Executive Committee (with financial contributions from a few wealthy revolutionaries) established its own printing operation before the month of August was out.[49] Shortly thereafter the group organized a dynamite workshop.[50]

While Kibalchich busied himself trying to perfect his handheld explosive devices, the leadership of the People's Will decided to supplement these devices with strategically placed mines buried underground. When the People's Will condemned the tsar to death, Alexander II was more than one thousand miles away in the Crimea. Yet the group viewed this as an opportunity rather than as an insurmountable hurdle.

One of the greatest challenges that faced the revolutionaries in their efforts to assassinate the tsar was the ability to anticipate Alexander II's location at any given moment and to thus direct their resources to that location at the necessary time. Alexander II's presence in the Crimea mitigated this difficulty. Inevitably the tsar would return to St. Petersburg at least partway by rail. Given Russia's relatively limited rail system, he would have only a few route options back to the capital. This allowed the People's Will to focus on limited stretches of isolated rail lines under which a mine could be laid. Once the mine was in place, revolutionaries would stand watch, ready to detonate the explosive device when the emperor's train passed by. Moscow, Alexandrovsk, and Odessa were chosen as the three points on which the revolutionaries would concentrate.[51] Dazzled by the prospect of such a dramatic undertaking, Vera peppered her colleagues with ardent requests to take part in the preparations for the tsar's assassination. Yet because of her good looks and engaging personality, her comrades thought it preferable to assign her to propaganda work in the capital.[52]

Despite the revolutionaries' self-perception as liberated individuals, they still harbored some traditional ideas about gender norms. In fact, regardless of the group's attempts to subvert the existing political and social order, long-held ideas about appropriate roles for men and women proved more difficult to abandon. Although one-third of the People's Will leadership was women, tasks assigned to its members followed a predictable gendered course. Men primarily served as the group's theorists until arrests and imprisonments necessitated otherwise. For the most part, the men in the organization lay the mines and threw the bombs, while their female comrades secured them posts, supplies, and wrote about their dramatic successes and tragic failures. If the revolution itself was tendered masculine, its underpinnings still were coded feminine.

The revolutionary movement in general and the People's Will in particular tacitly recognized both masculine and feminine notions of virtue and integrated these gendered ideals into revolutionary morality. While the occasional explosive, violent endeavors of the group epitomized masculine notions of heroism and self-sacrifice in battle, conceptions of feminine virtue abounded in the planning stages of each attack. Success depended on surprise; thus, in the days, weeks, and sometimes long months leading up to a terrorist event, revolutionaries invariably hid behind a veil of public anonymity and self-imposed silence as they patiently planned, plotted, and engaged in the often mundane preparations necessary to engineer an attack. As the planning of various terrorist attacks built toward a climax, the public sphere and the recognition that it had to offer beckoned the revolutionaries with the prospect of participation in the most public and dangerous roles. With the execution of each new violent attack, a select few engineers morphed into knights of the revolution, wielding handheld explosive devices and an occasional revolver or dagger, not just willing but eager to devote their last breath to the realization of their group's objectives. In the dramatic moments when their terrorist acts exploded onto the stage, individual terrorists emerged from the shadows and into the spotlight cast from the violent revolutionary glare. But for the majority who remained behind the scenes, consigned to supporting, unrecognized, and invariably feminine tasks, there was no spotlight. Instead they remained in the shadows, consigned to historical insignificance and anonymity. Although the first round in the violent battle between the state and the terrorists was literally fired by a woman (Vera Zasulich), the People's Will preferred their bomb throwers and assassins to be men.

Vera Figner refused to be excluded from the spectacular climax of the group's plans. She describes her ensuing ultimatum to be transferred to Odessa as being rooted in her conception of revolutionary morality and camaraderie. She contends, "It was intolerable to me that I should bear only a moral responsibility [for an act of terrorism] and not play a material part in an act for which the law threatened my comrades with the gravest penalties."[53] But Vera's insistence was predicated in her own egotism rather than in an inclination to self-abnegation. The "gravest penalties" to which she referred came on the heels of radical glory. She yearned to be recognized even if much of the recognition would come posthumously. When Vera committed to something, she did so completely. There were no gray areas with her; issues, decisions, and actions presented themselves to her in simple black and white terms. Thus, when she finally decided to devote herself to political violence, she had no intention of serving as a mere cog in the wheel that drove the People's Will. She longed to make a palpable difference in the group, her country, and in Russian history. She rejected the anonymity attached to a life lived quietly and anonymously in the revolutionary shadow of celebrated radicals in the same way that she renounced a life of obscurity as a provincial noblewoman. She had no interest in becoming a paragon of feminine virtue, be it revolutionary or otherwise; instead, she laid claim to masculine notions of heroism, valiance, and historical significance.

Vera's feelings epitomize the paradoxical motivations driving proponents of terror, both in the nineteenth century and the twenty-first. While putting one's life at the disposal of a larger political—or religious—mission may seem like the ultimate example of self-sacrificial behavior, it is based on egotism. Terrorists like Vera were, and are, willing and often eager to sacrifice their lives but not willing to sacrifice their personal significance. Be they jihadists or narodovol'tsy, terrorists retain *personal* objectives even as they give voice to the rhetoric of self-sacrifice and self-denial. As Vera herself admits, "Revolutionary figures desire to see some kind of concrete palpable manifestation of their own will and strength; [in late nineteenth-century Russia] such a manifestation was only possible through a terrorist act with its ensuing violence."[54] The valiant defense of cause and comrade may bring death, but it also holds the prospect of immortality in a way that few other life choices could engender.

Vera was a charming woman who knew how to get her way. A member of the People's Will for only a few weeks, she demonstrated her talents of persuasion on her fellow Executive Committee members. In September 1879 she did not find herself conducting propaganda in the capital as her colleagues had planned. Instead she made the long trek from St. Petersburg to the Black Sea port town of Odessa, carrying some clothes, personal necessities, and a suitcase full of dynamite intended to bring the autocracy to its knees.[55]

Riding the train from the imperial capital to Odessa over the same railroad lines she hoped the explosives she carried would soon destroy, Vera discovered yet another corner of her country. Before she left Russia for Switzerland, she had never ventured beyond her native province. But since her return from Western Europe, she had traveled from the imperial capital to Moscow, south along the Volga, and back again. Now in the fall of 1879, as she stepped from her railroad car, she found herself in the far southwestern corner of the empire in a town on the edges of the Black Sea. A city rich in history and heritage, this cosmopolitan city's "very location, far removed from the Russian imperial capitals and looking out on a teetering Ottoman Empire, allowed the city to become a hotbed of political intrigue."[56] With its population growing at a rate far beyond that of the other major cities in the empire, its widespread poverty, "a transient foreign population[,] and a constant stream of newcomers arriving by ship and overland carriage,"[57] Odessa offered the perfect atmosphere for revolutionary plots to be hatched and terrorist actions accomplished, because individuals and groups could easily disappear among the throngs of anonymous inhabitants in the city.

In Odessa Vera gained a new fictitious husband in the party's explosives expert Nikolai Kibalchich, and for the next few months she lived as "Mrs. Ivanitskii." Soon after the "Ivanitskiis" found an apartment, they were joined by three of their colleagues from the capital.[58] Together they devised a plan to gain access to a section of railway lines on the outer edge of town where they could lay a mine that could be used to assassinate Alexander II. In order to place the mine without being detected, the group plotted to have one of their male members hired as a railroad signalman. It fell to Vera to obtain her comrade the position by using her looks and charms to appeal to local authorities to give this job to her allegedly destitute acquaintance. After encountering some initial difficulties when she failed to look the part, she donned the dress and demeanor of, in her words, "a 'noble-doll," beseeched a local official, and accomplished her mission.[59]

By mid-October Mikhail Frolenko and his "wife," Tatiana Lebedeva, moved into a small sentry hut on the outskirts of Odessa, and preparations for the assassination moved into high gear. Under the leadership of Nikolai Kibalchich, this small cadre of revolutionaries stockpiled dynamite. Until they could transfer the dynamite to Frolenko's sentry hut, the group stored the explosives in Vera and Kibalchich's small apartment in town.[60] With little space available, explosives were concealed throughout the flat, with both Vera and Kibalchich aware that even a minor mistake could destabilize the explosives and spell an end not just to their designs but to their lives as well.[61]

Once Frolenko secured his position as a signalman, the Odessa narodovol'tsy transferred the dynamite to his sentry hut.[62] After several weeks of preparation and hard work, everything was ready; all that was left was to wait for word that Alexander II was on his way back to St. Petersburg. But in early November their plans came to an abrupt halt when Grigorii Goldenberg, the assassin of Kharkov governor Dmitrii Kropotkin, showed up in Odessa. With credible information indicating that Alexander II would not pass through the area on his way back to the capital, the Executive Committee, through Goldenberg, informed the Odessa group that their mission was aborted. Instead, the People's Will planned to concentrate their efforts on the rail lines around Moscow and thus ordered their colleagues in Odessa to turn their supply of dynamite over to Goldenberg, who would convey it to the Moscow assassins.[63]

The next day, Goldenberg left for Moscow. On the way, with his supply of dynamite in hand, he was arrested by the tsarist police in Elizavetgrad on November 14.[64] Consequently, the narodovol'tsy in Moscow never received the explosives intended for them. But the more serious consequences of Goldenberg's arrest began in early 1880, when he began to reveal everything he knew about the revolutionaries' plans.[65]

As Vera and her fellow terrorists abandoned their endeavor in Odessa, their comrades in Alexandrovsk and Moscow intensified their efforts. By mid-November explosives were in place in both locales. Good fortune appeared to be with the revolutionaries, as they received word that the tsar's train was scheduled to pass through both of the mined locations. On November 18 the emperor's train approached Alexandrovsk. As the royal train was about to pass over the stretch of rail that hid the explosives, Andrei Zheliabov joined the fuses that should have sparked the blast. Nothing happened. Instead, the tsar sat in his railway car oblivious to the fact that were it not for a mechanical glitch, he would have been in mortal jeopardy.[66]

The next day, in Moscow, uncertain of whether their Alexandrovsk comrades had met success or failure, the participants assigned to the Moscow assassination attempt waited for the tsar's train to come into sight. As the sounds of an approaching train echoed through the air, the terrorists miscalculated. Perhaps they were caught off guard, or perhaps, as they asserted, they assumed that timing made it improbable that this train carried the tsar. Letting the first train pass unmolested, the terrorists detonated the explosion directly under a second train. Iron, wood, and tattered clothing littered the tracks. But once again, Alexander II was unharmed. He had been riding in the first train; thus fate saved the sovereign on this late autumn day, while his baggage car lay in ruins.[67]

Although the Moscow assassination attempt did not kill the tsar, the explosion on the tracks outside of the old capital brought the People's Will the public attention and thus the opportunity for propaganda that it craved. Terrorist attacks are predicated upon their public nature along with the publicity that ensues from the carnage that the attack creates. For the members of the People's Will, "publicizing an attack—whether it be through media coverage or the terrorists' claim of responsibility—was in fact more powerful (and thus more important) for creating fear, anxiety, and disorder than the attack itself."[68] With the country's attention captivated, the Executive Committee issued a proclamation. Rather than painting the assassination attempt as a failure,[69] the party declared that the incident outside of Moscow was instructive and gave them renewed certainty that their future efforts would succeed.

The People's Will also used this occasion to reassert their position to the Russian people. Bringing about Alexander II's death, they explained, was only one of their immediate goals in the long-term struggle to free the Russian people.[70] Should the emperor willingly transfer his authority to an All-Russian Constituent Assembly, the narodovol'tsy would "leave Alexander II in peace and forgive his crimes."[71] But should the tsar maintain his present course of oppression, the Executive Committee would persist in their struggle. Although they resolved to continue the fight "as long as there is still a drop of blood in us,"[72] their task would be accelerated with the help of the people. Thus, the proclamation concluded with the following appeal to Russian society: "in order to destroy despotism and return justice and authority to the people we need your general support."[73]

With momentum building for the People's Will, the Figner family suffered two personal blows in November 1879. First, on the seventeenth, police arrested Peter N. Figner in connection with their investigation of Solovev's attempt on the tsar's life the previous spring.[74] Although he had nothing to do with the assassination plot, his informal association with his sisters' separatist group—which did include Solovev—was enough to warrant his arrest. In the heated atmosphere engendered by the battle between government and revolutionaries, an innocent Peter Figner spent almost two months in prison.[75]

Peter's brief but grueling ordeal coincided with the arrest of his younger sister Eugenia. Unlike her brother, Eugenia was an active part of the People's Will, having joined the group in the early fall.[76] When Vera insisted on going to Odessa, Eugenia had replaced her in the apartment she shared with Kviatkovskii. Only a week after Peter was arrested, a series of careless oversights on the part of the revolutionaries led gendarmes to Eugenia's apartment.[77]

Eugenia's arrest did not come as a complete surprise. As his sisters descended ever further into the revolutionary underground, Nikolai N. Figner enjoyed the benefits that came from being a well-placed nobleman in Imperial Russia. After attending the prestigious naval academy in St. Petersburg, he had distinguished himself as a warrant officer, fought in the Russo-Turkish War of 1877–1878, and was promoted to lieutenant. In mid-November he learned from friends in official circles that gendarmes were following Eugenia in the capital. With two children already in prison and frightened for her daughter's safety, Ekaterina Figner arranged a clandestine meeting with Eugenia, relayed to her what Nikolai had discovered, and begged her to leave the country.[78] Yet in spite of the danger, Eugenia refused to abandon the cause. Shortly thereafter gendarmes appeared on her doorstep in the middle of the night and arrested both Eugenia and Kviatkovskii. The cache of dynamite and illegal papers the police found in the apartment ensured that the "couple's" punishment would be severe.[79]

This began one of many difficult emotional periods that Vera spent in the revolutionary underground. Fretful about her sister's fate and the role her own actions played in these devastating arrests, Vera grew anxious. When Kibalchich, Frolenko, Lebedeva, and Nikolai Kolodkevich left Odessa in early January, she remained behind.[80] Alone, worried, and bored with the propaganda work in which she was engaged, Vera felt both lonely and restless.

For a brief period in early 1880, however, Vera found a charming distraction in F. N. Iurkovskii, who spent a little more than a month in Odessa. Although there is no evidence that the two shared a romantic relationship, Vera found the man who engineered the dramatic heist of the treasury in Kherson fascinating. Iurkovskii, who was also known as Sashka the Engineer, was a good-looking, dark-haired, bearded man of medium height and broad build whom Vera recalls it was impossible not to notice.[81] Never an official member of the People's Will, Iurkovskii had the spirit of a daring child and was a "black sheep" among his more serious, ascetic revolutionary counterparts.[82] Perhaps attracted by his independence, courage, nonconformity, and strong will, Vera knew Iurkovskii was cunning but admits that she "felt a certain weakness for him although it was clear that one had to be on their guard around him."[83] Unlike most of the male narodovol'tsy, Sashka the Engineer did not treat his female colleagues with pure camaraderie. Instead, he "courted, pleased and tried to fulfill the women revolutionaries' whims."[84] As he did, much to her chagrin, Iurkovskii "ignited a spark" in Vera.[85]

The spark that she admits Iurkovskii ignited in her is as close as Vera ever gets to confessing to a sexual relationship with a man. Although several men showed a romantic interest in her, she never admits to reciprocating their feelings. Even if she engaged in romantic dalliances, she cherished her independence and shied away from commitments. After her marriage ended, Vera discovered a sense of liberation and freedom that had been missing while she was tied to Alexei Filippov. The revolutionary movement and her work within it allowed her to enjoy her independence in a way few Russian women could. While the feminists of her day focused on achieving political and economic rights for women, the lived experiences of Vera and many of her fellow female radicals epitomize what later generations of feminists viewed as essential to women's emancipation. As Carla Hesse describes, women's liberation could not be realized "by the claims to political or juridical equality demanded by the feminist movement . . . but by financial and bodily independence— liberation from the coercion of the marital regime."[86] In a society in which women did not have the practical ability to achieve economic or even physical independence, the radical community offered an alternate path to relative material security and personal emancipation for women that was not predicated on marriage. With the group's collective fund-raising efforts and communal living arrangements providing for the needs of the men and women who comprised the Executive Committee of the People's Will, the women of the revolutionary organization, including Vera, discovered a feeling of liberation that few of their legal counterparts experienced.

Iurkovskii provided a needed distraction for Vera in the early winter of 1880. Not only was she worried about what would happen to her sister Eugenia, but she also fretted about what incriminating information the police had found in the raided apartment. She had good cause to worry. Among the papers seized from Kviatkovskii and Eugenia's flat was a diagram of the Winter Palace with a prominent red cross marked on the spot denoting the royal family's private dining room. Although soldiers and gendarmes immediately searched the palace, they failed to make a potentially explosive discovery.[87]

Stepan Khalturin, a member of the People's Will, had been posing as an innocent carpenter at the palace since September. Gaining the trust and friendship of many palace employees, by early February he was able to stash one hundred pounds of dynamite in his room, two floors directly below the family's dining room (workers often slept on cots on lower floors of the palace).[88] On the evening of February 5, 1880, a little after six o'clock, Khalturin lit the fuse to the dynamite in his trunk and left the building. His plan, approved by the appropriate members of the Executive Committee, was for his improvised bomb to explode just as the royal family sat down to dinner. Once again, Alexander II cheated death. Late for their evening meal, no member of the tsar's family was injured in the blast, yet ten soldiers and one civilian lost their lives while another fifty-six people suffered injuries in the attack.[89]

Both the tsar's survival and the spilling of nonroyal blood gave the People's Will cause for lament. Despite their dedication to violence, as terrorism expert Bruce Hoffman notes, "*Narodnaia Volia* displayed an almost quixotic attitude to the violence it wrought," in that they believed it possible and desirable to avoid shedding "one drop of superfluous blood."[90] For her part, in her thousands of pages of autobiographical writings, Vera avoids discussing the civilian bloodshed that ensued from the campaigns launched by the People's Will. What little attention she devotes to the subject of political violence is designed to portray her and her comrades as reluctant assassins. Writing in the immediate aftermath of the brutal civil war and rampant episodes of violence on the part of the Soviets in their pursuit of a new revolutionary order, Vera hints at a measure of regret when she asserts that "in entering into combat with each other, the government [of Alexander II] and the party helped to corrupt the country."[91] But in 1880 the loss of innocent lives did not dissuade the revolutionaries.

Instead the People's Will basked in the glow of unprecedented publicity. The group's ability to attack the tsar within the sanctity of his palace belied their limited membership and influence. The attack was so astounding that many outside the imperial capital initially viewed the explosion as a baseless rumor. The coverage in the *Times* (London) is typical. From Berlin, the correspondent writes, "This morning's intelligence at first produced here a feeling of skeptical stupefaction, until official dispatches all too fully confirmed the horrible tidings."[92]

Fear pervaded official circles as the government of Alexander II desperately sought an effective way "to fight an unseen, but ubiquitous menace."[93] A diary entry written by Grand Duke Konstantin Nikolaevich in the days after the explosion illustrates the powerful potential of terrorism. He writes, "We are experiencing a time of terror like that of the French Revolution; the only difference is that Parisians in the revolution looked their enemies in the eye, whereas we do not see, do not know, do not have the slightest idea of their numbers . . . [Thus, there is] universal panic."[94] The government reacted by pursuing all suspected revolutionaries and mercilessly dealing with those in custody. In addition, the "Supreme Commission for the Maintenance of State Order" under the chairmanship of M. T. Loris-Melikov, attempted to erode popular support for the radicals by abolishing the salt tax and expanding the rights enjoyed by the press.[95]

Aroused by the news of the spectacular events in the capital, Vera rejoiced when her colleagues Sofia Perovskaia and Nikolai Sablin arrived in Odessa to begin preparations for a new attempt on the tsar's life in the city.[96] Surmising that Alexander II would pass through Odessa on his way to the Crimea in May, the party declared that all available resources be marshaled. Instead of placing dynamite beneath railroad tracks as they had planned the previous summer, the Executive Committee decided to lay an explosive device under Italianskaia Street, which served as the central thoroughfare between the railroad station and the steamboat wharf.

Vera exploited the connections she made over the preceding months to raise nine hundred rubles to lease a store along Italianskaia Street. There Perovskaia and Sablin posed as grocers during the day, and at night all available hands dug tirelessly through the heavy clay soil in order to lay the mine beneath the street. The danger inherent in their assignment was apparent when Grigorii Isaev, one of the group's leading technical experts, lost three fingers in an accidental explosion while handling the dynamite.[97] Although Vera reports that Isaev bore his wounds bravely,[98] his sacrifice was for naught. Just as he had the previous summer, Alexander II once again bypassed Odessa on his journey. Thus, on May 24 the grocery store was locked up for the last time and Sablin, Perovskaia, and Isaev returned to the capital.[99]

After almost a year in Odessa, Vera was slated to join her colleagues in St. Petersburg once Mikhail Trigoni arrived to replace her. But she pined to be in the midst of the revolutionary excitement in the capital. Craving both action and camaraderie, she could stand it no more. In July, before anyone arrived to fill her place, Vera left Odessa for St. Petersburg.[100] Her blatant disregard of the group's directives irritated some of the revolutionary leadership, including Andrei Zheliabov, who expected his colleagues to exhibit the "same blind obedience that he forced himself to observe."[101] Yet in spite of her violation of revolutionary norms, Vera suffered no repercussions from her display of selfish independence.

Back at the locus of imperial power, Vera and the other members of the Executive Committee plotted, planned, and enjoyed the social distractions of St. Petersburg. As the populist writer and friend of the narodovol'tsy Nikolai Mikhailovskii notes, despite police surveillance and the persistent threat of arrests, exile, and prison, "the most dangerous terrorists walked around [the capital] openly, with false passports, going to theaters and parties."[102] Regardless of the seriousness of the threat posed by the People's Will, the gendarmerie, who had long viewed conspiratorial work as dishonorable, "was ill-equipped to deal with the changed methods of subversion."[103] Adding to police ineptitude was the fact that Nikolai Kletochnikov, an Executive Committee agent, had been working undercover in the Third Department since January 1879.[104] As a result of the information supplied by Kletochnikov, including the names of 385 police informants,[105] the revolutionaries were often one step ahead of the police. As a result, many of the narodovol'tsy seemed to revel in the cat-and-mouse game they conducted with the gendarmes and would laughingly relate the stories of their close calls to their radical colleagues.[106]

The summer and fall of 1880 were undoubtedly a high point for the Executive Committee. Exploiting the more liberal press policies instituted by Count Loris-Melikov and the publicity garnered by the explosions under the Moscow railroad and in the Winter Palace, the party intensified their propaganda efforts and expanded their membership. Vera played a pivotal role in the party's propaganda campaign during the fall of 1880, as she established contacts with both students and members of the armed forces and served as the People's Will's secretary for relations abroad.[107]

Thanks to the efforts of Vera, Perovskaia, Zheliabov, and Kolodkevich, the People's Will established an affiliated Central Military Circle at the Kronstadt

naval base at the end of 1880.[108] The revolutionaries' ability to sway naval officers to their side speaks to the vulnerability of the autocracy. For most of the
officers in this circle, disillusionment with the government began during their
stints of service. As they witnessed the arbitrary nature of the tsarist regime
at close range, these men began to question the autocracy's legitimacy.[109]

In terms of the physical confrontation between the government and the
revolutionaries, the early autumn of 1880 was relatively uneventful.[110] Although years later Vera recalled that Loris-Melikov's attempt to herald the
possibility of reforms did not fool anyone,[111] the members of the People's Will
clearly adopted a cautiously hopeful attitude in these early autumn months
and abstained from terrorist attacks.[112] But hopes for reform were dashed
when two of those convicted in the "Trial of the Sixteen," including Vera's former roommate Kviatkovskii, were executed on November 4, 1880.[113] Another
member of the sixteen revolutionaries tried was Eugenia Figner. Although she
did not share Kviatkovskii's fate, her punishment was severe, just as the party
had expected, because of the cache of evidence police found in her apartment.
Fortunate to leave the courtroom with her life, Eugenia nevertheless faced a
sentence of twenty-one years in Siberian exile.[114] Calling Kviatkovskii and
Alexander Presniakov, the other executed revolutionary, martyrs, the Executive Committee warned the government that "there will be dozens more to replace them and with the cry 'Death to the Tyrants!' they will bring the people
to victory."[115] Thus, after a brief lull in terrorist activity, the People's Will re-
doubled their efforts to kill the tsar.

The Executive Committee decided to assassinate Alexander II using the
same method they had planned to use in Odessa the previous spring. Their
strategy was to lease a shop on a St. Petersburg street where the emperor inevitably traveled and bury a mine that could be exploded when he passed. In
the days following their friends' executions in November, eight revolutionaries
took turns shadowing the tsar's movements.[116] This surveillance team discovered that every Sunday, after attending morning religious services and sharing a meal with his family in the Winter Palace, Alexander II traveled across
town to the Mikhailovskii Riding School to review the troops. To traverse
this short distance, he could use one of two routes. The vast majority of the
time he chose the more direct path, having his carriage drive straight down
Nevskii Prospect and onto Malaia Sadovaia Street. The People's Will decided
that it was along this route that they would strike.

Posing as the Kobozevs, a married couple from the provinces, the revolutionary veterans Iuri Bogdanovich and Anna Iakimova opened a cheese shop in a basement flat on Malaia Sadovaia Street just after the new year.[117] At the same time, Vera and Grigorii Isaev moved into an apartment just around the corner at 25 Vosnesenskii Prospect. With entrances on two separate streets that could mask the comings and goings of its illegal visitors and a bathhouse nearby that made the presence of numerous young strangers less obvious to the neighbors, Vera's new dwelling suited the People's Will's conspiratorial needs.[118] As the necessary preparations for a new assassination attempt fell into place, she and the other Executive Committee members became consumed with the project. Putting aside all other distractions, the revolutionaries could talk of nothing "besides dynamite and bombs."[119]

Plotting another assassination attempt in the capital itself was audacious in spite of the ineptitude of the gendarmerie. Almost from the beginning of their latest hatched plan, it looked as if the revolutionary group might have overplayed its hand. Before the cheese shop was even rented, one of the strongest leaders of the People's Will, Alexander Mikhailov, was arrested. While the apprehension of Mikhailov was both a strategic and emotional loss, the arrest of Kletochnikov in the last days of January 1881 was devastating. Over the preceding two years, through his undercover position in the police department, Kletochnikov had thwarted the apprehension of numerous revolutionaries. As the group closed in on another assassination attempt, they realized that without Kletochnikov's deflecting attention, the party was in a much more vulnerable position. Thus, the Executive Committee decided that their latest attack against the tsar needed to occur at the earliest possible opportunity.

By February the People's Will ran on nervous energy. Exploiting the long hours of winter darkness in St. Petersburg, a dozen party members worked throughout the seemingly interminable nights removing the earth under Malaia Sadovaia Street so that they could lay the mine. By the evening of February 24–25 the tunnel was complete.[120] The group surmised that the next time the tsar would pass the cheese shop would be the following Sunday, March 1. At a meeting in Vera and Isaev's apartment, the Executive Committee agreed that beginning March 1 the People's Will would try to assassinate the tsar every Sunday until they achieved their goal or died trying.[121]

Learning from the lessons of their past assassination attempts, the Executive Committee decided to hatch a backup plan. In case of a mechanical error, or should the emperor alter his route, the party decided to station four revolutionaries armed with handheld explosive devices that could be hurled at Alexander II if need be. In addition, if all of the explosive devices failed or were unable to be used, the party planned to utilize a method that dated back to ancient Greece and Rome: Andrei Zheliabov would lie in wait with a dagger and fatally stab the tsar.[122]

The days preceding the assassination were incredibly tense and difficult ones for the revolutionaries. The Kobozevs' shop was attracting increased attention. To many neighbors something seemed amiss with the obviously well-bred shopkeepers and their poorly stocked business. Informed about the strange cheese chop on Malaia Sadovaia Street, on the morning of February 28, just twenty-four hours before the scheduled assassination, police detectives posing as sanitation officials arrived at the Kobozevs' shop for a "routine inspection." Amazingly, although General Constantine Mrovinskii, the lead inspector, perused all three rooms and questioned Bogdanovich about curious aspects of the shop, he left satisfied that nothing was amiss.[123]

On the heels of this "sanitation inspection," Bogdanovich rushed over to Vera and Isaev's apartment to inform the other members of the Executive Committee about the morning's events.[124] Although his news engendered a great sense of relief that their plans had not been discovered, for the time being at least, the members of the People's Will were already struggling with the ramifications of another unwelcome news bulletin. The night before, gendarmes had arrested Andrei Zheliabov, the unquestioned leader of the Executive Committee.[125] Not only was Zheliabov a critical linchpin in the party, but he was also supposed to play a crucial role in the next day's assassination attempt.

By three o'clock ten of the members of the Executive Committee gathered at the apartment on Vosnesenskii Prospect. Discussing the events of the past twenty-four hours, the group agreed the situation looked bleak. Police suspicions had been raised about the cheese shop, Zheliabov was in prison, the mine was not yet in place, and none of the four handheld bombs was ready.[126] Nonetheless, the group decided to continue with their plans.[127] The only thing that would change would be that Sofia Perovskaia would replace her arrested lover, Zheliabov, in directing the bomb throwers and overseeing the attack.

With these issues resolved, the revolutionaries sprang into action. Isaev went to the cheese shop to lay the mine; others cleaned out Zheliabov and Perovskaia's apartment before the inevitable arrival of the police; and at the group's conspiratorial apartment, Vera, Nikolai Kibalchich, Mikhail Grachevskii, and Nikolai Sukhanov assembled bombs for the next day.[128] Soon the latter group was joined by Sofia Perovskaia. Although much work remained to be done, at 11:00 PM Vera and her comrades convinced Sofia to go to bed so that she would be well rested for the next day. Vera remained at the table mixing chemicals and cutting up paraffin cans until 2:00 AM, when she, too, retired for the evening.[129]

By 8:00 AM the next morning, the bombs were assembled. Perovskaia then took the four bombs and gave them to Ignatii Grinevitskii, Timofei Mikhailov, Nikolai Rysakov, and Ivan Emelianov, who were discharged with throwing the devices.[130] She reiterated the committee's instructions to the men and informed them that she was directing the operation. Should the mine under Malaia Sadovaia Street fail to explode, or should the tsar take another route, Perovskaia would give the signal to these men to throw their bombs.

As her apartment emptied of its overnight visitors, Vera paced anxiously. If all went well, the assassination should occur in the early afternoon. In the aftermath, the scene on Malaia Sadovaia Street would be bedlam. Attention would quickly focus on the cheese shop, and Bogdanovich and Iakimova would be in grave danger. While the revolutionaries assumed that the bomb throwers would themselves be killed and Perovskaia apprehended, plans were made to hide and protect the rest of their circle. It was Vera's job to wait for the "Kobozevs" and then conceal them until they could be safely spirited away from the capital and Russia, if need be.[131] The moment the People's Will had prepared for over the past year and a half was only hours away. Alone in her apartment without news or distractions, Vera was on pins and needles, desperate to know what was happening on Malaia Sadovaia Street. The minutes felt like hours and the hours passed like days as Vera waited to hear if her comrades had finally succeeded in killing the emperor of Russia.

6

REVOLUTIONARY ICONOGRAPHY

As Vera paced nervously in the empty silence of her apartment, Tsar Alexander II rode in a horse-drawn carriage through the streets of his capital. Although it was just after 2:00 in the afternoon, the emperor had already had a full day. After attending religious services, he reviewed the troops at the Mikhailovskii Riding School and had a pleasant visit with his cousin, the Grand Duchess Ekaterina Mikhailovna.[1] The schedule he followed this March morning was typical for the emperor. He was a man comfortable with routine, and his day mimicked many of his Sunday mornings since his return from the Crimea a few months before. But Alexander II had not been to the riding school for several weeks. As the confrontation between his government and the People's Will escalated, the tsar canceled his review of the troops, choosing to remain in the palace and not expose himself to unnecessary danger. Yet the February 27 arrest of the terrorist leader Andrei Zheliabov reassured the emperor that his police forces had gained the upper hand; thus, he resumed his favored Sunday morning routine on March 1. Bowing to the continued concerns his new young wife expressed for his personal safety, however, Alexander agreed to vary his typical route to and from the Winter Palace. Instead of following his usual path along Nevskii Prospect and Malaia Sadovaia Street, he took a less open course along the Ekaterinskii Canal, a route that many close to him believed would offer more protection against a potential terrorist attack. Sitting in his supposedly bombproof carriage, a present from

Napoleon III, he was only a couple of miles from home when a violent blast shook the carriage.

In the People's Will apartment she shared with Grigorii Isaev, Vera did not hear the explosion on the nearby Ekaterinskii Canal. Waiting for some kind of news or indication that the People's Will had finally killed the tsar, she neither heard nor saw anything to give the impression that this day was different from any other Sunday. Fatigued from her late night of assembling bombs, and dejected that the People's Will had seemed so close to realizing their objectives but had been unable to finish the job, she felt compelled to leave the apartment. Assuming that no fellow conspirators would be fleeing a police dragnet if an assassination attempt had not occurred, she saw no need to wait for Bogdanovich and Iakimova as she had been instructed to do, and she headed for the flat of her friend Gleb Uspensky.[2] Closing the apartment door behind her, nothing seemed out of the ordinary. All signs indicated that the People's Will had failed yet again.

As Vera walked briskly to Uspensky's apartment, Alexander II stepped from his carriage. Napoleon III's present to the tsar had saved his life. Shaken but unharmed, Alexander looked to his guards. Seeing the emperor out of the carriage, a member of his security detail, Colonel Dvorzhitskii, rushed to Alexander's side and assured him that all was well and that the bomb thrower had been apprehended.[3] Heaving a sigh of relief, the tsar walked along the sidewalks of the canal, surveying the damage. In answer to the anxious questions about his well-being, the tsar, not ten steps from the man who tried to end his life, responded, "Thank God, I escaped injury."[4] Hearing the words of the sovereign, the nineteen-year-old bomb thrower, Nikolai Ivanovich Rysakov, who was being restrained by onlookers and Imperial Guards,[5] wryly proclaimed, "We will see if you will still thank God."[6] Refusing to dignify his would-be assassin with a response, the emperor made his way back toward the carriage. Suddenly a second explosion rang out. Billowing smoke mixed with countless particles of snow sent rushing skyward by the blast. Bedlam and terror rippled along the canal. When the clouds of smoke and snow settled, several people lay either dead or injured on the now blood-soaked ground. One of the mortally wounded was the revolutionary Ignatii Grinevitskii, who had thrown the second bomb. Another was Alexander II. Although the tsar was conscious, his body was mangled and bloody and his breathing labored.[7] As soldiers and bystanders rushed to answer his barely audible cries for help, the

Russian emperor, losing massive amounts of blood,[8] complained of being cold and asked to be taken to the palace.[9]

Even this second explosion failed to attract Vera's notice. Just a few blocks from where her comrades had just thrown bombs at the feet of the emperor of Russia, it seemed like a mundane day. Vera arrived at Uspensky's flat feeling despondent that even with the number of safeguards and backup plans the party had put in motion, the latest assassination attempt had apparently ended in failure. Yet she was mistaken. Learning from the mistakes of the past, Sofia Perovskaia had responded to the tsar's route change and placed her four fellow conspirators with handheld bombs at the ready. Understanding the habits of the tsar's security forces as well as the urban space of the capital, Perovskaia achieved the party's murderous objectives in spite of Alexander II's attempts to elude his assassins.

The fate of the revolutionaries, their party, and the Russian autocracy collided violently that day along the picturesque canal in Alexander II's capital. Joined for a moment in the destruction unleashed by an exploding bomb, the trajectories of each group were forever changed. But in the minutes after the explosion, no one yet knew how. Instead both the revolutionaries and the men charged with protecting the tsarist state scrambled to safeguard what had not yet been destroyed. While Imperial Guards rushed the mortally wounded emperor to the Winter Palace, Perovskaia exploited the chaos and disappeared into the anonymous space of the city. Meanwhile, just a few blocks away, Vera was chatting with Gleb Uspensky, bemoaning her party's most recent failure, when Alexander Ivanchin-Pisarev rushed into Uspensky's apartment and relayed the rumors he had heard that the tsar had been killed.[10]

Overwhelmed with feelings of excitement and disbelief, Vera hurried home. Unlike the scene she had encountered less than an hour before, now the streets were filled with talk of explosions, blood, wounds, and the death of the emperor.[11] Finding a group of comrades in her apartment, Vera's overwhelming emotions barely allowed her to get the words out that Alexander II was dead as she broke down in tears. Standing in her apartment looking at the faces of the men and women with whom she had engineered the murder of the Russian emperor, Vera recalls, "I wept as did others that the heavy nightmare that had oppressed young Russia for ten years was over."[12] As she wept in relief, soldiers were raising a funeral flag over the Winter Palace.[13]

With Alexander II dead, members of the Executive Committee gathered in Vera's apartment to relish their success and plot their next move. Though they were unsure of how their victory would play out, the members of the People's Will leadership felt they had finally prevailed. Intoxicated by the clear manifestation of the party's will and power, Vera writes, "Neither the bayonets of hundreds of thousands of troops, nor throngs of guards and spies, nor all the gold in his treasury could save the sovereign of eighty million people as he fell at the hands of a revolutionary."[14]

In a document released the day after the tsar was killed, the terrorists publicly acknowledged their responsibility for the assassination. The Executive Committee argued that Alexander II's death "crowned two years of effort and costly sacrifices with success. Henceforth all of Russia will be convinced that the persistent continuation of the struggle is capable of destroying even centuries of the Romanovs' despotism."[15] The People's Will proclamation informed the public that while the revolutionaries did not relish bloodshed, Alexander II had left them no alternatives to this violent path. In maintaining the full force of the autocracy, the Executive Committee pronounced, Alexander was "an enemy of the people . . . and a tyrant," who thus deserved to die.[16]

Consistently thwarted in their attempts to work among the Russian masses, the terrorists had demonstrated their will by invoking the name of the people. After months and years during which their efforts to bring about meaningful change while publicly demonstrating their personal motivation and resolve had been frustrated by Alexander II's government, the revolutionaries of the People's Will exacted their revenge in a seemingly heroic and certainly dramatic manner and empowered themselves through the use of terrorism. Accustomed to feeling powerless, the realization of their potency was intoxicating.

But this empowerment came at a cost. Attracting the full fury and focus of the Russian police apparatus, the People's Will paid dearly for its success. In the days and weeks after the events of March 1, the party's leadership was nearly decimated as the captured bomb thrower, Rysakov, revealed all that he knew of the organization, its personnel, and its agenda.[17]

With the exception of Rysakov (whom police seized at the scene), the first major arrests in connection with the assassination came on March 3 when gendarmes stormed the apartment of Nikolai Sablin and Gesia Gelfman.[18] Apart from their sorrow at having lost two valuable comrades,[19] the members of the Executive Committee were unnerved that the police zeroed in on this apartment. Since so few narodovol'tsy even knew of this residence's existence, the party's leadership surmised that someone in police custody was disclosing revolutionary secrets to the authorities. Confident that it could not be the imprisoned leaders Zheliabov or Mikhailov, the Executive Committee correctly assumed that Rysakov was feeding the police information. This meant that the revolutionaries and their critical assets, including their stockpile of dynamite, their printing presses, and the unexploded and so far undiscovered mine under Malaia Sadovaia Street, were in immediate danger.

Wasting a resource such as the underground mine was unimaginable, but with Rysakov presumably confessing all he knew to the police, trying to utilize the bomb now seemed suicidal. Vera contends that she was one of a small minority who suggested maintaining the cheese shop in the hopes that it could be used against the dead tsar's eldest son and heir, Alexander III.[20] But most of the other leading narodovol'tsy disagreed with her, considering it too great a risk. Accusing her comrades of cowardice,[21] Vera demonstrated her increasingly fanatical sentiments. For a woman who had avoided confrontation with the tsarist authorities for so many years, the recklessness she exhibited in this instance demonstrates how much she had changed in the revolutionary underground. Living an illegal existence, she became consumed with the notion of revolution and the idea of assassination. She defined herself by her standing as a revolutionary and reconciled herself to martyrdom on behalf of the cause. In fact, she had done more than reconcile herself to the notion of revolutionary martyrdom; she sought and even craved it as the manifestation of her own will and autonomy. By the time the People's Will assassinated the emperor, Vera was so fixated on the notion of her own martyrdom that rational considerations and efforts toward self-preservation seemed like revolutionary sacrilege, and she viewed them as indicative of personal weakness. To live a life devoted to the public good and die on behalf of a higher cause was the ultimate goal to which she aspired. Thus, the danger posed by prospective detection by the gendarmes was nothing to fear. Instead, the continued display of power, force, and autonomy needed to be pursued in spite of the costs.

Vera yearned to demonstrate her daring, conviction, and strength of will in an immediate and personal way. To that end she disdained the notion that she would fill merely a supportive position in the escapades of the People's Will and openly lobbied to play a primary role in the most daring and dramatic of the group's exploits. In doing so she rejected feminized models of behavior—even feminized revolutionary behavior—and embraced more reckless, heroic, and thus masculine tasks. In a group that ostensibly put personal motives aside, Vera did not. While her ultimate aim was the desire to establish a more just and equitable country, an equally important motivation for her was the opportunity to allow for the manifestation of her own power and the celebration of her bravery and will.

Having survived the battle with the tsarist state, years later Vera used her memoirs to herald the self-image she consciously sought to create. Subsequently, many of her anecdotes describing the days before and after the tsar's assassination are intentionally dramatic. One in particular characterizes Vera's conception of herself as a daring renegade better than most. Having learned the role that Sofia Perovskaia played in the events of March 1, gendarmes combed the streets and alleys of the capital in an effort to apprehend the terrorist leader. Trying to avoid capture, Sofia wandered from one friend's apartment to the next. Given the gravity of her crimes, anyone found with Perovskaia would inevitably be prosecuted to the full extent of the law. However, the danger inherent in harboring Sofia did not dissuade Vera from coming to her friend's aid. Instead, she relished the opportunity to help Sofia and was energized by the potential danger associated with her revolutionary act of solidarity. Assuring Sofia that she was not afraid of what the tsar's police or courts could do to her, Vera showed her friend a revolver that she kept by her bed and said, "Whether you are here or not, if they come I will shoot them."[22]

Other members of the People's Will were more inclined to self-preservation than Vera. Despite her best efforts to sway her fellow revolutionaries, the Executive Committee decided that the cheese shop should be abandoned without delay. On the evening of March 3, Anna Iakimova closed the store, put money and a note for the butcher on the counter, and left the building on Malaia Sadovaia Street for the last time. "Mrs. Kobozev" then went to Vera's apartment, changed her clothes, and traveled to Moscow via Smolensk.[23] Her fictitious husband, Iuri Bogdanovich, had left St. Petersburg earlier that day. The following morning, the closed cheese shop attracted the authorities' attention for the second time in less than a week.[24] Unlike General Mrovinskii's inspection of the premises on February 28, on March 4 police investigators discovered the cheese shop's secret tunnel and the mine underneath Malaia Sadovaia Street and realized how close they had come to thwarting the recent assassination.[25]

Just as the revolutionaries tried to use the emperor's death as an occasion for propaganda, so, too, did his government. In an effort to arouse the ire and indignation of the populace and direct the people's long-standing frustrations away from the imperial state and toward the terrorists, the official press demonized the culprits and vowed revenge. Lamenting Alexander II's death, and mourning the ruler who "fell at the sacrilegious hands of assassins who made repeated attempts on his precious life,"[26] the Russian press spoke for the government when it declared the tsar's killers "enemies of the Russian people and the entire Slavic world."[27]

In the days and weeks after the assassination of Alexander II, police officials turned the capital into a virtual militarized state. Cossacks patrolled the roads in and around the city and carefully checked the identification papers of anyone entering or leaving the capital, while gendarmes combed the streets of St. Petersburg for the terrorists who had engineered the murder of the Tsar.[28] As rumors swirled of random house searches and the threat of imminent arrest hung over the heads of the conspirators,[29] each of the revolutionaries knew that at any time he or she could be the next one snared by the police dragnet. As a former member of the Executive Committee later recalled, these weeks reminded the young radical men and women that the life of a terrorist was "the life of a hunted wolf."[30] Many left the capital for other parts of the country, but some terrorists, like Sofia Perovskaia, did not manage to escape and fell into police custody.

Despite their losses in personnel, the remaining members of the People's Will consciously sought to cultivate an impression of strength and power. To that end the Executive Committee members who remained at liberty in the capital published a letter to Alexander III. Reminding him that regardless of the most concerted efforts of the late emperor, the revolutionary movement "tenaciously grew and spread," the Executive Committee warned that if the new sovereign did not change the government's repressive tactics, the movement would continue to grow in number and strength, and "terrorist acts [would] be repeated in ever more alarming and intensified forms."[31]

Less than two weeks after Alexander II's assassination, the committee knew that with its party's depleted forces it could not carry out the threats it issued in the letter.[32] But as with any terrorist group, the People's Will's power lay in the *threat* of continued action, not in the action itself. The "equation of terrorism" is that once a violent act is committed, more violent acts can be expected "unless certain things are done (or discontinued)."[33] In this regard the exact number of terrorist forces is secondary to the *appearance* of power and capability. As Martha Crenshaw notes, across the spectrum of organizations that engage in terrorism, the lack of proportion "between the material power of the actors and the fear their actions generate is typical."[34] As long as the implied or explicit *threat* of additional violent acts remains and the *illusion* of potential power is maintained, the terrorist's ability to influence targeted players and events is not diminished. "As much political theater as violence," terrorism is a form of politically motivated extortion.[35]

In the late spring of 1881 the remainder of the Executive Committee used the threat of continued violence in order to try to exact some concessions from the autocratic government. "Without a doubt . . . the government was inclined to consider the revolutionaries much stronger and more powerful than they were in reality."[36] Although the secret police captured more agents of the People's Will almost daily, the overwhelming impression remained that Alexander III's life was in danger. With each new arrest the extent of the conspiracy against the tsarist regime seemed to grow. On March 24 Alexander secretly moved from the capital to his palace at Gatchina to thwart any plans the People's Will had to take his life.[37] Although his flight from St. Petersburg secured his personal safety, it played directly into the hands of the People's Will. For many people in both the government and society, news of the emperor's exodus seemed only to confirm their impressions of the awesome power of the terrorists.[38]

As Russia waited for the People's Will to carry out another daring act of political violence, the remaining members of the Executive Committee hunkered down in an effort to salvage the remnants of their battered party. The first priority was to move the revolutionaries who had survived the police crackdown in March out of the capital. The headquarters of the Executive Committee were relocated to Moscow, and many agents set out for provinces throughout European Russia.[39] Vera, however, delayed leaving St. Petersburg. Although she contends that she was disinclined to separate herself from the revolutionary energy in St. Petersburg,[40] the reality is that her quest for martyrdom was not served by fleeing the capital. Employing the full force of her persuasive skills, she convinced the other members of the Executive Committee to grant her permission to remain in the city for the time being.[41] As the other luminaries of the party fled or were imprisoned, Vera's presence in the capital impressed many of the lower-tiered members of the People's Will. Her tenacity and dedication only seemed to confirm to her fellow radicals and their sympathizers the impression that she personified revolutionary commitment, courage, and selflessness; this in turn gave her great personal satisfaction.

Within weeks, though, Vera's position in the capital became untenable. After her roommate, Grigorii Isaev, fell into the hands of the police on April 1, it was obvious that Vera had to abandon St. Petersburg or be arrested herself. But before she could leave, she and her comrades needed to liquidate her apartment, which still stored a cache of dynamite, a rudimentary chemical lab, a printing press, and equipment used to manufacture false passports.[42] Confident that Isaev would not reveal his name or address, the revolutionaries knew they had some time to clear out the apartment, but they had no idea how much.

Throughout the day on April 2, Vera and four male comrades emptied the apartment of its precious revolutionary supplies.[43] The revolutionaries worked quickly and deliberately, unsure if they would suddenly be interrupted by a group of gendarmes. After the sun had set and the last box was carried out, there was no longer any reason to remain in the apartment. Yet Vera did anyway. Believing that if the police did not yet know the apartment's location they would not discover it in the late evening hours, she spent one last night on Vosnesenskii Prospect. While there is some credibility to her rationale that it was doubtful the police would discover Isaev's address before morning, there was no reason for Vera to tempt fate by remaining in the apartment. Yet perhaps she did not worry about possible capture because she was inclined toward it. Her last night in the party's apartment was also the last night of several of her comrades' lives. The martyrdom that Vera craved was hours away for Sofia Perovskaia, Andrei Zheliabov, Nikolai Rysakov, Timofei Mikhailov, and Nikolai Kibalchich, all five of whom were scheduled to be hanged on April 3.

Vera awoke on the morning of April 3 to an empty apartment devoid of both incriminating evidence and police agents. She made herself some tea, tidied up, and left. Police documents show that gendarmes discovered Isaev's true identity and address thanks to a house porter who was summoned relatively early in the day on April 3.[44] Immediately thereafter police descended upon the apartment on Vosnesenskii Prospect. Inside they found no inhabitants and no revolutionary supplies, only a still-warm samovar with which Vera had made herself some tea just hours before.[45]

Vera delights in describing how close she came to losing her freedom on this early April day. Recounting the events surrounding her narrow escape on April 3, she uses the imagery of the gendarmes' discovery of the warm samovar to give tangible evidence of her bravery and seemingly uncanny ability to make the police look like fools. As she relates cleaning an apartment that would soon be infiltrated by the muddy boots of gendarmes, Vera purposely attempts to cultivate the impression that the threat posed by the police meant nothing to her. This aggrandizes her person and her strength of will while speaking to the ultimate power that the People's Will exercised in this period. Against such reckless individuals who demonstrated so little concern for their own well-being that they were happy to risk penal punishment and death, the ultimate ability of the emperor and his many-man military to effectively deal with the terrorist threat was seriously compromised. In a state where sovereignty resided solely in the power of the tsar, his autocracy, and his military's ability to protect and defend his empire and himself, the disempowerment caused by the People's Will challenged the state's very raison d'être.

Shortly before the warm samovar was found in Vera's recently vacated apartment, her five comrades died at the hands of the state on Semenovsky Square. The execution of the regicides was a theatrical display of autocratic power performed before tens of thousands of spectators. Although it certainly was designed to punish, the public execution was intended to restore the autocracy's "sovereignty by manifesting it at its most spectacular."[46] As Michel Foucault argues, contained within the spectacle of the scaffold, "there must be an emphatic affirmation of power and of its intrinsic superiority" that involves marking, beating, and breaking the body of the condemned.[47] In other words, "the ceremony of punishment, then, is an exercise of 'terror.'"[48] While this exercise of terror may have impelled the masses to reject the propaganda of word and deed that was directed to them by the members of the People's Will, it only reinforced the commitment of the revolutionaries themselves. For those who were ready and even eager to die on behalf of a higher cause—those like Vera—the continued display of sovereignty, power, and violence on the part of the tsar's government only fueled the dreams of martyrdom and justified the blood spilled by the revolutionaries in an effort to redress the inequity of power in the state.

Utilizing the unusual flurry of activity in the streets caused by the spectacle of the regicides' execution (which was attended by thousands of the capital's inhabitants), Vera boarded a horse-drawn tram and left St. Petersburg. By the time evening fell, she was comfortably ensconced in the Kronstadt apartment of A. P. Shtromberg and F. I. Zavalishin, two naval officers who were members of the People's Will Central Military Circle.[49] Although gendarmes sought her in connection with the recent assassination, Vera did not hide behind closed doors. Passing herself off as Zavalishin's cousin, the exotic-looking beauty attracted a great deal of attention from the men in the tsar's navy, which she made no attempt to discourage. While she did try to indoctrinate some of these sailors with radical ideals, she did not proselytize all of the men she met. Instead she relished the social interaction and flattering attention of the military men whose company she kept to the point that she even accompanied several of them to a nearby music hall, where the group spent an evening singing and playing the piano.[50] According to her host, Vera made a wonderful impression on everyone with whom she came into contact.[51] Captivating these sailors and officers with her "intellect, energy, striking femininity and grace," Esper A. Serebriakov recalled that this "remarkable woman's stay [at the fortress] was a genuine celebration for our circle."[52]

Vera's stay in Kronstadt was short-lived; after only a week she departed the naval town for Moscow and then moved on to Odessa, where she took on the task of rebuilding the People's Will in the south.[53] With a significant radical tradition among the city's workers and a local group of the People's Will already in operation, Odessa's revolutionary potential seemed considerable.[54] Yet it soon became clear that the greatest potential in the Black Sea town lay with its sizable military population. Given the Russian masses' political apathy, which even so dramatic an event as the assassination of the tsar proved unable to destroy, the People's Will lost faith in the people. As Vera writes, "After the events of March 1 the people were silent and society remained dumb."[55] Unable to overturn the political immaturity of a people bogged down by illiteracy, ignorance, and poverty, the remaining members of the People's Will sought other, more politically conscious allies in their struggle with the autocracy. Increasingly, in the months that followed the assassination of Alexander II, the Executive Committee, and especially Vera, believed they had found this ally in the tsar's own military.

While circles of both students and workers emerged during this period in Kiev, Odessa, Nikolaev, Rostov, Tiflis, and Kharkov,[56] among no other group did the narodovol'tsy have such success as among officers of the Russian army and navy. Over the course of 1881, military organizations directly linked with the People's Will formed in a network of cities including Moscow, Orel, Smolensk, Riga, Vilna, Odessa, Nikolaev, and Minsk.[57] By the middle of 1882 there were over fifty circles with more than four hundred officers in assorted towns in European Russia.[58] The largest of these circles were in Odessa—the home port of approximately one-third of the Russian navy—and Nikolaev, where Vera, along with her colleague A. V. Butsevich played a primary role in creating local military groups and enlisting officers in the revolutionary cause.[59]

By the spring of 1882, General Vasilii S. Strelnikov, the military prosecutor in the region, held Vera directly responsible for the fact that "a criminal circle developed among officers of the 59th Liublinskii infantry regiment in

Odessa."[60] Using her personality and looks to charm the military men in her midst, Vera utilized the gendered expectations of the soldiers, sailors, and officers for the unladylike goal of revolution. The leading Soviet historian of the People's Will, S. S. Volk, contends that "few other narodovol'tsy besides Zheliabov did so much for the organization of military circles [as Vera Figner]. Her passion and personal conversations converted many of the officers who listened to her into revolutionaries."[61] To the radically inclined men serving far from home in the imperial military, Vera's influence among the military in the aftermath of the tsar's assassination was so great that revolutionary troops deemed her the "Mother Commander."[62]

With things going well in Odessa, in October 1881 Vera traveled to Moscow to meet with the other members of the Executive Committee who were still at large. Although she was happy to see old friends, the meeting was bittersweet. The leadership of the People's Will was only a shadow of its former self, with its ranks decimated by arrests, executions, and emigration. Given the group's paucity of human and financial resources, the accomplishments of Vera and her comrades in 1881 and 1882 are astounding. They continued to produce the revolutionary organs *Narodnaia Volia, Listok Narodnoi Voli,* and *Rabochnaia Gazeta,* even after several police raids and a series of arrests.[63] These efforts were herculean given the risks, but with each subsequent issue of a revolutionary publication, the People's Will gave evidence of its endurance and the viability of the party in the face of official persecution.

The party communicated their message of fortitude and resilience beyond Russia's borders as well in a continued quest to sway the sympathies of the European and American public to its side. In the foreign press the Executive Committee sought to depict themselves as the most reluctant of assassins. After James Garfield died in September 1881 from wounds sustained in an assassination attempt two months earlier, the Executive Committee published a letter expressing its outrage at the American president's assassin. In its public letter the party leadership asserted that political assassination was reprehensible in a democratic state. The statement alleges that in a country that provides its citizens with personal freedom and political rights, assassination is a "manifestation of that same spirit of despotism which we seek to destroy in Russia . . . violence is only justified when it is directed against violence."[64]

In spite of the revolutionaries' resilience, Alexander III's multilayered security apparatus wrought havoc on the narodovol'tsy and their operations as an increasing number of revolutionaries and radical sympathizers found themselves detained by the state. In order to "render defense and moral support" to their comrades in prison and exile,[65] the free members of the People's Will established a section within the party called the Political Red Cross. While this revolutionary group emulated its international nonpartisan counterpart through its effort to communicate with prisoners and exiles, it remained true to its revolutionary goals and methods by working to arrange prisoners' escapes.[66] By the fall of 1881, realizing the urgent need to provide assistance to the spiraling numbers of political prisoners, the Executive Committee recruited additional help from abroad. Using Peter Lavrov and Vera Zasulich as their representatives, the Political Red Cross waged a vigorous propaganda war against the tsarist regime and its treatment of prisoners and exiles in the Western European press.[67]

But it was the physical war with the terrorists that Alexander III feared most. Believing the bombastic rhetoric of the People's Will, for months after his father's murder the new tsar essentially hid in his palace at Gatchina.[68] He was unaware that his revolutionary adversaries lacked the resources to attack him. In Vera's opinion the group's paucity of resources could not distract the People's Will from continued acts of terror, but their focus needed to change. Thus, instead of killing the emperor himself, the Executive Committee decided to attack his officials, who represented what they believed to be the tyranny of the regime.

At Vera's behest, the People's Will settled upon Odessa's military prosecutor General Vasilii Strelnikov as its first victim.[69] In order to coordinate the assassination personally, Vera returned to Odessa at the beginning of December 1881. Living under the alias Elena Ivanovna Kolosova, she shadowed Strelnikov for weeks and recruited Stepan Khalturin to come to Odessa to kill him.[70] By mid-March everything seemed to be in place. In order to maximize her chances to remain free, Vera left the city in anticipation of the impending assassination. As one of only a handful of revolutionary leaders still at liberty in Russia, it was essential that she not be arrested. Putting the assassination in Khalturin's hands, she returned to Moscow.

On March 18 Vera's plans came to fruition. At approximately six o'clock that evening, Strelnikov took his usual post-dinner stroll. Toward the end of his walk, he sat down on a bench to enjoy the evening air when a well-dressed young man approached him and shot him at point-blank range.[71] Strelnikov died almost instantly. But Vera's preparations for a clean getaway for the assassins failed. Khalturin and his accomplice, Nikolai A. Zhelvakov, were apprehended immediately and hanged on March 22.[72]

Vera had been in Moscow for only a few days when she learned of Strelnikov's death and Khalturin's and Zhelvakov's subsequent executions. Pleased that she and her comrades had been able to successfully engineer the military prosecutor's assassination, she nonetheless was saddened that her plans to ensure the assassins' safety had faltered. The situation in Moscow did little to lighten her mood. In the weeks preceding her arrival, the People's Will had suffered a new wave of arrests. In addition to the loss of such experienced revolutionaries as Bogdanovich, Iakov V. Stefanovich, and Vera Lebedeva, the party's workers organization in Moscow was destroyed after being betrayed by a spy.[73] With their forces already severely compromised, the narodovol'tsy could ill afford these latest arrests. As the numbers of skilled and practiced revolutionaries continued to dwindle, those who remained felt increasingly vulnerable. In Moscow in the spring of 1882, many of the men and women living in the revolutionary underground, including Vera, had an "eerie, foreboding feeling."[74] Rumors began to circulate that someone in the Moscow group had turned police informant, and the revolutionaries started to leave the old capital in droves.[75]

While she was certainly anxious about her own arrest, Vera claims she felt great sadness as she watched her comrades scurry off to the provinces, St. Petersburg, and Western Europe like frightened mice. Yet she, too, left Moscow. Not only was she in imminent danger of arrest, but also, without sufficient human resources in the former capital, she was essentially incapacitated. In Moscow for less than a month, she left for Kharkov.

Living as Maria Brovchenko Frolova, Vera posed as a fel'dsher student pursuing her degree.[76] Every morning she left her apartment at eight o'clock as if heading out to class. But instead of going to a lecture on medicine, she spent long hours trying to consolidate the party's fortunes. In addition to leading Kharkov's local People's Will group, Vera spent the bulk of her time trying to find capable, experienced individuals whom she might recruit for the party's badly weakened center.[77] Although she encountered a number of energetic aspiring revolutionaries, she failed to find a potential ally with the expertise to help her lead the People's Will in such a desperate time.

During the late spring of 1882, supporters of the revolutionary party had occasion to believe that the fortunes of the People's Will were improving. Although the Moscow organization had been decimated, a number of Executive Committee members gathered in St. Petersburg and it seemed possible that the group might be reconstituting itself in the imperial capital.[78] Cultivating a plan to assassinate the viciously ardent police official Georgii P. Sudeikin,

Mikhail F. Grachevskii, Anna Pribyleva-Korba, and Alexander V. Butsevich established a dynamite workshop on Vasilevsky Island.[79] But any hopes for a revolutionary renaissance were soon dashed. After a worker in the dynamite workshop became a police informant in early June, the gendarmes arrested everyone involved in the project, including the Executive Committee agents listed above.[80]

Although the tsarist regime did not realize it, these arrests all but sealed the fate of the Executive Committee of the People's Will. The Moscow and St. Petersburg party organizations were completely wiped out. There were narodovol'tsy circles that continued to flourish throughout the empire, but the party's center was essentially destroyed. In the spring of 1882, Maria Oshanina emigrated to Western Europe for health reasons. After the arrests at the dynamite workshop in June, only two party leaders remained at liberty in Russia: Vera Figner and Lev Tikhomirov. While she was in Kharkov desperately trying to rebuild the center, Vera received heartbreaking news from her fellow committee member: Tikhomirov and his wife had decided to leave Russia. Despite her "strong admonishments," Vera could not change the Tikhomirovs' minds, and in the summer of 1882 they emigrated abroad.[81] Vera was left alone with the entire burden of the fate of the People's Will weighing on her slight shoulders.

"Sick[ened] and distressed" by the arrests of her St. Petersburg comrades and the emigration of Tikhomirov,[82] Vera was miserable during the summer of 1882. In a letter to her sister Olga, she sounds like a woman running out of time. Full of advice about how to live and persevere in the face of hardship, the letter appears to be Vera's good-bye to her sister. Feeling solely responsible for the fate of her party and completely cut off from her former revolutionary colleagues, every aspect of her life seemed hopeless and painful; even if she remained free, she did not know how much more she could endure. As the only member of the Executive Committee still at liberty in Russia, Vera Figner became the primary target of the tsarist security forces.[83] "Knowing the desperate condition of the party, the irreparable state of the cause at that moment[,] and the danger facing Vera Nikolaevna personally," Anna Pribyleva-Korba beseeched her friend from prison to emigrate and form a new Executive Committee abroad.[84] But Vera refused and insisted she was not going to abandon Russia.[85] As she wrote to Nikolai Morozov two years earlier, "The struggle [for political freedom] has thus far been bought at the price of so many of [our] comrades" that revolutionary solidarity demands "that all who are available should continue to fight as long as the struggle continues."[86] Continuing the fight, in Vera's mind, necessitated being on Russian soil.

During this period Vera endured much "more failure than success."[87] Tired and demoralized, she nonetheless persisted and marshaled her energy and will to carry "life like a cross."[88] Her perseverance in the face of enormous personal danger during this difficult period became legendary. As she stood alone preserving what was left of the People's Will from political and physical annihilation, Vera Nikolaevna Figner became "a living legend, idolized as a martyr by some and abhorred as a bloodthirsty monster by others."[89] With her good looks, intense convictions, and dauntless will, she was the perfect revolutionary heroine. Recognizing that she had given up everything, including "love, motherhood, family life and security,"[90] to devote herself to the emancipation of the Russian people (albeit through violence), those who believed in the cause could not help but respect Vera. In her party's most desperate hours, she became the symbol around which supporters of the revolutionary movement could rally. As an admirer in Western Europe contended decades later, "Everywhere she passes the ranks of men who cry with frenetic enthusiasm 'Hail Liberty!' grows."[91] A nineteenth-century living version of the revolutionary icon of liberty,[92] Vera became a "divine heroine" and a martyr for the cause.[93]

Vera's transformation into a legend, however, exacted an enormous personal price. From this point in her revolutionary career until her death (and even beyond), she became as much of a symbol as she was a woman. Ever conscious of her position and responsibility as an icon of the radical movement, she suppressed many of her true emotions, aspirations, and fears so as not to compromise the revolutionary myth that was Vera Nikolaevna Figner. In 1882 she wrote to her mother and youngest sister, saying, "All of my energy is spent hiding my inner state in an effort to be cheerful for others . . . even though I feel horror, despair and rage and am deeply unhappy."[94] Knowing that her optimistic endurance served as an inspiration to the entire movement, Vera lived a dual life. Racked by worry and doubts, she appeared hopeful and invincible. As the party increasingly relied on her and as her legend grew in turn, the amount of self-expression that she allowed herself to indulge in decreased. Like other notable female revolutionaries of her generation, as "the myth substituted itself for the reality, the image that was cultivated masked and to an extent devoured the personality."[95] Her close friend Gleb Uspensky wrote of Vera that she was "a person of the highest order, whose ideals could not be separated from her essence but instead harmoniously merged with her personal experiences."[96] Vera's private life and public image became inextricably fused. For most of her comrades, she "was not only an example of revolutionary bravery, but the embodiment of human perfection."[97]

By the summer of 1882 it was clear that Vera was "the actual leader of the People's Will."[98] Although she was overwhelmed by the responsibilities of directing a crippled revolutionary party, she focused on trying to rebuild an effective Executive Committee and establishing a new printing press.[99] These tasks proved difficult. As she traveled through the country and attempted to establish ties with radically inclined individuals, Vera sadly acknowledged that the young people whom she met "could not replace [her] old, experienced comrades."[100] The most promising radicals Vera encountered since the demise of the original Executive Committee were some of the men in the People's Will's military organization. Making it her priority to rebuild the center of the party, she decided to convince the top radical officers in the party's military organization to resign their commissions and become full-time members of the Executive Committee.[101]

Vera sent a recent radical recruit and former artillery officer named Sergei P. Degaev as her emissary on this mission. Without question, Degaev failed to rival his terrorist predecessors in either charisma or a penchant to self-sacrifice through radical violence; he had even been turned down as a prospective Executive Committee member before Alexander II's assassination. But with her ranks so seriously depleted in the fall of 1882, Vera decided that Degaev's intelligence and resourcefulness would make him a valuable comrade.[102] In October and early November 1882, Degaev traveled to St. Petersburg, Odessa, and Nikolaev to recruit military men who had been handpicked by Vera for the Executive Committee. M. Iu. Ashenbrenner and N. M. Rogachev were among those who answered the call.[103]

In the midst of trying to rebuild her tattered party, Vera received an unexpected visitor. On October 15, 1882, the noted literary figure Nikolai K. Mikhailovskii arrived on Vera's doorstep to discuss a possible truce between the People's Will and the tsarist administration.[104] Ignorant about the true dilapidated state of the terrorist group, well-placed persons with contacts at the highest levels of government had approached Mikhailovskii and other distinguished writers with revolutionary sympathies about mediating to end the three-year battle between the narodovol'tsy and the regime.

In an effort to ensure the tsar's safe and overdue coronation, a group of influential Russians with ties to the highest ranks of government constituted themselves as the "sacred brigade" and opened negotiations with carefully selected intermediaries. The representatives of this brigade promised to obtain the release of an influential revolutionary from prison or exile; provide for the appointment of an impartial commission to investigate charges of onerous conditions in the Kara mines; and explore the possibility of granting an amnesty for political crimes, freedom of the press, and the liberty for radicals to conduct socialist propaganda. In return the narodovol'tsy had to pledge to refrain from political violence until the coronation.[105]

Various sources that describe this mediation agree that the uppermost reaches of the government were aware that these negotiations were taking place.[106] There is perhaps no greater evidence that the conspiratorial and organizational methods adopted by the People's Will in the wake of the assassination of the tsar were at least partly successful. Though severely weakened by the loss of almost all members of the Executive Committee, the revolutionary party continued to function and in some places expand. In doing so Vera and a handful of other terrorists maintained the illusion that their ability to use violence to achieve their social and political ends was undiminished. As long as they were able to do so, the People's Will remained a powerful force in the country.

But although the illusion was of her making, Vera's initial reaction to the "sacred brigade's" potential deal was one of disbelief.[107] Knowing the abysmal state of her party, she could not conceive that the same regime that refused to work with the revolutionaries in the immediate aftermath of Alexander II's assassination would want to compromise after more than a year of relative silence from the terrorists. Vera believed that these alleged negotiations were just the police's latest ploy to capture the narodovol'tsy who remained at liberty, and her first inclination was to reject them out of hand.[108]

Long an admirer of Vera, Nikolai Mikhailovskii was dismayed at the toll the previous months had taken on this beautiful and spirited woman. With the weight of the party's burdens resting squarely on her shoulders, he found Vera "weary of her turbulent life" and despondent over the awful state of the revolutionary cause.[109] After she confessed that the state of the party was such that she could not even contemplate arranging new violent attacks against the regime, Mikhailovskii convinced Vera that if the party could not engage in terrorist activities, she had nothing to lose in undertaking negotiations. Still wary, Vera instructed him to tell his contacts that he was unable to find any Executive Committee members in Russia and that should the "sacred brigade" want to continue its mediation efforts, its envoys needed to deal with the party's agents abroad. In the meantime, Vera sent a message to Western Europe to apprise Oshanina and Tikhomirov of this latest turn of events.[110]

With a degree of revived hope after Mikhailovskii's visit, Vera directed five revolutionaries to reestablish the party's printing press in Odessa.[111] For a moment it seemed as if the fortunes of the People's Will could be improving. But any elation that Vera felt was fleeting. Less than one month after it was established, the apartment where the party's press was housed was infiltrated by the police, its inhabitants arrested, and its equipment confiscated.[112] Among the revolutionaries seized in this December 20 raid was Sergei Degaev, the agent in charge of the press. Although he was not a revolutionary of the caliber of an Alexander Mikhailov or a Sofia Perovskaia, Degaev was a member of the Executive Committee and Vera sharply felt his loss. But as the next few months would prove, his arrest was far more catastrophic for the People's Will than she ever anticipated. "Faced with decades in prison, Degaev's weak character sought a way out,"[113] and he became a traitor in the employ of the police.

Degaev's betrayal sealed the party's fate, because the information he provided shattered the People's Will's carefully constructed illusion of power. Almost immediately after he began to share revolutionary secrets with police officials, the "sacred brigade" abruptly abandoned its negotiations with the revolutionaries. According to Tikhomirov, Degaev's testimony "uncovered the government's eyes" and showed them the colossal mistake they were about to make in compromising with the terrorists.[114] As soon as the government learned that the People's Will was physically incapable of making good on their threats, the party's destruction was a foregone conclusion.

Without realizing the full ramifications of the shutdown of the Odessa press, Vera nevertheless descended into a new period of depression upon hearing the news. Once again she felt the responsibility for the loss of her comrades. Those whom she had recruited had been destroyed, and her recent undertakings had come to naught.[115] She writes of this period, "I was left alone . . . to travel this sorrowful path with no end in sight."[116] Having received a note from her mother and youngest sister, Vera responded, "If you want what is best for me, wish me the courage and strength to endure until the moment when I become adjusted to these new conditions, and with the lessons of the past, the party will begin again its march forward. Then I will be able to go to the scaffold with a smile."[117]

Vera's letter to her family reveals that the revolutionary leader did not fear arrest or death; instead the notion sustained her. What was difficult for her to endure was failure and isolation. Having directed the People's Will, she was terrified that the party's dramatic run would end in revolutionary ignominy and hence political insignificance. The prospect of her execution on the heels of a party rejuvenated through her own efforts, however, was cause for celebration. But the chance that her present state of solitude, both physical and emotional, and impotence, both political and social, would be the permanent reality of a long, ineffectual life was intolerable.

Perhaps because she was so desperate for success, Vera overlooked troubling signs of treachery when Sergei Degaev materialized alive and free in January 1883. Because she could not tolerate the thought that her work over the preceding years had been for naught, she gullibly accepted Degaev's tale of his escape from police custody,[118] as did her fellow revolutionaries. "All doors were opened for and all secrets revealed" to the gendarmes' most recent undercover agent.[119]

When Lieutenant Colonel Georgii Sudeikin, the notorious police investigator, convinced Degaev to betray his comrades, the first objective he assigned his newest traitor was to arrange for Vera Figner's arrest.[120] Subsequently, soon after Degaev returned to Kharkov, he started to question his "comrade" about her daily routine. Failing to see the sinister motives behind his curiosity, Vera candidly answered her colleague's questions.[121]

On the morning of February 10, 1883, Vera left her Kharkov apartment at 8:00 AM as she did every morning. A short distance from her flat, she recognized the notorious traitor Vasilii Merkulov, who had been pointing out revolutionaries to the gendarmes for the past two years. Knowing the police must be lurking nearby and would probably seize her at any moment, Vera looked around to see if an escape would be possible. Just as she realized that there was no way she could elude her would-be captors this time, the gendarmes seized her and threw her into a carriage bound for Kharkov police headquarters.[122]

From April 1881 until her arrest on February 10, 1883, the Third Department had relentlessly pursued this elusive woman to no avail.[123] As one police investigator contemptuously hissed, "Vera Nikolaevna is a . . . devil, not a woman."[124] Deemed "one of the most dangerous of the Central Committee of terrorists," her capture became a primary objective of the gendarmes, and officials delighted in the news of her arrest.[125] On hearing that the legendary terrorist was in custody, Alexander III made a simple notation in his journal about Vera's capture; it read, "She was finally caught."[126]

Vera's arrest engendered as much despair among revolutionaries as it did relief in official circles. News that the seemingly invincible radical leader was in police custody "demoralized the ranks and pushed the party to the brink of destruction."[127] Nikolai Mikhailovskii was unusually disheartened when he heard the news. Although scores of other young people he knew and respected had been lost to prison over the years, the famed literary figure "could not stop thinking about this unusual woman" after he heard about her arrest.[128]

Vera's capture spelled the end of the Executive Committee and the People's Will. In the weeks and months after her capture, with the information provided by Degaev the gendarmes apprehended more than one hundred people.[129] Almost the entire military organization of the party was extinguished by the summer of 1883. Only a few circles that Degaev did not know existed remained unscathed.[130] The revolutionaries had survived the police persecutions that ensued in the immediate wake of Alexander II's assassination, but Degaev's treachery in 1883 "inflicted a blow from which the party could not recover, and the People's Will as an organized revolutionary party [in Russia] ceased to exist."[131]

Vera Figner's activity in the aftermath of Alexander II's assassination until her arrest demonstrates that conventional historical conceptions of this period need to be reevaluated. Traditionally the months from the late spring of 1881 through 1882 have been viewed as a period when the fortunes of the People's Will were in decline, a time when the party was at the lowest point in its existence. But this idea is overly simplistic. Although the terrorists did not achieve their concrete political and social aims with the emperor's assassination, it must be noted that over the course of the party's existence, the People's Will had rarely enjoyed tangible success. On March 1, 1881, the revolutionaries accomplished their immediate objective of assassinating the tsar. But this was never a goal in and of itself. Tsaricide was not even a means to an end; rather it was a means to a means to an end. The party decided to kill the emperor in order to provoke a political revolution, or at least to obtain political concessions that would allow them to propagandize peasants and workers in order to effect a social revolution. Neither revolution nor concessions resulted from the tsar's assassination. But the People's Will came closer to realizing these ends in 1882 than it did at almost any other point in the party's existence.

Only once before had the narodovol'tsy been on the brink of extorting concessions from the government. During Mikhail Loris-Melikov's "dictatorship of the heart," the minister of the interior attempted to erode the revolutionaries' support base in society by instituting some moderate reforms while simultaneously intensifying police repression against the terrorists.[132] Begun in the wake of the bombing of the Winter Palace in February 1880, Loris-Melikov escalated his proposed reforms over the course of 1880 despite the fact that the People's Will failed to execute another significant terrorist act. On the very day of his assassination, Alexander II declared his intention to put Loris-Melikov's latest reforms into effect. The events of March 1 ended these plans. However, the same forces that drove Loris-Melikov and Alexander II to consider these reforms impelled the much more reactionary regime of Alexander III to negotiate with the regicides.

Peter Zaionchkovskii writes that on the eve of the tsar's murder, "despite the lack of new assassinations [during 1880], the government, mortally frightened by the past[,] had recognized gradually the need for concessions."[133] More than a year later, the new regime had even more cause to be alarmed. The People's Will had succeeded in killing Alexander II, forced his heir into hiding, formed various revolutionary circles of military officers throughout the empire, established the party's Political Red Cross, and killed the military prosecutor in Odessa. It does not matter that with the exception of Strelnikov's assassination, more terrorist acts did not ensue. There had been scant political assassinations before the tsaricide. Yet the "sacred brigade's" negotiations indicate that more than a year after Alexander II's assassination, the People's Will was once again on the verge of obtaining at least some limited political objectives. The reason lies not only in the shock generated by the assassination but also in the secrecy and conspiratorial tactics that were engineered and maintained by Vera in the wake of March 1 that spoke to the possibility of future violence.

It was only in December 1882, when Sergei Degaev became a traitor, that the government realized the party's strength was the result of its own paranoia and the terrorists' bombastic stance. Then the narodovol'tsy became virtually powerless. When Vera Figner, the icon of the indomitable perseverance of the revolutionary party, was arrested, both sides finally realized that the dramatic ride of the People's Will was over.

7

TRANSFORMATION

ON SEPTEMBER 24, 1884, THE Trial of the Fourteen opened in St. Petersburg amid circumstances much different from those of the well-publicized political trials of the previous decade. For years both the Romanov autocracy and the Russian public viewed the trials of accused revolutionaries and terrorists as "great political *causes célèbres*."[1] Except for Vera Zasulich's stunning acquittal, the verdicts doled out by the courts were mostly preordained, and thus no drama was involved in the deliberation of guilt or innocence; yet the proceedings were grand spectacles. Imperial courtrooms served as the stages on which a new type of modern political theater was performed; a curious public and anxious friends angled for admission to witness the drama as both the prosecution and defense presented cases and delivered lines designed to sway hearts and influence minds in a propaganda battle between the tsarist state and the revolutionaries who conspired to overthrow it. Although the imperial government had learned from early trials in the post-reform period and began to more strictly control the space in its courtrooms and the publicity emanating from them as the 1870s gave way to the more violent 1880s, the secrecy that surrounded the Trial of the Fourteen in 1884 was unparalleled. According to the foreign correspondent, for the *Times* of London, only nine coveted tickets were doled out for this latest trial.[2] The regime of Alexander III decided to try the latest defendants with as little external fanfare as possible in order to prevent the accused members of the People's Will from using the

defendant's box as a platform from which to remind the country of their exploits, sacrifice, and aspirations for a more equitable and just future for Russia. But Vera Figner had other plans.

Despite the small number of spectators in the courtroom, the most notorious of the defendants in the Trial of the Fourteen viewed the opportunity
to speak at the trial as the role of a lifetime. Having sat behind the impreg-
nable walls of the Peter and Paul Fortress for the last nineteen months, Vera
looked at her day in court as a unique opportunity to memorialize her dying
movement and her place within it. Convinced that she would be condemned
to death for her crimes, she viewed her trial and the opportunity to speak to
the court as the last opportunity to express herself, detail her achievements,
and make a case for her significance before "the curtain irrevocably lowered
on the tragedy" of her life.[3]

When Vera rose to address the court on the last day of the five-day trial, she
was a different woman from the one seized on the streets of Kharkov in 1883.
The days following her arrest were difficult ones. While she believed that her
capture was the first step along a journey to the martyrdom to which she aspired, she worried about what she would have to endure before her anticipated
release from this world. Adding to her anxiety was her despondence about
the apparent demise of the People's Will despite her fervent efforts to resusci-
tate this once deadly terrorist group. As she traveled under armed guard from
Kharkov to St. Petersburg, Vera's emotions overwhelmed her and she began
to show signs of the toll that the previous months had taken on her. One moment she was the picture of strength and revolutionary swagger, bemoaning
to her young guard the fact that she did not have her revolver with her when
she was arrested so that she could have murdered the traitor who identified
her; the next moment she sat silently looking out the window at the passing
Russian countryside, her bravery betrayed by the tears streaming down her
cheeks.[4]

Upon arrival in St. Petersburg, gendarmes transported Vera to the Peter
and Paul Fortress's Trubetskoi Bastion, the prison building constructed in
the 1870s specifically to hold political prisoners before their trial. Incarcerated in cell forty-three, she surveyed the sparse surroundings: with only a
small window situated above the eye level of the diminutive prisoner, her accommodations were limited to a cot with a thin mattress, a small wooden
stool, and an iron table chained to the wall. Exhausted from her multiday trip

from Kharkov, the journey she had traveled from the Rodionovskii Institute through Zurich, the Russian countryside, and the revolutionary underground to the prison that had hosted such radical luminaries as Fyodor Dostoevsky, Nikolai Chernyshevskii, and Sergei Nechaev seemed very long indeed.

Great excitement swirled in official circles about the arrest of Vera Nikolaevna Figner as relief and fascination made the tsar's security apparatus intensely curious about the long-sought-after member of the People's Will Executive Committee. Soon after she arrived in St. Petersburg, none other than Count Dmitrii Tolstoi, the minister of the interior and chief of the gendarmerie, arrived to see the infamous Vera Figner for himself. One terrorist sat alone facing the man ultimately charged with protecting the tsar and his empire from those of her ilk. Though they were enemies, there seemed to be a grudging respect between the two. After a prolonged conversation, Tolstoi rose to take leave of his notorious prisoner, telling her he was sorry that he did not have time to convince her of her mistakes. Amused by the notion, Vera replied in turn, "I too am sorry. I had hoped I could convince you to join the People's Will."[5]

Tolstoi had come to the fortress because he was interested in hearing how Vera might justify her violent actions over the previous few years, and she was more than happy to oblige. Expecting to be silenced forever on the scaffold, she longed to leave a record of her life and the life of her party for posterity. Eager to discover the inner workings and details of the organization that had terrorized the state for more than four years, police officials gave Vera paper, a pen, and a room in which to write—and she wrote voluminously. She described why a girl reared amid privilege was compelled to become involved in revolutionary activity and why nothing short of terrorist methods seemed sufficient in tsarist Russia.[6] Because Vera expected to live only a few months, her confession became her last will and testament. With no worldly goods to bequeath, the inheritance she bestowed was a description of the inner workings of a revolutionary disposition. The confession was a supremely personal document, but it demonstrated the extent to which Vera's revolutionary mission and sentiment had engulfed her inner life. In her confession she did not lament her fate, explore ruined hopes, or pine for love never realized. Instead she mourned the revolution to which she devoted her life but had never come to pass. She grieved for friends lost, but only as a means of celebrating their deaths as martyrs. Confident that she soon would follow her deceased com-

rades to the scaffold, Vera's confession was a conscious effort to publicly memorialize herself and her party. Like the life writings of early Christian martyrs, her narrative was intended to "draw attention to the production of the
martyr's self within the context of a much more public collective narrative."[7]

At the end of each day when Vera finished writing her confession, she returned to cell forty-three. The relatively relaxed atmosphere of Russian political prisons that she had experienced when surreptitiously visiting imprisoned friends in the mid-1870s had disappeared in a post-terrorism world. In
the 1880s tsarist prison administrations ardently worked to quell any collaboration between imprisoned revolutionaries and thus instituted conditions designed to ensure the complete isolation of prisoners "under conditions of strict
silence in combination with their continual control and observation."[8]

Vera arrived at the fortress in a state of nervous anxiety. For months she had
publicly silenced her inner turmoil and worries about the fate of her party and
comrades in order to present a strong countenance to friend and foe alike. But
any initial relief she may have felt at abandoning this charade was replaced by
the traumatic experience of prolonged isolation and silence.

Regardless of the various causes that may lead to extended periods of solitary confinement, the effects that ensue are remarkably homogenous. Be they
hostages, prisoners of war, or convicted criminals, human beings experience
debilitating effects from isolation that include palpable disturbances in the
central nervous system and quantifiable brain abnormalities after only several
weeks in seclusion.[9] A typical reaction to the physical and psychological disruptions caused by solitary confinement is an inclination to sleep for abnor-
mally extended periods of time. With her written testimony completed, Vera
literally yearned to sleep the days away. Only a state of unconsciousness, she
believed, would allow her to escape the pain caused by the loss of precious
comrades and the sad state of both her life and the condition of the revolutionary cause.[10]

When she was not asleep, Vera tried to lose herself in reading. She spent
hours engrossed in books that she either obtained through her mother or bor-
rowed from the prison library. During her first year in the Peter and Paul Fortress, she taught herself both English and Italian and by her own count read
116 books in a variety of languages.[11] As the months passed, she became convinced that her sanity and physical health depended on her continued intellectual engagement. So, even when her eyes ached and her vision blurred from

countless hours of reading in her dark cell, she continued to escape into books. Since novels failed to sufficiently distract her tortuous thoughts, she dove into scholarly works in fields as diverse as history, psychology, and biology.[12]

During the period of time between her arrest and her trial, Vera found distraction not only in books but also in bi-monthly visits from her mother and her youngest sister, Olga. But while these visits brought a diversion from her endless routine, they did not always bring solace. Desperate for physical contact, the metal grating that separated Vera from her loved ones taunted her with what she wanted but could not obtain. The proximity of the family members whom she could not embrace reminded Vera that with her arrest she unwillingly forfeited control over her body. Her autonomy was eradicated as the state assumed control over her actions and interactions. Unable to realize the solace she sought, she often thought it would have been easier to have no contact with her family at all. Explaining her frustration, she writes, "I am uncertain whether it is better to have no honey at all or a spoonful of honey in a tub of tar."[13]

But during the summer months it became clear that Vera yearned for a taste of honey no matter how small. In keeping with their annual custom, as the practically endless hours of sunlight in St. Petersburg signaled the arrival of summer, Ekaterina Figner, along with Olga, her only daughter not yet imprisoned or exiled by the tsarist state, left the capital for the countryside. Deprived of any human contact beyond her prison guards, Vera's mood considerably worsened. Her desperation is apparent both in the increased frequency of the letters she wrote to her family and the increasing personal tone of the correspondence. Unlike her written confession, private issues take prominence in the letters she wrote to her mother and sister during the summers of 1883 and 1884. Instead of the public memorializing and self-confident awareness apparent in Vera's written confession for the tsarist police, in these personal letters one discovers sibling rivalry, personal regret, private reminiscences, and an adult child's disappointment in a parent incapable of providing the motherly solace her daughter craves. Left alone in a hostile environment, the public self she constructed gradually receded while the private Vera Nikolaevna came to the fore.

In the letters she wrote during the first two summers of her incarceration, Vera's revolutionary dreams are immaterial. Instead she devotes herself to familial issues. Whether she is urging her brother Peter to move home to care for their mother; insulting Nikolai, her much exalted opera star brother, and his wife for their materialism and egotism; bemoaning the fact that she and Lidia have grown apart; or recalling tender childhood memories, Vera's letters resurrect her personal and private life. She even begins to acknowledge the personal costs associated with her revolutionary career. Writing to her mother, she apologizes for the grief she and her sisters have caused her through their radicalism but admits they could not have done otherwise and still have been true to themselves.[14] Thus, the relationship between the personal and the political is inverted from Vera's typical conception. Whereas in her formal autobiographical writings personal, private details are utilized only to underscore a political point, in this selection of her personal correspondence, Vera's public self is depicted as a natural consequence of who she is as a human being. Instead of depicting a private life that is subsumed within a public, political mission, her public self becomes overwhelmed by the personal. Thus, cut off from a dying revolutionary movement by the walls of the Trubetskoi Bastion, Vera's public life becomes immaterial or at least secondary to her personal, private self.

Without an apparent social or political purpose, Vera became increasingly fragile. But her infirmities did not ensue just from the psychological trauma caused by incarceration. With no one to speak to, she consequently never spoke, and silence became routine. Thus, by the time her mother and sister returned from the provinces and resumed visits with their imprisoned relative, the renewed human interaction caused Vera considerable anxiety and made apparent the physical effects of months of isolation and silence. After months without use, her voice had transformed from what had been a rich, musical contralto into a thin and shrill version of its former self.[15]

But apart from the silence and isolation she endured, Vera was not ill treated while at the Trubetskoi Bastion. Not yet a convicted criminal, in her first nineteen months in prison she was allowed to wear her own clothes and had her wardrobe regularly augmented with the blouses, skirts, and dresses that her mother brought her. Prison guards served her neither spoiled meat nor watery gruel; instead she enjoyed culinary delights, including partridge, wine, and fresh fruit. This was not unusual for someone of her class. Prison officials in the Peter and Paul Fortress accorded considerable privileges to their noble inmates. Before their trials, these elite revolutionaries dined on excellent food and regularly enjoyed courteous treatment from their guards.[16]

After more than a year in prison, Vera had yet to discover when her trial would take place. Waiting without news of when her fate would be decided reinforced the extent to which her arrest eroded her self-determination. In prison the power of the autocracy was vigorously reaffirmed for Vera as the tsar's prison officials dictated the terms of her access to books, letters, food, wine, sunlight, fresh air, and other people. Her sanity depended on her ability to acclimate herself to this new state of life. As the months passed, the routine imposed in the Trubetskoi Bastion became Vera's new reality. Learning what to expect allowed her solace, because it enabled her to forget that her daily routine was dictated by an entity apart from herself. But in the spring of 1884, two events disrupted the monotony of her existence. The first was welcome. In April, on the orders of the fortress's doctor, prison officials moved Vera to a new cell.[17] Cell fifty-five was smaller, but it was brighter and had more fresh air than her previous accommodations.[18] Allowed to keep the window open for an entire month, she relished the fresh air in her new cell and the sounds of music wafting in from the Summer Garden across the Neva River.[19]

But the second occurrence that interrupted Vera's routine that spring was devastating. She was summoned into an office in the administrative section of the fortress, where two high-ranking officials presented her with a large notebook and instructed her to examine its contents. She immediately realized that she was looking at the testimony of someone connected to her case, but she did not recognize the handwriting. Flipping to the end of the document in order to discern the author, Vera's stomach dropped as she read the name Sergei Degaev. For the first time, she realized that the man whom she had taken into her confidence and promoted to a leadership role within the party had betrayed her and her comrades.[20] Decades later she confessed that "to experience such a betrayal was a misfortune without equal," because it pierced her idealism and destroyed her faith in the beauty of "people, the revolution, and life itself."[21] Any effort she made to put Degaev's treachery out of her mind was useless. Yet even if somehow she could forget the extent of her former comrade's betrayal, she was forced to revisit it again in September 1884 when the details of Degaev's treachery were used as the cornerstone of the state's case again Vera and her co-defendants in the Trial of the Fourteen.

Late in the evening on September 22, as Vera prepared for bed, one of the prison gendarmes unexpectedly walked into her cell.[22] Handing the prisoner her coat and hat, the gendarme informed Vera that she was being moved to the House of Preliminary Detention immediately.[23] She realized that officials were moving her from the Peter and Paul Fortress in anticipation of the imminent start of her trial. Arriving at the new prison just before midnight, she was unable to quiet her nerves and spent a sleepless first night in her new surroundings.[24]

When the next day dawned, Vera was exhausted and agitated. She knew that since it was Sunday, she would have to wait at least one more day for her trial to begin, so she tried to settle her nerves as she waited for the inevitable. A measure of solace arrived with the appearance of Ekaterina and Olga Figner. Unlike the arrangements in the Peter and Paul Fortress, in the House of Preliminary Detention no glass or metal grating separated the prisoner from her loved ones. With no physical impediment between them, Vera lovingly kissed Ekaterina's hands and for several moments basked in the sensory pleasures of tender physical contact with her mother and sister.[25]

On the following morning, September 24, 1884, the event that Vera had been waiting for finally got under way when the Trial of the Fourteen began in the St. Petersburg Palace of Justice.[26] At 10:00 AM, armed gendarmes escorted her into a room in the imperial courthouse, where her thirteen co-defendants were already assembled.[27] At the sight of her comrades, even those she had never seen before, Vera felt a flurry of emotions. Having been isolated from her fellow revolutionaries for the previous year and a half, she was excited to be in the company of more than a dozen people who ostensibly shared her political viewpoints and dedication to the Russian people. She longed to embrace her co-defendants, but a gendarme with an unsheathed saber who stood between each pair of prisoners thwarted her aspirations.[28] The most troubling aspect of this somber reunion, however, rested in the unhealthy, blanched faces that she encountered. The physical appearance of those comrades whom she had known in freedom were especially troubling. Faces that previously had been so full of life were now pale and yellowed from their long months of incarceration.[29] Although Vera presents her sorrow at the physical state of her comrades rather altruistically, she was certainly unsettled by the realization that her fellow defendants' pallid countenances were a reflection of her own deteriorated appearance.

According to the judicial measures instituted in 1879 by Tsar Alexander II and Count Loris-Melikov, Vera was tried under the auspices of the St. Petersburg military district court.[30] Perhaps more than any other case prosecuted in the preceding years, her trial looked and felt like a court-martial. The judiciary tribunal was comprised of four colonels and General V. M. Tsemirov, who chaired the proceedings. But the military's presence was felt on the other side of the bench as well. Among the fourteen defendants were six officers of the Russian army and navy who were members of the People's Will military organization. Approximately one hundred of this group's members had been arrested, but only a small minority were formally brought to trial. The state wanted to punish its errant military men harshly; however, those in power thought it best to downplay the fact that there were so many insurrectionary forces in its ranks and officer corps.[31] Thus, the vast majority of this group's members were never tried and instead were dealt with through the extralegal means of administrative exile.[32] But the six military men tried along with the revolutionary leader Vera Figner were not as fortunate: M. Iu. Ashenbrenner, N. D. Pokhitonov, N. M. Rogachev, A. P. Shtromberg, I. P. Iuvatshev, and A. P. Tikhanovich were prosecuted to the fullest extent of the law.

In addition to Vera and these six military officers, the other seven defendants were L. A. Volkenstein and L. V. Chemodanova (both women), A. I. Nemolovskii, D. Ia. Surovtsev, A. A. Spandoni, V. I. Chuikov, and V. G. Ivanov.[33] Although there had been a series of political trials in the previous few years, contemporaries recognized that this was the most important prosecution of Russian revolutionaries since the trial "of the assassins of the late tsar" in late March 1881.[34] Those prosecuted in the Trial of the Fourteen not only symbolized the extent to which revolutionary ideology had permeated the armed forces but also represented the last bastion of the active People's Will movement in Russia. In this regard the most important defendant and the one who bolstered the significance of the trial was Vera Figner.

In their account of the trial, the *Times* of London deemed the "good looking and remarkably intelligent Figner . . . one of the moving spirits in nearly every plot and attempt at political assassination since 1878."[35] Capitalizing on her beauty, grace, intelligence, and fame, the *Times* perpetuated the dramatic myth of Vera. Even if one discounts the obvious exaggeration of her role in the revolutionary movement since 1878, it was unquestionable that she was regarded as "one of the most distinguished women revolutionaries in Russia," and that most people in both government and radical circles realized that "after the death of Andrei Zheliabov and Sofia Perovskaia [she] was the highest authority in [the People's Will.]"[36]

As the trial began, everyone knew that the outcome was already determined. It was only the sentences that the court would hand down to those convicted that were unclear. Without the need to objectively prove their case, the prosecution took great legal liberties, which included using the written testimony of witnesses who never materialized in court, including Sergei Degaev.[37]

The court made no effort to hide their prejudice against those on trial and repeatedly interfered with the defendants' efforts to address those assembled.[38] Even though the radicals on trial did not try to refute their guilt, they aspired to speak in court in order to make their convictions known.[39]

The five-day-long judicial affair was difficult for Vera to endure. Forced to wait until the end of the trial to speak on her own behalf, she sat helplessly as the prosecutor expressed his regret "that a woman like Figner, of noble background with an exceptional education . . . could be so bloodthirsty."[40] Forced to listen to the unpleasant portrait painted of her and unaccustomed to so much activity and human interaction, she found herself repeatedly overcome and on the brink of nervous exhaustion.

On the last day of the trial, when the presiding judge called Vera's name, an anxious curiosity directed the focus of all of those assembled toward the former leader of the People's Will.[41] The reputation of the woman who had single-handedly led her party in the aftermath of the tsar's assassination evoked tremendous fascination. While the members of the judicial tribunal had consistently interrupted Vera's co-defendants when they tried to speak, the judges gave her their undivided attention.[42] Whether it was the result of her beauty, regal bearing, dedication to her cause, or a combination of the three is unclear, but something about Vera elicited a polite, almost respectful, attitude from the court. Even the head of the tribunal, General Tsemirov, who rudely interrupted many of the other defendants, respectfully referred to the infamous revolutionary on occasion as Vera Nikolaevna instead of the usual "Defendant Figner."[43] When she took her place at the front of the courtroom, everyone assembled listened attentively as Vera Nikolaevna began to speak.

She informed the members of the court that before she had adopted violent measures against the tsarist state, all she wanted was to be socially useful in life.[44] She told her audience that for over a year she worked in the countryside engaged in what in any other country would be considered socially constructive or cultural activities.[45] But in Russia this work was illegal. She contended that after repeated frustration, she had come to the conviction that violent means were necessary in order to provoke real change in her homeland. She informed the court that as a leader of the People's Will, once she "theoretically recognized that only violent means could have any effect, [she felt] obligated to accept a part in any violent activities undertaken by the organization."[46] She revealed that the Executive Committee of the party wanted to use her for peaceful projects, but she had refused. As she knew that both the judiciary and public opinion reacted with the most ferocity against those who participated directly in violence, she believed that it would have been dishonorable to "push others down a road that [she] would not go down [herself]."[47]

Thus, Vera depicted herself as a woman of high principles whose altruism impelled her down a road toward revolution and the violence she believed was necessary to effect it. Surprisingly, Vera's public statement to the court was inherently personal; economic theories and proposed political systems had no place in her speech. Instead, her testimony before the court depicts a woman whose personal dreams about making a positive difference in the world were thwarted by political repression. In the last public words that she ever expected to utter, Vera did not lament the poverty of the masses nor did she castigate the autocracy. Rather, she bemoaned the fact that conditions in Russia were such that personal emancipation and autonomy were impossible. Extrapolating from her personal experience an assumption about the general order of things in Russia, Vera's testimony is rooted in personal frustration. As her speech came to a close, she noted, "I consider it most important and essential that there be conditions in our country that would allow the development of each individual's abilities and the application of these talents for the benefit of society. It seems to me that in our current situation such conditions do not exist. That is all that I want to say to the court."[48]

Vera then resumed her seat on the defendants' bench. As she recalled these events years later, she notes that at that moment her emotions and fatigue were so great that she would have been incapable of saying another word.[49] Relieved of her duty to her comrades and her party, for the first time in years Vera felt free. Expecting death to be imminent, with her social and political obligations fulfilled in her own mind, she no longer felt larger than life. The dehumanizing effect of her extraordinary responsibilities retreated into the past. For a brief time, Vera writes, "I was enveloped by a feeling of liberation from my duty to my country, society and party. I became only a person: the daughter of my mother, and the sister of my sister, who were the only ones left to me amidst my social ruin."[50]

When the court returned its verdict on September 28, Vera's sentence was what she had expected. Along with seven of her co-defendants, she was condemned to death by hanging.[51] The martyrdom that she had chased for years was now within her grasp. On September 30, two days after Vera's death sentence was announced, Ekaterina and Olga Figner came to visit her.[52] Seeing her eldest child, who was sentenced to die at the hands of the tsarist state, Ekaterina gave Vera an icon of the Virgin Mary with an inscription that read, "Most Holy Virgin of Unexpected Joy." Although she expected her daughter to be executed in the upcoming weeks, Ekaterina told Vera that she prayed that someday she would find some unexpected joy.[53]

Since the state had not yet set the date for Vera's execution, the convicted revolutionary never expected that this would be the last time she would see her relatives. Except for Ekaterina's blessing of her eldest daughter, there is no account of what the Figner women discussed at this visit or how long it lasted. But three years after this final encounter, Vera wrote about the lasting impression she took from this meeting. In an untitled poem written on New Year's Day 1888, she recalls that her mother left the visiting room without looking back at her.[54] Olga, however, "remained at the threshold in order to give a last glance. With a look of complete compassion, deep sorrow and melancholy, as a silent symbol of suffering, she stood before me."[55] As Vera watched her youngest sister standing by the door, her heart quickened, and the emotions of the moment began to overwhelm her. All the personal feelings of loss she had quelled by imagining the sanctity of her martyrdom reemerged as her gaze met Olga's. With the devastated countenance of a person awash in grief, her sister's presence and compassion brought home to Vera the reality of her impending doom and lost possibilities. But just as her emotions threatened to erupt, Olga lowered her eyes and abruptly turned. Within an instant, the door slammed shut behind her. While in later years she cherished her sister's "unspoken look of love,"[56] the sound of the slamming door resounded in Vera's consciousness. The heavy prison door irrevocably separated the condemned terrorist from the world of the living. Vera's former experiences, replete with personal connections and meaningful social work receded further and further into the past as her sister's steps echoed through the prison halls.

The following afternoon Vera sat in her cell in the House of Preliminary Detention. Although this was the first day of her life as a convicted criminal, the day seemed unexceptional. Life was no more onerous than it had been before. She was wearing a pretty blue dress that her mother had recently brought her and felt rather content as she sat in her cell eating fruit and chocolates.[57] But several hours later she found herself in much different circumstances after prison guards transferred her back to the Peter and Paul Fortress. Exhausted from the tumult of the preceding days, Vera settled into her new cell, asked her jailer to bring her some tea and her box of chocolates, and dozed off before the guard returned.[58] When she awoke the nightmare of the next stage of her life began.

Roused from her slumber by the harsh directives of the prison's commandant, Vera soon found herself transformed. Within minutes, in place of her elegant blue dress and sentimental icon of the Virgin Mary, she wore a "dirty peasant shirt of harsh, gray hemp, and a matching kerchief."[59] Under her rough, gray, moth-eaten skirt, her legs were wrapped in coarse linen. Her prison ensemble was completed by a pair of peasant shoes that were too big for her small feet and a gray cotton dressing gown with the yellow diamond that denoted a Russian convict on her back. The noblewoman who had always enjoyed the finer things in life now found herself in prison garb soaked with dirt, grease, and the sweat of its previous wearers.[60]

For Vera this transformation was not just an incidental element of her punishment. It did not merely denote her transition from accused to condemned; it also signaled a fundamental transformation of self along both gender and class lines. Born into the Russian nobility, before her arrest in February 1883 Vera could adopt transgressive behavior and don the cloak of revolutionary terrorist voluntarily while still retaining the ability to cast aside her more ascetic, nihilist guise and willingly reveal the proper, well-coiffed, noblewoman who lurked beneath. As she wrote to her mother from prison, "Although I am a nihilist I am not without aesthetic inclinations—I love beautiful faces, music, flowers, and nature."[61] For Vera, women's clothes in late nineteenth-century Russia had a theatrical property. As Lynn Patyk relates, "Attire appropriate to her social station [became] a disguise instrumentally employed, not expressive of her identity."[62] Before her imprisonment, Vera could affect the persona of a noble petitioner by dressing up in "peacock plumes" for a revolutionary mission, or assume the guise of a bourgeois lady by outfitting herself with the appropriate blouse and jewelry,[63] and then willingly cast these accessories aside and revert back to a more traditional revolutionary appearance. But the choice of which guise to don had been hers until she was sentenced in the Trial of the Fourteen. After that she was deprived of the rights of the class into which she was born and the right to construct the public manifestation of that class and her womanhood. The regime now acquired the ultimate power over her body, including the right to denote and signify her identity through her appearance, physical condition, and attire. The prison administration now bestowed upon Vera clothes that were designed to erase any vestiges of femininity and nobility. The definition of gender and class and the corporeal expression of these constructed identities became external to her as a convict, because the state acquired this right and power over her body and identity.

Vera's cell was similarly transformed. Guards replaced her double mattress with a sack of straw and took one of her two pillows away.[64] Just as the weather was starting to turn cold in St. Petersburg, the prison administration reclaimed her blanket and left her only an old piece of flannel as a defense against the cell's chill.[65] Earlier that day, she had dined on partridge and chocolates, but back in her old cell in the Peter and Paul Fortress, she was denied both tea and the delicate white china cup from which she had sipped. Now a convicted criminal condemned to death, she received only hot water in a rusty, jagged tin cup.[66]

Aware that a convict's identity has an internal component as well as an external one, the prison administration attempted to reclaim Vera's intellectual entitlement. Books on history and biology disappeared; in their place only the Bible remained. The tsarist state did not aspire to lend to its political criminals' intellectual development. It only sought to punish and possibly convert. For Vera, who had no interest in conversion, be it religious or political, the dearth of intellectual stimulation felt like a punishment worse than death. Desperate to retain her faculties in the days or weeks that preceded her expected death, she attempted to stave off insanity by mentally translating the Gospels into French and then into German.[67]

Vera soon realized that she would need to wage this battle against insanity much longer than previously expected. On October 4 the commandant of the Peter and Paul Fortress informed her that Alexander III had commuted her death sentence to life imprisonment at hard labor.[68] Averse to executing another woman, especially one as well-known as Vera Figner after the negative reaction that had ensued from the 1881 hanging of Sofia Perovskaia,[69] Alexander III's regime denied Vera the martyrdom she craved and replaced it with a variant she feared the most. She understood the commutation of her death sentence as an exercise in cruelty rather than a display of mercy and lamented that she "would have much preferred a simple, quick death on the scaffold to a long, slow death" in prison.[70]

In addition to Vera, five other defendants condemned to death in the Trial of the Fourteen also had their sentences changed to various periods of hard labor.[71] But two others met their end on the scaffold. On October 10, 1884, the death sentences of N. M. Rogachev and A. P. Shtromberg were carried out.[72]

Two days later, in the early morning hours of October 12, 1884, a gendarme quickly opened Vera's cell, handed her a pair of felt boots and an unlined sheepskin coat, and hissed at her to dress quickly.[73] Having lived without soap, a comb, and a toothbrush for ten days, Vera wrapped her legs in rags; put on her old, dirty, moth-eaten skirt, prison coat, peasant shoes, and white kerchief;[74] and realized that her physical metamorphosis from noble doll to asexual convict was complete. Vera became the quintessential "other." De-sexed and dehumanized, she was shackled and loaded onto a waiting car-riage. In an effort to reclaim control over her inner self, even as the manifes-tation of her inability to determine her physical state was glaringly obvious, she shouted at the guards, "Tell my mother! . . . no matter what they do to me I will remain the same!"[75]

As she sat in the carriage that flew through the still deserted streets of the capital, the minutes seemed like hours. But this was only the beginning of Vera's journey. Guards emptied the prisoner from her carriage at a boat ramp on the Neva River and loaded her onto a ship. As the boat left the dock, bound for an unknown destination, she sat alone in a small cabin with cur-tains shielding the outside world from her view. The hours passed. Even as the darkness of night lifted, no shadows or sounds materialized to give her an indication of where she was or how far from the capital her ship had jour-neyed. But after five hours, when the ship docked and guards brought her out of her cabin and up onto the deck, Vera knew where Alexander III's govern-ment had decreed she was to live out her days. She disembarked on an island at the mouth of the Neva where the river flows out of Lake Ladoga; before her she saw high white walls and towers. On a tall spire in the middle of what was obviously a fortress, a golden key glistened in the sun.[76] Vera had arrived at the dreaded Shlisselburg Fortress (the Key City), the prison specifically re-designed to house the most important and seemingly most dangerous mem-bers of the People's Will.[77] When guards brusquely escorted her inside the for-tress walls, the sight of the town on the other side of the lake vanished as did Vera's tangible connection with the outside world and life itself. Standing in-side the Shlisselburg prison on the afternoon of October 12, 1884, Vera real-ized that "the clock of life stopped";[78] yet her heart continued to beat. She had been brought here to die. The only questions that remained to be answered, she assumed, was when death would come to relieve her of the misery of the fortress and what the remnants of her life would look like until that time.

8

LIFE AND DEATH

MUCH OF THE JOY EKATERINA FIGNER felt upon learning that Vera's death sentence had been commuted dissipated when tsarist officials informed her that her daughter had been taken to Shlisselburg Fortress. While the state refused to end Vera's life on the scaffold, its judicial arm had no compunction about consigning her to a living death behind high fortress walls and a dangerous current at the mouth of the Neva River. Ekaterina spent years longing for news of her eldest child, but for more than a decade her anxious curiosity encountered only silence. It seemed that the prison administration intended to abide by the retributive promise made to the Figner matriarch in 1884 when an official ominously vowed that the next she would hear of Vera would be when she was "in her grave."[1] In spite of her fears, months and years passed and news of Vera's death never came. Although Ekaterina had no idea what her daughter's life was like, she found comfort in knowing that at least her firstborn was still alive. But for Vera the line between life and death blurred in Shlisselburg as she discovered a life that was much worse than her anticipated death. While each passing day without news of her daughter's death brought a measure of solace to Ekaterina, Vera's endless days in her tomblike cell led her to wistfully recall how close she had come to realizing the martyrdom on the scaffold that she had sought.

Although Shlisselburg Fortress was built in 1323, in the months after Alexander II's assassination the government had renovated the facilities at the edge of Lake Ladoga and erected a new forty-cell prison building to house "the most active and dangerous members" of the People's Will.[2] The prison was not meant for rehabilitation. It was intended to be a strictly punitive exercise in vengeance. To that end the prison regime was designed to be as arduous as possible. Inmates lived almost entirely within the narrow confines of their cells, isolated from the outside world and from each other.

Shlisselburg rapidly earned the reputation as a notoriously repressive prison, and its reputation was well deserved. To vengefully retaliate against the young men and women who violently attacked the state and the tsar, the fortress administration aspired to extinguish its inmates' spirits while it dominated their bodies through complete isolation, harsh discipline, and dehumanizing daily life. By suffocating the prisoners' personalities and smothering their wills, the Shlisselburg commandant, warden, and guards located punishment in and through the body. Everything about the prison—from the guards' demeanor, to the physical space, to the perpetual feeling of vulnerability that ensued— was designed to inscribe the prisoners' bodies with an absence of power and self-determination. Solace was difficult to find while torment lurked at every turn. The cumulative effect of years lived in this state left even those prisoners who survived the ordeal psychologically marred and emotionally damaged by the experience.

Vera's terrifying first day in Shlisselburg foreshadowed the grueling years to come. Immediately upon her arrival, guards ordered her to undress and stand naked before the prying gaze of a male prison doctor and his female assistant. The medical team studied Vera's body intently, noting all discerning features on the premise that familiarity with the newest inmate's body could abet the prison administration's control over it. Feeling completely vulnerable and utterly mortified, Vera tried to disengage her spirit from her exposed, naked body. In describing this moment decades later, she discloses a feeling of vulnerability that coexists with a grandiose conception of herself, her crimes, and her sacrifice when she compares this experience to that of young Christian women brought naked to the Roman Colosseum to be devoured by lions for the entertainment of the emperor and the assembled crowds. No sexual assault or corporal punishment ensued in this moment, but Vera likens the degradation she felt to torture and death. Stripped naked before two hostile strangers and denied the consideration typically afforded women, especially those of her class, she was forced to confront the extent of her bodily subjection.

With every physical feature noted and each freckle and mole mapped, the doctor allowed Vera to dress. Unlike the assortment of pretty dresses and delicate blouses she had worn during her pretrial incarceration, she now donned an ugly gray skirt, a gray-and-black oversized jacket, and a gray kerchief, which was to be the uniform of her incarceration.[3] Her female form receded behind the clothes that marked her as a political convict. With no mirror to taunt her, she was not forced to suffer her own image. Yet her surroundings spoke to her level of deprivation.

In order to reach cell twenty-six, the space to which she was assigned on the second floor of the building, Vera needed to traverse the length of the prison. Forty cell doors lined opposite sides of a hallway on two separate floors. Each of these doors spoke to the depressing regularity of the fortress and the regimented isolation of the inmates who languished inside. But perhaps most disconcerting was the net that separated the middle space between the two floors, the presence of which spoke to the potential inclination of prisoners to end their lives and the determined effort of the prison staff to deny them this prerogative.

Left alone with her thoughts inside cell twenty-six, Vera felt entombed. With black-painted asphalt floors and the walls blackened except for a wide strip of gray at the top, the one small window of opaque glass situated above the convicts' heads was insufficient to counter the depressing darkness of their physical space. Framed disciplinary directives hung in each cell. As the only adornment on the walls of the bleak, eleven-by-nine-foot cells, the delineation of rules governing life in the fortress visibly reminded inmates of what Michel Foucault describes as the "micro-physics of power," which was continually exercised over essentially defenseless prisoners.[4]

The guards and officials who ran Shlisselburg in the years after Vera arrived seemed to relish their power over the disenfranchised inmates and cruelly taunted the prisoners with their lack of control. While the total silence that predominated in the prison was disconcerting and nerve-racking, it was often suddenly and shockingly interrupted by the whim of a guard callously rattling the cell's casement window or bursting in through the door without provocation. As Mikhail Novorusskii describes it, the haphazard intervals at which guards threw open the cells' casement windows were purposely designed "so that [the inmates] would not be able to forget for even a single minute that they were not free."[5] Meals were regulated, and even basic hygiene

was demarcated by the regime as to time and place. I. P. Iuvatshev conveys the
emotional disruption that arose from this lack of control and the continual
potential for observation when he writes, "I passed the days in unbroken and
painful solitude, yet I was never left to myself. I could do absolutely nothing
without a witness."[6]

While these tendencies were universally unsettling for the prisoners, they
carried an extra burden for the women imprisoned in Shlisselburg. When the
tsarist state willingly incarcerated Vera and her fellow narodovol'tsy Ludmila
Volkenstein in a prison comprised of, guarded by, and administered by men,
they implicitly denied the female convicts' identities as women. Operating
from the premise that these women's adoption of political violence was analogous to a renunciation of womanhood, the state's decision to send Vera and
Ludmila to Shlisselburg indicated that their sex became secondary to their
crimes. But throughout their incarceration, Vera and Ludmila could never escape the unique position they occupied as women in an otherwise all-male
prison. For these two women the micro-physics of power exercised over their
bodies entailed a latent threat of sexual violation and voyeurism that did not
extend to the imprisoned men to the same degree. With no ability to lock or
cover the casement window in their cell doors, the women of Shlisselburg
had no defense against potentially lecherous male gazes on the other side of
the window. While Vera never explicitly relates this fear, it was unavoidable.
As a woman being supervised by all male gendarmes, she had to live with the
reality that even her most private moments, whether she was in a state of undress or tending to personal bodily functions, were liable to be observed and
thus not private at all.

Divesting inmates of their identities was central to Shlisselburg's punitive
mission. The fortress administration viewed the prisoners as wholly defined
by their crimes. Thus, education, class, family connections, personality, and
even health were immaterial. To remind both prisoners and guards alike that
the convicted revolutionaries housed in Shlisselburg abdicated their right to
individuality through their crimes, the prison administration replaced the inmates' names with numbers. Thus, when she entered the prison, Vera Nikolaevna Figner officially ceased to exist for the duration of her imprisonment;
in her place prisoner number eleven remained. She became solely a convicted
terrorist, a number—one of forty sentenced to live out their days in what ultimately became known as the Russian Bastille.

Vera might have gone mad in her early days in the fortress had she not had continual reminders that other men and women shared her fate. She knew that behind the forty iron doors she saw as she climbed the prison staircase to her cell, other kindred revolutionary souls lurked. In an attempt to stave off depression and madness, Vera kept telling herself that although she could not see their faces and did not know their names, she was not alone. This reassurance was easily indulged, since she regularly heard evidence of the existence of these anonymous souls. Employing a system designed by imprisoned revolutionaries of an earlier generation, the person beneath her tirelessly tapped out a message on the water pipes connecting the two cells. For more than a month Vera listened intently to the tapping but could not decipher the message. She had no neighbor in the Peter and Paul Fortress and thus had no experience with the nonverbal language of prison. But finally, after six puzzling weeks, she cracked the code. Prisoners divided the Russian alphabet into six lines with five letters in each so that a certain number of long and short taps corresponded to a particular letter. After coming to this realization in early December 1884, the walls began to speak when Vera realized that the inmate below her was tapping, "I am Morozov, who are you?"[7] Amazed that her old friend and comrade had found her in a place designed to kill revolutionary solidarity and friendship, she tentatively tapped back, "I am Vera."[8]

Vera quickly became adept at this nonverbal form of communication, and her tapping soon extended beyond her immediate neighbors. Throughout Shlisselburg, tapping "clubs" developed in which two inmates who shared a wall on the second floor would "converse" with the two inmates below them.[9] In this way it became possible to pass messages throughout the prison. Tapping was forbidden in Shlisselburg, and the guards continually reprimanded and threatened the culprits. But despite the gendarmes' best efforts, the tapping continued. Several prisoners spent extended periods of time in the fortress's ominous punishment cells for breaking the rule against tapping, but the "desire to share one's thoughts and feelings and learn who was there, who was healthy and if there was any other news was so strong" that most of the prisoners tapped to their neighbors on a regular basis.[10]

Amid the horrid conditions of Shlisselburg, tapping to comrades was a means of self-preservation. The regular sound of inmates' tapping was a positive reminder of the life that persevered behind prison walls. Yet sometimes the sounds that reverberated through the fortress seemed to emanate from the gates of hell. Agonizing groans of inmates in the throes of mental or physical illness carried across the cold stone floors of the prison. Haunted by the memory of this emotional torture, Nikolai Morozov notes that the wails, screams, and shouted profanities of fellow inmates who had lost their minds or who were close to losing their lives engendered unbearable heartache for their comrades as they listened helplessly to the demise of a friend and the sounds of their own potential fate.[11]

Little distinguished one day from the next in Shlisselburg. With no visitors to interrupt the monotony of their lives, correspondence with family and friends beyond Shlisselburg's walls being forbidden, and no human interaction beyond their illicit tapping and the hostile exchanges with guards and prison officials, prisoners were left alone with their own potentially maddening thoughts and with few resources beyond their own determination to stave off the madness that threatened to engulf them. In their poorly ventilated, unhealthy cells that smelled of kerosene and human waste,[12] several inmates physically withered away from insufficient food, exercise, and fresh air, while others mentally collapsed from their silent solitude. The prisoners ate little more than stale, often moldy black bread, water-based soups, and unpalatable kasha. With negligible meats, vegetables, or fruits in their diets and an insufficient caloric intake, the health of all of the inmates deteriorated to some extent. Throughout her tenure at Shlisselburg, Vera suffered from chronic anemia, tuberculosis, and rheumatism that left her health impaired for the rest of her life.[13] While some lived through their bouts with maladies like tuberculosis, other prisoners succumbed to their illnesses. From 1884 until 1891, thirteen of the forty Shlisselburg inmates died from disease. During this same period, the administration executed two prisoners, two inmates committed suicide, and another three went insane.[14] That is, one-half of the inmates lost either their lives or their minds during their first seven years of incarceration in Shlisselburg Fortress.

A great deal of the responsibility for the mental and physical breakdowns that ensued in Shlisselburg in the 1880s rests with Warden Matvei E. Sokolov, who established a regime that exceeded even the brutality advocated by Tsar Alexander III and his government. As early as September 1885, police headquarters in St. Petersburg issued a directive to the head of the Shlisselburg gendarme administration addressing the conditions of the fortress. While these instructions recognized the need to "maintain the unconditional strictness" of the prison, they also urged that some basic improvements be made in the lives of the inmates.[15] The Department of Police called on its Shlisselburg colleagues to keep the prisoners healthy and satisfy their spiritual requests; to improve the variety of books the inmates could read; to give the prisoners pencils and paper; to provide the materials needed for the women to engage in needlework; and to keep the air in the cells fresh by opening the window several times a day.[16] Yet for several more years the prison library was woefully inadequate, cell windows were opened only twice a day for short periods of time, and the prisoners were denied pencils and paper until 1887.[17] Given Sokolov's obvious disdain for the prisoners and their situation, the mandated silence between the convicted revolutionaries and their guards, and the prisoners' loss of the right of correspondence, the inmates had little recourse against this physically and mentally unhealthy environment.[18]

Since it was under the jurisdiction of the Department of Police and the Ministry of Internal Affairs, high-ranking officials from the capital periodically inspected Shlisselburg. Making the rounds of the fortress's forty cells, these dignitaries inquired about the prisoners' health and asked if there were any issues that needed redress. But the inmates received no more satisfaction from these visitors than they did from their local administration, because the visiting officials nonchalantly dismissed or blatantly ignored inmates' complaints and concerns. While proponents of basic civil rights might consider this unacceptable, it is not surprising given the animosity between the revolutionaries and the state and the general absence of civil rights in Imperial Russia. Yet some prisoners refused to reconcile themselves to the dismissiveness that gave expression to their fundamental lack of power.

Even after several years living under the Shlisselburg regime, Vera expected officials and guards to treat her with some basic consideration. During one inspection in 1887, in answer to a visiting official's inquiry, she complained that Warden Sokolov had verbally abused her for a relatively minor behavior infraction. She told the dignitary, "The warden spoke to me in a way that respectable people do not even use with servants. If this type of behavior continues I will answer with a formal complaint."[19] Vera's attitude and assumptions about civility in the midst of such a repressive, dehumanizing environment seem unfathomable, and the reader may be tempted to question the veracity of the exchange. But since her complaint is clearly evocative of her formerly privileged existence, and given the fact that she published this account in the wake of the Soviet revolution that vied to rid the country of noble privilege, one must assume that the basic contours of the incident are grounded in fact.

Furthermore, since this incident portrays Vera and the tsarist official in at least equally unflattering light, we must assume that her sense of entitlement ran so deep that even in the bowels of Shlisselburg Fortress, she clung to the vestiges of the social prerogatives that she had always enjoyed.

When the visiting official reminded Vera that she was a condemned criminal and that further action on her part "would only make [her] situation worse," the imprisoned terrorist expressed her shock and outrage.[20] Again, this is not indicative of delusion; instead, Vera's behavior is both a function of her personality and reflective of the self-preservation tactics she employed in Shlisselburg. One of the paradoxes of her character was her proclivity toward the vestiges of her privileged upbringing and former social station and her simultaneous aspiration to destroy the source of such privileges and social inequality. Although she willingly abandoned a life of privilege in Imperial Russia, she never lost her taste for the social and material niceties her noble position afforded. Similarly, the consciousness of her noble background never left her. Throughout her life, she felt superior to most of the people she encountered. In this regard, despite her crimes against the tsarist state, Vera always felt entitled to a measure of deference from those around her. Thus, even as she languished amid the squalor and deprivation of the so-called Russian Bastille, she did not think of herself as a criminal; rather she saw herself as a persecuted, banished princess who suffered for a cause that most Russians, and certainly the Shlisselburg administration, were too unrefined to understand.

This point of view comes across in a short story Vera wrote during her incarceration, fittingly titled "Banished Princess." While the story conforms to the genre of Russian fairy tales that Vera eagerly devoured at her niania's knee, it is also an allegory for the condemned terrorist's conception of her imprisonment. In this piece the title character is the daughter of the tsar, who has been unfairly banished to a deserted, isolated island by her wicked stepmother. With guards watching the royal prisoner from high towers, this chimerical island is clearly a metaphor for the island fortress of Shlisselburg, the stepmother a literary stand-in for the Imperial Russian government, and the tsaritsa an unsullied version of Vera herself. Because she continued to view her terrorist endeavors as her social and moral responsibility rather than as a set of amoral, criminal actions, Vera is able to cast herself as a brave, aggrieved victim of the tsarist regime without hesitation.[21]

After living for the revolutionary cause for so long, once it was defeated Vera initially could place herself in a context no wider than the walls of cell twenty-six. Before being arrested she had suppressed her trepidation and fears for the benefit of the rank-and-file members of the People's Will and her public image, but in prison, as she confronted only her immediate reality, she occasionally found herself overwhelmed by personal feelings of loss, fear, and betrayal. At a particularly desperate moment in Shlisselburg, Vera writes, "In melancholy, I shudder deeply . . . I am here alone. There is no need to lie and pretend. There is no one to watch me. I can give in to grief. There are no lively circles of hearts here. I will not trample on anyone's dreams. The weight of pretext sleeps. The constrained mind is freed and the person in me rises up— overwhelmed and oppressed."[22]

While Vera's poetic rumination might seem to convey a sense of liberation, it actually implies a potentially ruinous reality. Without the protection of the iconic figure into which she had fashioned herself, Vera was merely a woman bereft of her family, her comrades, her freedom, and her revolutionary mission. Had she languished in such a solitary, purposeless state, it is doubtful she would have survived. But by imagining her imprisonment as just the latest chapter in a life of self-sacrifice for a higher ideal, the "banished princess," subconsciously at least, continued to harbor the faint hope that her life might have some purpose. Believing her "persecution" was symptomatic of the larger oppression at work in Russia, as a notable revolutionary figure and veritable icon, Vera had to persevere and endure if for no other reason than to stand as an example to millions of faceless, persecuted Russians.

Finding enduring purpose in her incarceration would have been impossible if Vera's isolation had remained complete. But a little more than a year after her term in Shlisselburg began, she rediscovered human contact through a new prison friendship. In January 1886, after officials in the Ministry of Internal Affairs decided to let Shlisselburg prisoners in poor health walk in pairs in specially designed exercise cages, the prison administration extended the privilege to the two women entombed in the island fortress.[23] Spending time with Ludmila Volkenstein became a source of unadulterated joy for Vera; as a result of her newfound friendship, her "cell no longer seemed so gloomy and life no longer seemed so arduous."[24]

Shlisselburg's dire environment lightened even more in the spring of 1886 when the prison regime converted a section of the fortress courtyard into vegetable gardens for the prisoners. Only twenty-one feet long by three feet wide, and essentially blocked from the sun, these gardens nonetheless seemed like paradise to Vera.[25] Together with her friendship with Ludmila, after a year in the bleak hole of Shlisselburg life felt a bit more tolerable for her. Although she still languished in solitude for countless hours in her dark, dreary cell; endured humiliating weekly body searches by a female matron brought to the prison for the occasion; yearned for soft, delicate undergarments and clothes; missed her mother terribly; and lived with the knowledge that control over her body was independent of her will, she developed a friendship network, albeit an unconventional one, enjoyed fruitful work in her garden, and found solace in books.

When Vera arrived at Shlisselburg, mundane books well below the intellectual capabilities of the mostly college-educated inmates constituted the prison library's catalog.[26] Although the fortress allowed the prisoners to bring several books with them when they began their terms of imprisonment, these quickly grew stale amid the monotony of endless solitary days. In response to a suggestion from Vera, the warden sanctioned the common use of the prisoners' private collections of books and allowed them to donate their books to the fortress library. Consequently, the condemned revolutionaries experienced a veritable intellectual revolution. Losing themselves in reading eased interminable hours spent in their cells, enabled them to momentarily forget their dire reality, and subsequently helped them to survive years and decades of incarceration.[27]

After almost two years in Shlisselburg, by the summer of 1886 Vera found a precarious emotional balance. Yet this equilibrium, derived as it was from the privileges she coaxed from the prison administration, rested on the regime's continued acquiescence. After only a few months of living with these privileges, Vera found herself again deprived. However, her deprivation came not at the hands of the prison regime, but from her own as part of a political protest engineered by Ludmila Volkenstein.

Neither exercise time shared with a comrade nor work in the prison garden were universally extended to Shlisselburg inmates. Instead the prison administration selectively doled out these privileges to stimulate good behavior. As a result, although many inmates, like Vera and Ludmila, enjoyed the transformative effects of these prerogatives, some failed to gain access to them.[28] The inequity of this situation unsettled Ludmila, who resolved to use the only power at her disposal to rectify the situation. To that end, she suggested that she and Vera refuse their own privileges until the administration extended them to all inmates. Vera initially rejected the notion of such a sacrifice, but Ludmila's repeated coaxing and Vera's feelings of revolutionary solidarity finally prompted her in the autumn of 1886 to refuse her communal walks and agricultural pursuits until the warden extended these prerogatives to every prisoner.

Despite the long, lonely, difficult days that ensued, this protest was life-affirming, for it demonstrated that "amid general silence and submission, the prisoners would not react passively to what happened around [them]."[29] Consequently, it reminded Vera that although she had lost the right to control her body in Shlisselburg, her will remained her own. While the prison administration might aspire to break her will, her cooperation was necessary for it to succeed. Thus, this small protest—only five prisoners took part—was monumental, as it demonstrated the protesters' deliberate retention of their moral autonomy in a space designed to annihilate all vestiges of protest and individuality. It also speaks to the endurance and tenacity of Vera, Ludmila, and the three men who joined in. The quintet only abandoned their protest after more than a year when a newly appointed warden extended walks in pairs and the opportunity to work in the kitchen gardens to every inmate.

The Shlisselburg regime conceived these privileges as means through which to ensure docility among the prisoners. The administration supplemented this positive reinforcement with more coercive, insidious measures, of which the most frequently used was the transfer of unruly inmates to the fortress's punishment cells. Located two courtyards away from the rest of the prison, as Warden Sokolov ominously explained to Vera, the old prison's ill-famed solitary cells were far enough away from the general population of prisoners that not a soul would be able to hear what took place in them.[30] Although the prison administration did not expressly torture the prisoners in these cells, the level of physical deprivation significantly exceeded the already onerous circumstances of life for the inmates in the fortress's general population.

Vera's first experience in Shlisselburg's punishment cells came six months after she and Ludmila began their prison protest. One day as she tapped to her neighbor, Mikhail Popov, she suddenly heard the sounds of a struggle in his cell. Vera listened in horror as the sound of a slamming cell door and heavy-booted footsteps down the hall conveyed the obvious impression that guards were dragging Popov to a punishment cell in retaliation for his continued tapping. Overwhelmed with both terror and guilt for the role she played in

Popov's impending punishment, Vera shouted to the guards that she should be taken to the punishment cells as well.[31] Without hesitation, Sokolov and the guards obliged.

Within minutes Vera found herself in a small, unheated, musty, dirty cell in the old prison. There was a small wooden table with a chair and an iron bench but no mattress or bedding. Vera waited in vain for a guard to bring her something to lie down on or at least something to keep her warm. Wearing only a linen shirt and her regular prison skirt, she spent a long, frigid, sleepless night. The next day passed without any concessions or additional supplies. By the next night, fatigue overwhelmed her and she lay on the filthy floor, using her shoes as a pillow. The unpalatable and stark meal of old, moldy black bread that guards placed in her cell offered no respite from her physical ordeal.[32] As the days passed, she grew increasingly exhausted and demoralized. After five full days of this treatment, guards brought bedding and hot tea to Vera and Popov in their respective punishment cells. Two days later both members of the tapping pair were returned to their normal cells.[33] The weeklong experience ravaged Vera's nerves and appearance. After she returned to her cell, she felt as though she had aged ten years in the previous seven days. And although the experience did not break her, it took a serious toll. Consequently, she decided that she needed to pick her protests carefully and engage only in those that she was prepared to see through to the end, even if it meant bodily punishment or even death.

Shortly after her ordeal in the punishment cell, Vera and her fellow inmates received pencils and paper. Forbidden to communicate with the outside world, the prisoners began to use these writing implements to indulge their creative energies. Poetry flourished in the fortress. Prisoners composed poems to celebrate special anniversaries, buoy despondent comrades' spirits, lament the cruel turns of fate, and indulge previously unrecognized creativity. Often inmates would engage in a poetic conversation that gave expression to feelings that were too intimate to otherwise express.

One such exchange occurred between Vera and Herman Lopatin. Lopatin initiated the conversation in verse with a poem that bemoaned his ruined life.[34] As Vera listened to the tapped poem from the man who showed such vitality in freedom, she felt inclined to answer him. In the poem she tapped back to Lopatin, she expressed her belief that revolutionaries' personal comfort and happiness were insignificant; what mattered was the larger process to which they dedicated and sacrificed their lives. Although the particulars of their prison ordeal were unknown beyond Shlisselburg's walls, the suffering of condemned radicals retained meaning through its potential inspiration for new generations of radicals. In this way the men and women condemned to live lives of deprivation and isolation in Shlisselburg were the lucky ones. "We had the good fortune to devote our best forces to the struggle for freedom . . . Now we are ready to endure and suffer until they bury us for the cause of the *narod*! . . . Through your quiet suffering, young brothers will be called to the battle for freedom and equality."[35]

The revolutionary inspiration to which Vera referred resulted from a slow martyrdom in which the condemned exhibited herculean levels of patience and endurance. Yet there were some Shlisselburg inmates who rejected patience and embraced a more dramatic and immediate manifestation of sacrifice. Mikhail Grachevskii, one of the former explosives experts in the People's Will, was one such prisoner. In October 1887, after a prolonged stint in a punishment cell and repeated efforts to publicize the depths of the inhumane punishment doled out in Shlisselburg, Grachevskii doused himself with kerosene from his lamp and set himself on fire.[36] His horrific death became the ultimate sacrifice, as it impelled the Department of Police to replace both the warden and commandant of the island fortress.[37] The new administration was decidedly more humane, improving the quality of food served to the prisoners,[38] ordering new books for the library, granting all inmates the right to walk in pairs and work in their gardens, and allowing the prisoners to tap to one another to their hearts' content.[39] In Vera's words, "the dead lay breathless, but the living began to breathe easier."[40]

Grachevskii's suicide reaffirmed for Vera and several other Shlisselburg inmates that they retained a capacity for protest and an ability to effect change behind the fortress's walls, albeit at a potentially lethal price. Struggles over what outsiders might consider trifles confirmed the prisoners' sense of preserved vitality and human dignity.[41] The inmates viewed the various deprivations and prohibitions to which they were subjected as the administration's attempt to break their will and to control both their bodies and spirits. Thus, the prisoners' protest of what they deemed egregious abuses proved to them that while the tsarist regime could imprison, isolate, and even kill the revolutionaries, it could not break them. While some inmates viewed challenging the administration as inherently dangerous, for the most part the opposite was true, as almost all of the most troublesome prisoners survived their experience in the Russian Bastille.[42] Vera was notoriously disruptive in prison.

Even after a relatively accommodating administration under the direction of Warden Fedorov, prison officials continued to note Vera's "unsettled and restless behavior" in their reports to the capital.[43]

By the end of the 1880s, life in the fortress was less lethal than it had been earlier in the decade, thanks to the improvements made in the wake of Grachevskii's suicide. The endless days of cruel deprivation defined by monotony and isolation seemed a bitter, distant memory. But in the fall of 1889 the specter of those days threatened to reappear when the director of police ordered the prison library purged of what he considered politically inflammatory books. Viewing this action as a personal affront that deprived them of what little property they possessed, the Shlisselburg prisoners unanimously agreed to engage in a collective protest.[44]

Although of one mind that they must react to the removal of the books, the inmates did not agree about the best method of protest. Vera, M. R. Popov, and F. N. Iurkovskii wanted to embark on a hunger strike even if it meant that several of the imprisoned revolutionaries might die.[45] But others demurred. The reluctant prisoners' hesitancy disgusted Vera, as she considered it illustrative of their cowardice and fear of death. Staunch in her conviction and intolerant of divergent opinions, she and four other inmates began their hunger strike. While still uncommitted to this form of protest, feelings of revolutionary solidarity impelled the majority of the remaining prisoners to join them.

In her memoirs Vera depicts herself as essentially unaffected by her self-sustained starvation. Other inmates suffered tremendously. After nine days of refusing food, and with the prison administration showing no inclination to return the removed books, Mikhail Popov informed Vera that he was ending his hunger strike. Sickened by what she considered evidence of Popov's weak will and tenuous revolutionary commitment, she broke off all communication with her friend. When other inmates followed Popov's lead, her "burning disillusionment turned into unrestrained anger."[46]

As the hunger strike collapsed, Vera writes, "I saw before me not a united collective . . . but scattered personalities who were weak and unstable who could retreat like ordinary people."[47] In Vera's opinion, when she and her comrades dedicated themselves to the revolutionary cause, they relinquished the right to act like "ordinary people." She believed that as revolutionaries, she and her fellow inmates had to dispel human sensations of weakness and frailties. Self-righteous and intolerant of diverse opinions, Vera considered herself entitled to decide a course of action for the entire prison. She had let other perceived injustices pass. But once she decided that the administration's requisition of the prisoners' books was an intolerable offense, she would sanction no dissension. In her mind she was the moral authority on all matters revolutionary, so to disagree with her was to commit an act of revolutionary treason.

Considering herself free of any obligation to the group, Vera, now joined only by Iurkovskii, continued her hunger strike and made peace with her impending death. But once again she found her plans for martyrdom stymied. On the eleventh day of her strike, Popov and N. P. Starodvorskii informed Vera that if she died they would kill themselves.[48] Vera greatly resented this emotional extortion. She believed her comrades' threat was rooted not in camaraderie or affection but masculine vanity.[49] Obviously, despite the tsarist regime's efforts to deny the femininity of its female prisoners, gender endured as an essential category of difference for the inmates themselves.

But in truth the government's effort to promote gender equity in the sentencing of political prisoners was disingenuous. By sending Vera to Shlisselburg, the tsarist regime attempted to deny her gender, even though her sentence was predicated upon it. Crime and punishment had long been gendered. Across cultures and centuries, "the treatment of prisoners is especially clearly sexually linked—the kinds of punishments received, the kinds of crimes committed, the kinds of judgments (and what it is that is judged) are clearly different for the two sexes."[50] Given her crimes, Vera should have been executed. She was not, however, because she was a woman. Yet she was sent to an otherwise all-male prison (except for Ludmila Volkenstein) because an element of her offense was rooted in her violation of the norms of femininity, through which she relinquished all claims to deferential treatment as a woman. In the fortress, though, Vera's sex was acknowledged. As the punishment of Shlisselburg was constituted in and through the body and the regime's control over it, sexual difference could not be denied, because it constituted the essential physical or bodily difference between Vera and all but one of her fellow inmates. Thus, by existing as a female body in an overwhelmingly masculine space, Vera's gender was psychologically rehabilitated for both her fellow prisoners and their jailers.

The male revolutionaries condemned to Shlisselburg viewed the daily sacrifice exacted from Vera and Ludmila as especially pronounced because of their sex. Influenced by the Cartesian tradition of dualism, Darwin's theories of evolution, and Victorian myths about the comparatively physically weak middle- or upper-class female, the mostly educated men imprisoned in Shlisselburg internalized assumptions about the alleged frailty of women. Even though the incarcerated male revolutionaries thought of themselves as liberated, they subconsciously subscribed to ideas born in "essentialism, naturalism and biologism" that connected "women much more closely than men to the body."[51] Thus, when Vera and Ludmila demonstrated strength that bested their own, the male prisoners drew conclusions about the exceptional nature of their female counterparts.

For centuries there has existed an understanding in the Christian tradition "whereby [a] martyr's endurance comes to be linked explicitly with masculinity and tied also to images of masculinized athleticism and militarism."[52] Willing death on the scaffold demands moments of endurance, but a slow death in a fortress like Shlisselburg calls for years or even decades of fortitude. In such an environment, gendered notions of suffering and endurance become all the more potent. If martyrdom realized on the scaffold "uncouples the soul from the body" and thus allows gender to be a "dimension of worldliness that can be left behind with enthusiasm and without regret,"[53] the same cannot be said for the martyrdom that is realized in a political prison. For the man or woman condemned to an extended period behind unforgiving prison walls, body and soul fuse in a prolonged contest of perseverance, courage, and even physical and psychological athleticism in which strength determines success or failure. In this way, should a woman show more agility in her martyrdom than her male counterparts, her gender transgression has ramifications not only for her but also for the emasculated men who exhibited signs of relative weakness. Although recent scholarship argues that the "'maternal-sacrificial affective code' imposed by Western society convinces participants in radical subcultures . . . of women's special suitability for martyrdom," the gendered difference in endurance that became apparent in the Shlisselburg hunger strike evoked impressions of relative strength and weakness that challenged the men's self-conception.[54]

When Popov relayed his ultimatum that Vera's death would necessitate his own, she realized his male ego could not suffer such a dramatic demonstration of his comparable frailty. Yet she was unable to bear responsibility for a death he would not choose of his own volition, so she ended her hunger strike in despair.[55] In the wake of this failed protest, Vera endured a period of intense depression. She refused to communicate by tapping to her neighbors, but she could not stop herself from listening to the messages they exchanged. In the midst of her disillusionment, hurt, and anger, Vera contends that she listened as two comrades tapped about her. Obviously aware that she could hear their communications, her friends may have purposely assuaged her vanity in the hopes of ending her isolation. If so, their ploy worked, because they tapped exactly what she longed to hear. Herman Lopatin held Vera up as a model of exemplary revolutionary behavior. Through her dedication, leadership, and sacrifice, he argued, her life had significance beyond Shlisselburg, because "Vera does not belong to her friends, she belongs to Russia."[56]

These words confirmed for Vera that her experiences and actions in Shlisselburg were just as integral to her role in the revolutionary movement as were her activities with the People's Will leadership while she was free. She believed it was her responsibility to continue to be a model of dedication, endurance, and self-sacrifice throughout her tenure in Shlisselburg in order to inspire her weaker comrades. By and large, her fellow inmates agreed.

More than any other figure incarcerated in Shlisselburg, Vera was the moral authority in the prison. In 1902 a police department official noted that "prisoner number eleven directs the social opinion of the entire prison. All of the other inmates submit to her instruction without scarcely a word."[57] Vera's fellow prisoners unanimously corroborate this appraisal. For them, her "word was law."[58] Given the masculinized conception of martyrdom, this was a natural consequence. In order for the male inmates' masculinity not to be compromised or questioned, Vera needed to be glorified. Rather than depicting her as a woman who was more of a "man" than they were in terms of her endurance and strength, she became allegorically transformed into a sort of higher being. M. Iu. Ashenbrenner, whose fervent admiration of Vera never diminished, writes, "With the soul of an apostle . . . she suffered cruelly . . . yet forgot herself . . . and instead agonizing over the fate of others magnanimously took on their heavy burden and carried it herself."[59] Before her early release from Shlisselburg in 1896, the male inmates held Ludmila Volkenstein in a similar regard. Mikhail Frolenko notes that throughout his decades in prison, he was continually "astounded by the exceptional selflessness, tact, self-possession and pure, fraternal, loving behavior of these sweet, dear martyrs."[60]

For the first half decade of their imprisonment, Vera and Ludmila became for Shlisselburg's men unseen forces of solace, encouragement, and inspiration whose feminine, selfless spirits seemed untethered from their constrained bodies. But beginning in 1890 they reemerged as visible physical beings after the prison administration built workshops for the prisoners to use in the old prison. After years in prison with nothing to do beyond embroidery, gardening, and intellectual labor, Vera relished the opportunity for the physical labor afforded by the prison workshops. She took great pride in the furniture she built and the books she bound. These projects became integral to her physical health and emotional well-being.[61] The rewards that the inmates garnered from such projects were not merely intangible. The prisoners' craftsmanship was such that the prison administration regularly bought their wares, which allowed Vera and the other inmates to purchase books, food, and incidentals.[62] But the greatest transformation in prison life that the workshops allowed was the inmates' ability to drill holes in the fences that separated the men's exercise cages from the one occupied by Vera and Ludmila. Although their initial efforts resulted in reprimands and fence repairs, the male prisoners proved so determined that the administration eventually relented. Rather than try to permanently seal the holes in the fences, the gendarmes compromised and made coverings that could be placed over the openings when officials visited from the capital.[63] In explaining this obvious breach of protocol, Mikhail Novorusskii asserts that the warden approved the fence openings because Vera and Ludmila had spent so many years so unfairly isolated.[64] Realizing that no sexual impropriety would result through the drilled fences, the prison administration capitulated to ease some of the harshest burden of the women's imprisonment.

Almost immediately the prisoners' lives became focused on these openings in the fence.[65] Deprived of contact with women for years, the romantic fantasies of almost all of the male inmates centered on Vera and Ludmila.[66] Aspiring to be as close as possible to their two ladies, the male prisoners did all they could to please them. The Shlisselburg men composed loving poems brimming with respect and adoration for the female inmates and made countless gifts for them in their workshops. It became a veritable sport to try to please Vera and Ludmila, and jealousies were inflamed as the men competed for the women's affections.[67]

It was not simply sexual desire that prompted the men of Shlisselburg to compete for the affections of Vera and Ludmila. With their bodies confined and purged of sexual identity through their incarceration, the Shlisselburg women were more akin to unattainable revolutionary goddesses deserving of worship than they were prospective lovers whom the men sought to seduce. Through their prolonged isolation, which obviously entailed an absence of sexual encounters and relationships, Vera and Ludmila were stripped of their identity as active sexual agents. Like cloistered nuns, isolated for the secular religion of revolution, their sexuality became latent. This notion resonated with the revolutionary men of Vera's generation. For a group who verbally espoused gender equality in the radical ranks, these male revolutionaries most admired the women who exhibited control over their bodies and sexuality.[68] According to the revolutionary author Gleb Uspensky, whose fictional characters described his generation's quintessential radical woman, the ideal was an "ascetic, martyred, and inescapably Christ-like figure whose sexuality is concealed and sublimated."[69] Thus, irrespective of the degree to which either Vera or Ludmila had conformed to this revolutionary model before being imprisoned, their long incarceration sanctified them through their sacrifice and the sublimation of their sexuality.

Realizing their comrades' desperation to have some contact with them, Vera and Ludmila tirelessly indulged the male prisoners and stood for hours by their fence talking with their visitors. During the summer months such meetings were often pleasant; however, in winter, standing still in the frigid weather for extended periods of time was almost unbearable,[70] but neither woman had the heart to turn a comrade away. Thus, regardless of weather conditions, the men imprisoned in Shlisselburg remembered always finding support, encouragement, and friendship through the openings they drilled in the fences.[71] It was obvious that prison life did not mitigate notions of feminine virtue in the minds of the inmates; on the contrary, these notions took on new strength. The male inmates expected comfort to be rendered by their female comrades. For their part, even though they needed solace just as much as the imprisoned men, Vera and Ludmila smiled at, charmed, and cajoled their male friends for endless hours as part of their comradely and feminine duties.

In 1891 Shlisselburg welcomed a new administration. With the appointment of the educated and kindhearted Colonel I. I. Gangardt as commandant, an air of toleration and relative openness filled the fortress. Rather than repair the holes that he found in the fences, the new commandant had all of the fences lowered three feet on the pretext of allowing more sunlight for the prisoners' agronomic endeavors. Taking advantage of Gangardt's tolerant attitudes, the inmates built rostrums in their workshops, placed them next to the outdoor fences, and were able to stand on them and converse with several of their friends and comrades at once.

Soon the prisoners used the common space created by the lower fences and the rostrums for full-blown social gatherings. Approximately three to four times a year, Vera and Ludmila hosted name day or birthday celebrations in their garden. Gangardt allowed inmates to use stoves he set up in the old prison. The inmates used these to full effect as they prepared appetizers, desserts, candies, jam, and even homemade vodka for their festivities.[72] As Vera and Ludmila passed out food and beverages over the fence, the men would take turns eating, drinking, and visiting with one another and the two women. As they enjoyed these simple pleasures and each other's company, the early years in Shlisselburg, when inmates could spend weeks in the punishment cells simply for tapping through the walls, became distant memories of an unpleasant past.

Before long, the inmates, most of whom were educated, organized academic lectures on the rostrums in their gardens. Four or five inmates would gather at the point where Vera's and Ludmila's garden intersected with the exercise cages and listen to lessons prepared by one of their learned comrades.[73] While the participants varied slightly over time, Vera, Morozov, Novorusskii, and I. D. Lukashevich were constantly in attendance as either lecturers or pupils. Vera recalls Lukashevich with gratitude, deeming him a brilliant man who "tirelessly helped his prison comrades in the pursuit of knowledge."[74] But Novorusskii credits Vera herself for the success of these lectures. He writes, "The most zealous organizer of these lectures was always Vera Nikolaevna[,] who preserved until the end the most lively interest in all possible branches of knowledge and art and displayed great persistence and stubbornness in the pursuit of her academic and scientific goals."[75]

By the mid-1890s Vera's days were filled with activity. During the duration of Commandant Gangardt's tenure, guards allowed the male prisoners to move freely through the halls while they were in their workshops. The women's workshops remained locked, but their door's casement window was open. Through this window Vera and Ludmila hosted an unending stream of visitors who came to their workshop for conversation, to conduct joint scientific experiments, and even to receive knitting lessons. Unlike the early years, when she sat alone in her cell for almost twenty-fours a day, Vera was almost never "home." The gendarmes opened the inmates' cells at 8:00 AM, at which time the prisoners could go to their gardens, their exercise cages, or their workshops until noon, when they were brought back to their respective cells for an hour for lunch. At one o'clock in the afternoon, guards unlocked the cells and the inmates went back to work or stayed in their rooms resting and reading. In winter the convicted revolutionaries returned to their cells at 3:00 PM for tea and remained inside for the rest of the day. But during the summer months, when St. Petersburg's white nights rewarded the region for months of dark-ness and cold, the prisoners stayed outside or in their workshops until 9:00 PM.[76]

With a humane administration ensuring an improved quality of life,[77] Vera became reconciled to her life in Shlisselburg. Many inmates, though, con-tinued to dream of freedom. Once hopeless that they would ever leave the prison, when news of Emperor Alexander III's death reached the fortress in 1894, prisoners and guards alike expected that imminent liberty awaited the inmates. Even the warden felt so confident his current prisoners would be freed that he told Vera, "Soon you will be a lady again."[78] As the Shlisselburg administration waited for the expected word that its inmates would be am-nestied, various officials grew lax in their prohibitions. One day a gendarme left the door to Vera and Ludmila's workshop unlocked. Imbued with the spirit of expectation and relative freedom, all of the men joined the women and celebrated their anticipated release by singing and taking turns waltzing with them.[79] But as the months passed and no amnesty occurred, these liber-ties were discontinued.

Within two years, however, freedom did come for several inmates. Instead of a general amnesty, upon his coronation Nicholas II declared a selective re-duction in sentence for several revolutionaries who had been condemned at the beginning of his father's reign. As a result, on November 23, 1896, five in-mates left the fortress. Ludmila Volkenstein was one of them.[80]

Although happy for their friends, the inmates destined to remain in Shlis-selburg were saddened at the prospect of life without certain members of their surrogate family. Vera was especially hard hit by the thought of losing Lud-mila. But those who remained celebrated the release of their friends with a farewell feast and concert. They bestowed homemade gifts on the departing inmates and cooked them an extravagant dinner (by prison standards). Then Vera serenaded the men and woman who took their last morning walks as prisoners in Shlisselburg. After bidding their friends a personal farewell, the time finally came for Volkenstein, Surovtsev, Ianovich, Martynov, and Sheba-lin to depart. Standing on chairs by their cell windows, the prisoners whose sentences remained unaffected by Nicholas II's decree watched sadly while their comrades left the fortress. As their friends faded from sight, those who remained were left to deal with a "new, dark emptiness" that descended on their isolated part of the world.[81]

With such a small "family," the absence of five members could not help but be felt. Realizing that their sole "lady" was again alone, the other remaining inmates worked hard to coddle Vera. Using the money they earned through the wares they produced, several inmates bought her special treats like stockings, long underwear, and pretty skirts.[82] On warm spring and summer days, the male prisoners sought to abet her loneliness by sitting on the other side of her fence and reading aloud to her as she knitted in her garden.[83] Although their efforts brought her solace, Vera faced a fresh emotional crisis in early 1897 when she received a letter from her sister Olga.[84]

From the beginning of their imprisonment until 1897, the Shlisselburg inmates had been denied the right to correspond with their relatives. Following through on its intention to make these condemned revolutionaries disappear, the tsarist regime silenced the prisoners on the island fortress and forced them to live in blind ignorance of their loved ones' fate. For the first few years, the inmates did not even know if their relatives were alive or dead. By 1887 the regime decided that such a complete dearth of information was too severe even for revolutionary terrorists. Thus, officials in St. Petersburg began to send the prisoners terse notifications stating which of their relatives had died since they had been vanquished to Shlisselburg.[85] Anxious to learn of her mother's fate, Vera was relieved to hear that Ekaterina was alive and healthy.[86] Yet many of her comrades were forced to face years of accumulated misfortunes in one devastating blow.

As prison officials handed Vera her sister Olga's letter, they informed her that henceforth she would be able to correspond with her family twice a year. This information was cause for consternation rather than celebration. In her effort to survive Shlisselburg, Vera had forced thoughts of her family into the distant recesses of her mind. Doing so had not been easy. Initially she was obsessed with thoughts of her beloved mother and siblings and was overwhelmed by the grief of being without them. But with time came the acceptance that she would never see her family again, and she "gradually passed into a fog of forgetfulness,"[87] since it was too painful to continue to pine away for them.

Having suppressed the warm, loving feelings she had for her family for over a decade, in 1897 Vera was forced to resume contact. Unaccustomed to letter writing after a thirteen-year respite, and forbidden to divulge anything concrete about her fellow prisoners or their location, she uncomfortably stared at a blank page for more than a month as she faced the difficulty of resuscitating her "petrified soul."[88] Sitting in her cell, she tried to overcome her feelings of irreparable separation, but the words refused to come.

By virtue of their shared experience of suffering in Shlisselburg, the other prisoners in the fortress had become Vera's family. With them, fears could go unspoken but be understood. Small material gains that those unfamiliar with Shlisselburg would find trivial could be relished and celebrated in common. Though freedom and death dwindled their numbers after more than a decade of incarceration, those who remained enabled one another to survive. Bridging the gulf of the last thirteen years with her real family seemed impossible. Vera finally wrote to Olga and Ekaterina, but the process remained painful and arduous.

By the beginning of the twentieth century, only thirteen men and one woman were still imprisoned in the island fortress. With so many cells vacated by released and deceased comrades, each prisoner now had two cells for his or her personal use. All of the inmates lived in cells on the second floor and had another cell on the first floor that they used for study or manual labor.[89] The extreme deprivation that had prevailed during the prison's early years was but a distant, unpleasant memory. Now gardens and exercise cages remained unlocked, and prisoners had a rich intellectual life, corresponded with family members, and visited with their fellow inmates.[90] Although Vera was not permitted *in* the men's cells nor they in hers, the male prisoners would sit on a bench in the corridor outside her cell or she on a bench outside theirs, and through the open casement window in the door she and her two friends would chat and drink their tea.[91]

Vera appreciated these liberties but always feared losing them. In her 1893 story "Banished Princess," her alter ego finds happiness on her isolated island through her natural curiosity and an appreciation for pleasures found in nature. But when her wicked stepmother returns, with the capricious stamp of a foot, the princess encounters only ugliness and despair: "As if a cover fell from her eyes, she no longer saw any beauty."[92]

The small joys and vestiges of beauty that Vera and her fellow inmates discovered in Shlisselburg were jeopardized in 1902 when Viacheslav K. Plehve, the former police director, became the new minister of the interior and returned repression to the prison. Henceforth, according to the warden, acting on directives from the capital, the prison administration would tolerate no violation of the official rules.[93] For the fourteen prisoners who had lost their youth, strength, health, and endurance over the previous two decades, the potential reversion to the tortures of the past was inconceivable.

Tensions escalated in the fortress. As prisoners protested the change in policy, the warden threatened draconian measures, including confinement in the punishment cell, in a desperate effort to maintain order. After a particularly disturbing exchange between gendarmes and Sergei Ivanov in March

1902, Vera penned a letter to her mother in which she asked Ekaterina to appeal to the Ministry of Internal Affairs or the Department of Police to investigate the situation at Shlisselburg.[94] Vera never expected her mother to see the letter. She assumed that the note would get no farther than a gendarme's desk in St. Petersburg. Knowing that police officials inspected all correspondence emanating from Shlisselburg, she believed her letter would prompt an investigation by the St. Petersburg bureaucrats who oversaw the fortress. But as it turned out, Vera's letter never left the island.

On March 5 the warden returned Vera's letter to her and instructed her to rewrite it. Frustrated that her ploy had failed, Vera shouted at her jailer that he was violating procedures and demanded that he forward the letter to the capital. When he again refused, Vera angrily lunged at the warden, tore the epaulets from his uniform, and dramatically threw them on the floor.[95] Shocked at the assault on his person and position by the diminutive prisoner number eleven, the warden picked up his epaulets and left Vera's cell.

As news of this event spread throughout the prison, Vera's comrades panicked. A physical and personal affront of this magnitude would likely warrant her court-martial and execution. Well aware of the expected repercussions, Vera nonetheless implored her friends to behave with all possible restraint "out of respect and love" for her.[96]

Once again Vera awaited what she expected to be her inevitable execution. As she proudly faced death, the fifty-year-old revolutionary was pleased that she was still capable of protest after so many years.[97] While she found solace in her enduring radical spirit, most of her friends were inconsolable. Ashenbrenner conveys the collective horror of the prison when he recalls their feelings that "the best, most beloved and independent comrade whose moral influence was a salvation to the exhausted, had fallen into the jaws of the evil enemy."[98] Similarly, Morozov recalls that "her life was dearer to me than my own and her imminent execution seemed to signal the execution of my heart and spirit if I did not use all possible means at my disposable to save her."[99] Thus, Morozov decided to risk his friend's wrath to save her life. In a letter he wrote to the director of the police department in St. Petersburg, he painted Vera as an emotional wreck. Prone to emotional outbursts, given her sex and the conditions under which she had lived for the past two decades, most notably her practical seclusion as a woman in a man's prison, Vera, Morozov claimed, had assaulted the warden in a nervous fit and state of emotional breakdown.[100]

Morozov's tactic worked. Within a week an outside police investigator came to the fortress; questioned Vera, Morozov, and the prison doctor; and spared Vera's life due to the presumed extreme emotional stress inflicted on this fragile woman by her long imprisonment. Instead of executing Shlisselburg's only female inmate, the Department of Police deprived Vera of the right to correspond with her family, required that the fortress doctor make monthly reports on her state of mind, and changed the administration of the prison yet again.[101]

Captivated by the brief prospect of sealing her revolutionary exploits with a dramatic, final act of self-sacrifice, Vera was disappointed that the chance to die had been wrested from her yet again.[102] Whether she was simply energized by the magnitude of her recent protest or actively aspiring to weave her way to the executioner's block, her behavior became increasingly disruptive. In the reports he prepared for officials in the capital in early 1903, Shlisselburg's new warden notes that of the thirteen prisoners who remained in the fortress, Vera was the only one whose behavior was "unsatisfactory."[103]

Given the increased tension between her and the prison administration, Vera was understandably startled when the fortress's commandant brusquely walked into her cell on January 13, 1903. Without giving her time to react to his presence, the commandant began to read from a document that he held in his hands. He read, "His Majesty the Emperor, in deference to the entreaty of your mother . . . has graciously ordered your term of penal servitude for life to be converted to twenty years . . . Your term ends September 28, 1904. You are once again free to correspond with your family."[104]

More than any other news or occurrence since she arrived at Shlisselburg, this latest event dumbfounded Vera. For the woman who yearned to seal her revolutionary career with martyrdom, mercy at the hands of the government she had sought to topple was intolerable. What made matters worse was the realization that her mother had begged for her daughter's release. Wanting to share her comrades' fate to the end, Vera felt humiliated.[105] She was also perplexed. Why would her mother, who had bravely endured so many hardships over the last few decades, break down after so long and beg on her daughter's behalf? Within a few days, Vera had her answer. In a letter she wrote to her daughter on January 18, 1903, Ekaterina Figner informed Vera that she was dying of cancer.[106]

Vera was overcome with feelings of grief and sadness. In a letter to Ekaterina, Vera pleaded with her mother to fight the deadly illness. "Do you really want to give up and leave us forever? . . . We love you so much and so deeply respect you . . . if you die, the soul of the family will die with you."[107] Within a span of a few days, Vera's world fell apart. Not only did she learn that her revolutionary legend would be scarred by a final plea for mercy, but also the only connection that she felt she had with the outside world was literally dying. Facing the prospect of a world both beyond Shlisselburg and without her mother, Vera wrote to Ekaterina, saying, "I am so alone, and so unused to people that I do not know how I will return to life, how I will meet with anyone except for you—my mother, friend, comfort and great mentor in everything good and eternal."[108]

Still limited to biannual letters, as Vera composed her January 25 missive to her mother, she did not know if these would be the last words she would ever be able to share with her dear *mamochka*. Vera realized that this was not the time for recriminations about Ekaterina's decision to plead for her daughter's release; that time would never come. Instead, she asked the mother whom she had not seen for two decades for her forgiveness. She writes, "I love you, appreciate you and thank you endlessly for the help and support which you have always rendered me. I ask you to forgive me all my shortcomings and the sins that I committed in respect to you."[109] Only thirteen days after Vera wrote this letter to her mother, she received a response. For the first time since her incarceration, she felt as if her and her mother's hearts beat in unison.[110] As she read Ekaterina's reply to her last letter, Vera felt her mother's presence and solace. Wanting to forget the hurt of the past, Ekaterina informed her eldest daughter that "a mother's heart does not remember grief."[111]

Still limited in the frequency of her correspondence, Vera then languished without news for months. Wondering if Ekaterina was alive or dead while at the same time preparing to start her own life anew was torturous. In June Vera received news that her mother was still alive but that her health was rapidly deteriorating. For weeks she waited for the inevitable news that her mother had passed away. Finally, toward the end of the summer, she received a letter from Ekaterina in which her mother shared that although she was not well, she hoped to survive until she could see her eldest daughter again.

Reading Vera's letter to Ekaterina from September 30, 1903, one can feel the revolutionary's hesitance to close her missive. In the two decades since the two women had seen each other, they had been able to write just over a dozen times. Separated by prison walls, armed guards, illness, time, and Vera's life choices, mother and daughter had only a few pieces of paper in which to say their peace before death severed their connection. Unsure if she would ever be able to see or even write to her mother again, Vera struggled to find the balance between what needed to be said and what needed to remain buried. Overwhelmed by emotions, she yearned to convey her feelings to the mother she might never see again. Realizing that no words would fully suffice, Vera writes, "Although we are physically separated, know that I am always with you. I hope that you are not suffering too much. My dear, I kiss your hands. Vera."[112]

These were the last words that Ekaterina Figner ever received from her daughter. The Figner matriarch died on November 15,[113] months before Vera's next biannual letter was scheduled. When the warden informed her of her mother's November death on February 6, 1904,[114] Vera became despondent. She shunned her fellow inmates and remained secluded for weeks in her cell indulging her grief.[115] A month later she still found it difficult to discuss her mother's passing, even with the sisters who shared her sorrow. In a March 9, 1904, letter to them, Vera writes, "For twenty-one years she was the center of my feelings. I feel exhausted now because for the past year I have stood over her open grave in continual alarm, agitation and fear."[116]

Equally as painful as her mother's death was Vera's realization that she had not been available to her. Learning of her sisters' trip to Nikiforovo to bury Ekaterina, she discloses her hope that in some metaphysical way she may have been there with the other women of her family. She informed her siblings that soon after their mother's death, before she even knew Ekaterina was dead, she had a dream in which the four sisters were traveling over the snow-covered fields of provincial Russia.[117] After she learned of Lidia, Eugenia, and Olga's sad trip back to their family's estate, Vera hoped that "on the night that you brought mamochka home, my spirit somehow accompanied you."[118]

In spite of her mother's death, the commutation of Vera's sentence stood. She was slated to leave the prison where she had struggled to survive on September 28. At fifty-two years of age, Vera knew that her life was dramatically and forcibly changing. Now that her beloved mother was gone, she could find even less reason to leave Shlisselburg. Over the previous two decades, she had grown accustomed to her life behind the fortress's walls. Prison had become her reality and freedom was a frightening unfamiliar prospect. The only people with whom she felt comfortable were the men imprisoned in the fortress with her. Her release had come too late, because her "yearning for the world and all of its beauty had ceased to exist."[119]

As the day of her release approached, Vera sat in her cell leafing through the mementoes her comrades had given her over the past two decades and sobbing for the past and her own bleak future.[120] But on the day she bid her fellow prisoners farewell, she held back the tears. Although she told her friends that leaving their living grave was no reason to cry, she actually felt as if she were exchanging a familiar tomb for an enigmatic future that was worse than death. After losing her mother, Vera was now losing the people who had become her family and the center of her universe.[121]

Faced with the prospect of leaving the prison that had constituted her entire world for more than twenty years, Vera confronted the sad reality that she lacked control over her fate. She did not want to leave Shlisselburg, but the tsarist state was forcing her to make one of the most dramatic changes possible. Adding insult to injury, however, was the fact that liberation from Shlisselburg did not entail freedom. Although she was destined to leave the island fortress, she would remain a prisoner of the tsarist state. At the very least, she anticipated facing years of exile in a remote corner of the Russian Empire where she would be forced to labor alongside common criminals.[122] With her nervous system ravaged by her long incarceration, Vera was terrified.

As a final reminder that her fate was not her own, for unexplained reasons the Russian government unexpectedly delayed Vera's release by one day. Scheduled to depart Shlisselburg on September 28, she did not leave the fortress until September 29, when at 4:00 PM one of the noncommissioned officers opened Vera's cell for the last time.[123] As she walked through the dark hallways that had been her world for two decades, she was overcome with emotion and trepidation. While still within the prison's walls, she was able to hold her feelings in check, but when gendarmes led prisoner number eleven out of the prison and across the courtyard, her emotions poured forth. With tears streaming down her face, she turned and looked back at the prison. In the windows of the second floor, she saw her friends waving handkerchiefs and shouting good-bye.[124] As these faces faded from view, she confronted her new life alone. Stepping onto a steamer that would take her away from the island in Lake Ladoga, Vera realized that the clock of time had started to tick again. What she could not fathom, however, was what she would do with this time and how she would learn to live in a world beyond Shlisselburg again.

9

RESURRECTION IN EXILE

IN THE DAYS BEFORE VERA LEFT Shlisselburg, her dear friend Nikolai Morozov composed a poem to commemorate her release. In it he expressed his wish that fate would treat his cherished comrade well and that soon she would put the horrors of prison behind her.[1] But Vera had spent too many years in Shlisselburg to believe that Morozov's good wishes for her would be realized. She knew that inmates did not move easily from fortress to freedom. On the contrary, the steamer ride down the Neva from Lake Ladoga was just the first leg of a long journey that brought former Shlisselburg prisoners to new, untried terms of incarceration. For most this fresh incarceration was physical, as newly released Shlisselburg inmates faced periods of varying length in other prisons of the tsar or in distant exile settlements. But even those lucky few who quickly passed from imprisonment to freedom soon realized that they still remained captive to the fortress that had stolen their youth. Though the former inmates might never see the white walls of the fortress again, they never completely left Shlisselburg, nor did it leave them. As Vera explained almost a decade after her release, "I cannot erase twenty years during which I experienced more than in the rest of my life combined. Shlisselburg always hangs over me. I cannot shake it off, nor do I want to."[2]

Vera did not expect her release from Shlisselburg to bring liberation. She felt too damaged, too transformed. With her nerves frayed from years of near-total isolation and her spirit demoralized by decades spent without the power to control even the most basic elements of her life and body, she simply wanted to remain entombed under the conditions to which and with the people to whom she had grown accustomed. If she had retained any autonomy over her fate, she certainly would have rejected the "resurrection" that her now deceased mother and the tsarist government had foisted upon her.

Four weeks after she left the prison where she had been confined for two decades, Vera was still behind bars.[3] After almost a fortnight in the Peter and Paul Fortress, where the new electric lamps signaled the passage of time from her last stay, she landed in a prison in the northern town of Archangel.[4] Although she expected to be transferred to a distant exile outpost such as Irkutsk or Sakhalin Island in the eastern section of the country,[5] Russia's recent war with Japan dictated the need to send her north. As her family and officials from the Ministry of Internal Affairs debated about her ultimate place of exile, Vera waited, confined to the Archangel Prison. In spite of the government's intentions to send her to a remote location in the far northern part of the province, the state finally acceded to her family members' requests to place Vera in a less severe environment. Both parties settled on the small town of Nenoksa, a mere 128 miles northwest of the provincial capital.[6] Believing that their fifty-two-year-old sister had suffered through enough extremes in her life, the Figner siblings were heartened that despite the White Sea coastal town's extreme climate, Nenoksa had ample provisions, access to medical care, and lovely pine forests through which Vera could stroll.[7]

The female members of the Figner family realized how important these types of niceties could be in exile. Both Lidia and Eugenia had spent more than a decade each in Siberian exile for their revolutionary activities, while the youngest sister, Olga, though never convicted of a crime herself, followed her husband into exile. The Figner brothers, however, were strangers to the practical ramifications of a life lived challenging the tsarist state. Embracing the legitimacy and material gain that came through their positions as noblemen in Imperial Russia, Peter and Nikolai had eschewed radical politics for financial security and aristocratic privilege. For Vera, both sets of her siblings' experiences and life choices would bring salvation and solace in the decade after Shlisselburg.

When Vera first laid eyes on her sisters and brothers in 1904 after a twenty-year separation, she was jarred by what she encountered.[8] Gone were the fresh-faced youths who had lived in the distant recesses of her memory. The passage of time had transformed these boys and girls into middle-age men and women whose graying hair and expanding waistlines testified to the years that separated Vera from life. Even Olga, who was barely out of her teens when she had gazed mournfully at Vera as she walked away from her for the last time in this same fortress twenty years before, was now a grown woman in her forties with a husband, child, and life of her own. In 1884 Olga's glance had conveyed the depths of her anticipatory grief and fear; now her gaze was more hopeful. While it expressed a sad recognition of the devastation of the past, her countenance communicated her conviction that Vera's trials belonged to the past. But Vera neither shared her sister's optimism nor had the energy to search for the silver lining within the clouds that overwhelmed her present state.

Realizing the depths of their sister's desperation, the Figner siblings resolved to tend to Vera's financial and emotional needs. Both Peter and Nikolai assumed financial responsibility for their eldest sister. Utilizing some of the considerable resources that they had amassed, they enabled Vera to maintain a material lifestyle that exceeded any she had ever known. For their part, the more radical female branch of the family made every effort to smooth their sister's reentry into the world and soothe her battered spirit. Although they had no extra financial resources to offer her, they gave their time and shared their company in the hopes that this demonstration of affection would compel their sister to embrace life again.

The support that Vera's siblings extended to her conformed to an emerging trend among political exiles and their families. Families of revolutionaries with means channeled money to their relatives in various exile settlements while even the more impoverished became advocates on their convicted family members' behalf or provided companionship to ease the pain and loneliness of exile.[9] For more than a decade after Vera's release from Shlisselburg, her brothers and sisters regularly beseeched the tsarist state to make accommodations to ease her physical and emotional woes. Whether it was asserting their sister's right to a modicum of space from the gendarmes who shadowed her movements or requesting that the government allow her to move to a new city or village, Vera's siblings advocated for her right to some solace and peace after two decades in the Russian Bastille.

By November 1904 Vera was out of prison and living in a small house in Nenoksa. Adjusting to life outside prison walls was a near-impossible task. Vera's mind continually played tricks on her, leading her to believe that she had caught sight of fellow inmates from Shlisselburg. While her heart momentarily leapt with joy at the prospect of being reunited with her comrades, the sad realization that she was far from all she had known for so long and irrevocably separated from the only people with whom she felt at home brought her to a new level of desperation.

Realizing their sister's precarious emotional state, for weeks Olga, Lidia, and Eugenia took turns staying with Vera.[10] But as the holidays approached, they returned to their families and the newly freed Shlisselburg prisoner was left alone. As Katy Turton has shown, families played a critical role in easing a newly exiled person's lot in life. Yet the family members who typically made the most dramatic differences in offsetting an exile's loneliness were spouses.[11] Having devoted the years after her divorce to the cause of revolution and then languishing for two decades in prison, Vera had no spouse on whom to rely. Although her sisters did an admirable job devoting their time to their fragile older sister, they had their own families to tend to. So as her first Christmas in freedom in twenty-two years approached, save for the unwelcome presence of her surveillance detail, who lived directly across the street, Vera found herself alone in her little drafty Nenoksa house.

As the cold descended and the days grew short, Vera felt herself on an emotional precipice. Having been forced out into the world to greet life, she feared that her body and spirit were not up to the task. Realizing that freedom had brought imminent death to several former inmates who killed themselves soon after their release from prison,[12] she worried that she would follow her comrades along the path of mad desperation that led to suicide.

With her sisters gone and her Shlisselburg comrades hundreds of miles away, Vera attempted to cultivate new relationships that would bring meaning to her life. Although she found some companionship in Grusha, a servant girl whom she hired and tutored,[13] her real solace came in the form of a five-year-old boy named Vania. One morning Vania had knocked on Vera's door to beg for bread and tea for himself and his mother.[14] Vera readily handed over the provisions, and so began a daily routine that meant as much to her as it did to this little family living in poverty.

Vera soon enticed Vania to stay for brief visits. As he sat at her table, Vania would draw with the pencils and paper that Vera gave him, and her woes temporarily disappeared.[15] In 1904 and 1905, as a middle-age woman living alone in exile, she felt the personal ramifications of her life choices as a profound loneliness swept over her. Desperate for a deep and lasting loving connection with another human being, Vera even tempted the boy to abandon his mother and come live with her. The boy's adamant refusal and devotion to his mother underscored for Vera the harsh reality that she was "without attachments of love or tenderness, and instead left alone with [her] gloomy and bitter fate."[16]

While there is certainly some element of truth to Vera's tale of her enticement of Vania, relating this story to the readers of her third volume of memoirs serves Vera's larger purpose of self-promotion. Having subsumed the personal element of her life into her political reputation decades before, she consistently goes to great lengths to convey the depth of her sacrifice for the revolution. Denied the martyrdom realized by Sofia Perovskaia on the scaffold, she cultivates a new category of revolutionary martyrdom. As she paints an image of herself as a former political prisoner desperate enough to try to lure a poor little boy away from his mother, Vera tacitly reminds her readers how much she sacrificed for the Russian people.

The decision to dedicate herself to the revolutionary cause led Vera down a path that left no room for maternal concerns apart from those she expressed toward her radical comrades. This was the consequence of being a woman in the revolutionary movement. While Vera's male comrades seemed to have no trouble combining their personal lives and political commitments, their female counterparts almost invariably had to choose. For countless radical women, personal lives were deemed insignificant compared to their political devotion and public personas. Although these women found opportunities and access in the conventionally male world of political activism, their access came at a personal cost. Forging a female identity in a male domain necessitated the construction of a new ideal. Thus, the female revolutionary was intensely devoted, courageous to a fault, capable of the highest levels of sacrifice, and decidedly alone. Without the distractions of love and private interests, women could prove their worthiness. Purified through their sacrifice, these radical women, with their latent sexuality, became objectified as almost virginal paradigms of devotion and virtue.

Vera's description of her interaction with Vania points to an important trend in her autobiographical writings. When she writes about the years before her incarceration, there is no trace of self-pity. Instead the reader finds determination, resolve, courage, and often a yearning for glory. But in describing her life after her imprisonment in 1883, the leitmotif of Vera's autobiographical writings becomes her self-sacrifice. Thus, loneliness, emotional instability, physical ailments, and her fears of insanity become a primary focus. With her generation of revolutionaries past their prime, and unable to take a leading role in the radical causes born of a modern, industrialized world, Vera found meaning for her life in her sacrifice on behalf of the revolutionary cause.

In the years after her release from Shlisselburg, political events underscored the association between revolution and sacrifice and thus reaffirmed Vera's historical significance. Just a few weeks after Russians celebrated Christmas, on Sunday, January 9, 1905, tsarist troops fired live rounds into a peaceful crowd of protesters.[17] The death of more than one hundred of these demonstrators galvanized Russia and incited a wave of uprisings, strikes, and political protests that defined Russia's first revolution. Days after "Bloody Sunday," Vera wrote Ludmila Volkenstein that she longed to be "thirty or forty years old with no prison scars" so that she could place herself in the midst of Russia's revolutionary ferment.[18] However, both her emotional wounds from the past and her enforced restriction to little Nenoksa ensured that the Revolution of 1905 would progress without Vera.

Although Vera did not affect the contours of this revolution, it had great ramifications for her, since the events of 1905 ultimately buttressed her political significance. Symbolized by Bloody Sunday's massacre of peaceful protesters on Palace Square, the 1905 Revolution prompted the popular conception that personal sacrifice was integral to the process of revolution. With a growing number of subjects determined to wrest political change from the intractable government of Nicholas II and a reenergized terrorist campaign conducted by both the Socialist Revolutionary (SR) Party and its offshoot group, the Maximalists, violence between the state and the revolutionaries skyrocketed.[19] State persecution of radicals soared with an unparalleled number of Russians imprisoned, exiled, or executed.[20] This new round of political repression did not diminish the perception of Vera's twenty-year incarceration; instead, it assigned it continued cultural value and ensured her revolutionary clout.

In the early twentieth century, Shlisselburg became iconic in the same way that the Bastille entered the iconography of the French Revolution. As the most notoriously arduous place of imprisonment in the Russian Empire, Shlisselburg became a sacred place of "triumph and suffering" for those inclined toward revolutionary change.[21] Russian radicals and even many law-abiding members of Russian society viewed Shlisselburg as illustrative of the government's repression; symbolic of "the great spiritual beauty" of the revolutionary movement; and, most dramatically, emblematic of its inmates' "heroic martyrdom."[22] In 1905, while Russian prisons filled with new revolutionaries and then temporarily emptied, thanks to the amnesty contained in the October Manifesto, as one of only two female survivors of Shlisselburg, Vera's suffering became enshrined, and she became a high priestess at the altar of sacrifice and revolutionary martyrdom.

Early indications of her reinvigorated prestige among a new generation of radicals came in the form of curious visitors to Vera's Nenoksa home. Along the route to the far northern parts of the province, Nenoksa was a frequent stop for those making their way to exile. Hearing that the notorious revolutionary and Shlisselburg prisoner lived in town, a steady stream of young exiled men and women paid their respects to the woman who was quickly becoming a living legend.[23] For Vera this attention was monumental. Even though she spent relatively little time with these young people, the consideration of those whom she called her flock reaffirmed for Vera her importance and standing in the revolutionary movement.[24]

During the months that she spent in Nenoksa, Vera also enjoyed visits from several dear friends as well as her aunt Elizabeth Kuprianova and her cousin Natasha Kuprianova. She even received a cherished gift when her aunt and cousin brought her a puppy to try to salve her broken heart. Although Vera publicly derided expressions of sentimentality as beneath her position as a revolutionary, she happily confessed that she loved her puppy, Luchek, intensely.[25]

In spite of the solace Luchek brought her, Vera remained fragile. After several months with little improvement in her emotional state, her relatives lobbied the government to allow Vera to relocate to her native Kazan. Citing her angina, rheumatism, insomnia, and chronic gum disease, an assortment of relatives, including her ex-husband, Alexei Filippov, secured permission from the regime for Vera to move to the Kuprianov estate of Khristoforovka.[26] Accompanied by Alexandra Kornilova-Moroza, a revolutionary whom Vera had befriended in the 1870s; her sister Lidia Figner Stakhevich; Kornilova-Moroza's two sons; her puppy, Luchek; and her ever present surveillance team; Vera left the village of Nenoksa on June 19. As her entourage arrived at a nearby village to board a ship for the next leg of the journey, a crowd of exiles from Archangel, including many prominent Socialist Revolutionaries, gathered to send Vera off from her northern exile.[27] Her resonance with the new generation was clear as the crowd of revolutionaries clamored to have their picture taken with the legendary Shlisselburg prisoner and feted her with a chorus of radical songs.[28] Between this warm send-off and the feeling she experienced sitting on a ship sailing down the Volga, for the first time since her release from prison Vera felt a measure of peace.

Yet Vera's homecoming did not prove to be the palliative that she or her family members had hoped. After more than a month at Khristoforovka, she conveyed her feelings of dislocation to A. A. Spandoni. She writes, "In Shlisselburg I was used to camaraderie and collaboration. Even in Nenoksa, I felt animated ties with [my revolutionary] flock through visits with returning exiles. But here I have nothing."[29]

Vera felt especially hopeless as the revolutionary situation began to escalate in October and she was unable to take part. On October 17 Russia's months of political tumult bore fruit when Tsar Nicholas II issued the October Manifesto. In addition to (temporarily) granting freedoms of speech and assembly, and creating a legislative body in the form of the State Duma, the manifesto amnestied many of Russia's political prisoners. Vera was directly affected by the decree, because its stipulations limited her sentence in exile to four years, after which time she could choose her place of residence.[30] In addition, the gendarmes who had shadowed her since her release from prison were dismissed.[31] Yet Vera was disgusted that her exile was slated to continue at all. In a letter she wrote to her brother Peter, she noted that since she had served only one year of her exile term, she was still chained down for another three years, a period long enough for "a person to die several times over."[32]

While Vera bemoaned her own continuing period of exile, she rejoiced for her revolutionary brothers who had been freed from Shlisselburg Fortress by the October Manifesto. With the state's permission Vera relocated to Nizhny Novgorod and moved in with her sister Eugenia and her brother-in-law Mikhail Sazhin in January 1906. There, Vera reconnected with her fellow Shlisselburg inmates over the subsequent three months. Arriving in Nizhny Novgorod days after the last prisoners left the infamous fortress,[33] Vera saw Nikolai Morozov, Herman Lopatin, Mikhail Novorusskii, and Sergei Ivanov in the late winter and early spring of 1906.[34] As joyous as these reunions were, they were undoubtedly dampened by the sad news of Ludmila Volkenstein's death. On January 10, 1906, in the far eastern town of Vladivostok, Vera's cherished friend had been shot and killed when tsarist troops fired into an unarmed crowd of demonstrators.[35] Reeling from this tragedy, Vera readily agreed to write a short biography of Volkenstein for the new historical journal *Byloe* (The Past).[36] As she celebrated Ludmila's life and commemorated her death, Vera laid the foundations for a new genre of revolutionary writing for which she would serve as a pioneer and literary muse: revolutionary martyrology. But in 1906 her intentions went no further than memorializing her friend who had survived thirteen years in Shlisselburg only to be killed by tsarist bullets in the midst of a revolutionary year.

In Nizhny Novgorod, Vera saw old friends from almost every stage of her life. Former Land and Freedom leader Mark Natanson and his wife, Vania, with whom Vera had been friendly in medical school, and Anna Pribyleva-Korba, her close friend from the People's Will Executive Committee, rushed to visit their former comrade.[37] In the midst of so many politically conscious men and women, Vera began to explore the possibility of social work. Taking advantage of the more liberal atmosphere that prevailed after the 1905 revolution, she amassed funds to build a library, feed hungry peasants, and provide aid to Jewish and Tatar refugees in Tetiushi.[38]

Vera became acquainted with the new revolutionary groups vying to determine Russia's future. Not surprisingly, she felt an affinity toward the Socialist Revolutionary Party. Formed in 1901 from a variety of "neo-Populist groups,"[39] the SR Party was influenced by Marxism but rejected "its historical determinism and dismissal of the revolutionary potential of the peasantry."[40] In order to effect a revolution in Russia, the SRs "developed a coherent defense of terrorism as a method of political struggle, arguing that it had both a disruptive effect upon the government and an agitation effect upon society."[41] These twentieth-century radicals thought of Vera and the other members of the People's Will as their "direct predecessors and spiritual fathers."[42] Yet despite her affinity with the ideology of the SRs, Vera felt too emotionally fragile to commit to the group. For the time being, she thus dismissed the idea of joining any political party and focused on cultural and literary work.

Despite the October Manifesto promulgated by Tsar Nicholas II, over the winter of 1905–1906 the "very existence of autocracy" continued to be contested by Russian radicals.[43] By the spring of 1906 the regime had embarked on a systematic attempt to "water down the October reforms by further legislation and new restrictive interpretations of the laws already passed."[44] Thus, while Vera's attention focused on cultural issues, the younger generation of revolutionaries galvanized for decisive political battle with the tsarist government. Reminded of her inefficacy Vera left Nizhny Novgorod and returned to her brother Peter's estate in Kazan in April 1906.

When Vera returned to the Russian countryside, tensions were running high as peasants waged an agrarian war against noble landowners. In deference to the increasingly agitated atmosphere, Elizabeth Kuprianova sold half of Khristoforovka's holdings to neighboring peasants and Vera convinced her brothers to sell a portion of their estates as well.[45] Although her siblings expressed concerns about her safety since she was a convicted regicide in an area with a strong monarchist penchant, Vera felt confident that the locals viewed her as a "saint" rather than as a cold-blooded murderer of the Tsar Liberator.[46] But in her native district the resilience of the perception of Vera's populist sainthood, if it ever existed, was soon to be challenged.

In the spring of 1906, Vera's native region was gripped by near-famine conditions. In an effort to help local peasants, the editors of the journal *Russkoe Bogatstvo* (Russian Wealth), for whom Lidia Stakhevich worked, sent Vera eight hundred rubles to help ameliorate the conditions in Tetiushi. To that sum Vera's cousin Natasha added three hundred rubles.[47] Vera then set out to distribute the eleven hundred rubles to the needy on an individual basis. Operating out of her brother's manor house on his estate bordering Nikiforovo, Vera seemed like the quintessential noble in exercising the arbitrary power to decide whose burdens to alleviate and whose needs to ignore. With relatively limited funds and a seemingly endless stream of needy petitioners, her brief foray into philanthropy aroused mostly bitterness among the hungry peasants. The Tetiushi masses needed everything and wanted land most of all. With her scant amount of money, it was impossible for Vera to satisfy their aspirations. With their ambitions frustrated by this seemingly careless, stubborn noblewoman, the disappointed villagers expressed their indignation directly at Vera. Not willing to exchange her halo for derision, she abandoned her philanthropic efforts before all the funds were even dispersed.[48]

Vera's inability to satisfy the needs and demands of the local villagers came at an inopportune time.[49] The government's refusal to address the peasant land issue heightened tension in the countryside, and a "full-scale peasant assault" directed against landowners was under way.[50] As she sat in her bedroom in her brother's manor house on May 9, 1906, Vera experienced firsthand the extent to which peasant tempers were flaring. Shortly before midnight, her evening reading was interrupted by the sound of clanging bells. As she looked through her window, she saw a fire in the distance and soon realized that Nikiforovo was engulfed in flames. As the dust settled, it became apparent that an arsonist had torched Vera's childhood home in anger after she refused his request for money to buy a horse.[51]

The deliberately set fire on the Figner estate was symptomatic of the tensions of the time. "Peasant *jacqueries* ravaged central Russia from 1905 to 1907, destroying around 2,000 estates."[52] In one village after another, the images of fire and smoke were eerily similar. As one witness described it, it was a "terrible picture: in the villages the bells ring, columns of smoke are everywhere, and at night the horizon is ablaze."[53]

In the aftermath of the fire, Vera mourned the loss of her childhood home and all the memories it contained. She wrote her brother Peter that although portraits of their grandfather and mother had survived the blaze, various other treasures were lost, including the family's piano and more than two hundred volumes of books she had acquired since leaving prison.[54] But more than any of the material possessions that were lost, Vera grieved her betrayal by a member of the masses to whom she devoted her life.

Although she remained in the Kazan countryside for several more months, Vera grew eager to move. With no companions or meaningful social activity to distract her, her bitterness intensified. Political developments in Russia surely demoralized her as well. In addition to the peasants who directed their frustrations against noble landowners and local officials, the SR Party accelerated their terrorist campaign against Nicholas II's government. But because of Vera's compromised physical and emotional state, she remained on the sidelines of the renewed contest between revolutionaries and the autocratic state they sought to overthrow.

After temporarily suspending terrorist activities in the aftermath of the October Manifesto, the SR Party intensified its efforts in 1906 to great publicity. One of the most sensational elements of the violent battle between the government and the terrorists began to unfold in February 1906 when a liberal newspaper published a letter from a twenty-one-year-old woman in custody for the murder of a provincial councilor in Tambov. Maria Spiridonova readily admitted her guilt in Councilor Gavril N. Luzhenovskii's assassination, but that was the least sensational aspect of her letter. Spiridonova's description of the beating and torture that she endured at the hands of the police and Cossacks, and, most especially, her intimation that police officials sexually abused her in the days after her arrest, provoked widespread outrage among the radical community and society at large.[55] Immediately thereafter, Spiridonova "gained national recognition for her heroism," and the country gained a revolutionary martyr among the younger generation.[56] Articles and stories describing Spiridonova's self-sacrifice on behalf of revolutionary ideals resurrected memories of her nineteenth-century predecessors like Vera Zasulich, Sofia Perovskaia, and Vera Figner. Although the latter never publicly commented on Spiridonova's case directly, she inadvertently reaped the benefits of the mythologizing of this latest revolutionary martyr in the Russian press.

Forced by her infirmities to remain a spectator in this latest campaign of revolutionary terrorism, Vera experienced renewed doubts about her social purpose. Even if she had felt well enough to join the SRs and commit her energies to their violent projects, the situation was more complicated than it had been in 1881. While the new crop of Russian revolutionary terrorists considered themselves the heirs of the People's Will, they distinguished themselves from their radical forebears by their indifference to collateral damage. This was especially true of one branch of the SRs that eventually broke away from the left flank of the party over this very issue. The Maximalists operated from the perspective that few people were truly innocent in Russian society. Thus, unlike the members of the People's Will leadership, who actively sought to reduce casualties beyond highly placed government officials, the Maximalist campaign did not discriminate and casually accepted that a significant number of bystanders would perish in their assaults against political targets.[57]

A dramatic attack by the Union of SR-Maximalists at the dacha of Prime Minister Peter Stolypin in August 1906 points to this tendency. Maximalists planned their attack on the prime minister to coincide with a public reception at his home. Although he walked away physically unscathed, many other guests were not as fortunate, including his young son and daughter, who were both gravely injured. The SR Central Committee immediately repudiated this attack, noting that in the indifference it displayed toward innocent casualties it contradicted "those principles that the party considered and considers morally and politically obligatory for itself."[58] In their own statement the Maximalists challenged the true innocence of many of the victims and expressed sorrow only for the injured children, even though, as the authors sneered, "they are his children."[59]

Vera avoided commenting on this dissension or on the increasing casualty count in the battle between the regime and the revolutionaries, but the scope and the scale of the latter certainly unnerved her. Whereas only thirty-five assassinations occurred in Russia between 1877 and 1881, archival sources indicate that there were more than seventeen hundred terrorists acts in the country between January and August 1906.[60] Vera realized that despite the effort the People's Will Executive Committee took to ensure that only notorious government or police officials fell victim to her party's violence, she and her comrades had inaugurated the use of political violence in the revolutionary struggle, and thus she needed to assume some culpability for the latest manifestation of terrorism. Given her emotional fragility and physical infirmities, she yearned to distance herself from the upheaval that gripped her country and the revolutionary movement. Anxious and demoralized, she decided to apply for permission to leave Russia. On November 4, 1906, in answer to the appeal of Peter and Nikolai Figner, Russian authorities issued a passport to Vera that allowed her to travel abroad.[61] She immediately prepared to return to Western Europe for the first time in thirty years.

Alexandra Kornilova-Moroza agreed to accompany her friend to Western Europe.[62] Before the two women left Russia, however, they spent three lovely days in Moscow, where Nikolai Figner paid for a beautiful hotel room where his sister and her friend lived in a manner befitting the country's social elite. But it was not only the accommodations that made Vera's trip to Moscow so enjoyable. While she was there, the legendary revolutionary met with artists, literary figures, publishers, and old friends. Young girls presented her with flowers, and deputies from both the Union of Equal Rights for Women and the Higher Courses for Women stopped by her hotel room to voice their admiration for the former revolutionary leader.[63]

On November 20 Vera and Alexandra Kornilova-Moroza boarded a train bound for Western Europe.[64] After a jaunt through Italy that included stops in Sorrento, Capri, Pompeii, and Naples, they settled on the Riviera. Ironically, it was in this traditional playground of Europe's wealthiest citizens that Vera met two of the leaders of the Socialist Revolutionary Party.

In the Italian Riviera city of Alassio, Vera encountered Evno F. Azef, one of the three leaders of the SRs' Combat Organization and a man ultimately remembered for his treachery as an informant for the *Okhrana,* Russia's political police.[65] When this double agent, who had yet to be revealed as such, met Vera, he immediately beseeched her to join the Socialist Revolutionary Party. However, she declined his advances, noting that her nerves remained too shattered to engage in political work at the time.[66] Yet it seemed as if the SRs were difficult to avoid on the Riviera. Soon after her encounter with Azef, Vera met another of the three leaders of the SR's terrorist arm. Boris V. Savinkov completely charmed her from the start. He seemed to be the quintessential new breed of revolutionary, and for that reason she asserts that she "was extraordinarily interested in him."[67] Just as she had fallen under the spell cast by the daring charm of F. N. Iurkovskii almost thirty years earlier, Vera was completely susceptible to this handsome, notorious womanizer who personified courage and revolutionary commitment.[68] Although there is no clear evidence that a sexual relationship existed between Vera and this married man many years her junior, the two obviously shared an intense mutual attraction for over a year, and a physical relationship cannot be ruled out.[69] Still, despite her attraction, she declined to join the SR Party.

In the middle of April 1907 Vera moved to Paris, where she enjoyed all that the French capital had to offer. She visited the zoo, toured the Louvre, felt humbled by the architectural splendor of Notre Dame, saw Sarah Bernhardt perform, and attended several concerts, including one by Nikolai Rimskii-Korsakov.[70] In Paris Vera met the last member of the SR Combat Organization's leadership trinity when she encountered Grigorii Gershuni. After nearly six months abroad, she felt stronger than she had in years. Thus, when Gershuni asked her if she wanted to join the Socialist Revolutionary Party, she finally assented.[71]

Eager to be of use to her new party, Vera resettled in Vyborg, Finland, a town rife with Russian émigrés and exiles in the fall of 1907.[72] Many Socialist Revolutionaries and Social Democrats took refuge in Vyborg after Tsar Nicholas II dissolved the first State Duma in July 1906. As the months passed, an increasing number of Russian political exiles arrived in town, and before long Vyborg became home to the SR's Central Committee.[73] Although her responsibilities to the SRs were not yet defined, Vera spent most of her time in Vyborg with members of the party. For a time, she lived with the family of SR leader Viktor Chernov and as a result became even more connected to the group considered to be the ideological heirs of the People's Will.

Vera functioned as an elder stateswoman of sort for the SRs. By virtue of her role as a prominent populist and her two decades of deprivation in Shlisselburg, she elicited great respect from the new generation of Russian revolutionaries, who afforded her the reverence that her elevated position deserved. While those of the younger generation were delighted to count Vera among their number, most found the Shlisselburg veteran quite intimidating. Viktor Chernov's step-daughter Olga recalls the solicitude with which her parents and their friends reacted to Vera. Instructed by their parents never to bother or disturb their infamous guest, who suffered terribly from insomnia and who found the natural noises of children maddening, Olga and her siblings consciously avoided her while their parents assiduously tried to indulge her needs.[74]

In spite of such accolades, Vera felt hopelessly lonely. While she was living in Vyborg among a number of friends and countless admirers, she poured out her loneliness in a letter to her cousin Natasha Kuprianova. Lauding her living arrangements in Finland, she admitted that she could not have asked for better physical conditions. But her problem was that she found herself "without anyone to love."[75] As she watched her fellow Shlisselburg veterans fall in love and marry in rapid succession, she yearned for companionship. Although her letter to Natasha indicates that she had a romantic interest, it did not satisfy her emotional needs. Vera wrote, "I have one friend whom I like very much in all respects, but I see him infrequently."[76] Although she does not name this mystery man, it is likely that she was referring to the married but womanizing SR leader Boris Savinkov, since the descriptions of him in her published memoirs bear a considerable similarity to the depictions of her anonymous friend in letters to her cousin.[77]

By the beginning of 1908, in reaction to increased Okhrana activity in Finland, the SR's Central Committee moved from Vyborg to Paris. With a thriving Russian émigré community that was unrivaled in Western Europe, the French capital was the logical place to establish the headquarters of this radical party.[78] By the middle of February, Vera left Vyborg as well. Although she had planned to pass several months in either Germany or Switzerland before heading to Paris, Grigorii Gershuni's untimely death hastened her arrival in the City of Lights, where she joined scores of other prominent radicals for the SR leader's memorial service in March 1908.[79]

This began a period in which Vera crisscrossed Europe on a regular basis. After Gershuni's memorial service, she temporarily alighted in Great Britain, where she established a close friendship with the seventy-year-old anarchist Peter Kropotkin,[80] and then moved on to Switzerland in the summer of 1908. In the Alpine country where she had once studied medicine, Vera hosted Eugenia and Mikhail Sazhin and her niece Vera Stakhevich, who had emigrated to Western Europe to enroll in medical school in the wake of her own 1907 arrest.[81] In addition to maintaining her relationship with family members, while in Switzerland, Vera Nikolaevna cultivated her ties with the revolutionary community both in Western Europe and in Russia.

In this capacity, Vera soon became especially interested in the condition of political prisoners in her homeland. After failing to arrange the escape of several imprisoned revolutionaries,[82] she sought more legal means to work on behalf of prisoners and exiles. Back in Paris in September 1908, she outlined plans for a nonpartisan committee whose express purpose would be to aid political prisoners and exiles. Taking inspiration from the Committee to Help Administrative Exiles established by Sofia Kropotkina and her colleague Mrs. Howe in London,[83] Vera asked the editors of *Russkoe Bogatstvo* to undertake a questionnaire about administrative exiles. Immediately embracing this task, the journal soon sent Vera twenty-five hundred responses. Moved by the tales of hardship she read in these surveys, she compiled the statistics and resolved to publicize the ordeals that the exiles' responses conveyed.

But in the midst of preparing her literary accounts, Vera received a new assignment from the Socialist Revolutionaries; she accepted her most recent task reluctantly because it reminded her of some of the most despondent days of her life. In May 1908 Vladimir Burtsev, the former editor of *Byloe*, publicly accused Evno Azef of being a spy for the Russian police.[84] Although he was a committed radical, Burtsev was not a member of the SRs and the party leadership initially paid no attention to his charges. He continued to gather evidence against Azef, and with the support of testimony from a retired director of the Department of Police, he was able to persuade the Socialist Revolutionaries to undertake an investigation.[85] The first stage of this inquiry came at the end of September 1908 when the Central Committee asked three legendary and respected radicals to examine Burtsev's charges against Azef. The three revolutionaries burdened by this weighty task were Vera Figner, Peter Kropotkin, and Herman Lopatin.

Listening to the evidence compiled in Boris Savinkov's apartment, Vera and Lopatin were inclined to rely on the opinion of Azef's closest colleagues, who trusted in the accused man's innocence.[86] But the matter refused to be settled. Burtsev continued to amass evidence against Azef, and by December 1908 few could deny that one of the top men in the SR Party was a double agent in the employ of the tsarist police.[87]

Vera's precarious emotional equilibrium was shattered by this revelation. Memories of Sergei Degaev's treachery two decades before loomed large. Humiliated by her own credulousness, Vera's physical health deteriorated yet again, and she yearned to run away from Paris and her responsibilities to the SRs.[88]

For Vera and scores of other revolutionaries, the exposure of treachery's existence at the heart of the party corrupted the essence of the SR Party and terror as a method of political struggle. As Philip Pomper asserts, "The prerevolutionary era of the virtuous terrorist who killed and died in the name of the people thus came to an end with the Azef scandal."[89] Like so many other former advocates of terrorist tactics, in the wake of the Azef scandal Vera lost faith in herself, other people, and the cause. Although feelings of rage and revenge made her regret that the Combat Organization did not murder Azef in retaliation,[90] she refused to involve herself in the matter any further.[91] In the beginning of 1909, she resigned from the Socialist Revolutionary Party and for the remainder of her life refused formal membership in any political party. However, although she severed her formal ties with the SRs, she maintained a relationship with individual party members, including Boris Savinkov,[92] leading Okhrana agents in Europe to believe that she remained an active member of the SR leadership over the next several years.[93]

Ironically, Vera's nonpartisan status allowed her to find a semblance of meaning in her life and added to her stature in the revolutionary milieu. Alleging that a comrade had told her she "should not join any party because [she] belonged to all of them,"[94] Vera assumed the guise of a paragon of revolutionary virtue who stood above political treachery and intrigue. With her past sins and mistakes purged through the decades of deprivation and isolation that constituted her revolutionary martyrdom in Shlisselburg, she became the purified version of her former self.

Without current revolutionary responsibilities, Vera retreated into her past. For the next decade, her life became defined in and through her position as the only surviving female Shlisselburg prisoner. Accustomed to the reverence paid to her by the fortress's male inmates, she was long cognizant of the fact that there were few things as "fantastic as a female prisoner of Shlisselburg."[95] Her preliminary efforts on behalf of a new generation of political prisoners and exiles only confirmed her exceptional standing as a woman who had survived the Russian Bastille. Thus she melded her two interests into one: she embarked on the literary commemoration of her exploits while utilizing her stature and long martyrdom in Shlisselburg to raise awareness of and funds for the radicals who were currently incarcerated.

As the nineteenth-century writer Constance Pipelet asserted, for women, "as for men, being forgotten is the greatest of ill fates and it is the hope of escaping it that sends our thoughts to higher spheres."[96] As a woman whose private life had been subsumed into her public role as a revolutionary, but who found her inner self unable to navigate the stress and demands of revolutionary activism in the twentieth century, Vera found another avenue to continued public significance and cultural self-representation in her autobiographical writings. Embracing a tradition among Christians who chronicled their martyrdom in print, her memoirs were intended to contribute to her own memorialization through the textual production of her martyred "self within the context of a much more public collective narrative."[97] Having already written about comrades who fell in the fulfillment of their revolutionary duty, she added her life as a new, evolving chapter. By defining her incarceration, sacrifice, and the continuing struggles she faced as essential to and inextricable from her revolutionary generation's collective martyrdom, she redefined the very notion of political, secular martyrdom. With her task ameliorated by the widespread press coverage of Spiridonova's abuse at the hands of tsarist guards, Vera's description of her long incarceration in Shlisselburg gave evidence that in the revolutionary movement, death alone did not produce martyrs. Instead, her life writings gave textual testimony to the fact that often the most grueling and cruel martyrdom was that which was suffered slowly and indefinitely, through one's reluctant survival and continuing existence.

In the early part of 1909, after the public revelations of Azef's treachery, Vera retreated to her literary endeavors and relocated to Zurich, where she passed the majority of her time writing her memoirs.[98] Despite the inherent drama of her life, she made a conscious effort to frame her life as a narrative arc in order to make her memoirs as interesting and inspiring as possible. Much of her success in these literary endeavors stemmed from the constant feedback she received. Although she spent most days alone in her flat crafting her life story, she passed numerous evenings giving public lectures about her experiences in Shlisselburg as part of her campaign to raise money for political prisoners and exiles. In these efforts she often left Switzerland briefly to travel as an invited speaker to many of the urban locales of Western Europe. In this way she vetted her life writings before international audiences. Often hundreds of people would crowd into packed auditoriums to listen to the tales of suffering she had endured as an inmate of Shlisselburg Fortress. Weaving her own experiences with the sad fate of contemporary prisoners in the tsarist empire, Vera's accounts inspired her audiences to contribute considerable sums of money for the cause.

In her recollections about the speeches that she delivered throughout Europe, Vera notes how her own ordeals in Shlisselburg moved those assembled much more than did the tales of woe emanating from present-day prisons and exile settlements. Although she never acknowledges the part played by her gender and contemporary conceptions of femininity, it is undeniable that her sex exacerbated her audiences' outrage. Thus, while accounts of nutritional deficiencies and exposure to the elements provoked pity, her description of how she was forced to cut her luxurious dark hair after prison authorities continually denied her access to a comb evoked indignation from the crowds.[99] Since she was a noblewoman and not a member of the lower classes, her revolutionary sentiments could not be ascribed to simple self-interest. Instead, her radicalism appeared to speak to a selflessness in which she forsook privilege and comfort on behalf of the underprivileged masses. Thus, contemporary conceptions of gender and class reinforced each other, and in the juxtaposition that they presented to the conditions of Vera's life behind Shlisselburg's walls, these notions transformed her from just another liberated political prisoner into a long-suffering revolutionary martyr and icon for the cause.

Vera's appearance contributed to her growing myth. The exemplary proper-looking woman of the Edwardian age, with her impeccably white collars and cuffs, prim dark dresses, stylish hats, and neatly coiffed hair, Vera's image was the antithesis of her contemporaries' preconceptions of revolutionary women. Although she was a naturally striking woman, she exhibited no trace of sexuality and no indication of an immorality beyond her political radicalism. Vera's looks played into her public persona and the reception given to her by both fellow revolutionaries and law-abiding sympathizers, and she knew it. Consequently, as the years passed, she feared the chance that someday she might not be "pretty anymore" more than she did the debilitating effects of old age and illness.[100]

The disparity between Vera's appearance and noble heritage on one hand and her violent endeavors and their dire consequences in prison on the other incited an unusual fascination among European society in a post-Victorian age. For decades, emerging notions of psychology and evolution had intrigued educated Europeans. From gothic novels to the notorious characterizations imagined by Robert Louis Stevenson in *The Strange Case of Dr. Jekyll and Mr. Hyde,* the literary public in Western Europe delighted in discovering "the borderland between the normal and the abnormal."[101] In other words, literature reflected a contemporary cultural preoccupation with otherwise law-abiding, timid individuals' proclivity, or perhaps impulsion, to commit violent or even vicious acts. A primary element of this fascination rested in the dualism between the mind and body and the extent to which bodies and appearances could be utilized to accurately read or gauge the "mental chemistry" of a person.[102] Thus, the dichotomy between the image of the demure, privileged Vera Figner and the reality of her advocacy of terrorism and the sentence of extreme deprivation she endured as a result inflamed the imaginations of those who saw her and listened to the accounts of her life.

This is what allowed respectable citizens who personally eschewed radicalism to hail Vera as a brave, virtuous martyr for the cause of freedom. Characteristic of this attitude are the introductory remarks of Professor Edward

Claparede of the University of Geneva before Vera's scheduled lecture there in 1910. Claparede reminded the Swiss audience that those assembled were in no position to judge this former regicide's actions.[103] Instead, the Genevan professor suggested that the audience reserve its condemnation for the Russian government and direct its admiration toward Vera, who showed "magnificent courage" similar to that shown by "the first reformers of the Christian Church."[104] In Claparede's opinion the members of the People's Will were "valiant fighters who sacrificed their lives for an ideal," and of these "Madame Vera Figner is the most noble incarnation."[105]

In 1910, impressed with the reception she received throughout Europe and the willingness of her audiences to donate funds to the cause of political prisoners, in Paris Vera formed the Committee to Help Political Prisoners and Exiles Condemned to Hard Labor. The organization's operating expenses came from monthly fees that she collected from Russian émigrés as well as the proceeds from her speaking engagements.[106] In an effort to avoid partisan strife, she acted as chairperson and secretary of the organization and refused to allow any Socialist Revolutionary or Social Democrat representatives on the committee.[107] In her published appeal on the committee's behalf, Vera contended, "It is within our power to ease the physical sufferings of some prisoners. We believe in the solidarity of the human race, and we count on the sympathies of all feeling people and each nation to which they belong."[108] Unlike some of her earlier philanthropic efforts, this one enjoyed immediate success. Only a few months after it was formed, her new committee collected 20,738 francs, which it dispersed among five different prisons in Russia.[109]

Given the success that her Paris committee enjoyed, Vera established similar organizations in Brussels, Antwerp, Liege, Grenoble, Geneva, Dresden, Lausanne, and Munich.[110] Even Socialist Revolutionaries living in the United States became involved when they sent twelve thousand dollars to Vera's committees in Europe between November 1911 and November 1913.[111] Through these various benevolent groups, in addition to the funds from the Socialist Revolutionaries in America, between 1910 and 1914 the committees raised 136,970 francs in Europe and 10,185 rubles in Russia for political prisoners and exiles condemned to hard labor.[112] Flush with success, Vera also established an autonomous section in May 1912 to deal with exiles who were not condemned to hard labor but who were permanently resettled in Siberia. In the first eight months of its existence, this group sent 8,000 francs to Siberia.[113]

Vera personally deserves much of the credit for the success of these philanthropic organizations. During 1910 and much of 1911, she maintained a grueling schedule of public appearances and speeches. Despite recurrent health problems, she traveled through France, Belgium, the Netherlands, and Switzerland speaking about her experiences in the Russian Bastille and the current conditions that political prisoners in Russia faced.[114] These lectures were nerve-wracking for her. Although she never seemed to falter, she confided to a friend that when giving lectures, she was "ready to disappear through the floor," and that "even when reading [the text of the speech directly from prepared notes] it is only through a huge force of will that I kept from trembling."[115] Thus, in her mind and in the minds of those with whom she had personal contact, Vera's self-sacrificial behavior continued.

Settling in Switzerland to write her memoirs, Vera soon discovered that writing her personal narrative was more difficult than detailing the lives of other revolutionaries had been. While she was able to describe Ludmila Volkenstein's terrorist activity as an illustration of her elevated humanity, she avoided penning the chapters that detailed her own involvement in political violence. She was much more comfortable with her martyrdom than the reasons for it. Thus, she first turned her attention to writing about her years in Shlisselburg Fortress, because these eulogized her self-sacrifice.

Remembering this period of her life in detail was often difficult for Vera. When the emotions that ensued from recalling her twenty years in prison became too overwhelming, she turned her literary focus to less dire times.[116] But Shlisselburg and the sacrifice it symbolized never fully retreated. As Vera crafted the chapters from her youth and young adulthood, her two-decade-long incarceration loomed large. Building toward her inevitable martyrdom in Shlisselburg, her early experiences, education, and decisions acquired potent significance for the ways they determined her revolutionary commitment and subsequent sacrifice.

By focusing on her sacrifices rather than her political ideology, Vera's memoirs transcend party lines. Her personal sacrifice became a sacrifice for Russia rather than for the People's Will. Specific political aspirations receded into the background, and her willingness to offer herself for the sake of the Russian masses and the future of Russia itself became the decisive issue of her life. Subsequently, the means she employed were secondary. What tied her to the revolutionary tradition was neither her specific political aims nor the means she employed; rather her sacrifice and martyrdom became the basis of "the spiritual relationship that linked [her] with all revolutionary generations."[117]

As Vera fashioned this image of herself in her autobiography, it became the overriding theme that infused her personal narrative and anchored her place in the revolutionary tradition. But as the most prolific spokesperson for her generation of revolutionaries, she did more than cultivate her individual identity within the revolutionary movement. By providing a literary example of suffering and sacrifice on behalf of a lofty political cause, Vera constructed the framework according to which her entire generation of radicals defined themselves. Subsequently, her depiction of herself as a reluctant terrorist whose selfless devotion climaxed in her own symbolic martyrdom helped to craft the collective historical identity of the People's Will.

Although she continued to travel throughout Western Europe periodically, in October 1912 Vera settled in the little hamlet of Baugy on Lake Geneva, near Clarens, Switzerland.[118] There she tried to balance work on her memoirs with her responsibilities to her committees to help political prisoners. Yet once again the Russian government interfered with the intellectual and social satisfaction that she found in Switzerland. Still suspicious of Vera's Socialist Revolutionary connections,[119] the Okhrana made it increasingly difficult for her to transfer funds to Russian prisoners. With her once wonderfully successful venture experiencing difficulties,[120] she stepped down as secretary and chairperson of the Committee to Help Political Prisoners and Exiles Condemned to Hard Labor,[121] became absorbed with her memoirs, and looked into the possibility of returning to Russia.

At her urging, in 1913 Vera's family petitioned the Russian Ministry of Internal Affairs to allow her to return to Russia.[122] Because her last place of residence was Nizhegorod province, the minister of internal affairs referred the matter to the provincial governor, who rejected Vera's request.[123] Although Okhrana detectives in Western Europe informed their Russian supervisors that Vera was no longer a champion of terrorist activity or a member of the SR Party,[124] there continued to be much trepidation about this revolutionary legend in official circles. Thirty-three years after she had helped to assassinate Tsar Alexander II, Vera's reputation as a powerful and violent radical figure retained almost mythic proportions for the Russian authorities. In an effort to explain why she no longer belonged to the SR Party, the secret police never considered that her emotional or physical infirmities played a part. Instead, Okhrana agents surmised that she left the party because she was disgruntled with its lack of activity and success.[125] With the government still considering her a threat, as of May 27, 1912, Russian border guards received a standing order that should she try to enter the country, she should be placed under the most serious, persistent surveillance.[126]

As Vera waited to hear if her appeals to return to her native country would be approved, World War I shattered European peace. The war not only divided Europe but also created fissures within the socialist community. Weeks after hostilities began, Vera attended a lecture by Vladimir I. Lenin in Switzerland. Before a small crowd of Russian émigrés, Lenin described the need to transform what he described as an imperial war into a civil war that would enable socialist revolutions throughout Europe. Frustrated that the Bolshevik leader left the venue immediately after his speech without taking questions, Vera was unimpressed with Lenin's performance and unconvinced by his argument. Disheartened by the carnage that had occurred in only the first few weeks of war, Vera could not stomach the thought that such bloodshed and grief could continue for years.[127] As much as she believed in socialism and the revolutionary movement, by this point in her life she could not sanction the death and maiming of millions as a means to such ends.[128] Lenin made the case that Russia's defeat in the war would maximize the revolution's chance for success. Vera disagreed and surmised that a German victory would only bring more reaction in the Russian Empire.

The war intensified Vera's desire to return to Russia. Cut off from her homeland and her major source of income, she found herself in a potentially disastrous situation.[129] Refusing to lose precious time, even before she received permission from the government she began the preparations needed to leave Western Europe after almost a decade abroad. Paramount among her concerns was the fate of her still unfinished memoirs. Fearful that Russian border police might harass her and seize her possessions, she arranged to leave her manuscript in Western Europe.[130] Meanwhile, Nikolai's efforts on his sister's behalf paid off. Upon receiving her brother's letter in which he informed Vera that Nicholas II had granted her permission to return home, she was overjoyed. In a grateful letter back to Nikolai, Vera writes, "My heart leaps. Will I really be in Russia with all of you soon?!"[131] Weeks later everything was in place, and she left Western Europe to return home in mid-February 1915.

Travelling in the midst of war was not easy but it was possible. Vera decided to take a southern route through Europe back to Russia. She traveled by sea to Greece and then moved north through Serbia, Bulgaria, and Romania.[132] She encountered no danger or trouble on her way back to the tsarist empire until she arrived at the Russian border. But as she prepared to cross into her native land after an exhausting ten-day trip, she found herself in police custody.[133] Although officials had promised Nikolai Figner that the Russian police would not harass his sister as long as she stayed away from either Moscow or Petrograd,[134] an existing directive from the previous September called for her arrest. The order contended that the "famous Socialist Revolutionary" Vera Figner intends to come to Russia and that should she arrive, she should be arrested immediately, searched, and sent to St. Petersburg to the Department of Police.[135]

When border guards arrested the former radical, they conducted a detailed search of her person and baggage but found nothing incriminating.[136] Responding to their questions about her party affiliation, Vera avowed that she no longer belonged to the SR Party and that over the past few years she had been exclusively occupied in working to improve the material circumstances of political prisoners and exiles. In answer to questions about her motives in returning to Russia, she declared that she wanted to be with her family and to be of service to the Russian war effort, possibly by tending to wounded soldiers.[137] As a result of her continued protestations and Nikolai's assurances that his sixty-two-year-old sister was in poor health and posed no threat to the regime, the police released her.[138]

With Moscow, Petrograd, and any town considered militarily sensitive now off limits to her, Vera moved back to Nizhny Novgorod.[139] In spite of her haste to return to Russia, she faced the same problems and frustrations that she had left in 1906. Bored in Nizhny Novgorod, she left for Nikiforovo in the beginning of May 1915 and remained in her native district until September 23.[140] Over these four months, she spent her time with her siblings, aunts, cousins, and old friends. Unlike the summer before she left for Western Europe, her stay in Nikiforovo was restful. In compliance with her wishes, Peter had built her a small house of her own in the middle of one of the estate's gardens.[141] Isolated from the front and far from major population centers, during the summer of 1915 she almost felt as if there were no war dividing Europe.[142]

In the fall Vera returned with her sister Lidia to Nizhny Novgorod. Unlike Nikiforovo, which seemed immune to the toll of World War I, the effects of the hostilities had started to make themselves felt in Nizhegorod province. Despite the war's material manifestations, Vera maintained her interest in cultural affairs. Determined to resurrect the society to spread education in Nizhny Novgorod, she organized lectures and exhibitions, and she and Lidia collected almost two hundred volumes of books to be distributed to locals.[143] Vera also aspired to ease the burdens of the men who had been wounded in the war. Unable to render medical care, she decided to contribute to their cultural and political awareness. Thus, she delivered two lectures at a local hospital to wounded soldiers, whose severe and extensive injuries astounded her.[144]

Vera found a welcome respite from Nizhny Novgorod during a brief winter visit to Moscow. There she visited old friends, made new acquaintances, and delighted in the city's cultural and social diversions. Back in Nizhny on January 11, she wrote to her cousin Natasha telling her how good it had been "to be among those who love me" in Moscow.[145] Relishing an occasion to be celebrated by individuals who were sympathetic to the radical cause and her life experiences, Vera notes, "In Nizhny I always feel cold and alone, in Moscow they warmed me."[146] At sixty-two years of age, Vera was most comfortable in her role as a revolutionary celebrity. Lamenting her public insignificance in Nizhny Novgorod, she wrote that her return to the industrial city in the midst of war transformed her back again from "a princess to a slob."[147]

Vera faced new concerns in April 1916 when she learned of the death of her brother Peter.[148] While saddened at the loss of her sibling, Vera worried about how Peter's death would affect her personal financial situation. Since her release from prison, Peter Figner had assumed primary fiscal responsibility for his eldest sibling and each month sent money to sustain her, no matter where she was. Although Vera had refused any part of her brother's inheritance a decade earlier,[149] recently she had anticipated receiving some form of stipend that would allow her to maintain the level of material comfort to which she had become accustomed. When she finally learned that she would receive only 550 rubles a year plus a lump sum of 10,000 rubles, she was bitterly disappointed and concerned about how a financial shortfall would affect her quality of life and her philanthropic pursuits.[150]

The stress engendered by her brother's death compounded Vera's stress and health problems. But relief seemed to be in sight. In May 1916 the government gave Vera permission to live in Moscow, although she was still forbidden to reside in Petrograd.[151] Immediately thereafter she left Nizhny Novgorod for good. After spending two months at the Orel dacha of a pair of sisters whom she had befriended in Western Europe before the war,[152] Vera moved to Moscow as autumn neared. There, she lived with her friend and former comrade Vera Lebedeva in an opulent house in the center of the city. Feeling at home and rested after her summer in the countryside, Vera Nikolaevna read chapters of her memoirs to various literary figures who showered her with praise.[153] She enjoyed the weeks that she spent in Moscow; she went to literary evenings, attended the ballet and musical concerts, and found the city's residents very solicitous toward her.[154] In spite of the accolades she received and the cultural diversions she enjoyed in Moscow, she journeyed to Kharkov in November. There she spent time with her old friend Nikolai Morozov and received the much awaited news that tsarist authorities had granted her permission to move to the capital.

By early December 1916 Vera was back in Petrograd. After a brief stay in her brother's elegant home, she moved into the Sazhin family's modest apartment on Posadskaia Street.[155] It was from this apartment just two months later that the notorious revolutionary and Shlisselburg veteran watched as the common people of the capital effected a revolution. Despite the government's fears that she would incite Russia's disgruntled masses to revolution, in 1917 she was merely a spectator as the old political order collapsed and the revolution that she dreamed of was finally realized. In the months that followed, Vera sought to take an active part in the dramatic events that were unfurling around her. But as the year progressed, the revolutionary landscape became increasingly complicated as one revolution gave way to another, and Vera Figner was forced to find her way as an old revolutionary in a new revolution.

10

AN OLD REVOLUTIONARY IN A NEW REVOLUTION

IN THE LATE WINTER OF 1917, a series of rapidly growing protests and strikes toppled the three-hundred-year-old Romanov autocracy. No professional revolutionaries took the helm. Neither bombs nor assassinations played a part. Instead, mounting death tolls in a debilitating world war, economic and industrial inadequacy, ensuing food and fuel shortages, drastic socioeconomic disparity, and the long-term corrosive effects of the autocracy itself finally exhausted the patience of the people in the tsar's capital and forced the abdication of the last Romanov tsar.

As these dramatic events unfolded in the city to which Vera had so recently returned, she experienced a flurry of different emotions. Watching the mounting protests and hearing the news that a new Provisional Government had taken control, she felt "joy, sadness for the past, and a sense of alarm" about what the future held.[1] For a woman so familiar with the sacrifices demanded by radical political change, the first revolution of 1917 seemed too swift and the transfer of power too easily accomplished. In a letter to her cousin Natasha, Vera wrote, "The first days [of the revolution] were sad for me. I kept thinking of those who perished in the last thirty-seven years. I hope for a favorable outcome and the consolidation of freedom, but I expect difficulties will arise along the way."[2]

While the revolution ultimately presented challenges that surpassed even the most cynical expectations, it immediately engendered unprecedented possibilities for former radicals to reenter the political fray. After the Provisional Government declared an amnesty for political prisoners condemned by the tsarist regime, for the first time in her life Vera breathed the air of political and personal liberty in her homeland. The former revolutionary embraced her newly found freedom and became socially active. As her country sought to define its future, she lent her voice to the political dialogue. By her own esti- mation, in the months between the February and October Revolutions, she took the stage at more than sixty public events.[3]

At each event in these harried months, Vera enjoyed the adulation of those assembled and found the attention intoxicating. With the imperial order dis- graced and a new revolutionary era heralding the prospects of a brighter fu- ture, she and her generation of radicals became a sort of "revolutionary no- bility," whom the new authorities "honored in every possible way."[4] In the frenzy of political demonstrations and assemblies that followed the February Revolution, various groups vied to have the venerable Vera Figner adorn the dais at their events. Inspired by the sense that Russia had awakened from its apathetic slumber, she found it difficult to decline such invitations. Thus, as the icy winter gave way to a spring full of promise, among other engagements she attended trade union meetings, spoke at a concert for the Petrograd People's Conservatory, and was a featured participant in a demonstration for women's suffrage.[5]

Throughout her adult life Vera believed that women were entitled to enjoy equal rights with men, but she considered a women's movement in a country like tsarist Russia, where the state equally deprived both men and women of political and civil rights, pointless.[6] The liberal revolution of February 1917 changed this situation. On the eve of a new political order, as Russians over- threw the dynasty and demanded an active role in Russia's political future, Vera believed it was necessary for women to take part in the reconfiguration of their country. Consequently, in order to ensure that women shared equally in the fruits of the revolution, she lent her voice, presence, and prestige to the Russian League for Equal Rights for Women.

On a Sunday morning in March, just weeks after Russia's first revolution of 1917, the League for Equal Rights for Women held a demonstration demand- ing that women be given the right to vote in the upcoming elections for the Constituent Assembly. The day began with speeches by a handful of presti- gious women who were committed to the cause. Vera Figner was among them. At noon the speakers and protesters took to the streets en masse as part of a procession to present their demands for women's suffrage to the Provisional Government.[7] A group of women on horseback led the demonstration of forty thousand women from all walks of life. In the middle of this procession, riding in an automobile surrounded by schoolgirls were Vera and the president of the suffrage organization. In describing the scene the British feminist press touted Vera as "one of the greatest pioneers of Russian liberty" and noted that she was cheered by onlookers and showered with offerings of flowers.[8]

While some in the crowd may have found her advocacy of political violence abhorrent, the majority of those assembled seemed to recognize Vera as a revolutionary legend. A member of the hereditary nobility of Imperial Russia, she had climbed the radical equivalent of the Table of Ranks to become revolutionary nobility.[9] Her courage, self-sacrifice, and harrowing experience in prison, all on behalf of the Russian masses, made her larger than life. The president of the League for Equal Rights for Women acknowledged Vera's contribution to the cause of the Russian people's freedom and reminded those in attendance that their newfound liberty "had been prepared not only with the hands of men."[10]

> We have come here to remind you that the women were your faithful comrades in the gigantic struggle for the freedom of the Russian people; that they also have been filling up the prisons, and boldly marched to the galleys; the best of us looked into the eyes of death without fear. Here at my side stands V. N. Figner, who has been struggling all her life for what has now been attained.[11]

With no mention of bombs or bloodied bystanders, the speaker crafted an image of Vera as a selfless freedom fighter who had made the ultimate sacrifices for the cause of Russian liberty. By omitting the specifics of both the means and the ends of the People's Will, this advocate for women's rights demonstrates how Vera became historically significant for a new revolutionary age on the basis of her sacrifice and suffering.

Weeks after the suffrage demonstration, Vera mounted the dais yet again at an event that dwarfed the women's march. With a crowd that British ambassador George Buchanan described as "so immense," nothing like it has "ever been seen in Europe,"[12] she joined notables of varying political persuasions to honor the memory of those who died in the February Revolution. Dressed elegantly in a black coat trimmed with fur and a matching hat, the former terrorist leader slowly assumed her position of honor on the rostrum. She looked lovely and graceful. Unlike the beaming Vera Zasulich, who preceded her at the event, Vera Nikolaevna's countenance had only the smallest hint of a demure smile. Both her expression and the way she held her body suggested a noble bearing. With her face largely unmarred by wrinkles, she seemed to

defy the passage of time. The beauty about which so many commentators had
waxed poetic was clearly apparent; however, the ordeals of her past remained
visible. Dealing with chronic rheumatic disease, Vera had developed a slow,
impaired gait that betrayed her sixty-four years and decades of physical deprivation. As she walked with a cane and a pronounced limp to the right, the
woman whom a commentator heralded as the "world famous revolutionary
assassin" was gingerly supported by two escorts while a bevy of supporters
jockeyed for a spot close to her.[13]

An acclaimed figure of the Russian revolutionary movement, Vera held the
crowd under her spell as she disclosed her hopes and fears for the revolution.
The woman who had given decades of her life in the hopes of effecting the
radical amelioration of social, economic, cultural, and political conditions in
Russia disclosed to the assembled masses how happy she was to be alive as
Russia celebrated its new life.[14] She told the crowd that "the path to freedom
was difficult and it may be even more difficult to preserve and fortify the freedom that we so recently achieved . . . But if we are able to establish a democratic republic through our combined harmonious efforts, and we fortify our
political and civil rights, we will not only benefit Russia, we will fortify the
democracies of all European nations."[15]

As Vera delivered these words, she stood before her newly politically liberated compatriots as a cog in the wheel of revolution. When the people of
Petrograd toppled the autocracy, Vera did not confront tsarist soldiers nor
did she march in the streets demanding change. Nonetheless she viewed both
her political agitation in the 1870s and 1880s and her decades of suffering and
deprivation in Shlisselburg Fortress as critical aspects of the current Russian
Revolution. Vera told the men and women at the memorial for the fallen heroes of the February Revolution that those who point to limited casualties of
the revolution have a distorted perspective. Recalling a story titled "The Wall"
by Leonid Andreev, Vera made a connection between 1917 and the previous decades. She told the crowd that in Andreev's story there was a wall that hid the
glorious achievement of all of humanity. At first a group of people approached
the wall, tried to scale it, but fell to their deaths. Soon a second group arrived,
whose partial ascent was facilitated by the fallen bodies of their predecessors.
Yet they remained unable to reach the summit and perished as well. "So," Vera
said, "one after another, new groups of people approached the fatal wall and
perished. Piles of corpses stacked up. Consequently each group was able to
climb higher than the one before it. Finally, when the last group arrived they

easily reached the top by standing on the accumulated bodies of their predecessors."[16] Similarly, the achievements of the February Revolution came at
the cost not only of the relatively few revolutionaries who died in the streets
of Petrograd in 1917 but also of the countless souls who were lost to the scaffold and behind foreboding fortress walls.[17]

Vera feared that in time her compatriots would forget the sacrifices of those
who came before them. Even as prime ministers fell, ministries reorganized
and symptoms of instability threatened the fragile gains so recently made,
Vera resolved to commemorate Russia's revolutionary heritage by spearhead-
ing a campaign to build a Museum of the Revolution. As early as June 2, 1917,
she delivered a public speech in which she urged the government to build such
a museum at the earliest opportunity in order to document "the great struggle
for freedom" in Russia and in the process "render justice to those who were
tormented or destroyed" along the way.[18] Her efforts bore fruit. Thanks in
large part to her personal endeavors, the Museum of the Revolution was established in 1917 and housed in the former Winter Palace on the banks of the
Neva River. As Vera wished, it heralded Russia's *entire* revolutionary past and
transcended party lines.[19]

Vera's passion for the Museum of Revolution was matched by her dedication to several other causes. Sympathetic to the hordes of Russians who found
themselves recently freed from prison and exile by the Provisional Government's amnesty, Vera established the Committee to Help Liberated Political Prisoners and Exiles.[20] Applying the fund-raising skills that she honed in
European exile as the founder of the Committee to Help Political Prisoners
and Exiles Condemned to Hard Labor, Vera raised two million rubles for this
group in just a few months in the spring of 1917.[21] Alexander Kerensky, the Provisional Government's new minister of justice, was an important ally in this
regard. As he assumed his position, the Socialist Revolutionary, who soon
would become the Provisional Government's last prime minister, assured his
fellow Russians that foremost among his priorities was to provide for the recently emancipated political prisoners.[22] Intoxicated with the possibilities of
freedom and inspired by the sacrifices of those who valiantly fought to bring
liberty to their homeland, Russians beset with their own material struggles
gave selflessly to ameliorate the condition of liberated political prisoners.

In Vera's mind one of the greatest achievements that could be realized
from the revolution was an elevation of the Russian people's cultural maturity.
When her generation had attempted to educate the masses in the late nine-

teenth century, they faced endless local suspicion and official harassment. But in 1917 the Provisional Government shared the earlier populist viewpoint that true progress required an enlightened populace and "worked to bring high culture to the new democratic audiences."[23] With official policy in sync with her own priorities, Vera organized a variety of projects designed to increase the cultural development of the Russian people. To this end, in the months after the first Russian Revolution of 1917 she instituted a massive book drive and worked on establishing a library and a *Narodnii Dom,* or People's House, in her native province of Kazan.[24]

In the spring of 1917 Vera associated with political activists of various bents, yet she remained obstinate about not joining a specific political party. She believed the treachery and betrayal she had experienced at the hands of Evno Azef and Sergei Degaev illustrated the negative consequences of formal party membership. In addition, her feelings of camaraderie, cultivated by years in the radical underground and in tsarist prisons, overwhelmed differences in revolutionary doctrine and creed and made individual party membership irrelevant. The revolutionary camaraderie that Vera sought to cultivate proved difficult to realize by the summer of 1917. In spite of the jubilation that pervaded Petrograd in the immediate aftermath of the February Revolution, once the old order was overthrown there was more dissension than consensus about the steps the government needed to take to address the ongoing crises. Although the Provisional Government was the official ruling body in the immediate post-Romanov period, its effective power was compromised by the considerable influence wielded by the Soviets of Workers' and Soldiers' Deputies and, most especially, the Petrograd Soviet. Formed in the early days of the February Revolution, the Petrograd Soviet consisted of soldiers, workers, and socialist intellectuals and activists. Similar bodies sprang up in towns and garrisons across the country. Marshaling the loyalty of the working classes, the Soviets immediately served as a counterweight to the Provisional Government.

Although both the Provisional Government and the Petrograd Soviet convened daily in the Tauride Palace, the two bodies largely repudiated cooperation. With the exception of a few moderate socialists like Alexander Kerensky who served in both bodies, most of the members of the Petrograd Soviet's Executive Committee viewed the Provisional Government with suspicion, considering it a compliant tool of the bourgeoisie. Thus, a state of dual power existed that essentially prevented any coherent and consistent attempts on the part of either body to govern the country effectively.

The political landscape in Petrograd became even more complicated in May 1917 when a new representative body came into existence. In reference to the election of representatives to serve peasant interests in the Soviets of Peasants' Deputies, the newspaper *Den'* (Day) reported, "before our eyes a powerful new organization of revolutionary forces is coming into being."[25] Yet the Soviets of Peasants' Deputies made no concerted effort to circumvent the established channels of power or initiate a new revolutionary agenda. Instead, at the first general meeting or Congress of the Soviets of Peasants' Deputies, the delegates agreed primarily to promote the freedom and self-determination of individuals and nationalities within the country and to urge peasants to insist that the Constituent Assembly, whenever it was convened, would establish a federated democratic republic.[26] Although Mensheviks, Bolsheviks, and Socialist Revolutionaries filled the ranks of politically identified members of the Soviets of Workers' and Soldiers' Deputies, SRs dominated the Soviets of Peasants' Deputies. Among the SR notables elected were Alexander Kerensky and the so-called grandmother of the revolution, Ekaterina Breshko-Breshkovskaia. Despite the fact that Vera no longer belonged to the SRs, peasants continued to associate her with the agrarian party. As a result, she received the seventh-highest number of votes for this body, outpolling such revolutionary luminaries as the radical writer Maxim Gorky, the anarchist prince Peter Kropotkin, and the Bolshevik Vladimir Lenin.[27]

In spite of serving on this body with an impressive collection of notable SR figures, Vera continued to cling to her nonpartisan status. She eschewed constrictive political identification and took seriously the notion that she and her legacy belonged to the revolutionary movement as a whole.[28] As a veteran of "the Old Guard of the Russian Revolution,"[29] she had considerable political clout and notoriety. She belonged to an exclusive club of legendary Russian revolutionary women who risked their lives for the radical cause. Referencing her election to the Congress of Soviets of Peasants' Deputies, the Western feminist press described Vera's unique stature in Russia. According to the author,

> one needs only to recall the names of Sophia Perovskaia, of Vera Zasulitch, of Vera Figner, of Maria Spiridonova, of Katherine Breshkovskaia, to bring into memory whole chapters of great social and political movements. With the utmost disregard

for their own lives, they have avenged or attempted to avenge the outraged victims of the Czardom.[30]

Thus, peasants with little inclination or ability to disentangle the confusing web of revolutionary politics in the capital chose a woman whose decades of service and sacrifice on their behalf qualified her as a reliable representative of their interests.

When peasants selected Vera to represent them, the gains of the recent revolution seemed anything but assured. The economic and military crises that provoked the February demonstrations and directly led to the overthrow of the autocracy remained unresolved. Russia's future path was uncertain, with the Provisional Government determined to delay the convening of the Constituent Assembly until at least the late fall and, persuaded by pressure from their military allies, committed to continuing Russia's participation in World War I.[31] Although the Russian people now enjoyed civil and political rights, the realities of their daily lives and struggles remained unchanged.

The magnitude of these ongoing problems and the hectic pace Vera kept over the preceding months soon proved overwhelming for her. Exhausted and overwhelmed, just after her sixty-fifth birthday, in July, she fled the political tensions of the capital and went to Finland, where she remained for a month and a half.[32] Soon after she arrived in Finland, the so-called July Days reminded her how tumultuous Russian affairs continued to be after the revolution. With an increasing number of the tsar's former subjects disgruntled by the continued economic dislocation and ongoing military conflict, a group of radical workers and sailors and an assortment of Bolshevik Party members decided the time had come to seize power by force. Although Bolshevik ideology, as Vladimir Lenin conceived and expressed it, was predicated on the need for the vanguard of the proletariat, or the Bolshevik Party, to wrest political control by force, Lenin did not support this instance of insurrection, because he considered it premature. His instincts proved correct. After three days of protracted fighting, the Provisional Government's forces defeated and disgraced the insurgency. Although Lenin fled to Finland and escaped arrest, many members of his party were imprisoned for their role or suspected role in this attempted coup d'état.

With fissures in the revolution continually deepening, Vera's initial inclination that the revolution seemed too quick and easy appeared prescient. Hearing about this latest upheaval in July, Vera grieved the apparent lack of revolutionary solidarity in her native land and worried about what it portended for the future. A letter from Nikolai Figner points to her disquiet. He wrote, "I can imagine how you are suffering from all this disorder!!?!! ... Be healthy dear, and may God give you the strength and patience to live through this difficult time."[33]

When Vera returned from Finland in the last week of August, the situation seemed to be growing worse. Despite frantic and multiple efforts to reconfigure the Provisional Government, a state approaching anarchy prevailed in Russia. Workers didn't work; peasants didn't farm; trains didn't run; and soldiers didn't fight. As Alexander Kerensky, now the new prime minister, later recalled, Nicholas II bequeathed to his former subjects "a terrible war, an acute food shortage, a paralyzed transportation system, an empty treasury, and a population in a state of furious discontent and anarchic disintegration."[34] As a result, Petrograd was a hotbed of activity. Soldiers deserted their posts at the front en masse. Ukrainians and other nationalist leaders made overtures toward autonomy, and peasants seized land indiscriminately. But perhaps the greatest perceived threat came from General Lavr G. Kornilov, who appeared to be mounting a counterrevolutionary offensive against the Provisional Government. Although Kornilov's intentions remain debatable, Kerensky reacted to the suspected threat by releasing the Bolsheviks imprisoned in July and allying with various radical forces on the left to rebuff Kornilov and his forces. The Kornilov uprising failed, but Kerensky had to deal with an unexpected consequence when as a result of their participation in eliminating the Kornilov threat the Bolsheviks enjoyed a surge in popularity and achieved majority positions in both the Petrograd and Moscow Soviets.

In the aftermath of the Kornilov affair, both Kerensky and the Petrograd Soviet, at the behest of the Mensheviks and SRs, agreed to convene a Democratic State Conference in a desperate attempt to reestablish government control and authority. Approximately five hundred men and women comprised this council that was charged with the task of serving as an advisory body to the Provisional Government until a Constituent Assembly could be elected.[35] Among the members of this body, which was quickly renamed the Council of the Republic and informally called the Preparliament, were members of the Congress of Soviets of Peasants' Deputies, including Vera Figner.

The Menshevik newspaper *Den'* aptly described the overwhelming challenges facing this new body when it noted, "The Provisional Council of the

Russian Republic starts its work in the most difficult moment of the Russian Revolution."[36] In addition to the economic and military issues that demanded the council's attention, its very position as a unifying body was complicated by the Bolsheviks' determination to challenge the Preparliament's existence. Fifty-three Bolsheviks were among the original delegates to the Council of the Republic, but their tenure was short-lived. On October 7 the Bolshevik delegation entered the "stately white and crimson hall of the Mariinsky Palace" after the ceremonial opening of the Preparliament was under way.[37] Following a series of "patriotic declarations and appeals to law and order" from a number of prominent figures, the Bolshevik orator Leon Trotsky demanded the floor.[38] "Mounting the speaker's platform, Trotsky launched into a denunciation of the Provisional Government and the Preparliament as tools of the counterrevolutionary bourgeoisie."[39] Immediately thereafter, the entire Bolshevik delegation filed out of the hall. The October 7 edition of the Bolshevik organ *Rabochii Put'* (Workers' Path) echoed Trotsky's indictment when it contended that the Council of the Republic was comprised "of persons graciously 'invited' by the ruling Bonapartist clique."[40]

Despite the Bolshevik charges, the Preparliament continued its discussions and deliberations about Russian state policies. In addition to her daily obligations to the Preparliament, Vera retained her commitment to several other cultural and social projects. She continued her work on behalf of freed political prisoners and the Museum of the Revolution and collected food, money, and books for the people in her native province of Kazan. Working with her sisters Lidia and Olga and her cousin Natasha, she amassed so many contributions that she felt confident she would soon be able to build libraries and cultural centers in the province.[41] But unbeknownst to Vera, a second revolution would soon derail her cultural plans.

On October 25, 1917, Vera and the other members of the Council of the Republic gathered in the Mariinsky Palace as usual. As they traded political news and waited for the session to start, radical soldiers and sailors burst into the building.[42] A military revolutionary commissar ordered the building cleared "without delay.[43] Horrified that the Bolsheviks were trying to forcibly dismiss a peaceful assembly with legitimate aspirations, Vera was one of "a minority [within the group] who voted not to disperse and to be removed by force."[44] Impervious to the protests from Vera and other members of the Preparliament, Bolshevik guards escorted her and other delegates from the building. Suddenly Vera found herself in a situation that she never expected in a post-Romanov Russia. For the first time, she experienced an encounter with another group of revolutionaries who came not to honor her but to remove her from her position of prominence. Shocked and dismayed, she found the Bolsheviks' forceful expulsion of her and her fellow Preparliament members "humiliating."[45]

The scene enacted at the Mariinsky Palace was repeated at various official venues throughout Petrograd as the Bolsheviks quickly overthrew the Provisional Government and announced a new Soviet government. In February it had taken only a week for the Russian masses to topple the autocracy; in October Lenin went from fugitive to leader in a matter of hours.

In the immediate aftermath of the October Revolution and the dissolution of the Preparliament, Vera was incapacitated by shock. In early December she wrote her sister Lidia about her feelings in the wake of this second revolution of 1917. Vera lamented, "I was so troubled after October 25, . . . that I was flat on my back in a state of dismay. I stopped going anywhere . . . [as] I considered it better to stay home since it was impossible for my nerves to endure this mad tumult."[46] Yet as time progressed, she emerged from her self-imposed isolation and realized the magnitude and momentous nature of the Bolsheviks' upheaval. At the beginning of December, she wrote to Lidia that "in February, March and the eight months that followed there was not a revolution. The revolution has only just begun."[47]

As she carefully considered the events of the whole tumultuous year, although she resented the tactics he employed, Vera came to see Lenin's assumption of political control as more warranted.[48] Justifying her evolved perspective to her sister, she argued that the point of revolution was to secure a better future for the masses, but the Provisional Government accomplished very little in this regard.[49] Although the costs of the February Revolution had not been great, the material rewards were similarly sparse. As a member of the Congress of Soviets of Peasants' Deputies, Vera was witness to the fact that more than anything the Russian masses wanted and needed land. In a resolution presented to the congress, the peasants called for the land to be "enjoyed by all citizens (without distinction of sex) of the Russian state who desire to cultivate it with their own labor."[50] On the day after their assumption of power, Lenin and the Bolsheviks validated the peasants' aims when they promulgated the decree sanctioning the transfer of land to the peasantry. Thus, although she found their tactics disagreeable, Vera acknowledged that Lenin's party was pushing the country forward.

In a flurry of legislation, Lenin and the Bolsheviks seemed to be rapidly transforming the political, social, and economic order. The new state sanctioned the transfer of land to the peasantry, nationalized state enterprises and banks, put factories under workers' control, declared the equality of men and women as well as that of various ethnic groups and nationalities, and proclaimed their intention to enter into peace negotiations with Russia's enemies in World War I.[51] After months of practical inaction on the part of the Provisional Government, the Soviets' rapid and dramatic activity aroused optimism in the souls of many, like Vera, who had dedicated their lives to effecting radical change in Russia. These hopes were only reaffirmed when the Bolsheviks allowed the planned elections for the Constituent Assembly to take place soon after they assumed power. Even after the votes were tallied and it became clear that the Socialist Revolutionaries had polled significantly higher than the Bolsheviks, hope remained. Vera herself was elected as a representative to the Constituent Assembly by citizens choosing from a list of candidates approved by the Socialist Revolutionaries.[52] But as the citizens of the soon to be Soviet Union would quickly discover, in revolutionary Russia hopes were all too often and too easily dashed.

Although the Constituent Assembly convened in early January 1918, its refusal to acknowledge Soviet authority sealed its fate. The four hundred delegates to the Constituent Assembly deliberated and discussed Russia's future for exactly one day. After a long first session in which the tension between the Bolsheviks and their rival political parties became extraordinarily heated, both the Bolsheviks and Left SRs (a faction within the Socialist Revolutionary Party that rejected the authority of the Provisional Government, sided with the Bolsheviks in 1917, and comprised part of Lenin's government through early 1918) withdrew from the assembly in turn.[53] Justifying their departure, Feodor Raskolnikov spoke on Lenin's behalf in the wee hours of January 6. As a silence aroused by curiosity and trepidation gripped the hall, the Bolshevik spokesmen linked the Constituent Assembly with a bourgeois agenda and the subsequent exploitation of Russian workers. Thus, Raskolnikov continued, "Not for a minute wishing to hide the crimes of enemies of the people, we [Bolsheviks] hereby announce our withdrawal from this Constituent Assembly in order to let Soviet power decide on a policy toward the counterrevolutionary part of the Constituent Assembly once and for all."[54] When the Left SRs followed the Bolshevik lead, the Constituent Assembly was doomed. Although the remaining delegates met for several more hours, when they attempted to return to deliberate the next day, they found Bolshevik guards blocking their way. In a public statement the Bolshevik leadership announced the dissolution of the democratically elected body by arguing that without the Bolshevik and Left SR factions, the Constituent Assembly "was nothing more than a smoke-screen for attempts by the counterrevolution to overthrow Soviet power."[55]

Having previously publicly supported this body, the Bolsheviks' subse-quent dissolution of the Constituent Assembly signaled an apparent insincer-ity on the new leaders' behalf, and it greatly demoralized the Russians who remained outside of the party but who were still committed to transforming the country. Vera was among this number.[56] To her, as an elected member, the Constituent Assembly's dissolution was a fresh personal humiliation, but on a more theoretical level it also seemed tantamount to revolutionary betrayal and conjured up painful memories of Degaev's and Azef's treachery.[57] Yet de-spite Vera's growing disillusionment and fears for the future of her country, she continued to refrain from direct recriminations. She was sixty-five years old, in poor health, unsure of the dynamics of Russia's various political par-ties, and without the strength to lead an outright attack—even a purely verbal or symbolic one—against the well-armed Bolsheviks. For the first time in years, she kept quiet as a means of self-preservation. Although she was not concerned about winding up in prison, she did fear being consigned to inac-tivity and silence. Witnessing the ease with which Lenin dispelled the Con-stituent Assembly and the "fundamental indifference" that the Russian people showed in response,[58] it became clear to her that if she aspired to any sort of social existence, she would have to navigate her way within the boundaries established by the Bolsheviks and the Soviet state.

In early 1918 these boundaries were not yet clear; one could argue that they rarely were in the first decade of Soviet rule. With Lenin quick to apply counterrevolutionary labels to those outside the Bolshevik fold, public figures who refused or were denied membership in the party had a precarious and nebulous path to tread. This small group of nonparty figures soon realized that if they were to maintain this nuanced existence of apolitical social activism, they would have to be flexible, politically astute, and sometimes cunning.

Critical to non-Communists' ability to retain a public role in society was the necessity to remain focused on purely social and cultural work while es-chewing a political role. Since Vera avoided political contests and concen-trated on her humanitarian and cultural endeavors, she was able to remain relatively free of official harassment. Because she rejected political affiliation

of any kind, she sought fulfillment in a nongovernmental and nonpartisan capacity. Continuing the work she had begun in Western European exile, initially there was no reason for her to believe that apolitical work by those who
did not belong to the Bolshevik Party would be proscribed. Thus, she continued her cultural and literary activities and resumed her work on behalf of
the Museum of the Revolution and the Committee to Help Liberated Political
Prisoners and Exiles,[59] which became a recognized institution of the emerging Soviet state.[60]

With political tensions rising, on January 30, 1918, Vera submitted a written request (which she authored and signed) to the commissar of justice, ask-
ing him to approve the establishment of the Moscow Political Red Cross.[61] In
eighteen pages she outlined the objectives, methods, and means of this new
organization, which had its roots in the repression of the tsarist period but
was nourished by the fertile soil of early Soviet political oppression. As Vera
described it, the organization would aspire to provide moral support and material aid to prisoners regardless of their party affiliation. Both Russian citizens and foreigners imprisoned for political crimes were eligible for assistance. Vera's own long experience as a prisoner informed the organization's
goals for aid. Thus, in addition to tending to prisoners' physical needs by sending care packages, the Moscow Political Red Cross aspired to furnish political
prisoners with intellectual distractions and cultural enrichment. Vera noted
that her group would provide these incarcerated men and women with books,
journals, and newspapers and would arrange concerts, lectures, and literary
evenings. In addition, the nonpartisan humanitarian organization aspired to
render material assistance to the families of political prisoners and arranged
meetings between prisoners and their families.

Other work beckoned the former revolutionary as well. While she lived in
Europe, Vera made significant headway on her memoirs. She wrote prolifi-
cally about her childhood, education, and years in Shlisselburg Fortress. Yet
the words to describe her involvement in the terrorist activities of the People's
Will eluded her. Overall, she could not replicate the conviction with which she
had dedicated herself to the use of political violence in 1879. Too many years
separated her from the intoxicating rush of camaraderie, danger, self-sacrifice,
and the tacit approval of liberal society. Older, wiser, and knowing the tragic
consequences of the People's Will's actions, neither Vera nor her significant
literary talents could adequately justify her motivations, decisions, or actions
during this violent stage of her life.

Despite her best intentions to safeguard her manuscript in the midst of world war, Vera had difficulty retrieving her writings after she returned to Russia. Ironically, as she struggled to obtain the chapters she had written years before, the portions of her memoirs that previously baffled her suddenly materialized. In the wake of the revolution, the new government gave her access to the confession that she had penned in 1883 in the weeks following her arrest.[62] Written while she was still secure in her decision to adopt violent measures against the state and its representatives, this confession communicated the idealism and earnestness that she had been unable to recreate in the intervening years. Thus, Vera used her 1883 confession as the basis for the chapters that dealt with her engagement in political violence; this in turn enabled the aging terrorist to avoid further introspection into this morally complicated period of her life.

Vera hoped that along with the political and economic revolutions effected by the Bolsheviks there would be a corresponding cultural transformation of the Russian people. In fact, she believed that the education and enlightenment of the masses was the key element that would allow a true socialist revolution to flower and grow. In this way Vera remained true to her populist roots. But months after Lenin's party seized power, the majority of Russia's people still languished in ignorance and backwardness as the Bolsheviks directed their attention to the country's economic instability, involvement in the world war, and confrontations with their political adversaries. Determined to lend their input into the emerging socialist transformation of Russia, several of the country's political and literary luminaries took it upon themselves to redress Russia's cultural blight. In the spring of 1918, Vera, Maxim Gorky, Herman Lopatin, Vera Zasulich, Georgii Plekhanov, and other aging, political notables formed "The Educational Society in Memory of February 27, 1917, Culture and Liberty." Although the title of the society was later shortened to "Culture and Liberty,"[63] by memorializing the first Russian revolution of 1917 the organization's original name highlighted what the group considered to be the Bolsheviks' failure to address the cultural underpinnings necessary for freedom to prevail. Vera, the vice chairperson of the society, told the assembled crowd at its first meeting, in an enlightened and peaceful variant of an old Jacobin slogan, that "culture can never thrive without liberty; nor can there be liberty without culture."[64] She believed that in this period of radical social, economic, and political transformation, the best assurance that revolutionary Russia would not falter in its quest was for people to be both educated and free. If this were to occur, the Russian masses would serve a function similar to that filled by the Russian revolutionary intelligentsia in the nineteenth and early twentieth centuries; that is, they could be the moral watchdogs of the social and political order.

Given the enormity of the problems facing the Bolsheviks, it could seem disingenuous that Vera expected cultural enlightenment to be a centerpiece of the new government's policy. But she was sincere in her opinion that the spread of culture and education was vital to the revolutionary agenda. Vera, who despite her radical undertakings remained in terms of her cultural perceptions very much a nineteenth-century noblewoman, felt that Culture and Liberty could add to the revolution some of the sensibilities that the crasser Communists lacked. Although her aspirations for the immediate improvement of Russia's educational and cultural level were unrealistic, they were typical of her long-standing idyllic view of the revolutionary future of Russia. Neither she nor her colleagues in the People's Will ever had a realistic conception of the revolution that they hoped to effect. Instead they nurtured a romantic vision of a postrevolutionary Russia that mirrored the best aspects of their often privileged childhoods without any of the attendant oppression or exploitation.

Vera's preoccupation with cultural issues was rooted in both her populist past and her privileged upbringing. Although she had rejected the lot of a provincial noblewoman many decades before the revolutionary year of 1917, from the weeks after her release from Shlisselburg she reaped the benefits of her family's wealth and connections. She declined the personal inheritance that her brother Peter offered her because of her "socialist" principles,[65] but she had no compunction about accepting regular material assistance from her wealthy brothers. Especially helpful was the support provided by her brother Nikolai, whose inheritance was substantially augmented by the fortune he amassed as a richly celebrated operatic tenor. But along with the socialist revolution came changing economic fortunes for the Figners. The family's estate of Nikiforovo was nationalized in the first year after the revolution, and much of the income that had previously helped to support Vera in times of financial difficulty was gone. Nikolai Figner's formerly indulgent tendencies were stymied, and he found it impossible to reconcile himself to a revolutionary order that aspired to invert established hierarchies of power and privilege. According to Vera, the Bolshevik Revolution was "understandably more difficult for [Nikolai] than for the rest of [his siblings] because his lifestyle and convictions belong to the past."[66] Frustrated with the havoc the Bolsheviks were wreaking with his personal fortunes, Nikolai wrote Vera that "happy were those who died before the revolution."[67]

By the spring of 1918, Petrograd was a dangerous and cold city. With Petrograd threatened by a lack of food, the spread of disease, and attack by German and Finnish forces, the Soviet government relocated the nation's capital to Moscow.[68] Although food was in short supply, desperation and crime were abundant. As Bruce Lincoln notes, "The Russians stole from their government, their church, and each other with equal enthusiasm."[69] Crime was driven by despair. The food crisis began with the crippled infrastructure's inability to get food from the countryside to the cities, but it quickly escalated as German troops, with whom the Bolsheviks desperately tried to conclude a peace treaty, seized some of the most agriculturally productive areas in the Russian empire.[70] With the government gone, bakery shelves bare, and a burgeoning level of unemployment as factories closed due to a dearth of raw materials, many Petrograd inhabitants fled the city. Vera was among them.

Subsisting on as little as two ounces of bread and oats a day,[71] and anxiously watching as cholera ravaged the city, Vera and her sister Olga left Petrograd for Moscow in May 1918. But even in the newly established capital they found it difficult to find a reliable supply of adequate food. Desperate to find the necessary sustenance to maintain her increasingly precarious health, just weeks after she arrived Vera left Olga in Moscow and moved to Velikie Luki, a city in Pskov province. She ostensibly chose this city because it was an important railroad hub through which supplies regularly passed. At the same time, since the city was less crowded than either of the capitals, one could presume that the demand for commodities was not as intense there as it was in either Petrograd or Moscow. Finally, Vera had acquaintances who lived in the city and offered a readymade network of support. However, Velikie Luki did not prove to be the palliative that Vera hoped for. As she wrote a friend from the village, "It is a bad situation here. What little bread there is can only be secured at an exorbitant price and butter is nowhere to be found."[72] Although Vera's friends fed her "out of sympathy,"[73] when it became apparent that Velikie Luki was unable to provide the restorative opportunities she hoped for, she returned to Moscow.

Suffering in Soviet Russia was nearly universal by the summer of 1918. Lenin had remained true to his word and concluded a peace between Russia, renamed the Soviet Union, and the Central Powers in March 1918. Negotiating from a position of weakness, he agreed to peace terms in the Treaty of Brest-Litovsk, which cost the Soviets valuable territory in the western part of the country, where nearly half of the country's industrial infrastructure as well as some of their most productive farmland was located. In spite of dissent within his own party about the terms of this disastrous treaty, Lenin viewed the peace as essential and gambled that an imminent revolution in Germany would soon nullify the treaty's terms. Although the treaty was indeed nullified in November 1918 with the Triple Entente's victory in World War I, the ruinous peace agreed to during the previous spring ruptured precarious alliances in the Soviet government. When the Left SRs withdrew from Lenin's government in protest over the Treaty of Brest-Litovsk, there was little to stop the country's descent into civil war.

Outraged by one-party rule, draconian food policies, and the humiliating peace treaty, an assortment of Russians resolved to dislodge the Bolsheviks from power. By the summer of 1918, former tsarist military officers, members of persecuted political parties, disgusted and frightened nobles, and units of a displaced Czech Legion, all collectively referred to as the Whites, engaged the recently renamed Communist Party and its supporters in a bloody civil war. While the White offensive was primarily limited to the frontier areas of the empire, opposition parties and committed individuals determined to eject the Bolsheviks from power brought the battle to the heart of Lenin's dominions. Among the Bolsheviks' most vociferous enemies were their former colleagues, the Left SRs, who turned the terrorist tactics employed by the SRs Combat Organization before the Revolution against the Soviet state. Lenin himself fell victim to counterrevolutionary violence when an unaffiliated radical named Fanny Kaplan shot and seriously wounded him in August 1918. Although Kaplan acted alone, the Communists used the assassination attempt as an excuse to exterminate their opponents, most especially the SRs, and unleashed a general wave of terror.

With each battle and every incident of persecution, fear, desperation, and repression became more widespread. Leading the charge against the individuals and groups who stood in opposition against the Communists was the All-Russian Extraordinary Commission to Combat Counterrevolution and Sabotage (Cheka) led by Felix Dzerzhinskii. Using extralegal means, the Cheka consigned untold numbers of opposition members to prison, exile, or an early death before the firing squad. Included among those executed in this counterrevolutionary offensive were the members of the imperial family. Concerned that the family could be used to galvanize and unite the various elements comprising the White forces, the Communists decided to murder the family before Ekaterinburg, the Urals town to which the Romanovs had recently been relocated from the outskirts of Petrograd, fell to the enemy. Thus, during the night of July 16–17 local Bolsheviks executed Nicholas II; his wife, Alexandra; their five children; and several trusted members of their inner circle in a basement room of the Ekaterinburg house ominously referred to as the House of Special Purpose.

The cold-blooded execution of the Romanov family illustrates the violence and terror that characterized the Russian Civil War. In Vera's abundant correspondence from the summer of 1918, the war is barely mentioned. At no point does she discuss the political ramifications of this internecine battle or her inclination toward its resolution. Instead, she remains focused on the food shortages that prevail. Given Vera's revolutionary history, this is significant and her experience is instructive. If a woman who devoted her life to revolution is so overwhelmed by the struggles she faces to find the basic necessities of life that she abdicates interest in the political battle, it is unthinkable that less politically astute Soviet citizens would exhibit a preference rooted in ideology. Instead, support and opposition largely ebbed and flowed during the civil war of 1918–1920 according to issues of food, hunger, and physical suffering.

Back in Moscow after spending the summer in Velikie Luki, Vera balanced her time between writing *Shlissel'burgskie Uzniki* (Shlisselburg Prisoners), a series of biographical sketches of her fellow Shlisselburg prisoners, and numerous articles for political journals like *Byloe* along with the seemingly unending task of finding food. Although there were supplies in the newly established capital, they were priced out of the reach of most Russians. Vera's literary work provided her with a steady income, but the cost of living was so high that her earnings disappeared almost as soon as she received them. By the beginning of 1919, she was surviving, but as she told her aunt, her continued subsistence was in large part thanks to several friends who helped her procure food.[74] Just as she had discovered the previous summer, Vera learned that personal connections were essential to survival in the civil war.

The difficulties of daily life only compounded Vera's health problems. By the winter of 1918–1919, she suffered from frequent colds, chronic rheumatoid arthritis, sclerosis, and deteriorating eyesight.[75] Her emotional health was also increasingly fragile as she struggled to face the chronic loss and grief that seemed to plague her.

Vera barely had time to recover from her brother Peter's death when she learned that Nikolai Figner had passed away on December 13, 1918, in Kiev.[76] Because of Nikolai's stature as a world-renowned operatic tenor, Vera had always felt as if he were safeguarded from many of the dangers of life in the Soviet Union. Just before she heard of her brother's death, Vera wrote her aunt, "Nikolai will be protected because he is [such a] significant artist."[77] Indeed, Nikolai had enjoyed a brief respite from Communist rule in the months preceding his death. Working at the Kiev Conservatory, he had found himself in a region administered by the former tsarist general Pavlo Skoropadsky, in which the general, who enjoyed the protection of German forces, reinstituted "the old world of imperial privilege that the Revolution had swept away."[78] But as the German Empire collapsed, so too did this last bastion of the old Russia. As a new round of fighting gripped the region, Nikolai Figner died alone, far from his beloved St. Petersburg, from complications from diabetes.

Nikolai's death came at an especially difficult time for his eldest sister. Only weeks before, her close friend Herman Lopatin passed away, and after nine months with no letters from or news about Eugenia Sazhin, Vera feared that her sister was dead as well.[79] The Sazhins had moved to Grozny just before the October Revolution. Months later, as Chechen groups, Cossacks, and White armies struggled for control of the region, Grozny's oilfields were ablaze, its rail lines were destroyed, and Grozny was essentially cut off from the rest of the country.[80] Adding to Vera's emotional distress was the continual stress resulting from the deprivation in Moscow. Consequently, when Lidia Stakhevich moved with her youngest daughter, Vera, to Orel province, Vera Nikolaevna made plans to join them.[81]

Newly pregnant and unmarried, Vera Stakhevich left Moscow to take a medical job at a sugar factory in Lugan, several hundred miles to the south; her mother accompanied her to help with the baby when it was born. With the Stakhevich women away, Vera Nikolaevna experienced deep pangs of loneliness that the severe anemia that left her confined to bed for days at a time did nothing to improve. Although she worried about her youngest sister, Olga, who was hospitalized in Moscow with kidney disease, and the security of her apartment and possessions, given the pervasive crime and corruption in the capital, the state of her own health dictated a change of venue.

Traveling by train in a country torn by civil war was a difficult prospect. In the Soviet Union in 1919, in order to secure "a ticket and a seat on a train, one had to have an official traveling permit, obtained from Soviet government institutions," which could be obtained only through personal connections.[82] Given her revolutionary pedigree, Vera had personal connections with many prominent public figures. She took advantage of this situation in the spring of 1919. None other than Leonid Krasin, the newly appointed commissar of railroads, arranged for Vera to receive a third-class ticket, albeit in a private compartment, from Moscow to Lugan in May 1919. Writing to a friend, Vera brags that because of Krasin's personal directive, no one, not even the railroad employees, disturbed her from the time she boarded until she disembarked in Lugan.[83]

In spite of her private accommodations, the journey was physically exhausting for the almost sixty-seven-year-old woman, and her nose bled for days after she arrived. Although her chronic anemia worsened as a result, the food situation in Lugan was not as desperate as it was in Moscow, and after a few weeks Vera's health stabilized. Yet the struggles and uncertainty of the time took a toll. In a letter to her aunt Liza, Vera bemoaned the fact that "economic conditions are such that people like us, of the cultured class, are brought to death from exhaustion, illness and suicide."[84]

Vera's lament to her aunt points to one of the paradoxes of the revolutionary's personality and attitude. Despite the deprivation that she endured in Shlisselburg, and despite her voluntary renunciation of her inheritance, Vera still thought of herself as a member of a privileged class. From the time she left prison, and certainly ever since she left Russia in 1906, she had enjoyed the benefits of wealth. Provided for by her brothers, Vera had the luxury of living very comfortably in a number of venues throughout Western Europe while publicly bemoaning the inequities of socioeconomic privilege. She never acknowledged the paradoxes of her situation. Imagining herself as a noblewoman who sacrificed privilege for the Russian masses, apart from the years she spent as an unwilling guest of the Russian state penal system her deprivation was voluntary and partial. As a result, it could be donned and abandoned at will. But when the Soviet revolution inverted systems of privilege, she lost this control and experienced involuntary deprivation for the first time in more than a decade. Now relegated to being truly one of the masses, she grew uncomfortable and indignant.

The challenges Vera faced became more pronounced when Olga Florovskaia joined her sisters in Orel that summer. Although only recently released from a Moscow hospital, Olga made the arduous trek to Lugan. Unlike Vera, whose health had improved with her move to Lugan, Olga's quickly deteriorated. By the end of the summer, Vera spent much of her day feeding Olga and in general caring for her as she would a small child.[85] Exhausted from the daily struggles of life, and with her heart aching for the darling sister she watched slowly fade away, Vera felt physically exhausted and emotionally devastated. Although Vera's trials would continue, her youngest sister's ordeal came to an end when she passed away on September 25, 1919.[86]

Even after Olga's death, peace did not return to the Figner-Stakhevich household. With her niece having recently delivered a baby boy, Vera's nerves were frayed from the physical demands of tending to the house, listening to the cries of her infant nephew, and grieving for her sister Olga. But the greatest threat came with the encroaching civil war front. As Vera nursed her sister in her dying days, White armies captured Kursk and Voronezh and General Anton Denikin's forces captured the nearby city of Orel.[87] In the last days of her youngest sister's life, Vera and the other members of her household anxiously expected an invasion by the White general at any time.[88] As the war heated up only miles from Lugan, the roar of cannons seemed to threaten calamity. Certainly the stories of atrocities committed by the invading forces could have done little to ease fears in the Figner-Stakhevich household. Unable to flee because of their dying sister, the Figner women and their young charge were powerless to defend themselves. But almost as quickly as the White army advanced, its position became untenable. Fearing a counterrevolution more than Soviet rule, the Russian peasantry threw their support behind the Reds, and the White armies were forced to deal with upheaval at their rear.[89]

As the rifle fire of the nearby war receded, Vera settled into a period of relative normalcy after Olga's death. Coming to terms that she might never retrieve her half-completed memoir from abroad,[90] Vera set about rerecording her life experiences as she coped with her grief. To her surprise, in spite of all the disruptions in her life, she wrote quite a bit in a relatively short span of time. She also started to give academic instruction to two local schoolgirls. In the months after Olga's death, Vera taught geography to her cook's niece and French to the daughter of the local priest.[91] But a new crisis lurked.

As Vera lamented to a friend, a new "catastrophe befell" her family in December 1919 when Vera Stakhevich contracted typhus.[92] As her niece's health rapidly deteriorated, Vera Nikolaevna's sense of hopelessness escalated. Four days before the younger Vera succumbed to the disease, her aunt wrote a friend that she fully "expected that soon all of us will fall sick with this awful illness."[93] While no one else in the house contracted the virus, the repercussions of this bout with typhus were disastrous for the Figner-Stakhevich household. Within three weeks of Vera Stakhevich's infection, the young woman was dead and her son, Sergei, orphaned. Overcome with grief at her daughter's burial, Lidia suffered a debilitating stroke that left her unable to speak and caused irrevocable paralysis of her right side.[94]

Suddenly the sixty-seven-year-old Vera was immersed in caring for her sister and great-nephew and no longer had any time to write or teach. Instead she spent her days washing dishes and clothes and tending to all the needs of Lidia and little Sergei. Although she had a cook and a peasant nurse who were supposed to ease her burdens, Vera complained that these women were merely a drain on the family's meager resources.[95] She even suspected that one of the servants was robbing the family.[96] Without her niece's income from the sugar factory, the family's financial straits soon became desperate, and Vera began to assess which of her deceased niece's possessions she could sell for food. In January 1920 she wrote to a friend, "I would have to check the urge to scream if I only had the strength to scream."[97]

The only bright spot in Vera's life during this awful period was her dog, "Come-here." Found by her niece in an abandoned hut at the front, Come-here was lovingly adopted by the Figner-Stakhevich clan.[98] In the wake of so many illnesses and deaths, Vera found consolation and the love she craved in her canine friend. But in the early months of 1920, it looked like she might soon be separated from her faithful companion as well. After Come-here was bitten by a dog that was thought to be rabid, the local veterinarian gave Vera chloroform to use on her pet if it began to exhibit signs of rabies. Yet Vera knew she would never use the chloroform on her "friend." Instead, immersed in her own personal tragedy, she contemplated using the drug on herself and bringing an end to her ordeals.[99]

Throughout all the trials she endured in her life, Vera was never so desperate as she was in the winter of 1920. In the midst of her troubles she disclosed to a friend:

> If you knew what I have to endure, what it takes to finish the day, how I spend my nights. If you only knew! Unfortunately, I am completely unsuited for such a life. Although I was able to endure Shlisselburg, I am not sure that I can endure this.
> [. . .] I feel that if I am not saved in a couple of months I will have to emulate the Romans who died by cutting open their arteries.[100]

Vera's desperation is indicative of many Russians' situation in the midst of the civil war. Hunger and disease became Soviet citizens' constant companions. Young women prostituted themselves for food, and other desperate souls sold family heirlooms and scant possessions in order to fill their bellies until the struggle to survive began anew the next day. Death was everywhere. For some, fear and suffering were so intense that death seemed a welcome relief.

In answer to the desperate, almost suicidal letters that Vera circulated to her friends, Alexandra Bakh arrived. A doctor and longtime friend of Vera's, Bakh managed to traverse the war-torn nation to collect Vera and bring her back to Moscow.[101] In her preparations to leave Orel, Vera arranged to move her sister and great-nephew Sergei into the Poltava home of Lidia's other daughter, Tatiana Stakhevich. But Lidia never left Lugan. The sister who had introduced Vera to revolutionary activism died on March 9, 1920.[102] Vera did not grieve her sister's death. Instead, she considered the sister she knew to have died more than two months earlier, when Lidia was incapacitated by her stroke.[103] With her sister gone and her niece Tatiana scheduled to raise Vera Stakhevich's son, Sergei, Vera Nikolaevna did not even wait for Tatiana to arrive from Poltava before she abandoned the town where she had lived through so much grief. Instead, she left her great-nephew with friends in Lugan and moved to Moscow.[104]

Vera's situation improved with her relocation to the Soviet capital, but the trauma of the past year had taken its toll. The civil war had claimed three of her siblings as well as her niece and namesake. She had not heard from her sister Eugenia or from anyone in the Sazhin family for two years. Desperate to learn Eugenia's fate, Vera wrote her from Moscow: "It has been two years since I have had any news of you and I do not know if you are alive or dead. In the time since we have been in contact, both Russia and our family have endured terrible ordeals . . . Our family is dying."[105] She implored Eugenia to come to Moscow: "If money is needed in order to engineer your escape, I can send you some from my own funds and some from the coffers of the Political Red Cross."[106] Vera's pleas were answered, as the Sazhins survived the chaos of the civil war in the Caucasus and returned to Moscow in June. By that time, however, Vera was dealing with a terrible case of dysentery that left her emaciated and bedridden.[107] Unable to recover independently, she entered a sanitarium where she remained for almost six weeks.[108]

Soon after her release in the early autumn, Vera met Emma Goldman for the first time. Acquainted with the famed revolutionary's image through photos, Goldman was shocked to find Vera in such a weakened physical state. To encounter Vera, whom Goldman found so "gracious of manner, witty, [and] with infinite humanity," so woefully malnourished horrified the American expatriate.[109] Goldman realized the economic devastation in the country, but she also was aware of the special rations that the Soviet state extended to its prominent citizens, including the academic rations that it provided its politically reliable intellectuals. Discovering that Vera was not among those receiving academic rations from the state, Goldman notified Anatoly Lunacharsky, the commissar for education and enlightenment, who immediately rectified the "oversight."[110]

By mid-October Vera's deprivation seemed a thing of the past. She had moved in with her sister Eugenia and her family, and the extended family pooled their growing resources. In a letter to her niece Tatiana, Vera wrote that she wanted for nothing and had no need for care packages from the country. With the income from her copious writings and the academic ration bestowed on both her and her brother-in-law Mikhail Sazhin (also a former revolutionary) by the Soviet government, Vera asserted that she and the Sazhins now "lived like bourgeoisie."[111]

By the fall of 1920, Vera was one of a small group of Soviet citizens who enjoyed a semblance of privilege from the state. Well known as a survivor of tsarist repression and gaining notoriety as a chronicler of the revolutionary movement, Vera was an aging icon whom Lenin's government saw fit to accord some consideration as they claimed her as a radical forebear. Having framed the foundation of her revolutionary activism in and through her confrontation of the tsarist autocracy and her ensuing sacrifice in Shlisselburg, she was both a powerful and innocuous enough figure for the Communists to claim. With her aging and often infirm body preventing her from entering directly into the political fray, the Soviets had nothing to gain and much to lose if they harassed the sixty-eight year old revolutionary veteran. Thus, they co-opted her as a radical ancestor, dispensed material privileges and cultural honors to her, and effectively neutralized the possibility that she could be a figure around which the political opposition could rally.

Because she was a woman, and especially because she was an attractive woman, Vera's symbolic power was even more pronounced than that of her male counterparts. In much the same way that the purified and nonthreatening allegorical variants of real French women were used by French revolutionaries to elicit support and loyalty among their citizens, Vera's image as an aging, sanctified, and still beautiful revolutionary woman allowed her to become an effective representation of the new Soviet ideals. As a living martyr and revolutionary saint, her presence and even references to her evoked a multilayered emotional response that was grounded in reverence and veneration. The radical Peter Kropotkin's pronounced reaction to a visit from Vera is illustrative of an esteem and attraction that transcended party lines. After Vera spent two days with Kropotkin and his family in 1920, he noted in his journal, "Vera Figner just left. She is so beautiful, she is worthy of worship."[112]

Functioning as a symbol of the purified revolutionary ideals of the past allowed Vera the latitude she needed in order to carve out a public role for herself in the new Soviet state. It also afforded her the opportunity to commemorate the contributions and sacrifices that she and her generation had made to and for the revolutionary cause. An essential element of this celebration was the writing and publishing of the biographies and autobiographies of radicals who were active in the decades before the Bolshevik Revolution. By publishing her memoirs and encouraging other revolutionary veterans to do the same, Vera hoped to "save a trace of our lives, our aspirations, victories, and defeats," for a future generation.[113] She worked tirelessly to ensure that the story of the revolutionary movement before October 1917 was not forgotten. In addition to the seven volumes of her memoirs that she published, Vera wrote numerous articles, served on the editorial board of *Katorga i Ssylka* (Hard Labor and Exile), and even produced the notes for the section of *Granat's Encyclopedic Dictionary* of prominent figures in the Soviet Union and the October Revolution that pertained to figures of the 1870s and 1880s.[114]

The tone that Vera found for her memoirs in Western Europe served her well in the Soviet period. Her motif of self-sacrifice for the cause of the Russian people transcended party lines. By providing a literary example of suffering and sacrifice on behalf of a lofty political cause, she constructed the framework according to which her entire generation of radicals defined themselves. By framing their revolutionary experience in their collective sacrifice, she and the other nineteenth-century radicals who penned their memoirs defined their place within the Russian revolutionary tradition by their martyrdom. They subsequently sanctified their cause and purified their efforts. Theirs was the generation that abandoned privilege and personal aspirations in order to fight on behalf of the Russian masses. Theirs was a party in opposition to the tsarist state. They were the victims of the secret police. They were the souls incarcerated in political prisons for their efforts to emancipate the Russian masses. They were the ones forced to witness their comrades' demise on the scaffolds of the tsars. They did not define themselves by the violence they committed but rather by the violence they endured. Their own victims became practically inconsequential as surviving members of the People's Will defined themselves, their comrades, and their collective place within the Russian revolutionary tradition not according to their terrorist acts but according to the punishments they endured as a result.

With the Communists' victory over the White armies, and with the civil war settled, many Soviet citizens anticipated a return to relative normalcy by the end of 1920. For Vera this entailed returning to her literary efforts full-time. But increasingly the old revolutionary saw signs that *Gosizdat*, the state publishing house, was reining in non-Communist authors and interfering with their publications. Determined to protest the state's capricious intervention in the literary field, on December 23, 1920, Vera called upon non-Communist writers to demand that the Eighth All-Russian Congress of Soviets, which was then in session, safeguard "the freedom of authors which is now being turned over to the arbitrary rule of state publishing."[115]

Vera's concerns emanated from her personal experience. For weeks at the end of 1920 she and Zadruga, the independent publishing house with which she had recently signed, had lobbied the state publishing agency in order to get the necessary permission to print the first volume of Vera's memoirs. When bureaucratic silence resulted, she appealed directly to Anatoly Lunacharsky.[116] Her advocacy on her own behalf did the trick. Relaying her relief and excitement in a letter to her niece, Vera writes, "Today, unexpected joy! It seems thanks to my protests and conversations with Lunacharsky, State Publishing gave Zadruga permission to publish my books."[117] While thrilled with her personal triumph, Vera realized that not every author could navigate such an arbitrary publishing process as successfully as she could. In fact, she was not confident that she would find success a second time. Thus, she hoped that the Eighth All-Russian Congress of Soviets would address the issue and make an official recommendation for ensuring publishing freedom in the country.

Soon after Vera learned that her book would be published, she lost one of her key allies in her publishing battle when her close friend Peter Kropotkin passed away in February 1921. Deeply saddened by the loss of another friend, Vera channeled her grief into public efforts to perpetuate the anarchist's memory. As the chair of the committee to commemorate Kropotkin, she worked tirelessly to establish a museum in the house where he was born and to publish a monthly bulletin in his honor.[118]

The calendar year after Kropotkin died was politically decisive in the Soviet Union. Although the civil war ended in a Communist victory, Lenin and his party were just as determined as ever to eliminate any political opposition in the Soviet Union. Beginning in the spring of 1921, the regime unleashed a new wave of repression against rival political parties and their members. Vera watched this trend with increasing alarm. In a speech she gave commemorating both Kropotkin and the recently deceased V. G. Korolenko in 1922 on the first anniversary of Kropotkin's death, Vera highlighted the difference between these two men's ideals and the political reality in the Soviet Union. She contended that Kropotkin and Korolenko were "two luminaries of the ideas of humanity and justice."[119] At any point in history, she asserted, the deaths of two such men would be occasions of grief. But in the atmosphere created by the civil war and its repressive aftermath, where "bloody uprisings, executions and every possible repression," prevailed, the loss of these "apostles of humanity" was a tragedy.[120] In the midst of Russia's current "civil strife and economic and moral ruin," Vera asserted that "the best honor for [Kropotkin and Korolenko] would be to propagandize their humanitarian ideas of truth, justice, and social initiative."[121]

Vera used her remarks at this ceremony not only to propagate the ideals of the two men being commemorated but also as a means to implicitly convey her criticism of the regime's recent policies and decisions. Without directly indicting the Communists, Vera made her displeasure clear. Refusing to become involved in the party-directed collective lie that suggested a higher moral order was currently being implemented in the newly formed Soviet state, her daring indictment of the "moral and economic ruin" of the country was dangerous indeed. Vera's penchant for testing the limits of the Communists' patience was also apparent in a powerful speech she gave in memory of Egor Sozonov in 1921. In her description of the Socialist Revolutionary who assassinated the reactionary minister of the interior, Viacheslav Plehve, in 1904, Vera stressed the revolutionary continuity between the People's Will and the Social Revolutionary Party.[122] Less than a year after Lenin declared that "the place for rival socialists was behind bars or in exile,"[123] Vera's celebration of the SRs as the true heirs of the People's Will was brazen. Her point, however, was clear. In a state where the ruling party claimed to embody all that was celebrated in the rich revolutionary history of the country, one of the legendary figures of that history suggested an alternate successor, thereby deriding the political autocracy that was emerging in the Soviet Union.[124]

With the establishment of the New Economic Policy and its introduction of state capitalism and a measure of private trade in the spring of 1921, Lenin and his government found it all the more imperative to silence any possible political challenge to their authority, especially those emanating from the left. As a result, the number of both prisons and their inhabitants was on the rise and the treatment of socialist prisoners was deteriorating.[125] Vera was intimately involved with this issue through her work with the Political Red Cross. With its offices housed in the same building on Kuznetsky Most as the Cheka, the Political Red Cross and its representatives worked to improve the quality of food in political prisons, facilitated correspondence between prisoners and their families, and actively investigated charges of abuse on the part of prison administrations.[126]

Although the Political Red Cross was a legal organization, because of the sensitive nature of its work the Cheka occasionally harassed the group. As the government's suspicion of the political opposition grew, so too did their uneasiness with those who came into contact with it. On May 20, 1921, Cheka guards surrounded the offices of the Political Red Cross, detained both the workers and petitioners that they found there for the remainder of the day, and conducted a thorough search of the premises.[127] Although Vera did not experience this harassment directly, since she was temporarily hospitalized for some of her recurrent health problems at the time,[128] she was incensed at this new outrage. Despite the harassment of its members by the security police, both the membership and the revenues of the Political Red Cross continued to grow, and in Vera's estimation the organization's efforts to help political prisoners and exiles proved more effective.[129]

Another area of humanitarian aid to which Vera lent her efforts in 1921 was the movement to ease the suffering of victims of a devastating famine gripping the Volga region. "As news of the Volga famine began to reach the capitals in spring 1921, many intellectuals felt compelled to assume their customary place as helpmate to the Russian people, particularly in its hour of greatest need."[130] The magnitude of the crisis compelled Lenin and his colleagues to sanction these intellectuals' establishment of the All-Russian Committee to Aid the Starving. However, the Soviet government stipulated that the group's organizers would be joined on the committee by a contingent of Soviet officials. In addition, the government formed its own commission to deal with the crisis when it established the Central Commission to Aid the Starving, or *Pomgol*, under the Central Executive Committee.[131] While both organizations aimed to help the victims of the famine, their fields of activity were not identical. One of the areas in which the nongovernmental committee had an advantage was in the soliciting of funds from abroad. But this ability to appeal to disparate forces abroad also made the Soviet government suspicious and ultimately made the dissolution of the All-Russian Committee to Aid the Starving a foregone conclusion.

Formed in July 1921, the All-Russian Committee to Aid the Starving was an unusual organization in the post–civil war period. While the group claimed an impressive list of high-ranking Communists as members, in conformity with the stipulations demanded by the government, the heart of the organization was found in the humanitarian impulses of a prestigious array of non-Communist luminaries. As Communists like Lev Kamenev and Alexei Rykov represented the government's concerns, venerable public figures like Maxim Gorky; Lev Tolstoy's daughter, Aleksandra; Vera; and an assortment of writers, intellectuals, artists, and former political figures strove to help their fellow Russians who were on the brink of starvation. With the famine poised to claim millions of lives, this committee wasted no time in tackling its work. Focused on tending to the plight of children and invalids, the All-Russian Committee to Aid the Starving sent two railroad cars with enough provisions to feed six and a half million starving children in the Volga region by early August.[132] United by the humanitarian emergency gripping the nation, Communists and non-Communists seemed united in their resolve.[133]

But harmony between the two groups was illusory. Although Lenin originally sanctioned a delegation from the All-Russian Committee to Aid the Starving to travel abroad to solicit funds,[134] as the planned departure date grew closer, the state's trepidation grew. When Lenin's government signed an agreement with the American Relief Administration—a nongovernmental organization run by Herbert Hoover—on August 20, both the All-Russian Committee to Aid the Starving and their proposed fund-raising trip abroad became superfluous.

On August 27, 1921, just one month after the organization formed, and with the famine still raging, the Soviet government dissolved the All-Russian Committee to Aid the Starving.[135] With claims that its members were "slaves to political consideration,"[136] Cheka agents descended on a meeting of the committee and arrested its members. However, not all of the members in attendance were led to Soviet prisons. While thirty-two non-Communist members found themselves behind bars, Vera Figner and a handful of other notables were escorted home.[137]

Even with this organization disbanded and its membership harassed, Vera remained committed to her work helping famine victims. The vehicle she used was a group called the L. K. Tolstoy Moscow Committee to Render Help to Famine Sufferers, which she and several other notables formed even before the All-Russian Committee to Aid the Starving was dissolved. Unlike its national counterpart, this group's focus was regional and its members avoided international fund-raising. Subsequently, the Soviets permitted its continued existence, and the impact that it made was significant. Amassing funds in excess of thirty million rubles, or approximately twenty-five thousand dollars,[138] this committee opened feeding stations in Moscow, sent several train cars filled with provisions to Samara, relocated a commune from the famine area, and supported children's colonies in and around the capital.[139]

By the fall of 1921, Vera was able to objectively appraise her place in the new Soviet order. Although she occasionally encountered state-erected obstacles to the realization of her literary and cultural activities, she enjoyed considerable opportunities under the Communists. She was not a Communist herself, yet her revolutionary pedigree entitled her to an honorary place among the Soviets' radical genealogy. As the new Socialist regime erected monuments and obelisks commemorating the sacrifices of her deceased comrades from the nineteenth century, they confronted a living, breathing relic from this bygone radical age in the person of Vera Nikolaevna Figner.

In the first years after the Soviets came to power, Vera proved that she was many things. She was a philanthropist, a humanitarian, an activist, an author, and an insightful witness to some of the most dramatic events in recent Russian history. In the early 1920s it was clear to most Russians that she was a member of an elite, revolutionary nobility and an allegorical symbol of the radical sacrifices of the past. But as the next two decades would prove, she was more than that. As Lenin's government gave way to a new order rigidly overseen by Joseph Stalin, and as the Soviet Union encountered its most dangerous foe yet in Hitler's Nazi Germany, Vera Figner proved that in spite of her advanced age, physical maladies, and self-imposed exclusion from the Communist Party, she was not only a member of the Russian revolutionary nobility; she was also a true revolutionary survivor.

11

REVOLUTIONARY SURVIVOR

By the fall of 1921, Vera realized that she had a vested interest in the Soviet Revolution. She believed her revolutionary generation's struggles had prepared the way for her Communist successors, and thus she felt a certain responsibility for their actions. But her acceptance of the Soviet system was also predicated in eminently practical concerns. Having lived through the dislocation caused by the civil war and witnessed the ultimate survival of Lenin's regime and party, Vera accepted the inevitability of the Bolshevik victory and tacitly admired the Communists' resilience. She also appreciated the consideration that the new regime had accorded her personally. While she certainly did not relish the censorship and bureaucratic hurdles that she had to clear in order to publish her writings, and while she rued the persecution of other political parties in which the Soviets engaged, she was grateful for the material privileges the state extended to her and appreciated the cultural and social leeway the regime allowed her. Yet Vera also realized that the privileges she enjoyed were precarious and knew that her continued ability to pursue her literary and cultural projects depended on the sustained cooperation of the Soviet state. Likening social insignificance and political apathy to death, she resolved to navigate the complicated quagmire that defined the Soviet political arena in order to maintain her livelihood and social satisfaction. As she combined this level of accommodation with a continued commitment to issues of social justice, she proved herself adept at navigating the often precarious contours of contemporary revolutionary politics.

The Cheka's arrest of almost three dozen of Vera's fellow relief workers in the All-Russian Committee to Aid the Starving afforded her the opportunity to test the parameters of her ability to protest political repression without falling victim to such repression herself. Horrified that these innocent relief workers remained in prison weeks after the committee was dissolved, even though they had engaged in nothing more insidious than aspiring to render humanitarian aid in the same way she had, Vera nonetheless pursued their release through sanctioned means. Refusing to trumpet their case as a separate, independent campaign or to engage the regime on ideological grounds, she resolved to aid her imprisoned colleagues solely through the aegis of the Political Red Cross.[1]

The case of the imprisoned aid workers was just one of many that the Political Red Cross dealt with during 1921 and 1922. With rival political parties on the right already silenced through repression and emigration, both forced and voluntary, non-Bolshevik socialist parties found themselves harassed and persecuted in the wake of the civil war. As Lewis Siegelbaum contends, "The end of these parties' existence in Soviet Russia came in early 1921 not because of anything that they did, but rather because of Bolshevik fears of what they could do if given the opportunity."[2] With peasant uprisings escalating; workers' strikes reemerging; the factitious Workers Opposition within the Communist Party critiquing policy; and the pride of the revolution, the sailors at the Kronstadt Naval Base, rebelling against Bolshevik authority, Lenin's government sought to eliminate all political opposition.

A steady stream of political prisoners were dumped in various prisons and places of exile, so the Political Red Cross had more than enough cases to keep its members occupied. In the spring of 1921, the group worked to get numerous political prisoners transferred back to Moscow after a prison disturbance led the government to move these men and women out of the capital. As Vera noted, the transfer meant that their material condition plummeted, because they were now forced to subsist without visits or care packages from their loved ones.[3] After tireless work on the part of the Political Red Cross, by April 1922 all but nineteen of the prisoners were back in the Soviet capital.[4] The group had similar success increasing the rations for imprisoned socialists and anarchists throughout much of the country's prisons and exile settlements. As Vera's report noted, "Thanks to the Committee's efforts and the continued petitions it sent to the government, the rations of socialists and anarchists in Moscow, Petrograd, Yaroslavl, Vladimir, Orel and Riazan doubled."[5]

For several months Vera remained rigorously committed to her work with the Political Red Cross. Throughout the fall and winter of 1921 and 1922, she attended most of the weekly meetings the organization held, prepared reports, introduced motions, and visited prisons to survey the conditions under which the government held political prisoners.[6] Given the increasingly restrictive political climate in the Soviet Union, the continued existence and independent activity of the Political Red Cross was not a given. In light of this, in June 1922 Vera suggested to her fellow Political Red Cross members that they might soon need to decide if they would cower before the increasing pressure of the state or "expand [our efforts] and fortify [our] position as a non-party social organization whose aim it is to help victims of internecine strife."[7]

As the various members of the Political Red Cross took up Vera's challenge to fortify their position, she gradually diminished her involvement in the organization. Increasingly committed to her literary endeavors, she curtailed her work with the Political Red Cross. Although she remained a member of the society, she abdicated her leadership role.[8] Ekaterina Peshkova, Maxim Gorky's ex-wife, who had worked with Vera in the organization, assumed the mantle of control and the group was renamed the E. P. Peshkova Society to Help Political Prisoners.[9]

The month after the name change, Vera Figner turned seventy years old. Her July 7 birthday became an occasion on which a diverse array of Soviet citizens honored the legendary revolutionary figure. Months before her birthday, her fellow Political Red Cross members formed a committee charged with the task of organizing a birthday celebration worthy of their esteemed colleague.[10] Similarly, the Museum of the Revolution spent months preparing a commemorative publication describing the contours of Vera's life; a celebratory meeting in her honor, replete with speeches by other radical luminaries; and a museum exhibition devoted to her.[11] The organizers of these events argued that Vera Figner's significance was enormous. In the brief comments that introduced the commemorative pamphlet, the editors laud her importance to the revolutionary movement, noting that "the history of her life is the history of the People's Will."[12] The editors of the journal *Golos Minuvshego* (Voice of the Past) marked the occasion of Vera's birthday by "saluting the woman who was such a great fighter on behalf of the freedom of the Russian people."[13]

But it was not only her coworkers and close friends who felt the need to observe Vera's seventieth birthday. As she entered her eighth decade, she also received congratulatory sentiments and good wishes from a new generation who valued her contributions to the revolution. Among others, university students and young revolutionaries in the Red Navy sent her their wishes for a happy birthday and expressed their gratitude for all she had done for the cause.[14] While these young Socialists acknowledged the fact that Vera's generation had "divergent worldviews," from their own, they celebrated her "heroic struggles" and "great sacrifice."[15] Thus, although these young radicals acknowledged what they considered to be Vera's ideological errors and antiquated political vision, they honored her dedication, endurance, and social consciousness.

In spite of the Soviet government's penchant for memorials and commemorations, there were no organized official events celebrating Vera's seventieth birthday. Since she was a living revolutionary figure from the past who eschewed Communist membership, an official celebration of her birthday would have elicited questions about her nonpartisan status. It served both Vera and the government to leave her party affiliation ambiguous and thus forestall speculation into the motivation behind her apolitical status. But some younger political radicals assumed that official state silence about Vera's birthday signified something more sinister. In a letter sent to her from Taganka Prison, the political prisoners who authored the missive acknowledge what they perceived as the injustice of the minimization of the birthday celebrations. The Taganka inmates write, "On your 70th birthday, public homes and public offices will not remember your name, but we feel no sadness."[16] The prisoners argued that the Soviet regime could not publicly commemorate Vera's birthday, because her "morally pure image" only highlighted the Communists' revolutionary apostasy.[17] Identifying their current imprisonment with Vera's long incarceration decades before, the Taganka prisoners claimed her as their radical muse and called upon what they understood to be her revolutionary purity in order to sanction their own persecution and sacrifice. Invoking an intangible and ethereal iconic representation of Vera rather than the aging populist herself, the prisoners exalted the woman who served as "a forever-young and beautiful symbol of the Russian revolutionary movement."[18]

By the time she turned seventy years old, Vera had become a truly romantic figure for many Soviet citizens. Her shortcomings were ignored, the violence she advocated forgotten. The public at large knew nothing of her intolerance, haughtiness, or often demanding nature, nor did it care to. As the embodiment of the best of the radical tradition, Vera served as a potential counterpoint to the Communist regime. But precisely because of the leeway the Soviets allowed her for her nonpartisan ventures, her relationship vis-à-vis the regime was ambiguous for most Russians. Unlike imprisoned political prisoners who invoked her name and history in defense of their own, ordinary citizens did not necessarily disassociate Vera Figner from Lenin and his party. Having claimed her as a radical ancestor for their own ends, precisely because of her notoriety, the Communists gained more from the revolutionary luminary's continued presence and activity than they lost. While Emma Goldman argued that Lenin allowed Vera and others of her political bent and stature to remain at liberty, to "effectively disprove the charge that only the gun and the gag were applied under his dictatorship,"[19] Vera served Lenin's purposes in a much more profound manner than Goldman insinuates. Her significance was not so much in the way she served as an international example of a modicum of Soviet political tolerance as it was in the positive and quasi-national associations her continued presence evoked on the domestic front.

Even as the Soviet regime silenced an increasing array of non-Communists, Vera's voice and presence permeated the developing revolutionary dialogue. She belonged to a category of radical luminaries whose revolutionary contributions continued to be revered. As Leonard Schapiro maintains, during the early years of the Soviet regime, "Veterans like Vera Zasulich and Vera Figner could live unmolested."[20] However, it must be noted that not all revolutionary veterans were alike. While Vera Figner escaped arrest and persecution, she did so not solely because of her reputation and radical pedigree but also because she refrained from joining those who could be considered politically dangerous. Although she was not a Communist, she remained politically loyal. In her study of the Russian Revolution, Sheila Fitzpatrick notes that even "former members of opposition parties who remained [in the Soviet Union] were tolerated as long as they abstained totally from all oppositionist political activities [in the 1920s].[21] At the age of seventy, Vera did not pose a threat to the new regime despite her humanitarian and literary endeavors. On the contrary, her iconic presence and seemingly tacit endorsement of the Soviet government legitimized the Communists' credentials as heirs of an organically Russian radical movement. Well known both inside Russia and beyond its frontiers as a selfless aristocrat who gave her youth and freedom in order to achieve the political emancipation of her homeland, Vera enjoyed a "spiritual influence . . . in Russia and abroad."[22] In both her writings and her public speeches, she did not focus on specific political goals or institutions; rather her stories and pronouncements celebrated the emancipation of the masses and the suffering and sacrifice endured by radicals on their behalf. In this way her life became a useful chapter in the "narrative of revolution" that developed in the early Soviet period.[23]

The deprivation that Vera experienced in Shlisselburg Fortress was just as important, if not more so, in the construction of the mythic perception of this revolutionary icon than was her role in the assassination of Tsar Alexander II. In other words, it was not her radical creed that was revered but her martyrdom on its behalf. Vera was not alone in this regard. Until the 1930s, a stint in a tsarist prison for political offenses offered aging revolutionaries a sort of "diplomatic immunity" under the Soviets.[24] The sacrifices that these pre-Bolshevik Russian radicals made for a revolutionary ideal connected them to both their Communist counterparts and the Russian masses.

In many ways Marxism-Leninism was an alien political concept. Even though Lenin adapted Marx's ideas to fit Russia's reality, the ideology still retained substantial foreign elements. The tenets of the Socialist Revolutionaries were more natively Russian than those espoused by the Bolsheviks, but many of the adherents of this organically Russian movement found themselves in Soviet prisons or unmarked graves by the early 1920s.[25] In the wake of the civil war, Lenin and his party needed to unify their country. To help them do so, the Soviets needed to formulate a national myth and history that was both Russian and Soviet. Past Russian leaders had found a source of unity in the Russian Orthodox Church, but the Soviets cultivated a post-Orthodox Russian unity through the secular religion of revolution. Although Lenin was both prophet and messiah, this developing revolutionary culture relied on the image and stature of radical apostles and saints in Russia's past. To this end, Bolshevik culture celebrated "European revolutionaries like [Karl] Marx, [Georges] Danton, [Giuseppe] Garibaldi, [Louis] Blanqui, [and Charles] Fourier . . . [and] Russian radicals like [Alexander] Radishchev, [Alexander] Herzen, [Mikhail] Bakunin, [Sofia] Perovskaya, and [Nikolai] Chernyshevsky."[26] As the new Soviet government erected monuments to deceased revolutionary figures such as those cited above, Vera Figner's continued presence within the new state, as well as her biographical essays of deceased Shlisselburg prisoners and her autobiographical accounts of her own exploits and suffering, contributed to the emerging Russian revolutionary canon. According to Lenin, the members of the People's Will "displayed the greatest self-sacrifice . . . [which] contributed—directly or indirectly—to the ensuing revolutionary education of the Russian people."[27] In this way Vera and the other members of the People's Will became a part of a new Bolshevik culture that fused the Russian radical past with its Soviet present.

Although Vera's political activism and claim to radical fame were decades in the past, she remained in the public consciousness through her steady stream of publications. In addition to *Shlissel'burgskie uzniki*, which appeared in 1920, and the 1921 publication of the first volume of *Zapechatlennyi trud*, the publishing house Golos Minuvshego published Vera's second volume of memoirs in 1923. The second volume of *Zapechatlennyi trud*, subtitled *When the Clock of Life Stopped*, recounted Vera's years in Shlisselburg and reaffirmed the enormous sacrifices that she made on the Russians' behalf. These publications were followed by autobiographical accounts of her student years, *Studencheskie gody*, in 1924 and the tale of her post-Shlisselburg years prior to 1917 in *Posle Shlissel'burga* in 1925. In addition, Vera edited the section of *Granat's Encyclopedic Dictionary of Revolutionary Figures of the 1870s and 1880s*, and was a regular contributor to journals such as *Katorga i Ssylka*, *Golos Minuvshego*, *Ogoniok* (Little Flame), and *Byloe* (The Past).

Vera's efforts to recount her experiences in both the revolutionary underground and Shlisselburg Fortress were not uncommon in the early Soviet period. Many of the journals in which her writings appeared were formed with the expressed purpose of publishing "extended essays commemorating the lives of deceased revolutionaries."[28] What made Vera unique, however, is that she was not solely a biographer but an autobiographer as well. Unlike the deceased comrades whom she celebrated, she became an active participant in the literary creation of her own legend. Thus, she edited and revised according to her desired ends. In the final stages of editing the first volume of her memoirs for publication, she spent hours editing and "correcting" details from her 1883 confession.[29] A straight recounting of the details of her past was not enough. Vera wanted to inspire and move her audience just as she had from countless podiums in Western Europe in the prewar period. As she prepared sections of her memoirs, she often read them in person to interested parties. A few months before the first volume of *Zapechatlennyi trud* appeared, she seemed to take great satisfaction in knowing that some of these recollections brought audience members at a Political Red Cross benefit to tears.[30]

In the decades that followed the publication of her books, the memoirs of Vera and other revolutionary luminaries became a foundational part of a good socialist education. Thus, Eugenia Ginzburg could recall the lines of *Zapechatlennyi trud* verbatim during her own stint in a dank prison cell during the Great Purges of the 1930s.[31] Similarly, a young Communist woman and future author who attended an event at the Society of Former Political Prisoners and Exiles joyfully recalled her delight at meeting the illustrious Vera Figner. Galina Serebriakova noted that at this event in the mid-1920s, she "instantly recognized Vera Nikolaevna Figner."[32] Serebriakova recalled that although Vera was over seventy years old when she saw her, she was struck by the aging revolutionary's beauty. But as she later recalled, this was apropos because Vera Nikolaevna was "ageless."[33] After all, Serebriakova continued, "years and the passage of time were insignificant to a person like her."[34]

Galina Serebriakova recalled that she "had read *Zapechatlennyi trud* many times and listened to stories about Vera Nikolaevna Figner from [her] mother."[35] Tales of the revolutionary underground, bomb throwing, and prison stints became the foundational mythic narrative for many Soviet youth in the immediate postrevolutionary period. Just as Vera had listened with fascinated delight to her niania's stories about fairy-tale tsaritsas and courageous young mythical figures, a new generation of young Soviet girls reveled in hearing about the brave exploits of this young noble girl turned revolutionary heroine. Thus, when Serebriakova met Vera in person, it was overwhelming. She recalls desperately "wanting to kiss Vera's hand, but [she] didn't dare."[36] Standing before this revolutionary icon, Serebriakova felt humbled, for although "Vera Nikolaevna was defeated; she survived."[37]

Each time that Vera's tale of self-sacrifice was read or repeated, it reaffirmed traditional gender roles for Soviet women. The Soviet state sent ambiguous messages about what defined the ideal socialist woman. Although women were to assume public roles and embrace work outside the home, they were still laden with stereotypical expectations. That is, they were expected to fuse public activities and service to the state with conventional feminine values of self-sacrifice and humility. Vera's life served as a model. In her memoirs she went to great lengths to adopt a humble tone while she regaled readers with revolutionary drama. Ostensibly with no regard for her own comfort or glory, she sacrificed herself for what she considered the greater good. Languishing in prison and then exile for three decades, there seemed to be no limit to her capacity for self-sacrifice.

Young Soviet citizens who encountered Vera were initially curious to meet "a woman whose name stood with Zheliabov, Mikhailov, and Perovskaia."[38] Nearly forty years after his "unforgettable meeting" with Vera, I. Porokhin recalls that during a visit to the Museum of the Revolution in Leningrad in 1928, he was immediately intrigued by the elderly woman whom both employees and museum visitors treated with such respect. A woman of medium build, primly attired in a proper black suit with her gray-streaked dark hair pulled tightly into a bun, Vera delighted visitors with personal stories and explanations about many of the exhibits.[39] Eager to meet such a prestigious figure in the revolutionary movement, Porokhin finally marshaled the nerve to introduce himself to her. After a prolonged conversation, the young man was completely inspired. He writes, "There was no limit to my joy."[40]

While many in her generation left the Soviet Union for Western Europe and the United States, Vera remained in her homeland. She was invested in Russia's future. Her continued literary and humanitarian efforts after the 1917 revolutions were the concrete manifestations of her nonpartisan dedication to her country, the Russian people, and notions of socialist justice. As a woman who for more than fifty years had no recognized lover beyond the revolutionary cause, Vera appeared to her Soviet compatriots as an ascetic, virginal, yet beautiful radical saint. Without question, her much celebrated beauty enhanced the drama of her life. She was not a woman without options, romantic or otherwise, and thus her good looks made her personal sacrifices for her political agenda more palpable. As Elizabeth Jones Hemenway contends, "This pattern [of denying oneself a satisfying personal life] became a critical aspect of the plot of women's revolutionary narratives in the period after 1917."[41] However, Vera did not adopt the plot of self-sacrifice as a literary device in order to compete with the memorial literature of fallen Bolshevik heroines that was then being published. On the contrary, this theme had informed her autobiographical writings and speeches since her time lecturing and publishing on behalf of Russian political prisoners in the prewar period; her writing most likely influenced the hagiography of Bolshevik heroines rather than the other way around.[42] Because of the consonance between Vera's literary works and those celebrating Bolshevik figures, her memoirs became an accepted part of the revolutionary canon in the early Soviet period; thus, her non-Bolshevik activities were seen as pre-Bolshevik rather than anti-Bolshevik. Although the tactics that Vera embraced and the immediate political aims she advanced may have diverged from those of the Bolsheviks, their revolutionary spirits, lofty dreams for the Russian people, and capacity for denying themselves converged.

Vera accepted the Soviets and their revolution and enjoyed the perquisites that they offered her. More than anything, she enjoyed her access to a rich in-

tellectual life in the early Soviet period. Living in Moscow, she spent after-
noons combing through archival files from the imperial period, reading foreign newspapers in the Academy of Social Science library,[43] and working in
the Karl Marx Institute.[44] Early in the civil war period, Lenin granted Maxim
Gorky permission to establish the All-Russian Committee for the Improvement of the Lives of Scholars (KUBU) in an effort to ease the physical woes
of critical intellectuals and thereby secure their services and support. Vera
became a member of this organization. As such, she received better rations
than most Soviet citizens and was able to tend to her physical maladies at the
KUBU's sanitarium. Vera also joined the All-Russian Union of Writers, which
allowed for literary and cultural diversions for its members, monitored their
material needs, provided necessary aid, and functioned as a liaison with the
government through its "representatives in the Commissariat of Enlightenment and in the State Publisher."[45] In 1926 Vera received another honor from
the Soviet state when the Soviet Academy of Arts and Sciences recognized
her prodigious literary efforts and unanimously accepted the memoirist and
biographer as a member.[46] Thus, by the late 1920s Vera was not only socially
significant for her revolutionary service in the past, but she was also heralded
as a member of an elite group of celebrated and officially sanctioned intellectuals.

Vera's symbolic honors were matched by material rewards doled out by the
Soviet government. During the same year that she was accepted as a member
of the Soviet Academy of Arts and Sciences, she also learned that henceforth
she would receive a monthly pension of 225 rubles for the rest of her life for
the role she played in the assassination of Tsar Alexander II.[47] Although Stalin
would later ban the study and commemoration of the regicide of Alexander II,
in the 1920s this event was still recognized as a valiant and critical part of the
revolutionary tradition. Vera reaped benefits as a former Shlisselburg prisoner as well. Beginning in 1932, former tsarist political prisoners collected
200 rubles a month from the Soviet government. Either of these pensions
alone would have provided Vera with a decent amount of financial security.
But taken together they catapulted her into a materially privileged class in
the early Soviet period that was only enhanced through her literary earnings.
The pensions that she received from the government constituted a considerable amount of money in the Soviet Union, where average industrial workers
earned 50 rubles a month and even prominent party workers brought home
only 175 rubles monthly.[48]

Vera did not begin her literary career for financial reward. She published articles and books about her own life and the lives of many of her radical comrades in order to document the history of the People's Will and its struggle. But she soon discovered that these reminiscences paid. In letters to relatives and friends, she often marveled at how much publishers paid her for a relatively small amount of work. Just as the artistic abilities of her brother Nikolai augmented his familial inheritance in the imperial period, in the first two decades of Soviet rule Vera's literary earnings substantially enhanced her material fortunes. As she informed her niece Tatiana, her "standard of living would be only moderate" were it not for her lucrative publishing contracts.[49]

By 1931, as the Society of Former Political Prisoners and Exiles prepared her seven-volume *Polnoe sobranie sochinenii* (Collected Works) for publication, Vera's contract stipulated that the society's publisher would pay her approximately fifteen thousand rubles for the series.[50] Thus, as she entered her golden years, Vera realized the goal she had set for herself decades before. As a recent institute graduate, she had written a friend that she wanted to become economically independent, educated, and useful to others.[51] After an aborted medical career, a daring stint in the radical underground, a commuted death sentence, two decades in solitary confinement in a notorious Russian prison, a world war, and the emotional and physical upheaval caused by revolution and civil war in her homeland, Vera's teenage aspirations had been realized. Of course, when she was a girl she expected that medicine would be the means through which she would achieve her ends. Yet she achieved her goals through the most unconventional of means. Vera Nikolaevna Figner became economically independent, educated, and useful to others through her lifelong commitment to political and social revolution. Although the revolution that ultimately brought her symbolic honors and material rewards was not a revolution of her making, she gladly accepted the privileges that the Bolshevik Revolution had bestowed upon her.

While her family's position and her brothers' generosity afforded her a level of comfort and material well-being both before her revolutionary activity and after her incarceration, in her seventies and eighties Vera provided for herself and for others as well. With her disposable income and political connections, she took a personal interest in a variety of causes. From lobbying for medical treatment for a rheumatic worker from her native district of Tetiushi, to transferring fifteen hundred rubles to her "peasant comrades" in Bolshoe Frolovo in order for them to establish a garden *artel* (cooperative association), to securing more than five hundred books for a school in a distant village,[52] Vera used her influence and money for philanthropic causes. But the primary recipients of her largesse were her family members, most especially the surviving daughter and grandchildren of her deceased sister Lidia.

Although Vera had abruptly left her great-nephew in Lugan in March 1920, she always cared deeply for the boy, as she did for many of her nieces and nephews. After she returned to Moscow from her trying stint in Lugan, she repeatedly made inquiries about the orphaned Sergei Stakhevich. Desperate for word about the little boy she had helped to rear, Vera justified her abandonment of him by arguing that she did not want to bring him to Moscow, where he would have to deal with the damp, cold conditions.[53] Yet this was merely an attempt to rationalize her actions and assuage her guilt. When she left her young nephew in the spring of 1920, little Sergei had just lost both his mother and grandmother. Vera was the only remaining relative with whom the child had any personal connection. But because she was desperate both to save herself and to be free of the obligations and commitments that would come with raising her great-nephew, Vera ran away. Willing to sacrifice herself for the Russian masses, she proved unwilling or unable to sacrifice herself for this little boy.

Ironically, she had directed Tatiana Stakhevich never to abandon her young nephew, who Vera maintained was now as much Tatiana's son as her other children.[54] Vera felt the need to remind Tatiana of her responsibilities because they were burdens that Vera herself was never able to assume. She loved her nephew, but she could not bear the thought of being his primary caregiver. While this is not surprising given the fact that Vera was almost seventy years old when Sergei Stakhevich was orphaned, there was also an intentional emotional detachment at work. Her extended isolation in Shlisselburg complicated her ability to form close, prolonged emotional ties. As Vera herself admitted, she was often "in a foul mood and generally depressed."[55] Loud noises and disorder wreaked havoc on her nerves, and she often felt incapable of carrying on conversations.[56] She chose her companions carefully and avoided people who were not aware of or sympathetic to her emotional frailties. Although she doted on her nieces and nephews financially and monitored their lives through regular correspondence, she kept them at an emotional distance. Despite her affection for them, she made a point of instructing her niece Tatiana that her children, including Sergei, should never address her as Grandma or Aunt Vera; instead, the children should always refer to their famous great-aunt as Vera Nikolaevna.[57]

In many ways, in spite of the companionship of friends and relatives, Vera was perpetually lonely. Having fused her personal life into her public persona decades before, she was now unable to extricate it. "Diabolically proud,"[58] she never regained the ability to expose her personal vulnerabilities; thus, she held most people at arm's length. The sad truth of her later years was that even though she was "surrounded by almost universal worship,"[59] she was emotionally isolated. Lidia Dan, who enjoyed a relatively close relationship with her, wrote that Vera always remained in many ways alone. After Shlisselburg, "All of her prison comrades soon forged new personal bonds, married, created new families, and found some comfort in life; but Figner's lot entailed worship rather than love."[60] As one of her nieces alleged, Vera was so determined, principled, and unwavering, that she was "often unable to show any emotional softness or kindness."[61] She yearned for opportunities to be needed and useful, but she shunned circumstances that would expose her neediness. In this way, in the words of Lidia Dan, Vera was "more of a relic than a living woman."[62]

On the surface Vera appeared to be a doting aunt. She regularly sent her nieces and nephews money, books, and personal mementoes of their deceased parents.[63] She took an intense interest in their studies and subsidized their educations. She reprimanded them for bad behavior and promised rewards like trips to children's camps if they conducted themselves properly.[64] But she doled out these favors and funds as she did any other philanthropic aid. It was not enough for her to know that she made the lives of her siblings' descendants easier; she wanted to be thanked—and thanked properly. Writing to Tatiana Stakhevich, she complained, "I am not satisfied with your children. They are not grateful or polite. They rejoice in taking money from me, but they don't express their gratitude by writing me letters of thanks."[65]

Emotional distance rather than geographical distance was responsible for Vera's detachment. Even though she lived with the Sazhin family for years, she noted that she never felt like a true part of the family.[66] She even resented watching her only surviving sister adapt to her matriarchal role. Vera once wrote to Tatiana that she hoped to be able to find an apartment of her own as soon as possible so that she would not witness Eugenia's metamorphosis into "a real housewife."[67] She found it annoying to watch Eugenia bogged down with household chores as she worked to feed three generations of Sazhins, and she failed to see any charm in her sister's life of familial responsibility. Even though she remained unhampered by marital ties, Vera resented the limits that marriage and motherhood imposed on Eugenia. The years had done nothing to temper her hostility to the lot of married women in Russia. Now an elderly woman, she continued to view marriage and motherhood as a vise, just as she did as a teen.

Vera's impulse to flee the irritation she experienced in the Sazhin home is indicative of a tendency she displayed since her release from Shlisselburg Fortress. For two decades she had languished in prison without the right to determine what she could do or where she could do it. Then even after she left the so-called Russian Bastille, the terms of her sentence repeatedly forced her to beseech the tsarist government for the right to reside in certain locales. Subsequently, as she aged she came to equate freedom with movement. Unable or unwilling to confront the internal or emotional basis of her unhappiness, Vera looked to external factors and operated under the assumption that many of her problems and anxieties would be relieved with a change of location. Thus, her internal sense of alienation compelled her to become a sort of perpetual exile as she traveled between apartments, rest homes, sanitariums, and the homes of various friends and relatives for the rest of her life.

In what can be seen as a quest to assuage this persistent sense of alienation, Vera returned to her roots in 1923, 1924, and again later in 1927 when she traveled to her native district of Tetiushi. She described the impetus behind her first trip home in two strikingly different ways. In the short autobiographical essay that she wrote for *Granat's Encyclopedic Dictionary* of notable revolutionary figures, her typical public stoicism and personal pride are evident as she describes her trip "home" as motivated by a sense of personal curiosity. In this selection she explains that after the civil war ended, her experiences of the newly formed Soviet Union were limited. She lived exclusively in Moscow, among intellectuals who shared an identical psychology. Increasingly, Vera claims, she became convinced that "I was not seeing real life. I wanted to see the changes wrought in the countryside."[68] But in her memoir titled *Posle Shlissel'burga,* she candidly and surprisingly conveys a much more intimate motive. In this publication she notes a sense of alienation and isolation after her siblings Nikolai, Olga, and Lidia died in quick succession. Hoping to rediscover a connection with herself and her past, she traveled to "the place where we were born, raised, and prepared for life."[69] In Tetiushi, which was then part of the Tatar Republic, Vera sought out what was "close, dear and sweet."[70] Having been away from her native district for a number of years, she was eager to "touch the black, native land which called to [her]" even when she was thousands of miles away.[71]

Vera's inability to find a satisfying emotional life also compelled her to continue working despite her physical infirmities and the growing interference of the Soviet state. Both her literary endeavors and her humanitarian causes distracted her from her loneliness and anxiety. As she herself noted as she approached her eightieth birthday, "If I have work then I am satisfied."[72] Consequently, she set a tireless pace for herself, especially in terms of her literary projects. With her memoirs well acclaimed in the Soviet Union, she began efforts to have her writings translated into various languages and published abroad. From 1924 until 1930, Vera's memoirs were published in German, French, English, Hebrew, Swedish, Dutch, and Yiddish. Working through friends and colleagues living abroad, she found a new productive outlet in the preparation and negotiation of these publishing contracts.[73]

It was supremely important to Vera that her generation of revolutionaries' stories be told and safeguarded for the edification of her fellow Soviet citizens, interested foreign parties and individuals, and posterity. However, she did not believe that all memoirs and autobiographical accounts had equal merit. Commenting on the recently published memoirs of Lazar Goldenberg, Vera wrote, "These memoirs are quite tasteless; if I were an editor I would have never published them due to their boastful and tacky tone."[74] While it might seem as if autobiography is by its very nature a boastful literary form, the model established for memoir literature in the early Soviet period was informed by "quiet modesty."[75] Unlike the biographies that many of the same authors composed of deceased comrades, autobiographical writings should edify but not boast. In order to conform to this new revolutionary self-hagiography, authors of memoirs needed to write almost as reluctant witnesses to history and assume an air of humility as they described their radical tendencies and revolutionary careers without vainly glorifying themselves personally. The need for such self-editing was even more pronounced for non-Communist figures than it was for their Bolshevik counterparts. Heralding non-Bolshevik revolutionary movements in a one-party state that controlled all publishing outlets, the authors of memoirs needed to conform to the established model in order to maximize the likelihood of publication and minimize the chances that their stories would erode the potential sympathy of their readers or seem too self-congratulatory to an exceptionally sensitive regime.

Vera's inclination to mold the memorial literature being churned out by former revolutionaries in the 1920s is evident in a letter she wrote to one of the preeminent archivists of the Russian revolutionary movement, the former Menshevik Boris I. Nicolaevsky. Even after he, along with numerous other intellectuals, was expelled from the Soviet Union in 1922, Nicolaevsky continued the work that he had started in documenting the revolutionary movement as the director of the Historical Revolutionary Archive in Moscow. In these efforts he often felt the need to correspond with Vera about materials of potential interest dealing with the revolutionary movement of the 1870s and 1880s and Shlisselburg Fortress. Always respectful of her feelings and solicitous of her opinions, Nicolaevsky in no way deserved the dressing down that Vera directed his way in a 1925 letter.

Responding to the archivist's respectful request about some manuscripts written by Shlisselburg inmates that he had acquired, Vera showed little patience with Nicolaevsky when she wrote the following:

> Deeply respected, Boris Ivanovich,
>   I have received your letter but your handwriting is so poor and sloppy that it alone irritates me. Similarly, the content of your letter is most unpleasant. You write that when Shlisselburg Fortress was closed, some manuscripts were preserved. I don't know which ones but I do know this: not all of them deserve to be presented to the reading public. In recent times, we have been inundated with the publication of meaningless material. The press is like a wastebasket for worthless papers, and, if you ask me, I will say that it is impermissible to overload the attention of the press.[76]

Apart from the condescending and arrogant tone Vera uses in this letter, her remarks indicate that she viewed the literary commemoration of the past as more than just compilation and publication. In her opinion the memorialization of the revolutionaries of the last century and their suffering under the tsars needed to be carefully selected, edited, and crafted. Having established the theme and form according to which these literary commemorations needed to conform, she rued the efforts of some to throw discretion to the wind and inundate the public with a mass of documents and publications.

Vera soon followed up this original letter to Nicolaevsky with a second that apologized for her harsh and potentially offensive tone. In this second letter she confides that she worries that the publication of Shlisselburg documents en masse might detract from the honor of the authors "who were writing under the conditions of Shlisselburg," works that were not meant to be published.[77] Although she restated her concern that at the present time the public was "literally drowning in literary trifles, real rubbish,"[78] she apologized for the obvious irritation with which she had previously written. She closed this December 23 letter to Nicolaevsky by writing, "Please pardon Vera Figner, the angry one, wholeheartedly."[79]

Vera's angry response to Nicolaevsky partly aroused from the fact that they were discussing materials produced in Shlisselburg. More than any other element of her radical past, Vera's tenure in the Russian Bastille retained an almost sacred significance for her. Amid a lifetime of drama and history, for Vera, "Shlisselburg was decisive."[80] Because of this, as the Soviet regime continued to sentence its political adversaries to various terms in prison and exile, she felt an affinity for these men and women that was born of their unique shared experience. Although she needed no reminders of this fact, the birthday greetings sent by a group of imprisoned Socialist Revolutionaries to Vera in 1922 reaffirmed this point: "Your example inspired our first steps into the revolutionary movement in our youth. Your example stands before us now in what could be our final struggle."[81] Assuming responsibility for both the Bolsheviks and a generation of revolutionaries who fell victim to the political ambitions of the Soviet state, Vera resolved to use her political and social influence with the Bolsheviks to advocate on behalf of the men and women they imprisoned.

Even as she decreased her involvement in the E. P. Peshkova Society to Help Political Prisoners, Vera found other avenues to advocate for justice for the men and women imprisoned on political charges. Sometimes she wrote personal appeals to prominent officials on a specific prisoner's behalf. For example, when Ivan Lavrent'ev, an employee of the newspaper *Bednota* (The Poor), was arrested in her native Tetiushi in August 1931, Vera penned letters to both Emelian Iaroslavskii, head of the Society of Former Political Prisoners and Exiles, and to Mikhail Kalinin, the chairman of the Central Executive Committee.[82] Involving the titular head of state in a matter such as this was certainly bold, and it demonstrates a clear sense of privilege on Vera's part. As a revolutionary luminary she had connections, and she did not hesitate to use them. Not only did she feel entitled to direct her inquiry to Kalinin, but also it is clear that she felt confident that a query coming from her would elicit an appropriate response from the government and the GPU, or the State Political Directorate.[83]

This was not the first time Vera had sent personal appeals to prominent Soviet figures. In 1926 she wrote Iaroslavskii that the government was being counterproductive by sentencing its youth for political crimes. She noted that the persecution of thousands of young people of both sexes in exile settlements in the distant corners of Russia and Siberia was only arousing these youth's enmity to Soviet power.[84] Thus, she appealed to Iaroslavskii from a humanitarian perspective couched in pragmatic political concerns. She employed a similar tactic in a collective letter of protest she signed with just over a dozen aging revolutionaries in 1927. In a letter addressed to the Presidium of the Central Executive Committee of the USSR, the authors took issue with the Soviet government's use of the death penalty and with the political repression of men and women who posed no threat to the socialist order.[85] The collective of self-described "old revolutionaries" invoked their prestige and years of suffering under the tsars to contest the persecution of Soviet citizens on the basis of political ideology.[86] For those who penned the letter of protest, the types of extralegal practices and punishments in which the Soviet government currently engaged would have been expected from the tsarist autocracy but not from the regime established by their revolutionary and Socialist brethren.

Vera Figner belonged to an exclusive club of revered revolutionaries whose numbers diminished with each passing year. Acknowledging the ways their actions paved the way for the Bolshevik victory, Vera believed that the pain and suffering her generation of revolutionaries had endured under the tsars entitled them to a measure of peace, comfort, and respect in their later years. It was for this reason that she was so incensed when she learned about the conditions under which her friend Nikolai Pavlovich Kotov was living in 1934. Once again, Vera sent an appeal to Kalinin:

> I am ready to scream: Help!! . . . The honored revolutionary, Nikolai Pavlovich Kotov, a sick seventy-nine-year-old man, who was persecuted by the tsarist government . . . is currently living in Moscow in an unheated kennel with his wife and two small children. He appeals to you with a request to help him change his place of residence and I ask you to grant his request and give him the chance to live decently. He deserves the gratitude and support of the Soviet authorities.[87]

This attitude was not Vera's alone; it was consistent with the treatment that former political prisoners and exiles had received since the Bolshevik Revolution. During the first decade of Soviet rule, the men and women who had suffered in tsarist fortresses and exile settlements for their Socialist and radical activism were honored by their revolutionary heirs and given perquisites that most of their fellow citizens did not enjoy. Many of these privileges emanated through the Society of Former Political Prisoners and Exiles, formed in 1921. Over its fourteen-year existence, this society "rendered material aid, organized lectures and the reading of papers, held meetings, and collected, studied and published materials on the history of tsarist prisons, labor camps, and exile settlements."[88] One of the most enviable aspects of the society was the country home that its members enjoyed, which was approximately sixty kilometers outside of Moscow on the former Sheremetev estate. As an American visitor to the rest home remarked, the members of the society lived there "in the atmosphere of an aristocratic club of bygone days, with a private restaurant and picture gallery containing photographs, drawings, paintings, and etchings—many of them works of art—that depict the less pleasant side of prison life under the Czars."[89] The mansion was idyllic with a huge old library, a music room with a grand piano, and large open balconies. With pine and birch forests, clear artificial lakes, beautiful gardens, and ample space for the children and grandchildren of the members to play and enjoy nature,[90] the society's dacha (country home) was a favorite haunt for its members. Until the last few years of her life, Vera regularly spent her summers in this marvelous vacation spot basking in the company of other aging revolutionaries and former political prisoners. The society also printed the journal *Katorga i ssylka,* which published many reminiscences of this old guard, including many selections written by Vera Figner. But despite her association with the Society of Former Political Prisoners and Exiles, she never officially joined the organization.

From 1928 until 1935 Vera spent months at the society's residence every year, availing herself of the mansion's luxuries and the company provided by a large contingent of her old friends. In 1932, given Vera's longtime association with the society's rest home and its journal, the presidium of the group's Central Committee offered her an honorary membership in the Society of Former Political Prisoners and Exiles. It is doubtful that any of the members of the presidium expected the response their offer elicited.

In a letter dated July 17, 1932, addressed to the Presidium of the Central Executive Committee of the Society of Former Political Prisoners and Exiles, Vera declined the membership and proceeded to lambast the group's leadership for its political cowardice.[91] She alleged that because the society allowed itself to be dragged into politics, it rendered its tacit approval of the repressive tactics of the state, including the use of the death penalty and the actions of the GPU. In addition, she contended that in recent years the society had colluded with these high-handed tactics by conducting its own purge of non-

Bolshevik members "instead of lifting its voice against this method of control which contradicts all of our revolutionary ethics."[92] Although Vera directed this censure to the society's presidium and not the corresponding government or party agencies, this letter was quite daring and provocative.

After Vladimir Lenin died in 1924, the remaining members of Lenin's Council of People's Commissars and its analogous party body, the Politburo, struggled for power and hotly contested internal factional plans for state policy. But by 1928 Joseph Stalin had risen above the fray to become the uncontested leader of the party and the country. Stalin jealously guarded his power and vigilantly mitigated any potential political threats through fear, repression, and by the mid-1930s with a bloody, often indiscriminate purge of his own party that would ultimately claim millions of lives.[93] In the aftermath of the murder of Leningrad party chief Sergei Kirov in late 1934,[94] Stalin's political police, the recently reorganized and renamed NKVD (Narodnyi Komissariat Vnutrennikh Del, or People's Commissariat for Internal Affairs) mercilessly pursued any political opposition, both real and imagined. Pre-1917 revolutionary pedigrees and stints in tsarist prisons no longer insulated Soviet citizens from the gulag or even the firing squad. Yet Vera continued to live unmolested. Clearly one cannot argue that her role as a conspirator to the assassination of Alexander II brought a special type of privilege, because it failed to save her co-conspirator A. I. Pribyleva-Korba, who fell victim to Stalin's purge.[95] Neither can one make the case that the extent of her suffering under the Romanovs entitled her to special treatment, since one of the most famous political "victims" of the tsarist period, Maria Spiridonova, was condemned by a Stalinist court. Instead what most likely saved Vera's reputation and freedom were the chronic physical ailments that plagued her and limited her activity.

In the correspondence that Vera maintained with friends and relatives throughout the 1920s, but especially the 1930s, she continually notes her numerous illnesses and infirmities. While rheumatic disease and nosebleeds plagued her in her early seventies, her illnesses became even more debilitating as she approached her eighties. She experienced protracted and repeated bouts with colitis that left her weak and susceptible to disease. In the winter of 1930, her health was so poor that doctors doubted she would survive her latest illness.[96] Although she did live through it, her health was so compromised that she remained isolated and missed momentous public events, including the fiftieth-anniversary celebration of the founding of the People's Will.[97]

In addition to her ongoing health problems, Vera suffered a devastating blow in 1932 when her only remaining sibling, Eugenia, passed away in November. Although she avoided discussing her reaction to her sister's death in her correspondence at that time,[98] Vera never fully recovered from the passing of the sister with whom she had shared so much of her life and the debilitating effects of old age. Writing to Fritz Brupbacher in 1934, Vera noted, "My health and strength have weakened significantly since my sister's death two years ago."[99] Spending extended periods confined to bed, she became increasingly frustrated. As she wrote Brupbacher in July 1934 in response to birthday greetings he sent to her, "What a dirty trick it is to live to be 82! I don't wish it on anyone. I have lost my energy and lost my capacity for work."[100]

With diminished physical fortitude, Vera posed little threat to the Soviet regime even as Stalin's NKVD became more sensitive to potential dissent. Instead of asserting herself to the Communists about the conditions of political prisoners, she found herself arguing with her doctors about whether she needed to remain confined to bed.[101] By the end of 1934 she relied on the constant services of a nurse and had difficulties with mobility. In July 1935 she wrote Brupbacher again, saying, "My health is fragile and frail. I have to take care of myself and think of myself! I am getting tired of rendering favors for others."[102]

Even if Vera's health remained good, it is doubtful that by 1935 she would have been in a position to help anyone. As the momentum of Stalinist repression began to build toward the Great Purges, her influence in official circles declined. Her image and prestige as an early apostle of the revolutionary movement was no longer needed as Stalinism became the official dogma of the nation and alternate interpretations of revolution and society were dismissed as heresy. As Richard Stites writes, Stalinism offered "a single utopian vision and plan, drawn up at the pinnacle of power and imposed on an entire society."[103] Indicative of the Stalinist appropriation of revolutionary history and tradition was the changing interpretation of populism and the actions of the People's Will. Whereas Lenin lauded the sacrifices made by the members of the People's Will and the "heroism of the terrorist method of struggle" that contributed to the "ensuing revolutionary education of the Russian people,[104] his successor's regime derided "the negative contributions of former revolutionary paradigms, especially those connected to Populism and Terrorism."[105] Instead of glorifying the sacrifices of this earlier generation of revolutionaries, by the mid-1930s, Stalin chose to ignore them. Thus, the Stalinist revolutionary tradition was purged of its narodovol'tsy connections. In the mid-to late 1930s, Stalin identified more with figures like Ivan the Terrible and Peter the Great than he did with the populist Mark Natanson or the People's Will leader Andrei Zheliabov, and he subsequently had no interest in exalting the actions of regicides. From 1917 until 1934 the study of populism and the People's Will "was intensive and widespread," because it was seen to have great scholarly and political significance.[106] But then in 1934 there began a "persistent and systematic struggle against the good memory of a whole generation of revolutionaries," most notably the revolutionary populists.[107] Fostered by Soviet official theorists, historical literature began to portray populism and the activities of the People's Will as harmful phenomena and their proponents as "evil enemies of Marxism."[108] As Emelian Iaroslavskii wrote in 1937, "Comrade Stalin recognized that if we teach our people about the narodovol'tsy then we would be rearing terrorists."[109]

Timing is everything. While Vera benefited financially and symbolically from the public celebration of her revolutionary past in the 1920s, anonymity brought a greater measure of security in the 1930s. In many ways the acceleration of her physical illnesses at that time may have saved her life and preserved her freedom. Being a public figure during the Stalinist era brought risk. The more one avoided the intrusive, curious gaze of the party, the state, and the NKVD, the more likely one was to avoid being victimized by the purges.

Thus, Vera spent the last few years of her life out of the public limelight and fighting to retain some of the personal dignity that she held so dear. In April 1937 she confessed to a friend that she no longer went anywhere and that she had not been able to work in two years.[110] Struggling to keep her mind strong as her body increasingly failed her, she practiced her German in letters to friends like Fritz and Paulette Brupbacher, who were living abroad. But even correspondence challenged her at times. The number of extant letters written by Vera precipitously decline in the late 1930s and early 1940s, and those that remain are practically illegible.

One of the few letters Vera wrote at the end of her life was to her niece Tatiana. Written two years to the day before her death, the ailing revolutionary urged her niece to insist that her children finish their educations.[111] Writing to Tatiana from a sanitarium and clearly cognizant of her mortality, Vera struggled to pass on her wisdom to her sister's progeny. It is doubtful that Vera thought she would ever leave the hospital. As she noted in her letter to her niece, she had been confined to that sanitarium for over a year.[112]

Surviving against nearly insurmountable odds was what Vera had done for decades. Having witnessed so much tumult, destruction, and death in her homeland, she lived to experience even more of this when Nazi Germany invaded the Soviet Union. As the Germans encroached on Moscow and much of the city evacuated, she refused efforts to be relocated. Instead she allegedly told her would-be rescuers to "save [their] concern for the living."[113] But Vera was so moved by the threat that her native Russia faced at the hands of the Nazi invaders that she briefly wrote about the heroic efforts of Soviet women who "in these years of sacred, patriotic war," fight against "fascism in the rear and at the front tirelessly and selflessly."[114]

Just a few months later, in the midst of this Great Patriotic War on June 16, 1942, half of the fourth page of the party newspaper *Pravda* (Truth) was devoted to Vera Figner. In the middle of the page was a picture of a serious, elderly Vera with the caption "An Old Revolutionary Has Died."[115] With death and destruction from the war abounding, none other than Emelian Iaroslavskii, who just five years before had referred to members of the People's Will as evil enemies of Marxism, stopped to eulogize the nearly ninety-year-old revolutionary luminary. Informing the Soviet public that Vera died on June 15 after a prolonged illness, Iaroslavskii praised her as one of a handful of notable Russian women who devoted themselves to the struggle against tsarism. Remembering Vera's activism, Iaroslavskii points out that she became a populist and a member of the People's Will before Marxism developed in Russia and before radicals understood the role of the working class. Nonetheless, Iaroslavskii insists that Vera made great sacrifices and spent twenty long, arduous years imprisoned in Shlisselburg Fortress.

Vera's eulogy clearly demonstrates the ambiguous reverence with which the radical legend was regarded in the Soviet Union. Of course, Iaroslavskii was forced to acknowledge that she did not belong to the Communist Party. He excused both her non-Marxist revolutionary career and her failure to join the party after the Bolshevik Revolution as a function of poor timing. Because Vera devoted herself to the revolutionary cause at a time when the Marxist movement did not yet exist in Russia, and because she remained politically unaffiliated in the Soviet period because of old age and poor health, Iaroslavskii exonerates her of the sin of nonpartisanship. In an effort to lend credence to his insinuated argument that Vera sympathized with the Communists, he claims that in her last years she told friends that if she were to join any political party, it would have been the Communist Party.[116] Ignoring the obvious irony of this statement in the one-party state, Iaroslavskii clearly means to invoke Vera's name as a collaborator in the Soviet socialist system.

The day after she died, a citizens' requiem was held for Vera Nikolaevna Figner. Her cremated remains were placed in an urn and transferred to the Novodevichy Cemetery.[117] There, Vera joined other national luminaries like Nikolai Gogol, Anton Chekhov, and Stalin's first wife, Nadezhda Stalina. Not all former non-Bolshevik revolutionaries who passed away in the Soviet era received such recognition. In a period when Vera's generation of revolutionaries in general and the party to which she belonged more explicitly were deemed to be Marxist heretics and the study of their lives and exploits labeled potentially dangerous, why would the Soviet state so publically acknowledge the life and death of Vera Figner?

The answer lies in the Great Patriotic War. Vera died during a period of the war often referred to as the "Black Summer" because of the bleak military prospects then facing the Soviets.[118] At that moment, in the midst of the colossal fascist threat, the Soviet government needed the Russian people to fight and sacrifice. Thus, the passing of a venerable old woman whose life seemed synonymous with sacrifice provided an opportunity to inspire and emotionally connect with a new generation of Russian freedom fighters. For this reason, although she published thousands of pages of her writing, in his literary memorial to her Iaroslavskii chose to quote extensively from one of the poems that Vera wrote in Shlisselburg. The choice was not coincidental.

> Dreaming about our future, I wait for the day
> when our native country will breathe freely
> When among our native fields, the news of
> freedom spreads to the distant seas and
> everyone who now slumbers will awaken
> When they do and they spring to life, they will
> discard their heavy drowsiness, and they will
> embrace fruitful work, bringing along with
> them thousands of our people.[119]

Although the context in which Vera originally wrote these lines invoked political repression under the tsars, in the midst of the Nazi threat they seem to call the Soviet people to action, to fight and sacrifice in order to ensure the freedom of the Soviet Union. Thus, the theme of sacrifice that Vera had so artfully crafted for herself and her generation of revolutionaries decades before, allowed her to be venerated in death as she so often was in life.

In the wonderful collection of the International Institute of Social History Archives in Amsterdam, there is a unique photograph taken in 1935 (see final photograph in picture gallery). The photo depicts Nikolai Bukharin, a former Politburo member and then editor of *Izvestiia* (News) kissing the hand of an elderly woman outside of the newspaper's offices. The woman pictured with Bukharin is Vera Figner. Although the reason for her visit to the *Izvestiia* offices is unknown, Vera looks as elegant as she always did when she ventured out in public. Dressed in a dark coat with a light-colored scarf with a matching brimmed hat, she could easily be mistaken for a visiting foreign dignitary or royal as she genteelly proffers her hand to Bukharin. From Bukharin's respectful kiss to the indulgent grin on Vera's face, it is clear that both figures are fully aware that she is a revolutionary and national luminary. As she stands across from the Soviet intellectual who would fall victim to Stalin's purges in 1938, Vera looks like the noble that she was.

What was so unique about Vera Nikolaevna Figner is that she was born into one noble class and earned her entry into another. While both of the noble classes to which she belonged were persecuted at various times after the Bolshevik Revolution, Vera not only survived, she triumphed. Vera Nikolaevna Figner was one of a handful of people who were lionized on both sides of the revolutionary divide. Venerated by radicals and liberal sympathizers both in Russia and abroad before the revolutions of 1917, she became a quasi-official figure in the period between the two revolutions of that year. In the wake of the Soviet Revolution, she initially suffered from disillusionment and physical trials engendered by the hazards of civil war, but she survived. Making her peace with the Communist regime, she and the new order reached a modus vivendi that allowed her to remain socially and intellectually active while politically unaffiliated. Determined to commemorate her generation of revolutionaries and their motivations before they were dead and forgotten, the theme of self-sacrifice that Vera so artfully depicts in her memoirs transcended partisan lines and allowed her life story to become a foundational part of the Russian revolutionary narrative. Claimed as a radical ancestor of the Communists, she enjoyed socially useful pursuits, financial security, prestige, and literary acclaim in the Soviet Union. Although she became increasingly reclusive due to old age and illness, her isolation came at a fortuitous time as she emerged from Stalin's purges essentially unscathed. After Vera drew her last breath, in the midst of the dangerous days of the Great Patriotic War the Soviet gov-

ernment took the time to remind citizens of the sacrifices made by this revolutionary assassin turned octogenarian and to commemorate this extraordinary woman as a means to inspire its people. In doing so they hoped to invoke
Vera Nikolaevna Figner's name one last time and to celebrate the noble and
revolutionary spirit of this unique and historic woman.

NOTES

INTRODUCTION

1. Andrew Baruch Wachtel brilliantly describes how memoirists of Figner's generation presented their childhoods according to an established nineteenth-century gentry standard. See Andrew Baruch Wachtel, *The Battle for Childhood: Creation of a Russian Myth* (Stanford, Calif.: Stanford University Press, 1990).

2. Soon after I began researching the life of Vera Figner, Hilde Hoogenboom published the essay "Vera Figner and Revolutionary Autobiographies: The Influence of Gender on Genre." This smart and precise essay served as both inspiration and methodological reminder throughout the writing of this book. Hilde Hoogenboom, "Vera Figner and Revolutionary Autobiographies: The Influence of Gender on Genre," in *Women in Russia and Ukraine*, ed. Rosalind Walsh, 78–93 (Cambridge, U.K.: Cambridge University Press, 1996).

3. 1922 Museum of the Revolution Brochure, *Rossiiskii gosudarstvennyi arkhiv literatury i iskusstva* (hereafter, RGALI), fond 1185, opis' 1, delo 114.

1. IN THE TWILIGHT OF A FADING AGE

1. Serfdom developed over several decades in Russia. Beginning in the late sixteenth century, in an effort to garner the loyalty of Russian boyars, or nobles, a series of tsars increasingly restricted the peasantry's freedom of movement to afford the boyars a dependable source of agricultural labor so that the boyars could in turn serve the tsar. This arrangement became legal and permanent in 1649 with the codification of laws known as the *ulozhenie*. From this point until the emancipation of 1861, Russian serfs were tied to their designated estate and had to provide either labor service or cash payment to the estate's noble owners. Although the serfs legally belonged to the estate and not the owner of the land, this distinction was effectively ignored and for all purposes irrelevant.

2. Newly emancipated serfs received only a fraction of the lands they expected and had to pay for that land in redemptive dues that were scheduled to be paid over the next half century. In addition, the state decreed that emancipation would not be implemented for another two years. See Daniel Field, "The Year of Jubilee," in Ben Eklof, John Bushnell, and Larissa Zakharova, eds., *Russia's Great Reforms, 1855–1881* (Bloomington: Indiana University Press, 1994); W. Bruce Lincoln, *The Great Reforms: Autocracy, Bureaucracy, and the Politics of Change in Imperial Russia* (DeKalb: Northern Illinois University Press, 1990).

3. Vera Figner, *Studencheskie gody* (Moscow: Golos Truda, 1924), 81.

4. One *desiatina* equals 2.7 acres.

5. Peter Kolchin, *Unfree Labor: American Slavery and Russian Serfdom* (Cambridge, Mass.: Belknap Press, 1987), 52. In making this assessment, Kolchin refers to the work done

by A. Troinitskii on the 1858 Russian census, *Krepostnoe naselenie v Rossii, po 10-i narodnoi perepisi* (St. Petersburg: Izdanie statisticheskago otdela tsentral'nago statistticheskago komiteta, 1861).

6. Kolchin, *Unfree Labor*, 166.

7. A. P. Korelin, *Dvoriantsvo v poreformennoi Rossii 1861–1904gg.: Sostav, chislennost', korporativaia organizatsiia* (Moscow: Izdatelstvo Nauka, 1979), 40, 292. Also noteworthy is the essay "Russia" by Jerome Blum that appears in David Spring, ed., *European Landed Elites in the Nineteenth Century* (Baltimore: Johns Hopkins University Press, 1977), 71–74.

8. For a wonderful description of the often frivolous excess in which the highest strata of the Russian nobility indulged themselves, especially regarding the number of servants they utilized, see Priscilla Roosevelt, *Life on the Russian Country Estate: A Social and Cultural History* (New Haven, Conn.: Yale University Press, 1995), 102–18.

9. The Figners relocated to the estate of Khristoforovka in 1858 after spending several years in a remote forested region of Mamadysh, also in Kazan province, where Nikolai worked as a forester for the state.

10. Karl Baedeker, *Russia with Teheran, Port Arthur, and Peking: Handbook for Travelers* (Leipzig: Karl Baedeker, 1914), 352.

11. Alexander II inherited the throne in 1855 upon the death of his father, Nicholas I. The Crimean War was a three-year conflict between Russia and the combined forces of France, England, and the Ottoman Empire. The war ended in 1856 with a decisive Russian defeat.

12. Vera Nikolaevna Figner was born on June 24, 1852. This date is according to the Old Style Russian calendar. From 1700 until soon after the Bolshevik Revolution, Russia followed the Julian calendar. Most other Christian countries in the West have followed the Gregorian calendar since the sixteenth century. In the nineteenth century the Julian calendar was twelve days behind the Gregorian and thirteen days behind in the twentieth century. I consistently use dates in the Old Style in this book until the Russians adopted the Gregorian calendar in early 1918.

13. Good statistics on the number of both privately held serfs and state peasants are available in Geroid Tanquary Robinson, *Rural Russia under the Old Regime* (Berkeley: University of California Press, 1932), 63.

14. Vera Figner, *Zapechatlennyi trud: Vospominaniia v dvukh tomakh* (Moscow: Izdatel'stvo sotsialno-economicheskoi literatury Mysl, 1964), 1: 60.

15. All six of the Figner children were close in age. Just one year after Vera was born, Lidia arrived in 1853. The two eldest girls soon welcomed Peter in 1855, Nikolai in 1857, Eugenia in 1858, and finally Olga in 1862. Andrei Vladimirovich Voronikhin, "V. N. Figner v russkom osvoboditel'nom dvizhenii, 1873–1884gg," PhD diss., Saratov University, 1992, 37–43.

16. The Figner family would add to their brood the following year with the birth of their last child, Olga.

17. Like most members of the provincial gentry, the Figners retained strong emotional ties to their estates. For an interesting discussion of the sentimental function that the estate played for the provincial gentry, see Mary W. Cavender, *Nests of the Gentry: Family, Estate, and Local Loyalties in Provincial Russia* (Newark: University of Delaware Press, 2007), 51–58.

18. V. Figner, *Zapechatlennyi trud*, 1: 54.

19. Wachtel, *Battle for Childhood*, 116–21.

20. V. P. Semenov, *Polnoe geograficheskoe opisanie nashego otechestva* (St. Petersburg: Izdanie A. F. Devriena, 1901), 6: 13.

21. V. Figner, *Zapechatlennyi trud*, 1: 58–59.

22. See Wachtel, *Battle for Childhood*.

23. V. Figner, *Zapechatlennyi trud*, 1: 57.

24. Ibid., 1: 58.

25. In the wake of the emancipation, land prices dropped considerably. Consequently, Nikolai A. Figner bought extensive acreage in the village where Khristoforovka was located and built the family's new estate, Nikiforovo.

26. Michel Foucault, *Discipline and Punish: The Birth of the Prison*, trans. Alan Sheridan (New York: Vintage Books, 1979), 130–31.

27. Barbara Alpern Engel, "Transformation versus Tradition," in Barbara Evans Clements, Barbara Alpern Engel, and Christine D. Worobec, eds., *Russia's Women: Accommodation, Resistance, Transformation* (Berkeley: University of California Press, 1991), 136.

28. Laura Engelstein, *The Keys to Happiness: Sex and the Search for Modernity in Fin-de-Siècle Russia* (Ithaca, N.Y.: Cornell University Press, 1992), 5.

29. The term "Great Reforms" refers to the 1861 Emancipation of the Serfs and the attendant reforms that Alexander II enacted in the judiciary, military, educational system and system of local self-government in the towns and provinces from 1861 through 1874.

30. Barbara Alpern Engel, *Women in Russia, 1700–2000* (Cambridge, U.K.: Cambridge University Press, 2004), 68.

31. Engel writes, "People of diverse views and backgrounds debated and some eventually joined forces to work for the betterment of society during these early, optimistic years." Ibid., 69.

32. V. Figner, *Zapechatlennyi trud*, 1: 60.

33. Roxanne Easley, *The Emancipation of the Serfs in Russia: Peace Arbitrators and the Development of Civil Society* (London: Routledge, 2009), 61.

34. Ibid., 71. Terrence Emmons contends that the office of peace mediators attracted many true liberals and abolitionists. Terrence Emmons, *The Russian Landed Gentry and the Peasant Emancipation of 1861* (Cambridge, U.K.: Cambridge University Press, 1968), 328–32.

35. Easley, *Emancipation of the Serfs*, 3.

36. Vera Figner, *Polnoe sobranie sochinenii v semi tomakh* (Moscow: Izdatel'stvo vsesoiuznogo obshchestva politkatorzhan i ssyl'no-poselentsev, 1932), 5: 18.

37. Ibid., 5: 24.

38. N. N. Figner, *Vospominaniia, pis'ma, materialy* (Leningrad: Izdanie Muzyka, 1968), 7.

39. V. Figner, *Zapechatlennyi trud*, 1: 72.

40. Hoogenboom, "Vera Figner," 80.

41. V. Figner, *Polnoe sobranie sochinenii*, 5: 23.

42. Ibid., 5: 32.

43. David Ransel, ed., *The Family in Imperial Russia* (Urbana: University of Illinois Press, 1978), 23.

44. V. Figner, *Polnoe sobranie sochinenii*, 5: 9.

45. *Niania* can be translated as "nurse" or "nanny." This woman was directly responsible for Russian noble children in their early years. Until the age of seven, when noble children passed from their nurse's care into that of governesses and tutors, their niania provided for almost all of their emotional and material needs.

46. V. Figner, *Zapechatlennyi trud*, 1: 59.

47. Wachtel, *Battle for Childhood*, 106

48. Nianias play a significant role in the memoirs and autobiographies of their former charges. For an insightful discussion of Russian nianias and the literary mythologizing of them, see Steven A. Grant, *The Russian Nanny, Real and Imagined: History, Culture, Mythology* (Washington, D.C.: New Academia Publishing, 2012).

49. Jessica Tovrov, *The Russian Noble Family: Structure and Change* (New York: Garland, 1987), 82.

50. V. Ya. Stoiunipa, "Obrazovanie russkoi zhenshchiny (po povodu dvadtsatipiatiletia russkikh zhenskikh gimnazii)." *Istoricheskii vestnik* 12 (April 1883), 133.

51. V. Figner, *Zapechatlennyi trud*, 1: 60.

52. V. Figner, *Polnoe sobranie sochinenii*, 5: 23.

53. Christine Johanson, *Women's Struggle for Higher Education in Russia, 1855–1900* (Kingston: McGill-Queen's University Press, 1987), 3.

54. Hoogenboom, "Vera Figner," 85.

55. Ibid.

56. V. Figner, *Zapechatlennyi trud*, 1: 95–96.

57. Noble service to the state became obligatory under Peter the Great in the early eighteenth century. Although Peter III freed nobles from obligatory service in 1762, service to the state remained emblematic of nobility and a route to greater prestige, honors, and riches.

58. Joan Landes, *Visualizing the Nation: Gender, Representation, and Revolution in Eighteenth-Century France* (Ithaca, N.Y.: Cornell University Press, 2001), 116–28.

59. Quoted in Deborah Valenze, *The First Industrial Woman* (New York: Oxford University Press, 1995), 156.

60. Elizabeth A. Wood, *The Baba and the Comrade: Gender and Politics in Revolutionary Russia* (Bloomington: Indiana University Press, 1997), 176.

61. V. Figner, *Zapechatlennyi trud*, 1: 64–68; V. Figner, *Polnoe sobranie sochinenii*, 5: 14.

62. V. Figner, *Zapechatlennyi trud*, 1: 96.

63. Ann Hibner Koblitz, *Science, Women, and Revolution in Russia* (Amsterdam: Harwood Academic, 2000), 6.

64. Although this phrase from Seymour Becker was used to describe the lot of provincial nobles, it is equally applicable to the way of life of *institutki* in this period. Seymour Becker, *Nobility and Privilege in Late Imperial Russia* (DeKalb: Northern Illinois University Press, 1985), 54.

65. Russian students were divided into these groupings based on assessments determined by ability in addition to age.

66. Toby W. Clyman and Judith Vowles, eds., *Russia through Women's Eyes* (New Haven, Conn.: Yale University Press, 1996), 78.

67. *The Contemporary* was just one of a number of so-called thick journals in Russia. These journals used the guise of literary criticism to censure the contemporary political, social, and economic order as a way to circumvent censorship laws. The journals were a pivotal part of public discourse in nineteenth-century Russia. Franco Venturi, *Roots of Revolution: A History of the Populist and Socialist Movements in Nineteenth-Century Russia*, trans. Francis Haskell (New York: Knopf, 1960), 146.

68. One member of the 1860s generation recalled, "We read the novel almost like worshippers with the kind of piety with which we read religious books." Quote cited in Andrew M. Drozd, *Chernyshevskii's* What Is to Be Done?: *A Reevaluation* (Evanston, Ill.: Northwestern University Press, 2001), 9. This quote and an insightful discussion around it also appear in

Ana Siljak, *Angel of Vengeance: The "Girl Assassin," the Governor of St. Petersburg, and Russia's Revolutionary World* (New York: St. Martin's, 2008), 56–57.

69. Daniel R. Brower, *Training the Nihilists: Education and Radicalism in Tsarist Russia* (Ithaca, N.Y.: Cornell University Press, 1975), 91.

70. Venturi, *Roots of Revolution*, 179.

71. Semenov, *Polnoe geograficheskoe*, 6: 136.

72. Ibid., 6: 136–37.

73. V. Figner, *Polnoe sobranie sochinenii*, 5: 27.

74. E. N. Vodovozova, *Na zare zhizn'* (Moscow: Izadatel'stvo "khudozhestvennaia literatura," 1964), 1: 472.

75. Richard Stites, *The Women's Liberation Movement in Russia: Feminism, Nihilism, and Bolshevism, 1860–1930* (Princeton, N.J.: Princeton University Press, 1978), 5.

76. Johanson, *Women's Struggle*, 11.

77. V. Figner, *Zapechatlennyi trud*, 1: 87.

78. Ibid., 1: 86.

79. Wachtel, *Battle for Childhood*, 129.

80. Vodovozova, *Na zare zhizn'*, 1: 395–97; Clyman and Vowles, *Russia through Women's Eyes*, 91–92.

81. V. Figner, *Zapechatlennyi trud*, 1: 89.

82. V. Figner, *Studencheskie gody*, 92.

83. V. Figner, *Zapechatlennyi trud*, 1: 83.

84. "Museum of the Revolution Brochure Celebrating 70th Birthday of Vera Nikolaevna Figner," RGALI, fond 1185, opis' 1, delo 114.

85. "Personal File of Vera Nikolaevna Figner in Files of the State Academy of Artistic Sciences," RGALI, fond 941, opis' 10, delo 649, listok, 3.

86. V. Figner, *Zapechatlennyi trud*, 1: 69.

2. AGE OF CONSCIOUSNESS

1. "Rech Very Nikolaevny Figner (Filippovoi) proiznesesnnoe eye v Peterburgskom voenno-okhruzhnom sude 27 sentiabria 1884 goda." *Listok Narodnoi Voli* 3 (November 1886).

2. V. Figner, *Zapechatlennyi trud*, 1: 97.

3. Ibid.

4. Confession of Vera Nikolaevna Figner, *Gosudarstvennyi Arkhiv Rossiiskoi Federatsii* (hereafter, GARF), fond 102, 7th deloproizvodstvo, opis' 1884, delo 747, Protocol of February 19, 1883.

5. Jürgen Habermas, *The Structural Transformation of the Public Sphere: An Inquiry into a Category of Bourgeois Society*, trans. Thomas Burger (Cambridge: MIT Press, 1991), 60. In analyzing the development of a public sphere, Habermas accords great weight to Great Britain's elimination of the institution of censorship in the 1690s. As Alexander II eased censorship restrictions in the period surrounding the abolition of serfdom, a similar phenomenon created a literary public sphere and allowed for a creation of public opinion in Russia in the nineteenth century.

6. Nikolai Chernyshevskii, *What Is to Be Done?*, trans. Michael R. Katz (Ithaca, N.Y.: Cornell University Press, 1989).

7. V. Figner, *Zapechatlennyi trud*, 1: 69.

8. When writing in her memoirs about her conversion to the creed of Socialism, Vera repeatedly quoted moral lessons from the gospels. All speak to the value of asceticism, self-sacrifice, and devotion to one's friends. Vera Zasulich, another noteworthy female revolutionary, engages in a similar practice. Both women cite the Gospel of John that stipulates there is no greater example of love "than a man who lays down his life for his friends." The use of this particular maxim speaks to the stress that this generation of revolutionaries put on notions of self-sacrifice. Zasulich is quoted in Siljak, *Angel of Vengeance*, 30. Vera Figner's words can be found in her *Studencheskie gody*, 94.

9. V. Figner, *Studencheskie gody*, 92.

10. "Speech of Vera Nikolaevna Figner at the commemoration of the 25th anniversary of the death of Gleb I. Uspensky, the 25th anniversary of the death of Nikolai K. Mikhailovskii, and the 50th anniversary of the death of Nikolai A. Nekrasov," January 8, 1928. RGALI, fond 1185, opis' 1, delo 179.

11. Koblitz, *Science, Women, and Revolution in Russia*, 6.

12. Ibid., 8.

13. Ibid., 10.

14. Ibid.

15. N. P. Efremova, "Pervye shagi russkikh zhenshchin k vysshemu obrazovaniiu." *Voprosy istorii* 5 (May 1983): 74–75.

16. Koblitz, *Science, Women, and Revolution in Russia*, 11.

17. Thomas Neville Bonner, *To the Ends of the Earth: Women's Search for Higher Education* (Cambridge, Mass.: Harvard University Press, 1992), 34.

18. J. M. Meijer, *Knowledge and Revolution: The Russian Colony in Zurich, 1870–1873* (Assen, Netherlands: Van Gorcum and Co., 1955), 24.

19. *Soveta St. Peterburgskoi biologicheskoi laboratorii P.F. Lesgafta*, ed. Pamiati Petra Frantsevicha Lesgafta (St. Petersburg: Shkola i zhizn, 1912), 144–45.

20. Vera Figner, *V Borbe* (Leningrad: Izdatel'stvo Detskaia Literatura, 1966), 39.

21. Barbara Alpern Engel, "Women Medical Students in Russia, 1872–1882: Reformers or Rebels?" *Journal of Social History* 12 (1978): 396.

22. Ibid. Perhaps the best example of the cult-like devotion to science that many nineteenth-century Russians possessed is Ivan Turgenev's classic work *Fathers and Sons*. Ivan Turgenev, *Fathers and Sons*, trans. Rosemary Edmonds (New York: Penguin Books, 1975).

23. V. Figner, *V Borbe*, 40.

24. V. Figner, *Zapechatennyi trud*, 1: 102.

25. V. Figner, *V Borbe*, 40.

26. N. G. Kulyabko-Koretsky, *Iz davnikh let: Vospominaniia Lavrista* (Moscow: Izdatel'stvo vsesoiuznogo obshchestva politkatorzhan i ssyl'no-poselentsev, 1931), 40.

27. V. Figner, *Zapechatlennyi trud*, 1: 104.

28. V. Figner, *V Borbe*, 41.

29. V. Figner, *Zapechatlennyi trud*, 1: 105.

30. Kulyabko-Koretsky, *Iz davnikh let*, 40.

31. Wachtel, *Battle for Childhood*, 103.

32. V. Figner, *Zapechatlennyi trud*, 1: 105.

33. V. Figner, "Iz avtobiografii Very Figner," *Byloe* 2 (August 1917): 158.

34. Ibid., 159.

35. L. D. Filippova, "Iz istorii zhenskogo obrazovaniia v Rossii." *Voprosy istorii* (February 1963): 211.

36. *Soveta St. Peterburgskoi biologicheskoi laboratorii P.F. Lesgafta,* 37.

37. V. Figner, *Zapechatlennyi trud,* 1: 107–108.

38. *Soveta St. Peterburgskoi biologicheskoi laboratorii P.F. Lesgafta,* 43.

39. V. Figner, "Iz avtobiografii Very Figner," *Byloe* 2 (August 1917): 160.

40. V. Figner, *Polnoe sobranie sochinenii,* 6: 67.

3. PIONEERS DIVERTED

1. Karl Baedeker, *Switzerland and the Adjacent Portions of Italy, Savoy, and Tyrol* (Leipzig: Karl Baedeker, 1911), 48.

2. Koblitz, *Science, Women, and Revolution,* 11.

3. Peter Kropotkin, *Memoirs of a Revolutionist* (New York: Horizon Press, 1968), 269.

4. M. P. Sazhin, "Russkie v Tsiurikhe," *Katorga i Ssylka* 10 (1932): 28; Bonner, *To the Ends of the Earth,* 44.

5. V. Figner, *Zapechatlennyi trud,* 1: 101–102.

6. V. Figner, *Studencheskie gody,* 9.

7. V. Figner, "Iz avtobiografii Very Figner," *Byloe* 2 (August 1917): 160.

8. Ibid.

9. Ibid.

10. Kulyabko-Koretsky, *Iz davnikh let,* 40.

11. V. Figner, "Iz avtobiografii Very Figner," *Byloe* 2 (August 1917): 160.

12. Sazhin, "Russkie v Tsiurikhe," 33; A. P. Stepanov, "Shveitsartsy v Rossii i russkie v shveitsarii," *Novaia i noveishaia istoriia* 1, no. 1 (2006): 120–51.

13. V. Figner, *Studencheskie gody,* 30.

14. Simone de Beauvoir, *The Second Sex,* trans. H. M. Parshley (New York: Vintage Books, 1989), 679.

15. Habermas, *Structural Transformation,* 54.

16. Sazhin, "Russkie v Tsiurikhe," 34.

17. Roger Chartier, *The Cultural Origins of the French Revolution,* trans. Lydia G. Cochrane (Durham, N.C.: Duke University Press, 1991), 23.

18. E. A. Pavliuchenko, *Zhenshchiny v Russkom osvoboditelnom dvizheniii: Ot Marii Volkonskoi do Very Figner* (Moscow: Mysl, 1988), 162.

19. V. Figner, *Studencheskie gody,* 28.

20. Amy Knight, "The Fritschi: A Study of Female Radicals in the Russian Populist Movement," *Canadian-American Slavic Studies* 9 (Spring 1975): 1–17.

21. V. Figner, *Zapechatlennyi trud,* 1: 122.

22. Qtd. in Voronikhin, "V. N. Figner v russkom," 73.

23. For an excellent study of the changing and intractable attitudes toward and policies about both marriage and divorce in the late imperial period, see Barbara Alpern Engel, *Breaking the Ties That Bound: The Politics of Marital Strife in Late Imperial Russia* (Ithaca, N.Y.: Cornell University Press, 2011).

24. Qtd. in ibid., 3.

25. F. Ia. Kon and Vladimir Dmitrievich Vilenskii, eds., *Deiateli revoliutsionnogo dvizheniia v Rossii bio-bibliograficheskii slovar': ot predshestvennikov dekabristov do padeniia tsarizm,* vol. 2, *vypusk* III (Moscow: Izd-vo politkatorzhan, 1927), 1835.

26. Lavrists were followers of Peter L. Lavrov, a prominent political theorist and an advocate of populism and socialism who escaped exile in Russia and relocated to Western Europe.

After spending time in Paris and taking part in the Paris Commune of 1871, Lavrov temporarily moved to Zurich in 1872. In Zurich he and his supporters became theoretical rivals of Mikhail Bakunin, a fellow proponent of Russian populism. M. P. Sazhin (Armand Ross), *Vospominaniia, 1860–1880x g.g.* (Moscow: Vsesoiuznoe obshchestvo politicheskikh katorzhan i ssyl'no-poselentsev, 1925), 46, 60.

27. See Barbara Heldt, *Terrible Perfection: Women and Russian Literature* (Bloomington: Indiana University Press, 1987).

28. V. Figner, "Iz Avtobiografii Very Figner," *Byloe* 2 (August 1917): 163.

29. Gregory L. Freeze, "Bringing Order to the Russian Family: Marriage and Divorce in Imperial Russia, 1760–1860, *Journal of Modern History* 62, no. 4 (1990): 709.

30. Gregory L. Freeze, "Krylov vs Krylova: 'Sexual Incapacity' and Divorce in Tsarist Russia," in *The Human Tradition in Modern Russia,* ed. William B. Husband (Wilmington, Del.: Scholarly Resources, 2000), 7.

31. V. Figner, *Zapechatlennyi trud,* 1: 114.

32. V. Figner, *Studencheskie gody,* 76–81.

33. These women included Sofia Bardina, Lidia Figner, Varvara Aleksandrova, Dora Aptekman, Betya Kaminskaia, Alexandra Khorzhevskaia, Olga Liubatovich, Vera Liubatovich, Eugenia Subbotina, Maria Subbotina, Nadezhda Subbotina, Anna Toporkova, and Eugenia Tumanova. Knight, "Fritschi," 4.

34. V. Figner, *Zapechatlennyi trud,* 1: 122.

35. V. Figner, "Iz avtobiografii Very Figner," *Byloe* 2 (August 1917): 160.

36. The Subbotina sisters' wealthy widowed mother, Sofia, financially supported not only her daughters' Zurich venture but also the education of at least one of her daughters' friends. See Barbara Alpern Engel, *Mothers and Daughters: Women of the Intelligentsia in Nineteenth-Century Russia* (Evanston, Ill.: Northwestern University Press, 2000), 159.

37. Sazhin, "Russkie v Tsiurikhe," 30.

38. Kropotkin, *Memoirs of a Revolutionist,* 269.

39. Knight, "Fritschi," 17.

40. Meijer, *Knowledge and Revolution,* 68.

41. P. L. Lavrov, *Gody emigratsii: Arkhivnye materialy v dvukh tomakh,* ed. Boris Sapir (Dordrecht, Holland: D. Reidel, 1974), 2: 44–46.

42. V. Figner, *Zapechatlennyi trud,* 1: 115.

43. V. Figner, *Studencheskie gody,* 40–41.

44. Lavrov, *Gody emigratsii,* 2: 45.

45. Qtd. in "Russian Women Students," *Times* (London), June 10, 1873, 14.

46. Qtd. in Meijer, *Knowledge and Revolution,* 141.

47. Marie Claude Burnet-Vigniel, *Femmes Russes dans le combat révolutionnaire: L'image et son modèle a la fin du XIXe siècle.* (Paris: Institut d'études slaves, 1990), 15.

48. Bonner, *To the Ends of the Earth,* 44–45; Meijer, *Knowledge and Revolution,* 56, 59; Sazhin, "Russkie v Tsiurikhe," 48.

49. Anon. Art. II—"The Zurich University. The Englishwoman's Review of Social and Industrial Questions," *Women's Journal* 4, no. 13 (1873): 7.

50. See Joan B. Landes, *Women and the Public Sphere in the Age of the French Revolution* (Ithaca, N.Y.: Cornell University Press, 1988).

51. Carla Hesse, *The Other Enlightenment: How French Women Became Modern* (Princeton, N.J.: Princeton University Press, 2001), 90.

52. Qtd. in an August 10, 1873, letter to the editor from an unidentified source at the University of Zurich, in "Recall of Russian Female Medical Students from Zurich," *Boston Medical Surgical Journal* 89 (1873): 343.

53. Ibid.

54. "Russian Women Students at Zurich," *New York Times,* July 16, 1873, 3.

55. "Women Students at Zurich," *Women's Journal* 4, no. 29 (1873): 231.

56. V. Figner, *Zapechatlennyi trud,* 1: 120.

57. Ruth A. Dudgeon, "The Forgotten Minority: Women Students in Imperial Russia, 1872–1917," *Russian History* 9 (1982): 7.

58. Bonner, *To the Ends of the Earth,* 90.

59. V. Figner, "Iz avtobiografii Very Figner," *Byloe* 2 (August 1917): 165.

60. Ibid.

61. Johanson, *Women's Struggle,* 57.

62. Engel, *Mothers and Daughters,* 144–45.

63. Meijer, *Knowledge and Revolution,* 147.

64. Kulyabko-Koretsky, *Iz davnikh let,* 40.

65. V. Figner, *Zapechatlennyi trud* 1; 132.

66. V. Figner, *Studencheskie gody,* 70.

67. Barbara Alpern Engel, "Women Medical Students in Russia, 1872–1882: Reformers or Rebels?" *Journal of Social History* 12 (1978): 409.

68. Knight, "Fritschi," 8.

69. V. Figner, *Zapechatlennyi trud,* 1: 128.

70. Ibid., 1: 127.

71. Ibid.

72. N. A. Morozov, *Povesti moei zhizni* (Moscow: Izdatel'stvo Nauka, 1965), 1: 434.

73. V. Figner, *Studencheskie gody,* 145.

74. Morozov, *Povesti moei zhizni,* 1: 433.

75. Ibid., 1: 434.

76. Ibid.

77. Ibid.

78. V. Figner, *Zapechatlennyi trud,* 1: 129.

79. V. Figner, *Studencheskie gody,* 147; Morozov, *Povesti moei zhizni,* 1: 432–33.

80. V. Figner, *Zapechatlennyi trud,* 1: 129.

81. Morozov, *Povesti moei zhizni,* 1: 471.

82. Ibid., 1: 475–81.

83. Ibid., 1: 483.

84. V. Figner, *Polnoe sobranie sochinenii,* 6: 67; Voronikhin, "V. N. Figner v russkom," 67. The money that Ekaterina Figner collected never made it out of the province of Kazan. On the orders of Russia's minister of internal affairs, Kazan's chief of police held the money and compelled Ekaterina to return the funds that she raised. Referenced in Engel, *Mothers and Daughters,* 142–43.

85. Kon and Vilenskii, eds., *Deiateli revoliutsionnogo dvizheniia v Rossii,* 2/III: 1002–1003.

86. V. Figner, *Studencheskie gody,* 153.

87. Ibid., 151.

88. Ibid., 154.

89. Morozov, *Povesti moei zhizni,* 1: 482.

90. V. Figner, *Studencheskie gody*, 154–55.

91. V. Figner, "Iz avtobiografii Very Figner," *Byloe* 2 (August 1917): 165.

92. V. Figner, *Studencheskie gody*, 94.

93. V. Figner, "Iz avtobiografii Very Figner," *Byloe* 2 (August 1917): 160.

94. Ibid.

4. TOWN AND COUNTRY

1. V. Figner, *Zapechatlennyi trud*, 1: 156.

2. The opportunities in question resulted from the patronage of one of Alexei Filippov's influential uncles who intervened to secure Vera's brother Nikolai a spot in the St. Petersburg Naval Academy. With Nikolai thus enrolled, Ekaterina and the rest of her children moved to St. Petersburg. See V. Figner, *Polnoe sobranie sochinenii*, 5: 28–29.

3. William Elroy Curtis, *The Land of the Nihilist: Russia, Its People, Its Palaces, Its Politics* (Chicago: Belford, Clarke and Co., 1888), 22.

4. At this time Lidia was imprisoned in Moscow. Vera's next oldest sibling, Peter, was twenty years old and living at home. Nikolai, then eighteen, had just finished his schooling in the naval academy in St. Petersburg and was serving in the Russian navy. The seventeen-year-old Eugenia Figner, who completed her gymnasium studies only months before her eldest sister returned to Russia, lived with her mother on Sadovaia Ulitsa as did thirteen-year-old Olga Figner. See GARF, fond 102, 7th proizvodstvo, opis' 1884, delo 747.

5. When the family relocated to St. Petersburg, they did not bring their servants from Kazan with them. Even Niania remained at Nikiforovo until her death during Vera's first winter abroad.

6. V. Figner, *Studencheskie gody*, 171.

7. Ibid., 171–72.

8. Ibid., 172.

9. Ibid., 168–69.

10. V. Figner, "Eugenia Nikolaevna Figner," *Katorga i ssylka* 2 (1924): 20.

11. Adam Ulam, *Prophets and Conspirators in Prerevolutionary Russia* (New Brunswick, N.J.: Transaction, 1998), 235–36.

12. V. Figner, *Studencheskie gody*, 172.

13. Ibid., 178–80.

14. V. Figner, "Iz avtobiografii Very Figner," *Byloe* 2 (August 1917): 171.

15. V. Figner, *Studencheskie gody*, 184.

16. Ibid.

17. Ibid., 185.

18. Certification given to "the wife of the Secretary of the Province, Vera Nikolaevna Filippova" and signed by Dr. Dmitrii Matveevich Glagolev, RGALI, fond 1185, opis' 1, delo 1, l. 1.

19. Karakozov was a member of the radical group "Hell." His attempt to shoot Alexander II as the tsar strolled through the Summer Gardens in St. Petersburg was allegedly thwarted when a peasant jostled (whether it was accidental or intentional depends on the source) Karakozov's arm as he was about to fire.

20. Ulam, *Prophets and Conspirators*, 252.

21. V. Figner, *Studencheskie gody*, 187. Interestingly, Vera identifies the doctor as Doctor

Pirozhkov in her memoirs. However, in the official document that attests to Vera's three months of work in the hospital, the signature, though indecipherable, bears no resemblance to the surname of Pirozhkov. Although it was indeed signed by the chief of staff of Yaroslavl Provincial County Hospital, the surname of this doctor cannot be verified.

22. "Certification by the Chief of Staff of the Yaroslavl Provincial County Hospital to Vera Nikolaevna Filippova," dated April 24, 1876. RGALI, fond 1185, opis' 1, delo 1, l. 2.

23. V. Figner, "Iz avtobiografii Very Figner," *Byloe* 2 (August 1917): 464.

24. Freeze, "Krylov vs. Krylova," 8.

25. Engel, *Breaking the Ties That Bound*, 15.

26. Engelstein, *Keys to Happiness*, 49–51.

27. Boris I. Nicolaevsky Collection, Box 75, folder 1, page 103–104, Hoover Institution Archives, Letter from V. I. Smirnov to R. Idelson, dated December 10, 1877.

28. Ibid., 104.

29. Qtd. in Voronikhin, "V. N. Figner v russkom," 73.

30. V. Figner, *Studencheskie gody*, 196–98.

31. V. Figner, "Evgeniia Nikolaevna Figner," *Katorga i ssylka* 2 (1924): 20.

32. V. Figner, *Polnoe sobranie sochinenii*, 5: 200.

33. "Iz pokazanii Iu. N. Bogdanovicha 22 sentiabria 1882 g.," *Kransnyi arkhiv* 1 (1927): 213; S. N. Valk, ed., *Arkhiv "Zemli i Voli" i "Narodnoi Voli"* (Moscow: Izdatel'stvo politkatorzhan, 1932), 58–59.

34. M. N. Polonskaia, "K istorii partii Narodnaia Volia," *Byloe* 6 (1907): 3.

35. M. Iu. Ashenbrenner, *Voennaia organizatsiia Narodnoi Voli i drugie vospominaniia (1860–1904)* (Moscow: Obshchestvo byvshikh politkatorzhan i ssyl'no-poselentsev, 1924), viii.

36. V. Figner, *Zapechatlennyi trud*, 1: 140–41.

37. Venturi, *Roots of Revolution*, 577.

38. Ibid.

39. V. Figner, *Polnoe sobranie sochinenii*, 5: 201; Valk, *Arkhiv "Zemli i Voli" i "Narodnoi Voli,"* 70.

40. *Zemstvos* were organs of local self-government formed in 1864 in the aftermath of the Emancipation Manifesto as part of a series of Great Reforms designed for a post-serfdom Russia.

41. Testimony given by Vera N. Figner on February 17, 1883, GARF, fond 102, 7th delo-proizvodstvo, opis' 1884, delo 747.

42. Avraham Yarmonlinsky, *Road to Revolution: A Century of Russian Radicalism* (New York: Collier Books, 1968), 210–11.

43. For a discussion of the *intelligenty*-led demonstration and the lack of worker support, see Pamela Sears McKinsey, "The Kazan Square Demonstration and the Conflict between Russian Workers and *Intelligenty*," *Slavic Review* 44, no. 1 (1985).

44. V. Figner, *Zapechatlennyi trud*, 1: 144.

45. Ulam, *Prophets and Conspirators*, 254.

46. Vladimir Burtsev, *Za sto let, 1800–1896: Sbornik po istorii politicheskikh i obshchestvennykh dvizhenii v Rossii*, part 2 (London: Russian Free Press Fund, 1897), 87.

47. Ulam, *Prophets and Conspirators*, 254. Iakov Potapov, who was hardly a revolutionary, spent the rest of his life in exile.

48. Betia Kaminskaia did not stand trial. During pretrial detention the former medical student went insane and eventually committed suicide. See V. Figner, *Polnoe sobranie sochinenii*, 5: 180

49. Yarmolinsky, *Road to Revolution*, 202.

50. N. A. Troitskii, "Vospominaniia Very Figner, zapisannye akademikom N. M. Druzhinym," *Sovetskie arkhivy* 2 (1987): 65.

51. V. Figner, *Polnoe sobranie sochinenii*, 5: 187–88.

52. Venturi, *Roots of Revolution*, 586.

53. The text of Bardina's speech can be found in Burtsev, *Za sto let*, part 1, 124–27.

54. Ibid., 127.

55. Sergei Kravchinskii, *Underground Russia: Revolutionary Profiles and Sketches from Life* (New York: Charles Scribner's Sons, 1883), 34.

56. V. Figner, *Polnoe sobranie sochinenii*, 5: 188–89.

57. Ulam, *Prophets and Conspirators*, 255.

58. V. Figner, *Zapechatlennyi trud*, 1: 146.

59. Referencing both Friedrich Spielhagen's secular parable "One in the Field Is Not a Warrior" and the Gospels, Vera once wrote that to live like Leo (the protagonist of Spielhagen's story, who suffered and struggled for others) and die like Jesus was her ideal. See V. Figner, *Zapechatlennyi trud*, 1: 93.

60. Testimony of V. N. Figner, March 17, 1883, GARF, fond 102, 7th proizvodstvo, opis' 1884, delo 747.

61. V. Figner, *Studencheskie gody*, 202–203.

62. Testimony of V. N. Figner on February 17, 1883, GARF, fond 102, 7th proizvodstvo, opis' 1884, delo 747.

63. V. Figner, *Studencheskie gody*, 203–205.

64. Ulam, *Prophets and Conspirators*, 239.

65. V. Figner, *Studencheskie gody*, 206.

66. Ibid., 204–11.

67. Deborah Hardy, *Land and Freedom: The Origins of Russian Terrorism, 1876–1879* (New York: Greenwood Press, 1987), 30.

68. Ibid.

69. V. Figner, *Polnoe sobranie sochinenii*, 5: 201.

70. May 19, 1881, inquiry of Alexander Ivanovich Ivanchin-Pisarev, GARF, fond 112, opis' 1, delo 503, l. 43.

71. Morozov, *Povesti moei zhizni*, 2: 191.

72. Ibid., 2: 192–93.

73. V. Figner, *Zapechatlennyi trud*, 1: 152. Police reports cite that both Eugenia and Peter Figner had ties with the Samara group. But there is no evidence to suggest that Eugenia went to Samara with her older sister or that Peter joined the separatists in the countryside. GARF, fond 102, 3rd proizvodstvo, opis' 77, 1881, delo 911.

74. "Inquiry of Dr. Vasili Dmitriev Vitevskii, February 23, 1878," GARF, fond 112, opis' 1, delo 486, l. 98.

75. "Inquiry of N. S. Popov, February 16, 1878," GARF, fond 112, opis' 1, delo 486, l. 90.

76. Ibid.

77. V. Figner, *Zapechatlennyi trud*, 1: 153–54.

78. Ibid., 1: 154.

79. Ibid.

80. Ibid., 1: 153.

81. The Third Department was the section of the government charged with ensuring state security within the borders. The gendarmerie belonged to the Third Department.

82. December 20, 1877, decree issued in connection with the case of Vera Petrovna Che-purnova, GARF, fond 112, opis' 1, delo 486, l. 12.

83. Inquiry of Alexander Ivanovich Ivanchin-Pisarev, May 19, 1881, GARF, fond 112, opis' 1, delo 503, l. 43–44.

84. Inquiry of N. S. Popov, February 16, 1878, GARF, fond 112, opis' 1, delo 486, l. 90.

85. A. I. Ivanchin-Pisarev, *Khozhdenie v narod* (Moscow: Molodaia Gvardia, 1929), 88–89.

86. Inquiry of N. S. Popov, February 16, 1878, GARF, fond 112, opis' 1, delo 486, l. 90–91 ob.

87. Venturi, *Roots of Revolution*, 591. While at first glance the fact that so many were ac-quitted seems to suggest justice at work, one must bear in mind that the government lacked sufficient evidence against many of the defendants and that these young people had already served three to four years in prison when the trial began.

88. V. Figner, *Zapechatlennyi trud*, 1: 156.

89. Jay Bergman, *Vera Zasulich: A Biography* (Stanford, Calif.: Stanford University Press, 1983).

90. Kravchinskii, *Underground Russia*, 36.

91. After the acquittal, Zasulich's lawyer, P. A. Alexanderov, received a telegram com-mending him on a job well done. Among the three signatories was Vera Figner. See Troitskii, "Vospominaniia Very Figner," 64. In the words of Louise McReynolds, "Zasulich's trial sym-bolized a political point of no return: the civil society represented by jurors continued their inexorable separation from the autocracy." Louise McReynolds, "Witnessing for the Defense: The Adversarial Court and Narratives of Criminal Behavior in Nineteenth Century Russia," *Slavic Review* 69 (Fall 2010): 620.

92. Philip Pomper, *The Russian Revolutionary Intelligentsia* (New York: Thomas Y. Crow-ell, 1970), 122.

93. Ibid.

94. Morozov, *Povesti moei zhizni*, 2: 229.

95. Ibid., 2: 246.

96. Ivanchin-Pisarev, *Khozhdenie v narod*, 93.

97. GARF, fond 112, opis' 1, delo 503, l. 44.

98. Rex A. Wade and Scott J. Seregny, eds., *Politics and Society in Provincial Russia: Sara-tov, 1590–1917* (Columbus: Ohio State University Press, 1989), 49–72.

99. Morozov, *Povesti moei zhizni*, 2: 258–60.

100. Ibid., 2: 261.

101. This tendency can also be discerned about the women radicals of the 1860s. Although they were a smaller population than their female counterparts of the 1870s and 1880s, the 1860s radicals by and large remained childless. Koblitz, *Science, Women, and Revolution*, 72.

102. V. Figner, *Zapechatlennyi trud*, 1: 161.

103. "Narodovol'tsy v saratovskii gubernii," *Sovetskie arkhivy* 2 (1991): 80.

104. V. Figner, "Evgenia Nikolaevna Figner," 21.

105. V. Figner, *Zapechatlennyi trud*, 1: 162.

106. V. Figner, "Avtobiografii Very Figner," in *Deiateli SSSR: Revoliutsionnogo dvizheniia Rossi entsiklopedicheskii slovar' Granat* (Moscow: Sovetskaia Entsiklopediia, 1989), 466.

107. Hardy, *Land and Freedom*, 148.

108. S. S. Volk, ed., *"Narodnaia Volia" i "Chernyi Peredel": Vospominaniia uchastnikov revo-liutsionnogo dvizheniia v Peterburge v 1879–1882gg.* (Leningrad: Lenizdat, 1989), 7.

109. Confession of Vera N. Figner, March 4, 1883, GARF, fond 102, 7th proizvodstvo, opis' 1884, delo 747.

110. GARF, fond 102, 7th proizvodstvo, opis' 1884, delo 747.

111. V. Figner, *Zapechatlennyi trud*, 1: 164.

112. Petrovsk *uezd* lay in a very fertile section of Saratov province. Its rich black soil provided a higher standard of living than the more impoverished Studentsy village where Vera previously worked. See Wade and Seregny, *Politics and Society*, 18.

113. V. Figner, *Zapechatlennyi trud*, 1: 164.

114. "Rech Very Nikolaevny Figner," 280.

115. V. Figner, *Zapechatlennyi trud*, 1: 165.

116. Ibid., 1: 171.

117. "Narodovol'tsy v Saratovskii gubernii," 85, 87.

118. V. Figner, *Zapechatlennyi trud*, 1: 173.

119. Valk, *Arkhiv "Zemli i Voli" i "Narodnoi Voli,"* 57.

120. V. Figner, *Zapechatlennyi trud*, 1: 174.

5. THE TSAR'S DEATH SENTENCE

1. Richard S. Wortman, *Scenarios of Power: Myth and Ceremony in Russian Monarchy, From Peter the Great to the Abdication of Nicholas II* (Princeton, N.J.: Princeton University Press, 2006), 220.

2. Ibid., 235.

3. For conceptions of political violence as a justified method of struggle, see William Ascher, "The Morality of Attitudes Supporting Intergroup Violence," *Political Psychology* 7, no. 3 (1986): 403–25.

4. Martha Crenshaw, "Thoughts on Relating Terrorism to Historical Contexts," ed. Martha Crenshaw, *Terrorism in Context* (University Park: Pennsylvania State University Press, 1995), 42.

5. V. Figner, *Polnoe sobranie sochinenii*, 5: 195.

6. Ascher, "Morality of Attitudes," 404.

7. Ibid., 419.

8. A. V. Tyrkov, *K sobytiiu 1 marta 1881 goda* (Rostov-on-Don: Tipografiia donskaia rech, 1906), 8.

9. A. V. Iakimova-Dikovskaia, M. F. Frolensko, et al., eds., *"Narodnaia Volia" v dokumentakh I vospominaniiakh* (Moscow: Izdatel'stvo obshchestva politkatorzhan, 1930), 251.

10. Ibid., 92–93.

11. V. Figner, *Zapechatlennyi trud*, 1: 174.

12. Anna Iakimova, "Iz dalekogo proshlogo (Iz vospominanii o pokusheniiakh na Aleksandra II)," *Katorga i Ssylka* 1 (1924): 9.

13. V. Figner, *Zapechatlennyi trud*, 1: 205.

14. Morozov, *Povesti moei zhizni*, 2: 415–18; M. P. Popov, "Iz moego revoliutsionnago proshlago (1878–1879gg.)," *Byloe* 7 (1907): 274–76.

15. *"Narodnaia Volia"—Degaevshchina—Protsess 14-ti* (St. Petersburg: Izdanie i tipografiia S. M. Propper, 1907), 9.

16. Those present included both members of *Land and Freedom* and individuals who did not yet belong to the group but who were sympathetic to a terrorist struggle. They included A. I. Barannikov, A. I. Zheliabov, A. A. Kviatkovskii, N. N. Kolodkevich, A. D. Mikhailov, N. A. Morozov, M. N. Olovennikova-Oshanina, L. A. Tikhomirov, M. F. Frolenko, S. G. Shiriaev, and G. D. Goldenberg. See *"Kalendar' Narodnoi Voli"* in Iakimova-Dikovskaia et al., *"Narodnaia Volia,"* 260.

17. Morozov, *Povesti moei zhizni*, 2: 421.

18. Polonskaia, "K istorii partii Narodnaia Volia," 5.

19. David Footman, *Red Prelude: A Life of A. I. Zheliabov* (London: Barrie and Rockliff, 1968), 100.

20. A. P. Pribyleva-Korba and Vera Figner, *Narodovolets Alexandr Dmitrievich Mikhailov* (Leningrad: Gosudarstvennoe Izdatel'stvo, 1925), 135; G. S. Kan, *"Narodnaia Volia": Ideologiia i lidery* (Moscow: Izdatel'stvo "Probel," 1997), 54.

21. Popov, "Iz moego revoliutsionnago," 273.

22. S. S. Volk, ed., *"Narodnaia Voli" i "Chernyi Peredel": Vospominaniia uchastnikov revoliutsionnogo dvizheniia v Peterburge v 1879–1882 gg.* (Leningrad: Lenizdat, 1989), 6.

23. Ibid., 89.

24. Morozov, *Povesti moei zhizni*, 2: 427; Valk, *Arkhiv "Zemli i Voli" i "Narodnoi Voli,"* 54–57.

25. Volk, *"Narodnaia Voli" i "Chernyi Peredel,"* 52.

26. V. Figner, *Zapechatlennyi trud*, 1: 190.

27. Ibid., 1: 192.

28. S. S. Volk, *Narodnaia Volia, 1879–1882* (Moscow: Izdatel'stvo "Nauka," 1966), 94.

29. Nikolai Morozov urged that "dynamite and the revolver be the answer to these executions," while Alexander Mikhailov promised that "the government will pay dearly for its actions. See A. P. Pribyleva-Korba, *"Narodnaia Volia": Vospominaniia o 1870–1880-kh gg.* (Moscow: Vsesoioznoe obshchestva politicheskikh katorzhan i ssyl'no-poselentsev, 1926), 41.

30. Iakimova-Dikovskaia et al., *"Narodnaia Volia,"* 260.

31. Polonskaia, "K istorii partii Narodnaia Volia," 3.

32. Ibid.

33. Volk, *Narodnaia Volia, 1879–1882*, 95; Olga Liubatovich, *Dalekoe i nedavnee* (Moscow: Izdatel'stvo vsesoiuznogo obshchestva politkatorzhan i ssyl'no-poselentsev, 1930), 75.

34. "Rech Very Nikolaevny Figner (Filippovoi)," 280.

35. From *Narodnaia Volia*, 1 (October 1, 1879), in *Literatura Partii "Narodnaia Volia"* (Moscow: Izdatel'stvo vsesoiuznogo obshchestva politkatorzhan i ssyl'no-poselentsev, 1930, 1.

36. *Literatura Partii "Narodnaia Volia,"* 49.

37. Ibid., 50.

38. V. Figner, *Zapechatlennyi trud*, 1: 194.

39. *Literatura Partii "Narodnaia Volia,"* 1.

40. Iakimova-Dikovskaia et al., *"Narodnaia Volia"* 261.

41. Claudia Verhoeven, *The Odd Man Karakozov: Imperial Russia, Modernity, and the Birth of Modern Terrorism* (Ithaca, N.Y.: Cornell University Press, 2009), 4–6.

42. In 1762 Catherine II deposed her husband, Peter III, to claim the throne in the name of her eight-year-old-son, Paul. In the days that followed, conspirators murdered the deposed Peter III. Meanwhile Catherine retained the throne, refusing to step aside in favor of her son. Paul only became tsar in 1796, when Catherine the Great died. Paul in turn was overthrown in a coup d'etat that left him dead and his son Alexander on the throne in 1801.

43. V. Figner, *Zapechatlennyi trud*, 1: 208.

44. Qtd. in James H. Billington, *Fire in the Minds of Men: Origins of the Revolutionary Faith* (New York: Basic Books, 1980), 409.

45. Ibid., 388.

46. Ibid., 408.

47. Ibid.

48. V. Figner, *Zapechatlennyi trud*, 1: 197–98.

49. Volk, *"Narodnaia Voli" i "Chernyi Peredel,"* 166.

50. Mikhail Frolenko, *Sobranie sochinenii v dvukh tomakh* (Moscow: Izdatel'stvo vsesoiuznogo obshchestva politkatorzhan i ssyl'no-poselentsev, 1932), 2: 62.

51. See Footman, *Red Prelude*, 115–21; Kan, "Narodnaia Volia," 69–70.

52. V. Figner, "Avtobiografii Very Nikolaevny Figner," in *Deiateli SSSR*, 469.

53. V. Figner, *Zapechatlennyi trud*, 1: 210.

54. Ibid., 1: 285.

55. V. Figner, "Iz avtobiografii Very Figner," *Byloe* 3 (September 1917): 188.

56. Charles King, *Odessa: Genius and Death in a City of Dreams* (New York: W. W. Norton, 2011), 88.

57. Ibid., 135–36.

58. V. Figner, *Zapechatlennyi trud*, 1: 211.

59. Ibid., 1: 212.

60. Iakimova-Dikovskaia et al., "Narodnaia Volia," 189; Frolenko, *Sobranie sochinenii v dvukh tomakh* 2: 112.

61. V. Figner, "Avtobiografiii Very Nikolaevny Figner," in *Deiateli SSSR*, 469.

62. V. Figner, "Iz avtobiografii Very Figner," *Byloe* 3: 189.

63. V. Figner, *Zapechatlennyi trud*, 1: 212; Iakimova-Dikovskaia et al., "Narodnaia Volia," 261.

64. Iakimova-Dikovskaia et al., "Narodnaia Volia" 261.

65. Pribyleva-Korba, "Narodnaia Volia": *Vospominaniia*, 48. By all accounts Goldenberg was duped into becoming an informant, convinced by government investigators' assurances that the information he provided them would allow the two sides to compromise on some liberal reforms. When he ultimately realized his mistake, Goldenberg committed suicide.

66. Footman, *Red Prelude*, 115; Venturi, *Roots of Revolution*, 682.

67. Pribyleva-Korba and Figner, *Narodovolets Alexandr Dmitrievich Mikhailov*, 142.

68. Alexis Peri and Christine Evans, "How Terrorists Learned to Map," in *Petersburg, Petersburg: Novel and City, 1900–1921*, ed. Olga Matich (Madison: University of Wisconsin Press, 2010), 152.

69. Understandably, the Executive Committee never mentioned that this was only one of three failed attempts. In referring to the failed attack outside of Moscow in the official proclamation, the terrorists state, "We do not find it convenient to publish at the present time the reason of the failure." Reprinted in "The Doom of the Czar," *New York Times*, December 25, 1879, 3.

70. Iakimova-Dikovskaia et al., "Narodnaia Volia" 93.

71. Ibid.

72. Ibid.

73. Ibid.

74. GARF, fond 102, 3rd proizvodstvo, 1881, opis' 77, delo 911.

75. Ibid. Peter Figner was released from the House of Preliminary Detention on January 7, 1880. Finally cleared of all culpability in July 1881, he pursued business interests and, unlike his sisters, became a respectable member of society. See F. Ia. Kon et al., *Deiateli revoliutsionnogo dvizheniia v Rossii*, II/III, 1829.

76. V. Figner, "Evgenia Nikolaevna Figner," 22.

77. V. Figner, *Zapechatlennyi Trud*, 1: 210.

78. V. Figner, "Evgenia Nikolaevna Figner," 22.

79. When Eugenia and Kviatkovskii were sentenced in the "Trial of the Sixteen," their punishments were harsh indeed. Figner was deprived of all rights and exiled to Siberia for

twenty-one years. Kviatkovskii was condemned to death and executed on November 4, 1880. See V. Burtsev, *Za sto let,* part 2, 104.

80. "Iz pokazanii V. N. Figner," 31.

81. V. Figner, *Zapechatlennyi trud,* 1: 216.

82. Ibid., 1: 215–16; Pribyleva-Korba, "*Narodnaia Volia,*" 42.

83. V. Figner, *Zapechatlennyi trud,* 1: 216.

84. Ibid.

85. Ibid.

86. Hesse, *Other Enlightenment,* 152.

87. Yarmolinsky, *Road to Revolution,* 250.

88. Ibid., 251.

89. Ibid.

90. Bruce Hoffman, *Inside Terrorism* (New York: Columbia University Press, 2006), 5–6.

91. V. Figner, *Zapechatlennyi trud,* 1: 285.

92. "Explosion in the Imperial Winter Palace," *Times* (London), February 19, 1880, 5.

93. Wortman, *Scenarios of Power,* 237.

94. Qtd. in Peter A. Zaionchkovskii, *The Russian Autocracy in Crisis, 1878–1882,* ed. and trans. Gary M. Hamburg (Gulf Breeze, Fla.: Academic International Press, 1979), 92.

95. Ibid., 115–16, 119, 140–43, 158–64, 187.

96. "Iz pokazanii V.N. Figner," 32.

97. Ibid., 33.

98. Vera Figner, *Shlissel'burgskie uzniki, 1884–1905g.: Biograficheskie ocherki* (Moscow: Zadruga, 1920), 62.

99. Iakimova-Dikovskaia et al., "*Narodnaia Volia,*" 262.

100. V. Figner, *Zapechatlennyi trud,* 1: 226.

101. Footman, *Red Prelude,* 145.

102. N. K. Mikhailovskii, *Vospominaniia* (Berlin: Izdanie Gugo Shteineshcha, 1906), 14. Similarly, Ivanchin-Pisarev details a New Year's Eve party on December 31, 1880. Although a crucial time in the group's history, many narodovol'tsy gathered for a boisterous party despite the risks. See Ivanchin-Pisarev, *Khozhdenie v narod,* 391.

103. Iain Lauchlan, "The Okhrana: Security Policing in Late Imperial Russia," in *Late Imperial Russia: Problems and Prospects,* ed. Ian D. Thatcher (Manchester, U.K.: Manchester University Press, 2005), 45–46.

104. See Ashenbrenner, *Voennaia Organizatsiia Narodnoi Voli,* 87; Venturi, *Roots of Revolution,* 619–20.

105. Jonathan Daly, *Autocracy under Siege: Security Police and Opposition in Russia, 1860–1905* (DeKalb: Northern Illinois University Press, 1998), 30.

106. V. Figner, *Shlissel'burgskie uzniki,* 57.

107. Valk, *Arkhiv "Zemli i Voli " i "Narodnoi Voli,"* 123; "Iz pokazanii V. N. Figner," 37.

108. Volk, "*Narodnaia Voli" i "Chernyi Peredel,*" 199–200.

109. Ashenbrenner, *Voennaia Organizatsiia Narodnoi Voli,* 69–70.

110. There were no terrorist acts or attempted assassinations in the last few months of 1880. "*Narodnaia Volia"—Degaevshchina-Protsess 14-ti,* 24.

111. V. Figner, *Zapechatlennyi trud,* 1: 232.

112. Even the *Times* (London) noted that the Will of the People "has already adopted a less offensive and threatening tone" in the wake of "Melikoff's [Melikov's] pacification." See *Times* (London), November 13, 1880, 6.

113. Iakimova-Dikovskaia et al., "*Narodnaia Volia,*" 263.
114. V. Figner, "*Eugenia Nikolaevna Figner,*" 23; Burtsev, *Za sto let,* 104.
115. Iakimova-Dikovskaia et al., "*Narodnaia Volia,*" 96–97. High-ranking officials seemed to take the terrorists at their word. By later November, Loris-Melikov refused to venture out without an escort of four guards. See GARF, fond 1762, opis' 4, delo 625, l. 21.
116. Tyrkov, *K sobytiiu 1 marta 1881 goda,* 12.
117. Ibid., 11.
118. V. Figner, *Zapechatlennyi trud* 1: 248.
119. Polonskaia, "K istorii partii Narodnaia Volia," 7.
120. Iakimova, "Iz dalekogo proshlogo," 12.
121. "Iz pokazanii V. N. Figner," 39.
122. V. Figner, *Zapechatlennyi trud,* 1: 262.
123. Iakimova, "Iz dalekogo proshlogo," 13.
124. Ibid., 14.
125. Footman, *Red Prelude,* 176–81.
126. Yarmolinsky, *Road to Revolution,* 265.
127. V. Figner, *Zapechatlennyi trud,* 1: 265.
128. Ibid., 1: 266.
129. Ibid.
130. Ibid.
131. Ibid.

6. REVOLUTIONARY ICONOGRAPHY

1. Iakimova, "Iz dalekogo proshlogo," 16.
2. V. Figner, *Zapechatlennyi trud,* 1: 268.
3. Rossiskii gosudarstvennyi Istoricheskii Arkhiv (hereafter RGIA), fond 1405, opis' 80, delo 8141, listok 2.
4. Ibid., l. 2.
5. Timofei Mikhailov was supposed to throw the first bomb, but his nerves got the better of him and he fled the scene without throwing the bomb. Tyrkov, *K sobytiiu 1 marta 1881 goda,* 16.
6. RGIA, fond 1405, opis' 80, delo 8141, l. 2.
7. Ibid., l. 2–3.
8. As the newspaper *Sankt-Peterburgskikh Vedomostei* reported the next morning, Alexander II's extensive blood loss made it immediately clear that the situation was hopeless. "Pokushenie na zhizn' gosudaria imperatora," *Sankt-Peterburgskikh Vedomostei,* Osoboe pribavlenie, 2 (14) Marta 1881.
9. RGIA, fond 1405, opis' 80, delo 8141, l. 3.
10. V. Figner, *Zapechatlennyi trud,* 1: 268.
11. Ibid.
12. Ibid.
13. Volk, "*Narodnaia Volia*" i "*Chernyi Peredel,*" 30. In addition to the tsar and his assassin, three other individuals died from the two blasts, including a small boy. Twenty additional people were injured. See Venturi, *Roots of Revolution,* 713.
14. V. Figner, *Zapechatlennyi trud,* 1:251.
15. "Proklamatsiia po povodu 1 Marta 1881 go," included in Iakimova-Dikovskaia et al., "*Narodnaia Volia,*" 98.

16. Ibid., 98.

17. See Viktor Kel'ner, *1 marta 1881 goda: kazn' imperatora Aleksandra II, dokumenty i vospominaniia* (Leningrad: Lenizdat, 1991), 19–42, 234–77; Volk, *"Narodnaia Volia" i "Chernyi Peredel,"* 40.

18. "O 58 litsakh," GARF, fond 102, opis' 1881, 3rd proizvodstvo, delo 79, ch. 1, reel 1.

19. Sablin, with whom Vera had been friends since Switzerland, shot himself before the police could apprehend him. He died instantly.

20. V. Figner, *Zapechatlennyi trud*, 1: 307.

21. Ibid.

22. Lecture given by V. N. Figner titled, "Feminizm i rol' zhenshchiny v borbe za svobodu v Rossii," RGALI, fond 1185, opis' 1, delo 187, l. 20.

23. Iakimova, "Iz dalekogo proshlogo," 16.

24. Ibid., 17.

25. Kel'ner, *1 Marta 1881 goda*, 19; Iakimova-Dikovskaia et al., *"Narodnaia Volia,"* 265. Crews removed the mine on March 5.

26. "Pokushenie na zhizn' gosudaria imperatora," *Sankt-Peterburgskikh Vedomostei*, Osoboe pribavlenie, 2 (14) Marta 1881.

27. 3 (15) Marta 1881, *Sankt-Peterburgskikh Vedomostei*, 1.

28. *Times* (London), April 4, 1881, 5. Since the Western calendar was twelve days ahead of the Russian calendar, April 4 in London was March 22 in St. Petersburg; S. S. Volk, *Narodnaia Volia, 1879–1882* (Moscow: Izdatel'stvo Nauka, 1966), 114.

29. V. Figner, *Zapechatlennyi trud*, 1: 278–79.

30. Qtd. in Richard Pipes, *The Degaev Affair: Terror and Treason in Tsarist Russia* (New Haven, Conn.: Yale University Press, 2003), 17.

31. *Literatura partii "Narodnaia Volia,"* 316–17.

32. V. Figner, *Zapechatlennyi trud*, 1: 302–307; Volk, *"Narodnaia Volia" i "Chernyi Peredel,"* 40.

33. Konrad Kellen, *Terrorists: What Are They Like?* (Santa Monica, Calif.: Rand Corporation, 1970), 9.

34. Crenshaw, "Thoughts on Relating Terrorism," 4.

35. Robert A. Paper, *Dying to Win: The Strategic Logic of Suicide Terrorism* (New York: Random House, 2006), 9.

36. P. Shchegolev, "Posle pervogo marta 1881 goda," *Byloe* 3 (1907): 290.

37. Ibid., 294; Volk, *Narodnaia Volia, 1879–1882*, 134.

38. Alexander Polovtsov noted in a March 27 journal entry that "in the city they are saying, 'C'est [la] fuite de Varenne.'" This remark references the attempt of Louis XVI and his family to flee France as the Revolution intensified in 1790. See Zaionchkovksii, *The Russian Autocracy in Crisis*, 197.

39. Polonskaia, "K istorii partii Narodnaia Volia." 9.

40. V. Figner, "Iz pokazanii V. N. Figner," *Byloe* 7 (July 1906): 41.

41. Ibid.

42. V. Figner, *Zapechatlennyi trud*, 1: 270; P. Kantor, "K istorii voennoi organizatsii 'Narodnoi Voli,' pokazaniia F. I. Zavalishina," *Katorga i Ssylka* 5 (1925): 221; Volk, *"Narodnaia Volia" i "Chernyi Peredel,"* 205–206.

43. V. Figner, *Zapechatlennyi trud*, 1: 271; Volk, *"Narodnaia Volia" i "Chernyi Peredel,"* 205.

44. *"O gosudarstvennoi prestuplenie Vere Filippovoi*, GARF, fond 102, 3rd proizvodstvo, opis' 1881, ch. 1, reel 6.

45. V. Figner, *Zapechatlennyi trud*, 1: 271.

46. Foucault, *Discipline and Punish,* 48.

47. Ibid., 49.

48. Ibid. Making the executions even more egregious for some was the ineptitude with which they were carried out. Especially horrific was the hanging of Timofei Mikhailov, for whom three separate attempts had to be undertaken before his slow torture came to an end and he was finally dead. See *Times* (London), April 18, 1881, 5.

49. RGALI, fond, 1185, opis' 1, delo 114; Volk, "*Narodnaia Volia*" i "*Chernyi Peredel,*" 207–208.

50. Volk, *Narodnaia Volia, 1879–1882,* 208.

51. Kantor, "K istorii voennoi organizatsii 'Narodnoi Voli,'" 221.

52. Volk, "*Narodnaia Volia*" i "*Chernyi Peredel,*" 208.

53. Kantor, "K istorii voennoi organizatsii 'Narodnoi Voli,'" 221; V. Figner, *Zapechatlennyi trud,* 1: 290.

54. V. Figner, *Zapechatlennyi trud,* 1: 291–92.

55. Ibid., 1: 345.

56. A. N. Bakh, *Zapiski Narodovol'tsa* (Leningrad: Molodaia gvardiia, 1929), 26–42; "K istorii narodovol'cheskogo dvizheniia sredi voennykh v nachale 80-kh godov," *Byloe* 8 (1906): 159–86; *Narodovol'tsy posle 1-go marta 1881 goda* (Moscow: Izdatel'stvo vsesoiuznogo obshchestva politkatorzhan i ssyl'no-poselentsev, 1928), 29–60, 116–27.

57. "K istorii narodovol'cheskogo dvizheniia sredi voennykh v nachale 80-kh godov," 178, 182–85.

58. L. N. Godunova, "Arkhivnye istochniki o voennoi organizatsii partii Narodnaia Volia," *Sovetskie Arkhivy* 1 (1971): 77.

59. "Iz pokazanii V. N. Figner," 42; "K istorii narodovol'cheskogo dvizheniia sredi voennykh v nachale 80-kh godov," 163–64.

60. "K istorii narodovol'cheskogo dvizheniia sredi voennykh v nachale 80-kh godov," 159.

61. Volk, *Narodnaia Volia, 1879–1882,* 328.

62. Bakh, *Zapiski Narodovol'tsa,* 41.

63. See *Literatura partii "Narodnaia Volia"* and Iakimova-Dikovskaia et al., "*Narodnaia Volia,*" 266–69.

64. October 23, 1881, edition of *Narodnaia Volia,* included in *Literatura partii "Narodnoi Volia,*" 127.

65. "Dokumenty dlia istorii obshchestva krasnago kresta partii Narodnoi Voli," *Byloe* 3 (1906): 288.

66. Ibid., 290.

67. Ibid., 288.

68. On May 3 the correspondent for the *Times* of London referred to the emperor's "retirement at Gatchina." *Times* (London), May 3, 1881, 5.

69. "Iz pokazanii V. N. Figner," 42.

70. Ibid., 43.

71. "*Narodnaia Volia*"—*Degaevshchina*—*Protsess 14-ti,*" 31.

72. Iakimova-Dikovskaia et al., "*Narodnaia Volia,*" 268.

73. V. Figner, *Zapechatlennyi trud,* 1: 325–26; Pribyleva-Korba, "*Narodnaia Volia,*" 170; Volk, *Narodnaia Volia, 1879–1882,* 141.

74. V. Figner, *Zapechatlennyi trud,* 1: 325.

75. Ibid., 1: 326.

76. V. Figner, *Zapechatlennyi trud,* 1: 359.

77. V. Figner, "Avtobiografiia Very Nikolaevny Figner," in *Deiateli SSSR,* 471.

78. "Iz 'obzora' sostavlennago departamentom politsii za 1882 god," *Byloe* 11 (1906): 261.

79. Ibid., 252; Pribyleva-Korba, *"Narodnaia Volia,"* 172; Volk, *Narodnaia Volia, 1879–1882,* 142.

80. "Iz 'obzora' sostavlennago departamentom politsii za 1882 god," 261; Pribyleva-Korba, *"Narodnaia Volia,"* 172; Volk, *Narodnaia Volia, 1879–1882,* 142.

81. V. Figner, *Zapechatlennyi trud,* 1: 326.

82. V. Figner, *Polnoe sobranie sochinenii,* 6: 23.

83. "Iz 'obzora' sostavlennago departamentom politsii za 1882 god," 261.

84. Pribyleva-Korba, *"Narodnaia Volia,"* 172.

85. Ibid.

86. Letter from Vera Figner to N. A. Morozov dated April 18, 1880, GARF, fond 1762, opis' 4, delo 625, l. 1.

87. V. Figner, *Polnoe sobranie sochinenii,* 6: 10.

88. Ibid.

89. Vera Broido, *Apostles into Terrorists: Women and the Revolutionary Movement in the Russia of Alexander II* (New York: Viking Press, 1977), 203.

90. Boris I. Nikolaevsky Collection, box 616, series 263, folder 14, 189–90.

91. Ibid., 190.

92. Joan Landes's discussion of the liberty icon as a female representation is instructive when considering the role that Vera Figner and other women radicals played in the Russian revolutionary movement. Landes, *Women and the Public Sphere,* 158–63.

93. The concept of Russian revolutionary women as divine heroines is discussed in Marie-Claude, Burnet-Vigniel, *Femmes Russes dans le combat révolutionnaire: L'image et son modelé à la fin du XIXe siècle* (Paris: Institut d'études slaves, 1990), 14.

94. V. Figner, *Polnoe sobranie sochinenii,* 6: 13.

95. Burnet-Vigniel, *Femmes Russes dans le combat révolutionnaire,* 21.

96. Qtd. in Ivanchin-Pisarev, *Khozhdenie v narod,* 307.

97. Volk, *Narodnaia Volia, 1879–1882,* 147.

98. Godunova, "Arkhivnye istochniki o voennoi organizatsii," 80.

99. Bakh, *Zapiski Narodovol'tsa,* 32.

100. V. Figner, *Polnoe sobranie sochinenii,* 5: 338.

101. V. Figner, *Zapechatlennyi trud,* 1: 348.

102. Pipes, *Degaev Affair,* 12–13.

103. V. Figner, *Zapechatlennyi trud,* 1: 348; *"K istorii narodovol'cheskogo dvizheniia sredi voennykh v nachale 80-kh godov,"* 168–69.

104. V. Figner, *Polnoe sobranie sochinenii,* 5: 333; Mikhailovskii, *Vospominaniia,* 6–7; "Dokumenty i materialy k istorii peregovorov Ispolnitel'nago Komiteta s Sviashchennoi Druzhinoi," *Byloe* 9 (1907): 213.

105. K. A. Borozdin, "Sviashchennaia Druzhina i Narodnaia Volia," *Byloe* 10 (1907); "Dokumenty i materialy k istorii peregovorov Ispolnitel'nago Komiteta s Sviashchennoi Druzhinoi," 208–13; L. Tikhomirov, "Neizdannye zapiski L. Tikhomirova," *Krasnyi Arkhiv* 4 (1928): 159–62.

106. Tikhomirov, "Neizdannye zapiski L. Tikhomirova," 158.

107. V. Figner, *Polnoe sobranie sochinenii,* 5: 335.

108. Ibid., 5: 337.

109. Mikhailovskii, *Vospominaniia,* 8, 13.

110. V. Figner, *Zapechatlennyi trud,* 1: 351; V. Figner, *Polnoe sobranie sochinenii,* 5: 340–46.

111. V. Figner, *Zapechatlennyi trud,* 1: 352.

112. Ashenbrenner, *Voennaia organizatsiia Narodnoi Voli,* 101; *Narodnaia Volia—Degaevshchina—Protsess 14-ti,* 37–38.

113. "Degaevshchina (materialy i dokumenty)," *Byloe* 4 (1906): 35–36. For a more sympathetic view of Degaev, see his sister's account, N. P. Makletsova (Degaeva), "Sudeikin i Degaev," *Byloe* 8 (1906). On his own behalf, years later Degaev wrote Tikhomirov that people who say he is a villain and betrayed "that woman [Figner]" do not have all the facts. Instead, he argued, it was a much more complicated matter. See letter from S. P. Degaev to L. A. Tikhomirov dated January 1885, quoted in full in Lavrov, *Gody emigratsii,* 2: 154.

114. Tikhomirov, "Neizdannye zapiski L. Tikhomirova," 163.

115. V. Figner, *Zapechatlennyi trud,* 1: 354.

116. Ibid., 1: 354.

117. V. Figner, *Polnoe sobranie sochinenii,* 6: 14.

118. Valk, "Pobeg Sergeia Degaeva," 221. In order to capture those Degaev implicated, the police arranged for his fictitious escape on January 14.

119. Pribyleva-Korba, "*Narodnaia Volia,*" 174.

120. Volk, *Narodnaia Volia, 1879–1882,* 148.

121. V. Figner, *Zapechatlennyi trud,* 1: 358–59.

122. Ibid., 1: 359–60.

123. "*O prestuplenie Vere Filippovoi,*" GARF, fond 102, opis' 1881, 3rd proizvodstvo, delo 79, ch. 1; GARF, fond 102, opis' 78, 3rd proizvodstvo, delo 602, l. 36; GARF, fond 102, opis' 181, 1884, 7th proizvodstvo, delo 747, ch. 4; fond 1764, opis' 1, delo 28.

124. A. A. Spandoni, "Stranitsa iz vospominaniia," *Byloe* 5 (1906): 23.

125. "Iz 'obzora' sostavlennago departamentom politsii za 1882 god," 261.

126. Volk, *Narodnaia Volia, 1879–1882,* 148.

127. N. A. Troitskii, "Protsess 14-ti," *Sovetskoe gosudarstvo i pravo* 9 (1984): 120.

128. Mikhailovskii, *Vospominaniia,* 11.

129. Volk, *Narodnaia Volia, 1879–1882,* 148.

130. Ashenbrenner, *Voennaia organizatsiia Narodnoi Voli,* 101.

131. *Narodovol'tsy posle 1-go Marta 1881 goda,* 116.

132. Zaionchkovskii, *Russian Autocracy in Crisis,* 143.

133. Ibid., 184.

7. TRANSFORMATION

1. *Times* (London), March 30, 1881, 7.

2. *Times* (London), October 14, 1884, 5; *Times* (London), October 15, 1884, 9.

3. V. Figner, *Zapechatlennyi trud,* 1: 388.

4. GARF, fond 102, 3rd proizvodstvo, opis' 1883, delo 122.

5. V. Figner, *Zapechatlennyi trud,* 1: 362.

6. GARF, fond 102, 7th proizvodstvo, opis' 1884, delo 747.

7. Elizabeth Castelli, *Martyrdom and Memory: Early Christian Culture Making* (New York: Columbia University Press, 2004), 70.

8. Constantine Logachev, ed., *The Peter and Paul Fortress,* trans. Kathleen Carroll (Leningrad: Aurora Art, 1989), 128.

9. Atul Gawande, "Hellhole," *New Yorker,* March 30, 2009, 36.

10. In a letter to her family, Vera recalled that from 1877 until 1884, five of her friends "committed suicide, eight went insane, eleven died unnatural deaths, seven died natural

deaths but under unnatural circumstances, and one hundred twenty lost their freedom." See V. Figner, *Polnoe sobranie sochinenii*, 6: 113, 20. For an examination of the effects of solitary confinement, including extended periods of sleep, see Gawande, "Hellhole," 36.

11. V. Figner, *Polnoe sobranie sochinenii*, 6: 41, 55, 77, 116, 134.

12. Ibid., 6: 166.

13. Ibid., 6: 135.

14. Ibid., 6: 39.

15. V. Figner, *Zapechatlennyi trud*, 1: 366.

16. Ulam, *Prophets and Conspirators*, 239.

17. V. Figner, *Polnoe sobranie sochinenii*, 6: 137.

18. V. Figner, *Zapechatlennyi trud*, 1: 374.

19. V. Figner, *Polnoe sobranie sochinenii* 6: 153.

20. V. Figner, *Zapechatlennyi trud*, 1: 369.

21. Ibid., 1: 370.

22. RGIA, fond 1288, opis' 1, delo 1138, l. 21.

23. V. Figner, *Zapechatlennyi trud*, 1: 376.

24. Ibid.

25. Ibid.

26. *Times* (London), October 14, 1884, 5.

27. V. Figner, *Zapechatlennyi trud*, 1: 376.

28. Ibid., 1: 377.

29. Ibid.

30. Motivated by Alexander Solovev's April 1879 attempt on the life of the emperor, the tsarist government transferred the cases of those accused of attacks against the state or its officials to the jurisdiction of military courts in the spring of 1879. Without a doubt, the government wanted to avoid another embarrassing judicial debacle like the acquittal of Vera Zasulich in March 1878. See Zaionchkovskii, *Russian Autocracy in Crisis*, 52.

31. Troitskii, "Protsess 14-ti," 120.

32. Ibid. Troitskii notes that some of these men even received the exceptionally light sentences of demotion and police supervision.

33. See Burtsev, *Za sto let*, part 2, 121–22.

34. *Times* (London), October 14, 1884, 5.

35. Ibid.

36. Troitskii, "Protsess 14-ti," 122.

37. Ashenbrenner, *Voennaia organizatsiia Narodnoi Voli*, 109; Spandoni, "Stranitsa iz vospominaniia," 15. By this point Degaev was living in Western Europe after having murdered Lieutenant Colonel Sudeikin, the man who recruited him as a traitor for the government, in December 1883. See Pipes, *Degaev Affair*, 63–109.

38. Troitskii, "Protsess 14-ti," 122.

39. V. Figner, *Zapechatlennyi trud*, 1: 378; This was typical of People's Will members on trial in the 1880s. Almost all readily acknowledged their guilt. At the Trial of the Fourteen, one exception was L. V. Chemodanova. Vera writes that Chemodanova was so adamant in denying she belonged to the party that Figner, who had dispatched her on several missions, almost started to believe her.

40. Spandoni, "Stranitsa iz vospominaniia," 32.

41. V. Figner, *Zapechatlennyi trud*, 1: 381.

42. Spandoni, "Stranitsa iz vospominaniia," 35.

43. Troitskii, "Protsess 14-ti," 122.

44. "Rech Very Nikolaevny Figner," 279–80.

45. Ibid., 280.

46. Ibid., 281.

47. Ibid.

48. Ibid.

49. V. Figner, *Zapechatlennyi trud*, 1: 388.

50. Ibid., 1: 389.

51. Ibid.; Ashenbrenner, *Voennaia organizatsiia Narodnoi Voli*, 111.

52. V. Figner, *Zapechatlennyi trud*, 1: 390.

53. Ibid., 2: 78.

54. V. Figner, *Polnoe sobranie sochinenii*, 4: 247.

55. Ibid.

56. Ibid., 4: 248.

57. V. Figner, *Zapechatlennyi trud*, 1: 390.

58. Ibid., 1: 391.

59. Ibid.

60. Ibid.

61. V. Figner, *Polnoe sobranie sochinenii*, 6: 82.

62. Lynn Patyk, "Dressed to Kill and Die: Russian Revolutionary Terrorism, Gender, and Dress," *Jahrbucher fur Geschichte-Osteuropas* 58, no. 2 (2010): 202.

63. V. Figner, *Zapechatlennyi trud*, 1: 212; V. Figner, *Polnoe sobranie sochinenii*, 6: 85.

64. V. Figner *Zapechatlennyi trud*, 1: 392.

65. Ibid., 1: 393.

66. Ibid.

67. Ibid.

68. RGIA, fond 1288, opis' 11, delo 16, l. 2 ob; fond 1328, opis' 2, delo 1.

69. Mikhail Novorusskii, *Zapiski Shlissel'burgzhsa, 1887–1905*, ed. N. A. Morozov (Moscow: Izdatel'stvo vsesoiuznogo obshchestva politkatorzhan i ssyl'no-poselentsev, 1933), 292. Across Europe both radicals and liberals decried the execution of Sofia Perovskaia as a "disgraceful and ignominious act" and a "return to the barbarism of the Middle Ages." See "Nihilists in London," *Times*, April 18, 1881, 10, and anonymous letter, *Times*, April 27, 1881, 7.

70. V. Figner, *Zapechatlennyi trud*, 1: 394.

71. Ashenbrenner, *Voennaia organizatsiia Narodnoi Voli*, 112.

72. Burtsev, *Za sto let*, 122.

73. V. Figner, *Zapechatlennyi trud*, 2: 3.

74. Ibid., 2: 4.

75. Ibid., 2: 5.

76. Ibid., 2: 7.

77. RGALI, fond 1185, opis' 1, delo 180, l. 3.

78. *When the Clock of Life Stopped (Kogda chasy zhizni ostanovilis)* is the English translation of Figner's second volume of memoirs in *Zapechatlennyi trud*.

8. LIFE AND DEATH

1. V. Figner, *Zapechatlennyi trud*, 2: 14.

2. Unpublished speech given by Vera Figner in 1909 about Shlisselburg Fortress, RGALI, fond 1185, opis' 1, delo 180, l. 3.

3. V. S. Pankratov, *Zhizn' v Shlissel'burgskoi kreposti, 1884–1898* (Petrograd: Izdatel'stvo Byloe, 1922), 10.

4. Foucault, *Discipline and Punish,* 139.

5. Novorusskii, *Zapiski Shlissel'burgzhtsa,* 51.

6. I. P. Iuvatshev, *The Russian Bastille,* trans. A. S. Rappoport (London: Chatto and Windus, 1909), 32.

7. V. Figner, *Zapechatlennyi trud,* 2: 140.

8. Ibid.

9. Novorusskii, *Zapiski Shlissel'burgzhtsa,* 97.

10. Pankratov, *Zhizn' v Shlissel'burgskoi kreposti,* 14.

11. Morozov, *Povesti moei zhizni,* 3: 12.

12. Novorusskii, *Zapiski Shlissel'burgzhtsa,* 50.

13. V. Figner, *Polnoe sobranie sochinenii,* 6: 197.

14. Boris I. Nikolaevsky Collection, box 192, folder 9, Hoover Institution Archives.

15. GARF, fond 98, opis' 1, delo 81, 1885, l. 1.

16. Ibid.

17. Ashenbrenner, *Voennaia organizatsiia Narodnoi Voli,* 115, 122; V. Figner, *Zapechatlennyi trud,* 2: 46; Frolenko, *Sobranie sochinenii v dvukh tomakh,* 2: 176.

18. I. Manucharov, "Epizod' iz zhizni v Shlisselburgskoi kreposti," *Byloe* 8 (1906): 81–82.

19. V. Figner, *Zapechatlennyi trud,* 2: 160.

20. Ibid.

21. "Banished Princess," RGALI, fond 1185, opis' 1, delo 190.

22. V. Figner, *Polnoe sobranie sochinenii,* 4: 259–60.

23. V. Figner, *Zapechatlennyi trud,* 2: 24.

24. Ibid., 2: 27.

25. Ibid., 2: 28.

26. Ashenbrenner, *Voennaia organizatsiia Narodnoi Voli,* 115, Frolenko, *Sobranie sochinenii v dvukh tomakh,* 2: 176.

27. Frolenko, *Sobranie sochinenii v dvukh tomakh,* 2: 180.

28. V. Figner, *Zapechatlennyi trud,* 2: 33.

29. Ibid., 2: 35.

30. Ibid., 2: 38,

31. Ibid., 2: 39.

32. Ibid., 2: 41.

33. Ibid., 2: 44.

34. V. Figner, *Polnoe sobranie sochinenii,* 4: 243.

35. Ibid.

36. V. Figner, *Zapechatlennyi trud,* 2: 88.

37. Pankratov, *Zhizn' v Shlissel'burgskoi kreposti,* 36.

38. The prison menu henceforth regularly included borscht, cabbage soup, cheese, sour cream, and frequently herring, meat cutlets, meat pies, and milk. Report on the state of Shlisselburg Prison, GARF, fond 98, opis' 1, delo 121.

39. Pankratov, *Zhizn' v Shlissel'burgskoi kreposti,* 36.

40. V. Figner, *Zapechatlennyi trud,* 2: 58.

41. Novorusskii, *Zapiski Shlissel'burgzhtsa* 288, Ashenbrenner, *Voennaia organizatsiia Narodnoi Voli,* 136.

42. Pankratov, *Zhizn' v Shlissel'burgskoi kreposti* 32

43. Report on the state of Shlisselburg Fortress and the inmates' behavior, GARF, fond 98, opis' 1, delo 113.

44. V. Figner, *Zapechatlennyi trud,* 2: 69.

45. Ibid., 2: 69–70

46. Ibid., 2: 73.

47. Ibid.

48. Ibid., 2: 74.

49. Ibid.

50. Elizabeth Grosz, *Volatile Bodies: Towards a Corporeal Feminism* (Bloomington: Indiana University Press, 1994), 157.

51. Ibid., 14.

52. Castelli, *Martyrdom and Memory,* 62.

53. Ibid.

54. Qtd. in Sally A. Boniece, "The Spiridonova Case, 1906: Terror, Myth, and Martyrdom," *Kritika: Explorations in Russian and Eurasian History* 4 (Summer 2003): 584.

55. V. Figner, *Zapechatlennyi trud,* 2: 74.

56. Ibid., 2: 18.

57. Report about the state of Shlisselburg Prison, GARF, fond 98, opis' 1, delo 891, l. 12.

58. Ashenbrenner, *Voennaia organizatsiia Narodnoi Voli,* 146.

59. Ibid., 154.

60. Frolenko, *Sobranie sochinenii v dvukh tomakh,* 2: 208.

61. V. Figner, *Polnoe sobranie sochinenii,* 6: 232.

62. Report about the state of Shlisselburg Prison, GARF, fond 98, opis' 1, delo 891, l. 100b.-120b.

63. Ashenbrenner, *Voennaia organizatsiia Narodnoi Voli,* 128, Frolenko, *Sobranie sochinenii v dvukh tomakh,* 2: 208.

64. Novorusskii, *Zapiski Shlissel'burgzhtsa,* 298.

65. Frolenko, *Sobranie sochinenii v dvukh tomakh,* 2: 208.

66. Morozov, *Povesti moei zhizni,* 3: 17.

67. Novorusskii, *Zapiski Shlissel'burgzhtsa,* 299–300. See also report about the state of Shlisselburg Prison, GARF, fond 98, opis' 1, delo 891, l. 12.

68. Henrietta Mondry, "With Short Cropped Hair: Gleb Uspensky's Struggle against Biological Gender Determinism," *Russian Review* 63 (2004): 483.

69. Ibid.

70. Novorusskii, *Zapiski Shlissel'burgzhtsa,* 106.

71. Frolenko, *Sobranie sochinenii v dvukh tomakh,* 2: 209.

72. Ashenbrenner, *Voennaia organizatsiia Narodnoi Voli,* 135; 145; Frolenko, *Sobranie sochinenii v dvukh tomakh,* 2: 224. Gangardt bought three small kerosene stoves for the workshops. With these the inmates made their cakes, pies, and rolls. The vodka, however, was made surreptitiously under the guise of a chemical experiment.

73. Novorusskii, *Zapiski Shlissel'burgzhtsa,* 110.

74. V. Figner, *Shlissel'burgskie uzniki,* 246.

75. Novorusskii, *Zapiski Shlissel'burgzhtsa,* 111.

76. Frolenko, *Sobranie sochinenii v dvukh tomakh,* 2: 221. Vera referred to these long days outside as her summer vacation. V. Figner, *Polnoe sobranie sochinenii,* 6: 227.

77. In contrast to her first years in Shlisselburg, the 1890s were much more peaceful. Whereas twenty people died or went insane from 1884 to 1891, there were only three deaths

and one case of insanity from 1892 to 1905. See Boris I. Nikolaevsky Collection, box 192, folder 9, Hoover Institution Archives.

78. V. Figner, *Zapechatlennyi trud,* 2: 110.

79. Ibid.; Frolenko, *Sobranie sochinenii v dvukh tomakh,* 2: 224.

80. Boris I. Nikolaevsky Collection, box 192, folder 9, Hoover Institution Archives.

81. V. Figner, *Zapechatlennyi trud,* 2: 112.

82. GARF, fond 98, opis' 1, delo 891, l. 12–13.

83. V. Figner, *Polnoe sobranie sochinenii,* 6: 227.

84. V. Figner, *Zapechatlennyi trud,* 2: 134–35.

85. Frolenko, *Sobranie sochinenii v dvukh tomakh,* 2: 176

86. V. Figner, *Shlissel'burgskie uzniki,* 18.

87. Iuvatshev, *Russian Bastille,* 38–39.

88. V. Figner, *Zapechatlennyi trud,* 2: 137.

89. GARF, fond 98, opis' 1, delo 891, l. 80b.

90. Ibid., l. 100b.; Novorusskii, *Zapiski Shlissel'burgzhtsa,* 287; Frolenko, *Sobranie sochinenii v dvukh tomakh,* 2: 232.

91. Frolenko, *Sobranie sochinenii v dvukh tomakh,* 2: 232; GARF, fond 98, opis' 1, delo 891, l. 8.

92. RGALI, fond 1185, opis' 1, delo 190, l. 17.

93. GARF, fond 98, opis' 1, delo 891, l. 17.

94. V. Figner, *Zapechatlennyi trud,* 2: 190.

95. GARF, fond 98, opis' 1, delo 891, l. 170b.

96. Ashenbrenner, *Voennaia organizatsiia Narodnoi Voli,* 151.

97. V. Figner, *Zapechatlennyi trud,* 2: 200.

98. Ashenbrenner, *Voennaia organizatsiia Narodnoi Voli,* 151–52.

99. Morozov, *Povesti moei zhizni,* 3: 35.

100. Ibid., 3: 33–37.

101. Ibid., 3: 38–39.

102. V. Figner, *Zapechatlennyi trud,* 2: 201.

103. GARF, fond 98, opis' 1, delo 891, l. 170b.

104. Nicholas II approved this change in Vera's sentence on January 2, 1903. See RGIA, fond 1328, opis' 2, delo 1, l. 510b., and GARF, fond 98, opis' 1, delo 891.

105. V. Figner, *Zapechatlennyi trud,* 2: 206.

106. V. Figner, *Polnoe sobranie sochinenii,* 6: 231.

107. Ibid.

108. Ibid.

109. Ibid., 6: 234.

110. Ibid., 6: 236.

111. Ibid., 6: 237.

112. Ibid., 6: 240.

113. V. Figner, *Zapechatlennyi trud,* 2: 214.

114. V. Figner, *Polnoe sobranie sochinenii,* 6: 243.

115. V. Figner, *Zapechatlennyi trud,* 2: 215.

116. V. Figner, *Polnoe sobranie sochinenii,* 6: 241.

117. Ibid., 6: 242.

118. Ibid., 6: 243.

119. V. Figner, *Zapechatlennyi trud,* 2: 217.

120. Ibid., 2: 221–23. Since the Department of Police would examine everything that she took with her, Vera decided to burn these treasures after looking at them for a final time.

121. Ibid., 2: 226.

122. Ibid., 2: 213. Once again, Vera's social prejudices are apparent. Although she was a convicted terrorist, the thought of living alongside "common criminals" who had wronged the state for reasons no more lofty than their own gain or gratification horrified her.

123. RGIA, fond 1328, opis' 2, delo 1, l. 510b.

124. V. Figner, *Zapechatlennyi trud*, 2: 227.

9. RESURRECTION IN EXILE

1. Morozov, *Povesti moei zhizni*, 3: 40.

2. V. Figner, *Polnoe sobranie sochinenii*, 7: 197.

3. The decree that commuted Vera's sentence to twenty years in prison served as of September 1904 did not specify a length of time for her subsequent exile. "Memos from the Ministry of Internal Affairs for 1904," RGIA, fond 1328, opis' 2, delo 1, l. 510b.

4. "Okhrana Collection," box 200, reel 366, series XVIIn, folder 1B, Hoover Institution Archives.

5. V. Figner, *Zapechatlennyi trud*, 2: 213.

6. Letter from Vera Figner to Eugenia Sazhina, October 28, 1904, RGALI, fond 1185, opis' 1, delo 242, l. 3.

7. Ibid., l. 3.

8. V. Figner, *Zapechatlennyi trud*, 2: 235.

9. Katy Turton, "Keeping It in the Family: Surviving Political Exile, 1870–1917," *Canadian Slavonic Papers* 52 (September–December 2010): 396–407.

10. V. Figner, *Polnoe sobranie sochinenii*, 3: 29, 6: 274, 281.

11. Turton, "Keeping It in the Family," 407.

12. V. Figner, *Polnoe sobranie sochinenii*, 3: 37; 6: 311. These men were L. Ianovich, B. Martynov, and P. Polivanov.

13. Ibid., 3: 31.

14. Ibid., 3: 36.

15. Ibid., 6: 284.

16. Ibid., 3: 36.

17. For details concerning Bloody Sunday and the Revolution of 1905, see Abraham Ascher, *The Revolution of 1905: Russia in Disarray* (Stanford, Calif.: Stanford University Press, 1988).

18. V. Figner, *Polnoe sobranie sochinenii*, 6: 300.

19. Susan K. Morrissey cites archival sources that demonstrate the incidence of violence was staggering: "Between January 1 and August 20, 1906, for example, 1,782 terrorist acts" occurred. State violence was not to be outdone. Morrissey notes that in the five years after the October Manifesto in 1905, "military courts sentenced 6,992 people to death, of whom 3,741 were executed." See Susan K. Morrissey, "The Apparel of Innocence": Toward a Moral Economy of Terrorism in Late Imperial Russia," *Journal of Modern History* 84 (September 2012): 614–17.

20. As Jonathan Daly has shown, the number of punishments for political activity spiked in the years after Nicholas II's ascension to the throne and skyrocketed in 1905–1907.

See Jonathan Daly, "Political Crime in Later Imperial Russia," *Journal of Modern History* 74 (March 2002): 82–84.

21. Ibid., 90.

22. "Ot Shlissel'burgskago Komiteta," *Byloe* 1 (January 1906): 315.

23. V. Figner, *Polnoe sobranie sochinenii,,* 3: 26, 35.

24. Ibid., 6: 335.

25. Ibid., 6: 317, 320, 341.

26. Ibid., 6: 327.

27. "O Vere Figner," GARF, fond 102, opis' 1905, Osobyi Otdel, delo 1280.

28. Ibid.; V. Figner, *Polnoe sobranie sochinenii,* 3: 58.

29. V. Figner, *Polnoe sobranie sochinenii,* 6: 335.

30. "Memoranda of the Ministry of Internal Affairs," RGIA, fond 1288, opis' 11, delo 16, l. 4.

31. V. Figner, *Polnoe sobranie sochinenii,* 3: 91. Still, multiple police reports show that the Okhrana continued to closely watch Vera's actions until the 1917 revolution.

32. V. Figner, *Polnoe sobranie sochinenii,* 6: 347.

33. The last prisoners left Shlisselburg on January 8, 1906. See "Ot Shlissel'burgskago Komiteta," 321.

34. V. Figner, *Polnoe sobranie sochinenii,* 3: 103.

35. V. Figner, *Shlissel'burgskie uzniki,* 49.

36. V. Figner, *Polnoe sobranie sochinenii,* 6: 362.

37. Ibid., 3: 103.

38. "Okhrana report dated November 10, 1905," GARF, fond 102, opis' 1905, Osobyi Otdel, delo 1281, reel 2.

39. Anna Geifman, *Thou Shalt Kill: Revolutionary Terrorism in Russia, 1894–1917* (Princeton, N.J.: Princeton University Press, 1993), 45.

40. Morrissey, "Apparel of Innocence," 620.

41. Ibid.

42. Teodor Shanin, *Russia, 1905–1907: Revolution as a Moment of Truth* (New Haven, Conn.: Yale University Press, 1986), 46.

43. Ibid., 45.

44. Ibid., 49.

45. V. Figner, *Polnoe sobranie sochinenii,* 6: 352, 357.

46. Ibid., 3: 149.

47. Ibid., 3: 112, 6: 380.

48. Ibid., 6: 381.

49. Abraham Ascher, *The Revolution of 1905: A Short History* (Stanford, Calif.: Stanford University Press, 2004)

50. Shanin, *Russia, 1905–1907,* 96.

51. V. Figner, *Polnoe sobranie sochinenii,* 3: 133.

52. Lauchlan, "Okhrana: Security Policing," 59. The term *jacquerie* derives from the period of the French Revolution. Jacqueries are peasant uprisings or revolts.

53. Qtd. in Shanin, *Russia, 1905–1907,* 96.

54. V. Figner, *Polnoe sobranie sochinenii,* 6: 383.

55. Boniece, "Spiridonova Case, 1906," 574.

56. Ibid., 575.

57. For a fascinating discussion of notions of guilt, innocence, heroism, martyrdom, and

the moral economy of terrorism among early twentieth-century Russian terrorists, see Morrissey, "Apparel of Innocence," 607–42.

58. Ibid., 637.

59. Ibid., 631.

60. Ibid., 614.

61. Okhrana Collection, box 200, reel 246, series XVIIIn, folder 1B, Hoover Institution Archives.

62. V. Figner, *Polnoe sobranie sochinenii*, 3: 151.

63. Ibid., 7: 13.

64. "O Vere Figner," GARF, fond 102, opis' 1905, Osobyi Otdel, delo 1280.

65. For Azef's association with the tsarist police, see Jonathan W. Daly, *Autocracy under Siege*, 90–91.

66. V. Figner, *Polnoe sobranie sochinenii*, 3: 160.

67. Ibid., 3: 174.

68. Geifman, *Thou Shalt Kill*, 53–54.

69. V. Figner, *Polnoe sobranie sochinenii*, 3: 165–74, 181.

70. Ibid., 3: 188, 7: 22–23.

71. Ibid., 3: 187.

72. Shanin, *Russia, 1905–1907*, 53.

73. V. Figner, *Polnoe sobranie sochinenii*, 3: 194.

74. Olga Chernov Andreyev, *Cold Spring in Russia*, trans. Michael Carlisle (Ann Arbor, Mich.: Ardis Press, 1978), 30–34.

75. V. Figner, *Polnoe sobranie sochinenii* 7: 51–52.

76. Ibid., 7: 52.

77. Ibid., 3: 181 and 7: 52.

78. Frederic S. Zuckerman, *The Tsarist Secret Police Abroad: Policing Europe in a Modernizing World* (New York: Palgrave Macmillan, 2003), 42–43.

79. "O Vere Figner," GARF, fond 102, opis' 1905, Osobyi Otdel, delo 1280; Okhrana Collection, box 140, reel 236, series XIIIC (1), folder 1C, Hoover Institution Archives.

80. V. Figner, *Polnoe sobranie sochinenii*, 3: 259.

81. Ibid., 7: 69–72. Vera's namesake and niece was arrested for her alleged involvement with the SRs. For information on Vera Stakhevich and her relationship with her aunt Vera, see Lidiia Dan, *Iz vstrech c V. N. Figner* (New York: Inter-University Project on the Menshevik Movement, 1961), 2–9.

82. Vera tried to arrange the escapes of both Maria Spiridonova and her friend Lidia Brupbacher. See V. Figner, *Polnoe sobranie sochinenii*, 3: 228, 7: 86, 174, and file 49, Felix Brupbacher Archive, International Institute of Social History, Amsterdam, The Netherlands.

83. V. Figner, *Polnoe sobranie sochinenii*, 3: 318.

84. Geifman, *Thou Shalt Kill*, 234.

85. Ibid.

86. V. Figner, *Polnoe sobranie sochinenii*, 3: 284–85.

87. Phillip Pomper, "Russian Revolutionary Terrorism," in *Terrorism in Context*, ed. Martha Crenshaw (University Park: Pennsylvania State University Press, 1995), 97.

88. V. Figner, *Polnoe sobranie sochinenii*, 3: 308, 7: 82, 87.

89. Pomper, "Russian Revolutionary Terrorism," 97.

90. V. Figner, *Polnoe sobranie sochinenii*, 3: 299.

91. Letter from V. N. Figner to Felix Brupbacher, file 49, Brupbacher Archive, International Institute of Social History, Amsterdam, The Netherlands.

92. "Spravka o Vere Figner," GARF, fond 102, opis' 1905, Osobyi Otdel, delo 1280.

93. GARF, fond 102, Osobyi Otdel, delo 1281, reels 1 and 2.

94. V. Figner, *Polnoe sobranie sochinenii*, 3: 309.

95. Ibid., 3: 220.

96. Qtd. in Hesse, *Other Enlightenment*, 136.

97. Castelli, *Martyrdom and Memory*, 70.

98. V. N. Figner's letters to Felix Brupbacher, file 49, Brupbacher Archive, International Institute of Social History.

99. Vera Figner, *Posle Shlissel'burga* (Leningrad: Kolos, 1925), 337.

100. V. Figner, *Polnoe sobranie sochinenii*, 7: 224–25.

101. Ed Block Jr., "James Sully, Evolutionist Psychology, and Late Victorian Gothic Fiction," *Victorian Studies* 25 (Summer 1982): 444.

102. Michael Davis, "Incongruous Compounds: Re-reading Jekyll and Hyde and Late-Victorian Psychology," *Journal of Victorian Culture* 11 (Autumn 2006): 208, 210.

103. "Conference of Madame Vera Figner at the University of Geneva, November 28, 1910," Boris I. Nikolaevsky Collection, box 94, folder 4, l. 3.

104. Ibid., l. 5.

105. Ibid., l. 7–8

106. Documents of the Paris Committee to Help Political Prisoners and Exiles Condemned to Hard Labor, Boris I. Nikolaevsky Collection, box 94, folder 4, Hoover Institution Archives.

107. V. Figner, *Polnoe sobranie sochinenii*, 3: 358–60.

108. January 1910 Founding Document, Boris I. Nikolaevsky Collection, box 94, folder 4, Hoover Institution Archives.

109. Okhrana Collection, box 215, series XXVb (2j), reel 401, Hoover Institution Archives.

110. Felix Brupbacher Archive, file 49, International Institute of Social History; Boris I. Nikolaevsky Collection, box 94, folder 4, Hoover Institution Archives; Vera Nikolaevna Figner, *Parizhskii komitet pomoshchi politicheskim katorzhanam otchet za 1911-i god* (Paris, 1912).

111. January 12, 1914, dispatch, GARF, fond 102, opis' 1905, Osobyi Otdel, delo 1281, reel 2; Okhrana Collection, box 215, series XXVa, folder 1C, reel 400, Hoover Institution Archives.

112. Okhrana Collection, box 215, series XXVb, folder 2r, Hoover Institution Archives; Boris I. Nikolaevsky Collection, box 94, folder 4.

113. Boris I. Nikolaevsky Collection, box 94, folder 3, Hoover Institution Archives,

114. Okhrana Collection, box 141, series XIIIC (1), folder 1D, Reel 245, Hoover Institution Archives; Okhrana Collection, box 215, series XXVA, folder 1C, reel 400, Hoover Institution Archives; Okhrana Collection, box 215, series XXVB (1), reel 400, Hoover Institution Archives; Felix Brupbacher Archive, file 49, International Institute of Social History.

115. V. Figner, *Polnoe sobranie sochinenii*, 7: 141.

116. Ibid., 7: 211.

117. V. Figner, *Posle Shlissel'burga*, 309.

118. Clarens was a major focal point for Russian émigrés because it was home to the

largest Russian library in Switzerland. In addition to Vera, other patrons of the library included V. I. Lenin, Anatole Lunacharsky, and G. V. Plekhanov. See Alfred Erich Senn, *The Russian Revolution in Switzerland, 1914–1917* (Madison: University of Wisconsin Press, 1971), 9.

119. "Spravka o Vere Figner," GARF, fond 102, opis' 1905, Osobyi Otdel, delo 1280; Okhrana Collection, box 147, series XIIIC (1), folder 1G, reel 265, Hoover Institution Archives.

120. V. Figner, *Polnoe sobranie sochinenii,* 7: 218.

121. Ibid., 3: 393.

122. January 16, 1914, dispatch, RGIA, fond 1288, opis' 11, delo 16, l. 4.

123. Ibid., l. 40b.

124. Incoming dispatch, 1913, Okhrana Collection, box 189, series XVIb (3), folder 4, Hoover Institution Archives.

125. June 1, 1912, dispatch, GARF, fond 102, opis' 1905, Osobyi Otdel, delo 1281, reel 1.

126. May 27, 1912 dispatch, GARF, fond 102, opis' 1905, Osobyi Otdel, delo 1280.

127. V. Figner, *Polnoe sobranie sochinenii,* 3: 397.

128. Ibid.

129. Ibid., 7: 239.

130. Letter dated February 11, 1915, to Felix Brupbacher from Vera Figner, file 50, Brupbacher Archive, International Institute of Social History.

131. V. Figner, *Polnoe sobranie sochinenii,* 7: 249.

132. Ibid., 3: 396–402.

133. Ibid., 7: 250.

134. RGALI, fond 553, opis' 1, delo 1320, l. 80.

135. September 22, 1914, dispatch, GARF, fond 102, opis' 1905, Osobyi Otdel, delo 1281, reel 1.

136. March 1915 dispatch, GARF, fond 102, opis' 1905, Osobyi Otdel, delo 1281, reel 2.

137. Ibid.

138. RGALI, fond 553, opis' 1, delo 1320, l. 80.

139. GARF, fond 102, opis' 1905, Osobyi Otdel, delo 1281, reel 2.

140. Ibid.

141. V. Figner, *Polnoe sobranie sochinenii,* 7: 257.

142. Ibid., 7: 261.

143. Ibid., 3: 411.

144. Ibid., 3: 410.

145. Ibid., 7: 274.

146. Ibid., 7: 273.

147. Ibid., 7: 273–74.

148. Ibid., 3: 413.

149. Ibid., 3: 149.

150. Ibid., 7: 283.

151. RGALI, fond 898, opis' 1, delo 12.

152. V. Figner, *Polnoe sobranie sochinenii,* 3: 414.

153. Ibid., 3: 414.

154. Ibid., 7: 295.

155. Ibid., 3: 419.

10. AN OLD REVOLUTIONARY IN A NEW REVOLUTION

1. Vera Figner, "Avtobiografii Very Nikolaevny Figner," in *Deiateli SSSR: Revoliutsion-nogo dvizheniia Rossii: Entsiklopedicheskii Slovar' Granat* (Moscow: Sovetskaia Entsiklope-diia, 1989), 478.

2. Letter from Vera Figner to Natasha Petrovna Kuprianova, dated March 14, 1917, RGALI, fond 1185, opis' 1, delo 231, listok 89.

3. V. Figner, "Avtobiographii Very Nikolaevny Figner," 478, in *Deiateli SSSR.*.

4. Rene Fulop-Miller, *The Mind and Face of Bolshevism: An Examination of Cultural Life in Soviet Russia* (New York: Knopf, 1928), 381.

5. Program of the Concert-Meeting of the Petrograd People's Conservatory on May 1, 1917, RGALI, fond 993, opis' 1, delo 112; *Rabochaia Gazeta,* March 19, 1917, 3, and March 21, 1917, 3.

6. See V. Figner, *Polnoe sobranie sochinenii,* 5: 382–427; RGALI, fond 1185, opis' 1, delo 149.

7. *Rabochaia Gazeta,* March 21, 1917, 3; Alexandra Kollontai, *Rabotnitsa za god revoliutsii* (Moscow: Knigoizdate'lstvo Kommunist, 1918), 8.

8. "How the All-Russian League of Women's Enfranchisement Strove to Obtain Elec-toral Rights for Russian Women during the Revolution," *International Women's News* 2/12 (November 1, 1917), 25–26.

9. The Table of Ranks was a system put in place by Tsar Peter the Great that rewarded ability and experience by promoting state servitors through the ranks. The Table of Ranks granted noble status to both civil servants and members of the nobility who were promoted to a certain level.

10. "All-Russian League," 26.

11. Ibid.

12. Film footage of the "Funeral for the Martyrs of the February Revolution," reel 17 (4/296), Axelbank Collection, Hoover Institution Archives.

13. Ibid.

14. V. Figner, *Polnoe sobranie sochinenii,* 5: 437.

15. Ibid.

16. Ibid., 5: 438.

17. Ibid., 5: 438–39.

18. Ibid., 5: 446.

19. Throughout the 1920s the Museum of the Revolution provided a space where the rich history of the Russian revolutionary movement remained alive. For much of its exis-tence, Vera continued to take a key interest in the project and often toured the facility and made forceful suggestions about the direction the museum should take. See "Nezabyvae-taia Vstrecha," in RGALI, fond 2223, opis' 2, delo 295; Emma Goldman, *My Disillusionment in Russia* (New York: Thomas Y. Crowell, 1970), 57; Emma Goldman *Living My Life* (New York: Dover Publications, 1970), 2: 861.

20. "Vera N. Figner's application to the State Academy of Arts and Sciences," RGALI, fond 940, opis' 10, delo 649, l. 3; V. Figner, "Avtobiografii Very Nikolaevny Figner," in *Deiateli SSSR,* 478.

21. V. Figner, "Avtobiografii Very Nikolaevny Figner," in *Deiateli SSSR,* 478.

22. Anonymous news brief in *International Women Suffrage News* (8/11), May 1, 1917, 119.

23. Daniel T. Orlovsky, "The Provisional Government and its Cultural Work," in *Bol-shevik Culture: Experiment and Order in the Russian Revolution,* eds. Abbott Gleason, Peter

Kenez, and Richard Stites, *Bolshevik Culture* (Bloomington: Indiana University Press, 1985), 51.

24. *Narodnii Dom* were cultural and educational centers established for the benefit of the working masses. Letter from Vera Figner to Natasha Petrovna Kuprianova, dated September 3, 1917, RGALI, fond 1185, opis' 1, delo 231, l. 112; V. Figner, "Avtobiografii Very Nikolaevny Figner," in *Deiateli SSSR*, 478.

25. Robert Paul Browder and Alexander F. Kerensky, eds., *The Russian Provisional Government, 1917: Documents* (Stanford, Calif.: Stanford University Press, 1961), 1286.

26. Ibid., 1288.

27. "M. Kerensky at Odessa," *Times* (London), June 4, 1917, 8.

28. Ia. V. Leont'ev and K. S. Iur'ev, "Nezapechatlennyi trud: Iz arkhiva V. N. Figner," *Zven'ia* 2 (1992): 425.

29. Ekaterina Breshko-Breshkovskaia, *The Little Grandmother of the Russian Revolution: Reminiscences and Letters of Catherine Breshkovsky,* ed. Alice Stone Blackwell (Westport, Conn.: Hyperion Press, 1973), 317.

30. J. B. Ohsol, "Concerning Women Suffrage in Russia," *Women's Journal* 1, no. 1 (1917): 17.

31. Vera agreed that Russia needed to see the war through to the end.

32. Letter from Vera Figner to Natasha Petrovna Kuprianova, dated September 3, 1917, RGALI, fond 1185, opis' 1, delo 231, l. 112.

33. N. N. Figner, *Vospominaniia, Pis'ma, Materialy,* 148.

34. W. Bruce Lincoln, *Red Victory: A History of the Russian Civil War, 1918–1921* (New York: Da Capo Press, 1989), 38.

35. Alexander Rabinowitch, *The Bolsheviks Come to Power: The Revolution of 1917 in Petrograd* (New York: W. W. Norton, 1976), 164.

36. Browder and Kerensky, *Russian Provisional Government,* 1721.

37. Rabinowitch, *Bolsheviks Come to Power,* 201.

38. Ibid.

39. Ibid.

40. Browder and Kerensky, *Russian Provisional Government,* 1723.

41. Letter from Vera Figner to Natasha Petrovna Kuprianova, dated September 3, 1917, RGALI, fond 1185, opis' 1, delo 231, l. 112.

42. Rabinowitch, *Bolsheviks Come to Power,* 276.

43. Ibid.

44. V. Figner, "Avtobiografii Very Nikolaevny Figner," in *Deiateli SSSR,* 479. Alexander Rabinowitch notes that the "members of the Preparliament steering committee . . . hurriedly agreed to protest the Military Revolutionary Committee's attack but to make no attempt to resist it." See Rabinowitch, *Bolsheviks Come to Power,* 276.

45. V. Figner, "Avtobiografii Very Nikolaevny Figner," in *Deiateli SSSR,* 479.

46. Letter from Vera Figner to Lidia Nikolaevna Stakhevich, dated December 8, 1917, RGALI, fond 1185, opis' 1, delo 246, l. 17.

47. Ibid..

48. Ibid.

49. Ibid.

50. William Chamberlin, *Russian Revolution: 1917–1921* (New York: Grosset and Dunlap, 1965), 1: 248.

51. Ronald Grigor Suny, *The Soviet Experiment: Russia, the USSR, and the Successor States* (New York: Oxford University Press, 1998), 52–72.

52. For information on the ten women elected to the Constituent Assembly, see Rochelle Goldberg Ruthchild, *Equality and Revolution: Women's Rights in the Russian Empire, 1905–1917* (Pittsburgh: University of Pittsburgh Press, 2010), 235.

53. Lincoln, *Red Victory*, 121–22.

54. Qtd. in Alexander Rabinowitch, *The Bolsheviks in Power: The First Year of Soviet Rule in Petrograd* (Bloomington: Indiana University Press, 2007), 122.

55. Ibid., 125.

56. V. Figner, "Avtobiografii Very Nikolaevny Figner," in *Deiateli SSSR,* 479.

57. Ibid.

58. Rabinowitch, *Bolsheviks in Power,* 127. As Oliver Radkey relates, "While the democratic parties heaped opprobrium upon [Lenin] for this act of despotism, their following showed little inclination to defend an institution which the Russian people had ceased to regard as necessary to the fulfillment of its cherished desires." See Oliver H. Radkey, *Russia Goes to the Polls: The Election to the All-Russian Constituent Assembly, 1917* (Ithaca, N.Y.: Cornell University Press, 1990), 4.

59. Letter from Vera Figner to her cousin L. P. Kuprianova, dated December 6, 1917, RGALI, fond 1185, opis' 1, delo 195.

60. A. D. Protopopov, "Predsmertnaia zapiska s predisloviem P. R. Russa," *Golos Minuvshego Na Chuznoi Storone* 2, no. 15 (1926): 167.

61. Archives of the Communist Party and Soviet State, Microfilm Collection, Hoover Institution Archives, fond R-8419, reel 3.6820, file 1.

62. As Frederick Corney argues, in the early months and years of their reign the Bolsheviks actively tried to construct a revolutionary narrative that would reinforce their claims to legitimacy. In the process, many Bolsheviks were entrusted with archival materials in an effort to write the history of October. But as Corney mentions, "Nonparty people who were well known and had shown complete loyalty to the party could have access" to the limited archival materials that existed. Clearly, Vera was counted among that select group. See Frederick C. Corney, *Telling October: Memory and the Making of the Bolshevik Revolution* (Ithaca, N.Y.: Cornell University Press, 2004), 106.

63. *Letopis zhizni i tvorchestva A.M. Gorkogo,* vyp. 3 (Moscow: Izdatel'stvo Akademii Nauk SSSR, 1959), 68.

64. Wada Haruki, "Vera Figner in the Early Post-Revolutionary Period," *Annals of the Institute of Social Science* 25 (1983–1984): 45; *Novaia Zhizn'* (April 9, 1918), 4.

65. V. Figner, *Posle Shlissel'burga,* 146.

66. Letter from Vera Figner to Lidia Nikolaevna Stakhevich, dated December 8, 1917, RGALI, fond 1185, opis' 1, delo 246, l. 16.

67. Ibid., l. 16 ob.

68. The most detailed account of the catastrophic state of Petrograd this spring can be found in Alexander Rabinowitch, *Bolsheviks in Power.*

69. Lincoln, *Red Victory,* 55.

70. Ibid., 59–61.

71. V. Figner, "Avtobiografii Very Nikolaevny Figner," in *Deitaeli SSSR,* 479.

72. Letter from Vera Figner to Iulii Savel'evicha Gessen, dated July 16, 1918, RGALI, fond 1185, opis' 1, delo 220, l. 10.

73. Letter from Vera N. Figner to Mikhail Vasilevich Novorusskii, dated June 12, 1918, RGALI, fond 1185, opis' 1, delo 627, l. 211–13.

74. Letter from Vera Figner to Elizaveta Viktorovna Kuprianova, dated January 25, 1919, RGALI, fond 1185, opis' 1, delo 229, l. 23 ob.

75. Letter from Vera Figner to Lidia Nikolaevna Stakhevich and Vera Sergeevna Stakhevich, dated December 30, 1918, RGALI, fond 1185, opis' 1, delo 246.

76. Letter from Vera Figner to Elizaveta Viktorovna Kuprianova, dated January 25, 1919; A. M. Prokhonov, *Bolshaia Sovetskaia Entsiklopediia* (Moscow: Izdatel'stvo Sovetskaia Entsiklopediia, 1977), 27: 337.

77. Letter from Vera Figner to Elizaveta Viktorovna Kuprianova, dated January 25, 1919, RGALI, fond 1185, opis' 1, delo 229, l. 23 i ob.

78. Lincoln, *Red Victory*, 308.

79. Letter of Vera Figner to Elizaveta Viktorovna Kuprianova, dated January 25, 1919.

80. Alex Marshall, *The Caucasus under Soviet Rule* (New York: Routledge, 2010), 70.

81. Letter from Vera Figner to Lidia Nikolaevna Stakhevich and Vera Sergeevna Stakhevich, dated December 30, 1918, RGALI, fond 1185, opis' 1, delo 246, l. 18; Dan, *Iz Vstrech c V. N. Figner*, 8.

82. Andreyev, *Cold Spring in Russia*, 121.

83. Letter from Vera Figner to Iulii Savel'evich Gessen, dated May 23, 1919, RGALI, fond 1185, opis'1, delo 220, l. 12

84. Letter from Vera Figner to Elizaveta Viktorovna Kuprianova, dated August 4, 1919, RGALI, fond 1185, opis' 1, delo 229, l. 27ob.

85. Letter from Vera Figner to Elizaveta Viktorovna Kuprianova, dated September 26, 1919, RGALI, fond 1185, opis' 1, delo 229, l. 32.

86. Ibid.

87. Lincoln, *Red Victory*, 223–24.

88. Letter from Vera Figner to Iulii Savel'evich Gessen, dated December 22, 1919, RGALI, fond 1185, opis' 1, delo 195.

89. Lincoln, *Red Victory*, 224–25.

90. Vera still continued her efforts to retrieve her original manuscript. Letter from Vera Figner to Felix Brupbacher, dated October 22, 1920, file 51, Brupbacher Archive Correspondence, International Institute of Social History.

91. Letter from Vera Figner to Iulii Savel'evich Gessen, dated December 22, 1919.

92. Letter from Vera Figner to Valentina Iakovlevna Borodino, dated January 12, 1920, RGALI, fond 1185, opis' 1, delo 217. l. 1.

93. Ibid., l. 1 ob.

94. Ibid.

95. Ibid l. 2.

96. Letter from Vera Figner to the Political Red Cross in Moscow, dated February 24, 1920, Archives of the Soviet Communist Party and the Soviet State, Microfilm Collection, Hoover Institution Archives, fond R-8419, opis'1, delo 10, l. 3.

97. Letter from Vera Figner to Iulii Savel'evich Gessen, dated January 8, 1920, RGALI, fond 1185, opis' 1, delo 195.

98. V. Figner, "Avtobiografii Very Nikolaevny Figner," in *Deiateli SSSR*, 480.

99. Ibid.

100. Letter of Vera Figner to Valentina Iakovlevna Borodino, dated January 12, 1920, l. 2.

101. V. Figner, "Avtobiografii Very Nikolaevny Figner," in *Deiateli SSSR*, 480.

102. Kon and Vilenskii, *Deiateli revoliutsionnogo dvizheniia v Rossii* III/III: 1828.

103. Dan, *Iz Vstrech c V. N. Figner,* 10.

104. Letter from Vera Figner to Tatiana Sergeevna Stakhevich, dated April 26, 1920, RGALI, fond 1185, opis' 4, delo 18, l. 1–2. Although Vera essentially abandoned her great-nephew, she continued to care deeply about him. She had assumed that Tatiana would arrive within days of her departure, but by April Tatiana was still not in Lugan and Vera began to grow increasingly anxious. It is unclear when Tatiana arrived in Lugan, but by July 1920 Sergei was living in Poltava with his mother's sister.

105. Letter from Vera Figner to Eugenia Nikolaevna Sazhin, dated March 30, 1920, RGALI, fond 1185, opis'1, delo 241, l. 108.

106. Ibid.

107. Letter from Vera Figner to Iulii Savel'evich Gessen, dated June 13, 1920, RGALI, fond 1185, opis' 1, delo 195.

108. Letter from Vera Figner to Iulii Savel'evich Gessen, dated August 17, 1920, RGALI, fond 1185, opis' 1, delo 195.

109. Goldman, *Living My Life,* 2: 894.

110. Ibid.

111. Vera notes that she received ten thousand rubles a month from the cooperative publishing house Zadruga, and she received forty thousand rubles for one article from *Golos Minuvshego*. Letter from Vera Figner to Tatiana Stakhevich, dated October 12, 1920, RGALI, fond 1185, opis' 4, delo 18, l. 10; ibid., 18, l. 12.

112. Qtd. in N. M. Pirumova, *Peter Alekseevich Kropotkin* (Moscow: Izdatel'stvo Nauka, 1972), 206.

113. V. Figner, *Zapechatlennyi trud,* 1: 43.

114. Application of Vera Figner to the State Academy of Arts and Sciences, RGALI, fond 941 (fond of the State Academy of Arts and Sciences), opis' 10, delo 649, l. 2. The biographical dictionary referenced is *Deiateli SSSR*.

115. Letter from Vera Figner to Peter A. Kropotkin, dated December 23, 1920, RGALI, fond 1185, opis' 1, delo 227, l. 5–6.

116. Letter from Vera Figner to Tatiana Stakhevich, dated December 19, 1920, RGALI, fond 1185, opis' 4, delo 18, l. 15 ob.

117. Ibid.

118. *Materialy vsesoiuzskogo obshchestvennogo komitet po uvekovecheniem pamiat Kropotkina P. A.,* RGALI, fond 1185, opis' 1, delo 97, l. 7.

119. V. Figner, *Polnoe sobranie sochinenii,* 5: 459.

120. Ibid., 5: 460.

121. Ibid., 5: 460–61.

122. Ibid., 5: 447–52.

123. Qtd. in Paul Avrich, *Kronstadt, 1921* (Princeton, N.J.: Princeton University Press, 1970), 221.

124. Although no harm befell Vera as a result of her words, in the published version of this speech the editors added a footnote that read, "The editors consider this opinion of V. N. Figner to be erroneous." V. Figner, *Polnoe sobranie sochinenii,* 5: 449.

125. Report on the meeting of the Political Red Cross Committee's activities for 1921 held in June 1922, RGALI, fond 1185, opis' 1, delo 176, l. 2–3.

126. Archives of the Communist Party and Soviet State, Microfilm Collection, fond R-8419, reel 3.6820, file 1, Hoover Institution Archives.

127. Report on the meeting of the Red Cross Committee's activities for 1921 held in June 1922, RGALI, fond 1185, opis' 1, delo 176, l. 3.
128. Letter from Vera Figner to Tatiana Stakhevich, dated July 11, 1921, RGALI, fond 1185, opis' 4, delo 18, l. 26.
129. Report on the meeting of the Political Red Cross Committee's activities for 1921, RGALI, fond 1185, opis' 1, delo 176, l. 1–13.
130. Stuart Finkel, *On the Ideological Front: The Russian Intelligentsia and the Making of the Soviet Public Sphere* (New Haven, Conn.: Yale University Press, 2007), 20.
131. Ibid., 21.
132. "Russian Relief Body May Upset Soviet," *New York Times,* August 6, 1921, 5, Frank A. Golder Collection, box 23, folder 15 A, American Relief Administration file, Hoover Institution Archives.
133. "Soviets' Famine Decree," *New York Times,* July 27, 1921, 2.
134. The Soviet government's ability to raise funds abroad was compromised by the fact that few nations recognized the legitimacy of the Soviet Union and its government.
135. Letter from Vera Figner to Tatiana Sergeevna Stakhevich, dated September 10, 1921, RGALI, fond 1185, opis' 4, delo 18, l. 31–32.
136. "Reds Arrest Relief Workers," *Times,* September 1, 1921, 1.
137. Letter from Vera Figner to Tatiana Stakhevich dated September 10, 1921, RGALI, fond 1185, opis' 4, delo 18, l. 31; Finkel, *On the Ideological Front,* 35.
138. "Report of the L. K. Tolstoy Committee to Render Help to Famine Sufferers, August 1921-April 1922," RGALI, fond 1185, opis' 1, delo 23, l. 3.
139. Ibid., l. 1–4.

11. REVOLUTIONARY SURVIVOR

1. Archives of the Communist Party and Soviet State, Microfilm Collection, Hoover Institution Archives, fond R-8419, reel 3.6820, file 1. Most of the imprisoned aid workers were released by mid fall. Several, however, remained in prison until they were first exiled to remote locations within the Soviet Union and then deported out of the country.
2. Lewis Siegelbaum, *Soviet State and Society between Revolutions, 1918–1929* (Cambridge, U.K.: Cambridge University Press, 1992), 54.
3. "Report of VNF detailing the activity of the Red Cross Committee for 1921," RGALI, fond 1185, opis' 1, delo 176, l. 10b.
4. Ibid., l. 2.
5. Ibid., l. 3.
6. Archives of the Communist Party and Soviet State, Microfilm Collection, Hoover Institution Archives, fond R-8419, reel 3.6820, file 1.
7. "Report of VNF detailing the activity of the Red Cross Committee for 1921," RGALI, fond 1185, opis' 1, delo 176, l. 1.
8. D. Minim, "Eshche o Politicheskom Krasnom Kreste," *Pamiat,* vyp. 3 (Moscow, 1978/Paris, 1980): 523–24; O. Markov, "Ekaterina Pavlovna Peshkova i ee pomoshch politzakliuchennym," *Pamiat,* vyp. 1 (1978): 317.
9. Archives of the Communist Party and Soviet State, Microfilm Collection, Hoover Institution Archives, fond R-8419, reel 3.6820, file 1. Under Peshkova the organization flourished for a time thanks in large part to the positive working relationship it enjoyed with Felix Dzerzhinskii, the first head of the Cheka and its successor the GPU. Although the group per-

severed after Dzerzhinskii's 1926 death, in the 1930s its fund-raising efforts were paralyzed when the government restricted access to foreign funds. Without the money necessary to effectively tend to the growing population of political prisoners, the official liquidation of the E. P. Peshkova Society to Help Political Prisoners in 1937 was little more than a formality.

10. Archives of the Communist Party and Soviet State, Microfilm Collection, Hoover Institution Archives, fond R-8419, reel 3.6820, file 1.

11. RGALI, fond 1185, opis' 1, delo 114.

12. Ibid., l. 1.

13. *Golos Minuvshego* 2, October 1922, 147.

14. RGALI, fond 1185, opis' 1, delo 113.

15. Ibid., l. 3, 4.

16. Letter from Taganka Prison Political Prisoners to Vera N. Figner, Boris I. Nicolaevsky Collection, box 586, file 34, Hoover Institution Archives.

17. Ibid.

18. Ibid.

19. Goldman, *Living My Life,* 2: 820.

20. Leonard Schapiro, *The Origin of the Communist Autocracy: Political Opposition in the Soviet State, First Phase, 1917–1922* (Cambridge, Mass.: Harvard University Press, 1977), 187–88.

21. Sheila Fitzpatrick, *The Russian Revolution, 1917–1932* (Oxford: Oxford University Press, 1982), 89.

22. Emma Goldman, *My Further Disillusionment in Russia* (Garden City, NY: Doubleday, Page and Company, 1924), 134.

23. Elizabeth Jones Hemenway, "Mothers of Communists: Women Revolutionaries and the Construction of a Soviet Identity," in *Gender and National Identity in Twentieth-Century Russian Culture,* eds. Helene Goscilo and Andrea Lanoux (DeKalb: Northern Illinois University Press, 2006), 77.

24. Sandra Pujals, "When Giants Walked the Earth: The Society of Former Political Prisoners and Exiles of the Soviet Union, 1921–1935," PhD diss., Georgetown University, 1999, 204.

25. In 1922 the Society of Former Political Prisoners and Exiles protested the arrest of a group of Social Revolutionaries who had been imprisoned under the old regime and secured their release. Pujals, "When Giants Walked the Earth," 196. For information about this 1922 arrest and trial that included a dozen former members of the SR party, see Leont'ev and Iur'ev, "Nezapechatlennyi trud," 438.

26. Richard Stites, "Iconoclastic Currents in the Russian Revolution: Destroying and Preserving the Past," in *Bolshevik Culture: Experiment and Order in the Russian Revolution,* eds. Abbot Gleason, Peter Kenez, and Richard Stites (Bloomington: Indiana University Press, 1985), 18.

27. V. I. Lenin qtd. in Iu.A. Krasovskii, "Zhenshchina russkoi revoliutsii: Literaturnye psikhologicheskie aspeky arkhiva Very Figner," *Vstrechi s proshlym,* vyp. 4 (1982): 351.

28. Hemenway, "Mothers of Communists," 79.

29. Letter from Vera Figner to Tatiana Sergeevna Stakhevich, dated October 12, 1920, RGALI, fond 1185, opis' 4, delo 18, l. 11.

30. Letter from Vera Figner to Tatiana Sergeevna Stakhevich, dated February 12, 1921 RGALI, fond 1185, opis' 4, delo 18, l. 17 ob.

31. Eugenia Semyonovna Ginzburg, *Journey into the Whirlwind,* trans. Paul Stevenson and Max Hayward (New York: Harcourt, 1995), 71–72.

32. Recollections of Galina I. Serebriakova, RGALI, fond 2594, opis' 1, delo 75, l. 52.

33. Ibid.

34. Ibid.

35. Ibid.

36. Ibid., l. 520b.

37. Ibid.

38. I. Porokhin, "Nezabyvaetaia Vstrecha," *Pravda Severa,* January 8, 1967, in RGALI, fond 2223, opis' 2, delo 295, l. 1.

39. Ibid., l. 1.

40. Ibid.

41. Hemenway, "Mothers of Communists," 80–85.

42. As Beth Holmgren's study of twentieth-century Russian women's autobiography has shown, "Narratives of committed oppositional self-sacrifice established an inspirational model for an entire generation." Beth Holmgren, "For the Good of the Cause: Russian Women's Autobiography in the Twentieth Century," in Toby W. Clyman and Diana Greene, eds., *Women Writers in Russian Literature* (Westport, Conn.: Greenwood Press, 1994), 129.

43. RGALI, fond 1185, opis' 4, delo 18, l. 100b.

44. RGALI, fond 1185, opis' 4, delo 18, l. 510b.

45. Finkel, *On the Ideological Front,* 95.

46. RGALI, fond 941, opis' 10, delo 649.

47. RGALI, fond 1185, opis' 1, delo 5. The government bestowed this pension on all the living conspirators in the March 1, 1881, assassination.

48. For description of earnings in the early Soviet period, see Mervyn Matthews, *Privilege in the Soviet Union: A Study of Elite Life-Styles under Communism* (London: Allen and Unwin, 1978), 67.

49. RGALI, fond 1185, opis' 4, delo 20, l. 2.

50. Letter from Vera Figner to Tatiana Stakhevich, dated September 8, 1931, RGALI, fond 1185, opis' 4, delo 19, l. 38 ob.

51. V. Figner, *Studencheskie gody,* 5–6.

52. Letter from Vera Figner to Natalia Peterovna Kuprianova, dated June 5, 1926, RGALI, fond 1185, opis' 1, delo 232, l. 2, l. 15

53. Letter from Vera Figner to Tatiana Stakhevich, dated April 26, 1920, RGALI, fond 1185, opis' 1, delo 18, l. 31.

54. Letter from Vera Figner to Tatiana Stakhevich, dated July 11, 1921, RGALI, fond 1185, opis' 1, delo 18, l. 27.

55. Letter from Vera Figner to Tatiana Stakhevich, dated November 3, 1929, RGALI, fond 1185, opis' 4, delo 19, l. 12.

56. Letter from Vera Figner to Tatiana Stakhevich, dated April 15, 1924, RGALI, fond 1185, opis' 4, delo 18, l. 540b.

57. Letter from Vera Figner to Tatiana Stakhevich, dated February 27, 1923, RGALI, fond 1185, opis' 4, delo 18, l. 47.

58. Dan, *Iz vstrech c V. N. Figner,* 10.

59. Ibid., 11.

60. Ibid., 12.

61. V. Figner, *V Borbe,* 225.

62. Dan, *Iz vstrech c V. N. Figner,* 12.

63. RGALI, fond 1185, opis' 4, delo 18, RGALI, fond 1185, opis' 4, delo 19.

64. Letter from Vera Figner to Sergei Stakhevich, dated September 1, 1931, RGALI, fond 1185, opis' 1, delo 244, l. 1.

65. Letter from Vera Figner to Tatiana Stakhevich, dated October 23, 1931, RGALI, fond 1185, opis' 4, delo 19, l. 420b.

66. Letter from Vera Figner to Tatiana Stakhevich, dated April 9, 1932, RGALI, fond 1185, opis' 4, delo 19, l. 350b.

67. Ibid.

68. V. Figner, "Avtobiografii Very Nikolaevny Figner," in *Deiateli SSSR,* 480.

69. V. Figner, *Posle Shlissel'burga,* 148.

70. Ibid.

71. Ibid.

72. Letter from Vera Figner to Natalia Kuprianova, dated July 1932, RGALI, fond 1185, opis' 1, delo 232, l. 1300b.

73. Boris I. Nicolaevsky Collection, box 479, folder 9, Hoover Institution Archives; Brupbacher Archive, file 51, International Institute of Social History; RGALI, fond 1185, opis' 4, delo 19.

74. Letter from Vera Figner to Boris Nicolaevsky, dated December 9, 1925, Boris I. Nicolaevsky Collection, box 479, folder 9, Hoover Institution Archives.

75. Hemenway, "Mothers of Communists," 84.

76. Letter from Vera Figner to Boris I. Nicolaevsky, dated December 9, 1925, Boris I. Nicolaevsky Collection, file 479, folder 9.

77. Letter from Vera Figner to Boris Nicolaevsky, dated December 23, 1925, Boris I. Nicolaevsky Collection, box 479, folder 9, Hoover Institution Archives.

78. Ibid.

79. Ibid.

80. V. Figner, "Avtobiografii Very Nikolaevny Figner," in *Deiateli SSSR,* 481.

81. Greetings from Imprisoned SRs to Vera Figner on July 7, 1922, RGALI, fond 1185, opis' 1, delo 113, l. 2.

82. Letter from Vera Figner to Natalia Kuprianova, dated August 19, 1931, RGALI, fond 1185, opis' 1, delo 232, l. 87.

83. GPU is the acronym for the Gosudarstvennoe politicheskoe upravlenie, which was the political police. Ibid., l. 87–98

84. Letter from Vera Figner to Emelian Iaroslavskii, dated December 23, 1925, RGALI, fond 1185, opis' 3, delo 9, l. 10b.

85. Letter of Old Revolutionaries to the Presidium of the TsIK, SSSR, RGALI, fond 1185, opis' 3, delo 1, l. 5–6. This letter can be read in its entirety in Leont'ev and Iur'ev, "Nezapechatlennyi trud," 433–36.

86. As Ia. V. Leont'ev and K. S. Iur'ev argue, since the letter's authors included a number of members of the People's Will, their denunciation of the death penalty indicates an evolution in their thinking away from violent revolutionary endeavors and toward legal social activity. See Leont'ev and Iur'ev, "Nezapechatlennyi trud," 430.

87. Letter from Vera Figner to Mikhail Ivanovich Kalinin, dated April 19, 1934, RGALI, fond 1185, opis' 1, delo 226, l. 1.

88. Prokhorov, *Bolshaia sovetskaia entsiklopediia,* 18: 248.

89. James E. Abbe, *I Photograph Russia* (New York: National Travel Club, 1934), 226.

90. Ibid., 227–31.

91. Letter from Vera Figner to Presidium of the Central Committee of the Society of Political Prisoners and Exiles, dated July 17, 1932, RGALI, fond 1185, opis' 1, delo 85, l. 2.

92. Ibid.

93. As Stephen F. Cohen contends, "How many Soviet citizens perished in the terror [un-

leashed by Stalin] is still a matter of dispute, even among specialists and even after consider-able (but not full) access to long secret archives. Leaving aside the nation's 26.5 million war deaths, considered estimates range from 12 to 20 million during Stalin's rule from 1929 to 1953." Stephen F. Cohen, *The Victims Return: Survivors of the Gulag after Stalin* (Exeter, N. H.: Publishing Works, 2010), 2.

94. Petrograd was renamed Leningrad after Lenin's death. Although the evidence re-mains circumstantial, it is widely believed that Stalin ordered Kirov's murder and then used it as an excuse to round up a vast assortment of so-called culprits.

95. Pujals, "When Giants Walked the Earth," 247.

96. Letter from Vera Figner to Tatiana Stakhevich, dated January 20, 1930, RGALI, fond 1185, opis' 4, delo 19, l. 20.

97. Letter from Vera Figner to Tatiana Stakhevich, dated November 3, 1929, RGALI, fond 1185, opis' 4, delo 19, l. 12.

98. RGALI, fond 1185, opis 4, delo 19.

99. Letter from Vera Figner to Fritz Brupbacher, dated July 1934, Brupbacher Archive, file 51, International Institute of Social History.

100. Ibid.

101. Letters from Vera Figner to Natasha Kuprianova, dated October 5 and October 8, 1934, RGALI, fond 1185, opis' 1, delo 232, l. 24–260b.

102. Letter from Vera Figner to Fritz Brupbacher, dated July 30, 1935, Brupbacher Archive, file 51, International Institute of Social History.

103. Richard Stites, *Revolutionary Dreams: Utopian Vision and Life Experiments in the Rus-sian Revolution* (New York: Oxford University Press, 1989), 226.

104. Qtd. in Krasovskii, "Zhenshchina russkoi revoliutsii," 351.

105. Qtd. in Pujals, "When Giants Walked the Earth," 229.

106. M. G. Sedov, "Sovetskaia literatura o teoretikakh Narodnichestva," *Istoriia i istoriki: Istoriografiia istorii SSSR* (Moscow: Izdatel'stvo Nauka 1965), 256.

107. Ibid.

108. Ibid.

109. Qtd. in ibid., 256–57.

110. Letter from Vera Figner to Frida Grigorevna Rappoport, dated April 8, 1937, RGALI, fond 1185, opis' 4, delo 4, l. 4.

111. Letter from Vera Figner to Tatiana Stakhevich, dated June 15, 1940, RGALI, fond 1185, opis' 4, delo 22, l. 41.

112. Ibid.

113. V. Figner, *V Borbe*, 226.

114. E. Iaroslavskii, "Umerla stareishaia revoliutsionerka," *Pravda*, June 16, 1942, 4.

115. Ibid.

116. Ibid.

117. "An Old Revolutionary Has Died," RGALI, fond 3102, opis' 1, delo 1352, l. 313.

118. Suny, *Soviet Experiment*, 325.

119. Iaroslavskii, "Umerla stareishaia revoliutsionerka," 4.

BIBLIOGRAPHY

ARCHIVAL SOURCES

GARF, Gosudarstvennyi arkhiv Rossiiskoi federatsii, Moscow, Russia
    fond 98, Shlissel'burgskaia tsentral'naia katorzhnaia tiur'ma
    fond 102, Departament Politsii
Hoover Institution Archives, Stanford University, Palo Alto, California
    Archives of the Soviet Communist Party and the Soviet State Microfilm Collection
    Axelbank Collection
    Boris I. Nicolaevsky Collection
    Frank A. Golder Collection
    Okhrana Collection
International Institute of Social History, Amsterdam, Netherlands
    Brupbacher Archive
RGALI, Rossiiskii gosudarstvennyi arkhiv literatury i iskusstva, Moscow, Russia
    fond 898, N. N. Figner
    fond 940, D. S. Bortniaskii
    fond 941, Gosudarstvennaia akademiia khudozhestvennyikh nauk
    fond 993, Sobranie teatral'nykh program
    fond 1185, V. N. Figner
    fond 1744, sobranie vospominanii narodovolets
    fond 2223, V. F. Panova
    fond 2594, G. I. Serebriakova
    fond 3102, V. G. Lidin
RGIA, Rossiiskii gosudarstvennyi istoricheskii arkhiv, St. Petersburg, Russia
    fond 1288, Glavnoe upravlenie po delam mestnogo khoziastva MVD
    fond 1328, Upravlenie dvortsovogo komendanta MIDV
    fond 1405, Ministerstvo iustitsii

PUBLISHED SOURCES

1 marta 1881 goda: Po neizdannym materialam. Petrograd: Izdatel'stvo Byloe, 1918. 13–62.
Abbe, James E. *I Photograph Russia.* New York: National Travel Club, 1934.
Andreyev, Olga Chernov. *Cold Spring in Russia.* Translated by Michael Carlisle. Ann Arbor, Mich.: Ardis Press, 1978.
Anon. Art. II: "The Zurich University. The Englishwoman's Review of Social and Industrial Questions." *Women's Journal* 4, no. 13 (1873): 6–11.
Anonymous news brief in *International Women Suffrage News* (8/11). May 1, 1917.

Ascher, Abraham. *The Revolution of 1905: A Short History*. Stanford, Calif.: Stanford University Press, 2004.

———. *The Revolution of 1905: Russia in Disarray*. Stanford, Calif.: Stanford University Press, 1988.

Ascher, William. "The Morality of Attitudes Supporting Intergroup Violence." *Political Psychology* 7, no. 3 (1986): 403–25.

Ashenbrenner, M. Iu. *Voennaia organizatsiia Narodnoi Voli i drugie vospominaniia, 1860–1904*. Moscow: Obshchestvo byvshikh politkatorzhan i ssyl'no-poselentsev, 1924.

Avrich, Paul. *Kronstadt, 1921*. Princeton, N.J.: Princeton University Press, 1970.

Baedeker, Karl. *Russia with Teheran, Port Arthur, and Peking: Handbook for Travelers*. Leipzig: Karl Baedeker, 1914.

———. *Switzerland and the Adjacent Portions of Italy, Savoy, and Tyrol*. Leipzig: Karl Baedeker, 1911.

Bakh, A. N. *Zapiski Narodovol'tsa*. Leningrad: Molodaia gvardiia, 1929.

Becker, Seymour. *Nobility and Privilege in Late Imperial Russia*. DeKalb: Northern Illinois University Press, 1985.

Bergman, Jay. *Vera Zasulich: A Biography*. Stanford, Calif.: Stanford University Press, 1983.

Billington, James H. *Fire in the Minds of Men: Origins of the Revolutionary Faith*. New York: Basic Books, 1980.

Block, Ed, Jr. "James Sully, Evolutionist Psychology, and Late Victorian Gothic Fiction." *Victorian Studies* 25 (Summer 1982): 443–67.

Blum, Jerome. "Russia." In *European Landed Elites in the Nineteenth Century*, edited by David Spring, 71–74. Baltimore: Johns Hopkins University Press, 1977.

Boniece, Sally "The Spiridonova Case, 1906: Terror, Myth, and Martyrdom." *Kritika: Explorations in Russian and Eurasian History* 4 (Summer 2003): 571–606.

Bonner, Thomas Neville. *To the Ends of the Earth: Women's Search for Higher Education*. Cambridge, Mass.: Harvard University Press, 1992.

Borozdin, K. A. "Sviashchennaia Druzhina i Narodnaia Volia." *Byloe* 10 (1907): 123–67.

Breshko-Breshkovkskaia, Ekaterina. *The Little Grandmother of the Russian Revolution: Reminiscences and Letters of Catherine Breshkovsky*. Edited by Alice Stone Blackwell. Westport, Conn.: Hyperion Press, 1973.

Broido, Vera. *Apostles into Terrorists: Women and the Revolutionary Movement in the Russia of Alexander II*. New York: Viking Press, 1977.

Browder, Robert Paul, and Alexander F. Kerensky, eds. *The Russian Provisional Government, 1917: Documents*. Stanford, Calif.: Stanford University Press, 1961.

Brower, Daniel R. *Training the Nihilists: Education and Radicalism in Tsarist Russia*. Ithaca, N.Y.: Cornell University Press, 1975.

Burnet-Vigniel, Marie Claude. *Femmes Russes dans le combat révolutionnaire: L'image et son modèle à la fin du XIXe siècle*. Paris: Institut d'études slaves, 1990.

Burtsev, Vladimir. *Za sto let, 1800–1896: Sbornik po istorii politicheskikh i obshchestvennykh dvizhenii v Rossii*. London: Russian Free Press Fund, 1897.

Castelli, Elizabeth A. *Martyrdom and Memory: Early Christian Culture Making*. New York: Columbia University Press, 2004.

Cavender, Mary W. *Nests of the Gentry: Family, Estate, and Local Loyalties in Provincial Russia*. Newark: University of Delaware Press, 2007.

Chamberlin, William. *The Russian Revolution: 1917–1921*. New York: Grosset and Dunlap, 1965.

Chartier, Roger. *The Cultural Origins of the French Revolution.* Translated by Lydia G. Cochrane. Durham, N.C.: Duke University Press, 1991.

Chernyshevskii, Nikolai. *What Is to Be Done?* Translated by Michael R. Katz. Ithaca, N.Y.: Cornell University Press, 1989.

Clements, Barbara, Barbara Alpern Engel, and Christine Worobec, eds. *Russia's Women: Accommodation, Resistance, Transformation.* Berkeley: University of California Press, 1991.

Clyman, Toby W., and Judith Vowles, eds. *Russia through Women's Eyes.* New Haven, Conn.: Yale University Press, 1996.

Cohen, Stephen F. *The Victims Return: Survivors of the Gulag after Stalin.* Exeter, N. H.: Publishing Works, 2010.

Corney, Frederick C. *Telling October: Memory and the Making of the Bolshevik Revolution.* Ithaca, N.Y.: Cornell University Press, 2004.

Crenshaw, Martha, ed. *Terrorism in Context.* University Park: Pennsylvania State University Press, 1995.

Curtis, William Elroy. *The Land of the Nihilist: Russia, Its People, Its Palaces, Its Politics.* Chicago: Belford, Clarke and Co., 1888.

Daly, Jonathan W. *Autocracy under Siege: Security Police and Opposition in Russia, 1866–1905.* DeKalb: Northern Illinois University Press, 1998.

———. "Political Crime in Later Imperial Russia." *Journal of Modern History* 74 (March 2002): 62–100.

Dan, Lidiia. *Iz vstrech c V. N. Figner.* New York: Inter-University Project on the Menshevik Movement, 1961.

Davis, Michael. "Incongruous Compounds: Re-reading Jekyll and Hyde and Late-Victorian Psychology." *Journal of Victorian Culture* 11 (Autumn 2006): 207–25.

De Beauvoir, Simone. *The Second Sex.* Translated by H. M. Parshley. New York: Vintage Books, 1989.

"Degaevshchina (materialy i dokumenty)." *Byloe* 4 (1906): 18–38.

"Dokumenty dlia istorii obshchestva Krasnago Kresta partii Narodnoi Voli." *Byloe* 3 (1906): 288–97.

"Dokumenty i materialy k istorii peregovorov Ispolnitel'nago Komiteta s Sviashchennoi Druzhinoi." *Byloe* 9 (1907): 208–13.

Dudgeon, Ruth A. "The Forgotten Minority: Women Students in Imperial Russia, 1972–1917." *Russian History* 9 (1982): 1–26.

Drozd, Andrew M. *Chernyshevskii's What Is to Be Done? A Reevaluation.* Evanston, Ill.: Northwestern University Press, 2001.

Efremova, N. P. "Pervye shagi russkikh zhenshchin k vysshemu obrazovaniiu." *Voprosy istorii* 5 (May 1983).

Easley, Roxanne. *The Emancipation of the Serfs in Russia: Peace Arbitrators and the Development of Civil Society.* London: Routledge 2009.

Emmons, Terrence. *The Russian Landed Gentry and the Peasant Emancipation of 1861.* Cambridge, U.K.: Cambridge University Press, 1968.

Engel, Barbara Alpern. *Breaking the Ties That Bound: The Politics of Marital Strife in Late Imperial Russia.* Ithaca, N.Y.: Cornell University Press, 2011.

———. *Mothers and Daughters: Women of the Intelligentsia in Nineteenth-Century Russia.* Evanston, Ill: Northwestern University Press, 2000.

———. "Transformation versus Tradition." In *Russia's Women: Accommodation, Resistance, Transformation,* edited by Barbara Evans Clements, Barbara Alpern Engel, and Christine D. Worobec, 135–47. Berkeley: University of California Press, 1991.

————. *Women in Russia, 1700–2000.* Cambridge, U.K.: Cambridge University Press, 2004.

————. "Women Medical Students in Russia, 1872–1882: Reformers or Rebels?" *Journal of Social History* 12 (1978): 394–414.

Engelstein, Laura. *The Keys to Happiness: Sex and the Search for Modernity in Fin-de-Siècle Russia.* Ithaca, N.Y.: Cornell University Press, 1992.

"Explosion in the Imperial Winter Palace." *Times* (London), February 19, 1880.

Field, Daniel. "The Year of Jubilee." In *Russia's Great Reforms, 1885–1881,* edited by Ben Eklof, John Bushnell, and Larissa Zakharova, 40–57. Bloomington: Indiana University Press, 1994.

Figner, N. N. *Vospominaniia, pis'ma, materialy.* Leningrad: Izdanie Muzyka, 1968.

Figner, Vera. "Evgeniia Nikolaevna Figner." *Katorga i Ssylka* 2 (1924): 20–27.

————. "Iz avtobiografii Very Figner." *Byloe* 2 (August 1917): 153–82.

————. "Iz avtobiografii Very Figner." *Byloe* 3 (September 1917): 166–91.

————. "Iz avtobiografii Very Figner." *Byloe* 4 (October 1917): 57–89.

————. "Avtobiografii Very Nikolaevny Figner." In *Deiateli SSSR: Revoliutsionnogo dvizheniia Rossi: Entsiklopedicheskii slovar' Granat.* Moscow: Sovetskaia Entsiklopediia, 1989.

————. *Parizhskii komitet pomoshchi politicheskim katorzhanam, otchet za 1911-i god.* Paris: 1912.

————. *Polnoe sobranie sochinenii v semi tomakh.* Moscow: Izdatel'stvo vsesoiuznogo obshchestva politkatorzhan i ssyl'no-poselentsev, 1932.

————. *Posle Shlissel'burga.* Leningrad: Kolos, 1925.

————. *Shlissel'burgskie uzniki, 1884–1905g.: Biograficheskie ocherki.* Moscow: Zadruga, 1920.

————. *Studencheskie gody.* Moscow: Golos Truda, 1924.

————. *V Borbe.* Leningrad: Izdatel'stvo Detskaia Literatura, 1966.

————. *Zapechatlennyi trud: Vospominaniia v dvukh tomakh.* Moscow: Izdatel'stvo sotsialno-economicheskoi literatury Mysl, 1964.

Filippova, L. D. "Iz istorii zhenskogo obrazovaniia v Rossii." *Voprosy istorii* (February 1963).

Finkel, Stuart. *On the Ideological Front: The Russian Intelligentsia and the Making of the Soviet Public Sphere.* New Haven, Conn.: Yale University Press, 2007.

Fitzpatrick, Sheila. *The Russian Revolution, 1917–1932.* Oxford: Oxford University Press, 1982.

Footman, David. *Red Prelude: A Life of A. I. Zheliabov.* London: Barrie and Rockliff, 1968.

Foucault, Michel. *Discipline and Punish: The Birth of the Prison.* Translated by Alan Sheridan. New York: Vintage Books, 1979.

Freeze, Gregory L. "Bringing Order to the Russian Family: Marriage and Divorce in Imperial Russia, 1760–1860." *Journal of Modern History* 62, no. 4 (1990): 709–47.

————. "Krylov vs. Krylova: 'Sexual Incapacity' and Divorce in Tsarist Russia." In *The Human Tradition in Modern Russia,* edited by William B. Husband. Wilmington, Del.: Scholarly Resources, 2000.

Frolenko, Mikhail. *Sobranie sochinenii v dvukh tomakh.* Moscow: Izdatel'stvo vsesoiuznogo obshchestva politkatorzhan i ssyl'no-poselentsev, 1932.

Fulop-Miller, Rene. *The Mind and Face of Bolshevism: An Examination of Cultural Life in Soviet Russia.* New York: Knopf, 1928.

Gawande, Atul. "Hellhole." *New Yorker,* March 30, 2009, 36–45.

Geifman, Anna. *Thou Shalt Kill: Revolutionary Terrorism in Russia, 1894–1917.* Princeton, N.J.: Princeton University Press, 1993.

Ginzburg, Eugenia Semyonovna. *Journey into the Whirlwind.* Translated by Paul Stevenson and Max Hayward. New York: Harcourt, 1995.

Godunova, L. N. "Arkhivnye istochniki o voennoi organizatsii partii Narodnaia Volia." *Sovetskie Arkhivy* 1 (1971): 77–83.

Goldman, Emma. *Living My Life*. New York: Dover Publications, 1970.

———. *My Disillusionment in Russia*. New York: Thomas Y. Cromwell, 1970.

———. *My Further Disillusionment in Russia*. Garden City, NY: Doubleday, Page, and Company, 1924.

Grant, Steven A. *The Russian Nanny Real and Imagined: History, Culture, and Mythologizing*. Washington, D.C.: New Academia Publishing, 2012.

Grosz, Elizabeth. *Volatile Bodies: Towards a Corporeal Feminism*. Bloomington: Indiana University Press, 1994.

Habermas, Jürgen. *The Structural Transformation of the Public Sphere: An Inquiry into a Category of Bourgeois Society*. Translated by Thomas Burger. Cambridge: MIT Press, 1991.

Hardy, Deborah. *Land and Freedom: The Origins of Russian Terrorism, 1876–1879*. Westport, Conn: Greenwood Press, 1987.

Haruki, Wada. "Vera Figner in the Early Post-Revolutionary Period." *Annals of the Institute of Social Science* 25 (1983–1984): 43–73.

Hemenway, Elizabeth Jones, "Mothers of Communists: Women Revolutionaries and the Construction of Soviet Identity." In *Gender and National Identity in Twentieth Century Russian Culture*, edited by Helena Goscilo and Andrea Lanoux, 75–92. DeKalb, Illinois: Northern University Press, 2006.

Heldt, Barbara. *Terrible Perfection: Women and Russian Literature*. Bloomington: Indiana University Press, 1987.

Hesse, Carla. *The Other Enlightenment: How French Women Became Modern*. Princeton, N.J.: Princeton University Press, 2001.

Hoffman, Bruce. *Inside Terrorism*. New York: Columbia University Press, 2006.

Holmgren, Beth. "For the Good of the Cause: Russian Women's Autobiography in the Twentieth Century." In *Women Writers in Russian Literature*, edited by Toby W. Clyman and Diana Greene, 127–48. Westport, Conn.: Greenwood Press, 1994.

Hoogenboom, Hilde. "Vera Figner and Revolutionary Autobiographies: The Influence of Gender on Genre." In *Women in Russia and Ukraine*, edited by Rosalind Marsh, 78–93. Cambridge, U.K.: Cambridge University Press, 1996.

"How the All-Russian League of Women's Enfranchisement Strove to Obtain Electoral Rights for Russian Women during the Revolution." *International Women's News* 2/12. November 1, 1917.

Iakimova, Anna. "Iz dalekogo proshlogo (Iz vospominanii o pokusheniiakh na Aleksandra II)." *Katorga i Ssylka* 1 (1924): 9–17.

Iakimova-Dikovskaia, A. V., M. F. Frolenko, et al., eds. *"Narodnaia Volia" v dokumentakh i vospominaniiakh*. Moscow: Izdatel'stvo obshchestva politkatorzhan, 1930.

Iaroslavskii, E. "Umerla stareishaia revoliutsionerka." *Pravda*, June 16, 1942.

Iuvatshev, I. P. *The Russian Bastille*. Translated by A. S. Rappoport. London: Chatto and Windus, 1909.

Ivanchin-Pisarev, A. I. *Khozhdenie v narod*. Moscow: Molodaia Gvardiia, 1929.

"Iz 'obzora' sostavlennago departamentom politsii za 1882 god." *Byloe* 11 (1906): 244–62.

"Iz pokazanii Iu. N. Bogdanovicha 22 sentiabria 1882 g." *Krasnyi arkhiv* 1 (1927): 212–14.

Johanson, Christine. *Women's Struggle for Higher Education in Russia, 1885–1900*. Buffalo, N.Y.: McGill-Queen's University Press, 1987.

"K istorii narodovol'cheskogo dvizheniia sredi voennykh v nachale 80-kh godov." *Byloe* 8 (1906): 158–87.

Kan, G. S. *"Narodnaia Volia": Ideologiia i lidery.* Moscow: Izdatel'stvo Probel, 1997.

Kantor, P. "K istorii voennoi organizatsii 'Narodnoi Voli,' pokazaniia F. I. Zavalishina." *Katorga i Ssylka* 5 (1925): 210–40.

Kellen, Konrad. *Terrorists: What Are They Like?* Santa Monica, Calif.: Rand Corporation, 1970.

Kel'ner, Viktor. *1 marta 1881 goda: Kazn' Imperatora Aleksandra II, dokumenty i vospominaniia.* Leningrad: Lenizdat, 1991.

King, Charles. *Odessa: Genius and Death in a City of Dreams.* New York: W. W. Norton, 2011.

Knight, Amy. "The Fritschi: A Study of Female Radicals in the Russian Populist Movement." *Canadian-American Slavic Studies* 9 (Spring 1975): 1–17.

Koblitz, Ann Hibner. *Science, Women, and Revolution in Russia.* Amsterdam: Harwood Academic, 2000.

Kolchin, Peter. *Unfree Labor: American Slavery and Russian Serfdom.* Cambridge, Mass.: Belknap Press, 1987.

Kollontai, Alexandra. *Rabotnitsa za god revoliutsii.* Moscow: Knigoizdatel'stvo Kommunist, 1918.

Kon, F. Ia., and Vladimir Dmitrievich Vilenskii, eds. *Deiateli revoliutsionnogo dvizheniia v Rossii bio-bibliograficheskii slovar': ot predshestvennikov dekabristov do padeniia tsarizm,* vol. 2, vypusk III. Moscow: Izd-vo politkatorzhan, 1927.

Korelin, A. P. *Dvoriantsvo v poreformennoi Rossii 1861–1904gg.: Sostav, chislennost', korporativaia organizatsiia.* Moscow: Izdatel'stvo Nauka, 1979.

Krasovskii, Iu. A. "Zhenshchina russkoi revoliutsii: Literaturnye i psikhologicheskie aspeky arkhiva Very Figner." *Vstrechi s proshlym.,* vyp. 4 (1982): 330–63.

Kravchinskii, Sergei. *Underground Russia: Revolutionary Profiles and Sketches from Life.* New York: Charles Scribner's Sons, 1883.

Kropotkin, Peter. *Memoirs of a Revolutionist.* New York: Horizon Press, 1968.

Kulyabko-Koretsky, N. G. *Iz davnikh let: Vospominaniia Lavrista.* Moscow: Izdatel'stvo vsesoiuznogo obshchestva politkatorzhan i ssyl'no-poselentsev, 1931.

Landes, Joan. *Visualizing the Nation: Gender, Representation, and Revolution in Eighteenth-Century France.* Ithaca, N.Y.: Cornell University Press, 2001.

———. *Women and the Public Sphere in the Age of the French Revolution.* Ithaca, N.Y.: Cornell University Press, 1990.

Lauchlan, Iain. "The Okhrana: Security Policing in Late Imperial Russia." In *Late Imperial Russia: Problems and Prospects,* edited by Ian D. Thatcher, 44–63. Manchester, U.K.: Manchester University Press, 2005.

Lavrov, P. L. *Gody emigratsii: Arkhivnye materialy v dvukh tomakh.* Edited by Boris Sapir. Dordrecht, Holland: D. Reidel, 1974.

Leont'ev, Ia. V., and K. S. Iur'ev. "Nezapechatlennyi trud: Iz arkhiva V. N. Figner." *Zven'ia* 2 (1992): 424–88.

Letopis' zhizni i tvorchestva A. M. Gorkogo. Moscow: Izdatel'stvo Akademii Nauk SSSR, 1959.

Lincoln, W. Bruce. *The Great Reforms: Autocracy, Bureaucracy, and the Politics of Change in Imperial Russia.* DeKalb: Northern Illinois University Press, 1990.

———. *Red Victory: A History of the Russian Civil War, 1918–1921.* New York: Da Capo Press, 1989.

Literatura partii "Narodnaia Volia." Moscow: Izdatel'stvo vsesoiuznogo obshchestva politkatorzhan i ssyl'no-poselentsev, 1930.

Liubatovich, Olga. *Dalekoe i nedavnee*. Moscow: Izdatel'stvo vsesoiuznogo obshchestva polit-katorzhan i ssyl'no-poselentsev, 1930.

Logachev, Constantine, ed. *The Peter and Paul Fortress*. Translated by Kathleen Carroll. Leningrad: Aurora Art, 1989.

"M. Kerensky at Odessa." *Times* (London), June 4, 1917.

Makletsova, N. P. "Sudeikin i Degaev." *Byloe* 8 (1906): 265–72.

Manucharov, I. "Epizod iz zhizni v Shlissel'burgskoi kreposti." *Byloe* 8 (1906): 81–83.

Markov, O. "Ekaterina Pavlovna Peshkova i ee pomoshch politzakliuchennym." *Pamiat*, vyp. 1 (1976): 314–19.

Marshall, Alex. *The Caucasus under Soviet Rule*. New York: Routledge, 2010.

Matthews, Mervyn. *Privilege in the Soviet Union: A Study of Elite Life-Styles under Communism*. London: Allen and Unwin, 1978.

McKinsey, Pamela Sears. "The Kazan Square Demonstration and the Conflict between Russian Workers and *Intelligenty*." *Slavic Review* 44, no. 1 (1985): 83–103.

McReynolds, Louise. "Witnessing for the Defense: The Adversarial Court and Narratives of Criminal Behavior in Nineteenth-Century Russia." *Slavic Review* 69 (Fall 2010): 620–44.

Meijer, J. M. *Knowledge and Revolution: The Russian Colony in Zurich, 1870–1873*. Assen, Netherlands: Van Gorcum and Co., 1955.

"Melikoff's [Melikov's] Pacification." *Times* (London), November 13, 1880, 6.

Mikhailovskii, N. K. *Vospominaniia*. Berlin: Izdanie Gugo Shteineshcha, 1906.

Minim, D. "Eshche o Politicheskom Krasnom Kreste." *Pamiat*, vyp. 3. Moscow (1978)/Paris, (1980): 523–34.

Mondry, Henrietta. "With Short Cropped Hair: Gleb Uspensky's Struggle against Biological Gender Determinism." *Russian Review* 63 (2004): 479–92.

Morozov, N. A. *Povesti moei zhizni*. Moscow: Izdatel'stvo Nauka, 1965.

Morrissey, Susan K. "The Apparel of Innocence: Toward a Moral Economy of Terrorism in Late Imperial Russia." *Journal of Modern History* 84 (September 2012): 607–42.

"Narodnaia Volia"—Degaevshchina—Protsess 14-ti. St. Petersburg: Izdanie i tipografiia S. M. Propper, 1907.

Narodovol'tsy posle 1-go marta 1881 goda. Moscow: Izdatel'stvo vsesoiuznogo obshchestva politkatorzhan i ssyl'no-poselentsev, 1928.

"Narodovol'tsy v Saratovskii gubernii." *Sovetskie arkhivy* 2 (1991).

Novaia Zhizn', April 9, 1918.

Novorusskii, Mikhail. *Zapiski Shlissel'burgzhtsa, 1887–1905*. Edited by N. A. Morozov. Moscow: Izdatel'stvo vsesoiuznogo obshchestva politkatorzhan i ssyl'no-poselentsev, 1933.

Ohsol, J.B. "Concerning Women Suffrage in Russia." *Women's Journal* 1, no. 1 (1917).

Orlovsky, Daniel T. "The Provisional Government and Its Cultural Work." In *Bolshevik Culture: Experiment and Order in the Russian Revolution*, edited by Abbot Gleason, Peter Kenez, and Richard Stites, 39–56. Bloomington: Indiana University Press, 1985.

"Ot Shlissel'burgskago Komiteta." *Byloe* 1 (January 1906): 315–16.

Pankratov, V. S. *Zhizn' v Shlissel'burgskoi kreposti, 1884–1898*. Petrograd: Izdatel'stvo Byloe, 1922.

Paper, Robert A. *Dying to Win: The Strategic Logic of Suicide Terrorism*. New York: Random House, 2006.

Patyk, Lynn. "Dressed to Kill and Die: Russian Revolutionary Terrorism, Gender, and Dress." *Jahrbucher für Geschichte-Osteuropas* 58, no. 2 (2010): 192–209.

Pipes, Richard. *The Degaev Affair: Terror and Treason in Tsarist Russia*. New Haven, Conn.: Yale University Press, 2003.

Pirumova, N. M. *Peter Alekseevich Kropotkin*. Moscow: Izdatel'stvo Nauka, 1972.

"Pokushenie na zhizn' gosudaria imperatora," *Sankt-Peterburgskikh Vedomostei*, Osoboe pribavlenie, 2 (14) Marta 1881.

Polonskaia, M. N. "K istorii partii Narodnaia Volia." *Byloe* 6 (1907): 1–11.

Pomper, Philip. *The Russian Revolutionary Intelligentsia*. New York: Thomas Y. Crowell, 1970.

———. *Sergei Nechaev*. New Brunswick, N.J.: Rutgers University Press, 1979.

Popov, M. P. "Iz moego revoliutsionnago proshlago (1878–1879gg.)." *Byloe* 7 (1907): 241–79.

Pribyleva-Korba, A. P. "*Narodnaia Volia*": *Vospominaniia o 1870–1880-kh gg*. Moscow: Vsesoiznoe obshchestvo politicheskikh katorzhan i ssyl'no-poselentsev, 1926.

———, and Vera Figner. *Narodovolets Aleksandr Dmitrievich Mikhailov*. Leningrad: Gosudarstvennoe Izdatel'stvo, 1925.

Prokhonov, A. M., ed. *Bolshaia sovetskaia entsiklopediia*. Moscow: Izdatel'stvo Sovetskaia Entsiklopediia, 1977.

Protopopov, A. D. "Predsmertnaia zapiska s predisloviem P. R. Russa." *Golos Minuvshego na Chuznoi Storone* 15, no. 2 (1926).

Pujals, Sandra. "When Giants Walked the Earth: The Society of Former Political Prisoners and Exiles of the Soviet Union, 1921–1935." PhD diss. Georgetown University, 1999.

Rabinowitch, Alexander. *The Bolsheviks Come to Power: The Revolution of 1917 in Petrograd*. New York: W. W. Norton, 1976.

———. *The Bolsheviks in Power: The First Year of Soviet Rule in Petrograd*. Bloomington: Indiana University Press, 2007.

Radkey, Oliver H. *Russia Goes to the Polls: The Election to the All-Russian Constituent Assembly, 1917*. Ithaca, N.Y.: Cornell University Press, 1990.

Ransel, David L, ed. *The Family in Imperial Russia*. Urbana: University of Illinois Press, 1978.

"Recall of Russian Female Medical Students from Zurich." *Boston Medical Surgical Journal* 89, 1873.

"Rech Very Nikolaevny Figner (Filippovoi) proiznesesnnoe eye v Peterburgskom voenno-okhruzhnom sude 27 sentiabria 1884 goda." *Listok Narodnoi Voli* 3 (November 1886).

"Reds Arrest Relief Workers." *Times* (London), September 1, 1921.

Robinson, Geroid Tanquary. *Rural Russia under the Old Regime*. Berkeley: University of California Press, 1932.

Roosevelt, Priscilla. *Life on the Russian Country Estate: A Social and Cultural History*. New Haven, Conn.: Yale University Press, 1995.

"Russian Medical Students." *Times* (London), June 10, 1873.

"Russian Women Students at Zurich." *New York Times*, July 16, 1873.

Ruthchild, Rochelle Goldberg. *Equality and Revolution: Women's Rights in the Russian Empire, 1905–1917*. Pittsburgh: University of Pittsburgh Press, 2010.

Sazhin, M. P. "Russke v Tsiurikhe." *Katorga i Ssylka* 10 (1932): 25–79.

———. (Armand Ross). *Vospominaniia, 1860–1880x g.g.* Moscow: Vsesoiznoe obshchestvo politicheskikh katorzhan i ssyl'no-poselentsev, 1925.

Schapiro, Leonard. *The Origins of the Communist Autocracy: Political Opposition in the Soviet State, First Phase, 1917–1922*. Cambridge, Mass.: Harvard University Press, 1977.

Sedov, M. G. "Sovetskaia literatura o teoretikakh Narodnichestva." In *Istoriia i istoriki: Istoriografiia istorii SSSR*, edited by Institut Istorii (Akademiia Nauk SSSR), 240–69, Moscow: Izdatel'stvo Nauka 1965.

Semenov, V. P. *Polnoe geograficheskoe opisanie nashego otechestva*. St. Petersburg: Izdanie A. F. Devriena, 1901.

Senn, Alfred Erich. *The Russian Revolution in Switzerland, 1914–1917*. Madison: University of Wisconsin Press, 1971.

Shanin, Teodor. *Russia, 1905–1907: Revolution as a Moment of Truth*. New Haven, Conn.: Yale University Press, 1986.

Shchegolev, P. "Posle pervogo marta 1881 goda." *Byloe* 3 (1907): 290–306.

Siegelbaum, Lewis. *Soviet State and Society between Revolutions, 1918–1929*. Cambridge, U.K.: Cambridge University Press, 1992.

Siljak, Ana. *Angel of Vengeance: The "Girl Assassin," the Governor of St. Petersburg, and Russia's Revolutionary World*. New York: St. Martin's, 2008.

Soveta St. Peterburgskoi biologicheskoi laboratorii P. F. Lesgafta. Edited by Pamiati Petra Frantsevicha Lesgafta. St. Petersburg: Shkola i zhizn, 1912.

Spandoni, A. A. "Stranitsa iz vospominaniia." *Byloe* 5 (1906): 14–36.

Spring, David, ed. *European Landed Elites in the Nineteenth Century*. Baltimore: Johns Hopkins University Press, 1977.

Stepanov, A. P. "Shveitsartsy v Rossii i russkie v shveitsarii." *Novaia i noveishaia istoriia* 1 (2006): 120–51.

Stites, Richard. "Iconoclastic Currents in the Russian Revolution: Destroying and Preserving the Past." In *Bolshevick Culture: Experiment and Order in the Russian Revolution*, edited by Abbot Gleason, Peter Konez, and Richard Sites, 1–24. Bloomington: Indiana University Press, 1985.

———. *Revolutionary Dreams: Utopian Visions and Experimental Life in the Russian Revolution*. New York: Oxford University Press, 1989.

———. *The Women's Liberation Movement in Russia: Feminism, Nihilism, and Bolshevism, 1860–1930*. Princeton, N.J.: Princeton University Press, 1978.

Stoiunipa, V. Ya. "Obrazovanie russkoi zhenshchiny (po povodu dvatsatipiatiletia russkikh zhenskikh gimnazii)." *Istoricheskii vestnik* 12 (April 1883).

Suny, Ronald Grigor. *The Soviet Experiment: Russia, the USSR, and the Successor States*. New York: Oxford University Press, 1998.

"The Doom of the Czar." *New York Times*, December 25, 1879.

Tikhomirov, Lev. "Neizdannye zapiski L. Tikhomirova." *Krasnyi arkhiv* 4 (1928): 154–74.

Tovrov, Jessica. *The Russian Noble Family: Structure and Change*. New York: Garland, 1987.

Troinitskii, Alexander. *Krepostnoe naselenie v Rossii, po 10-i narodnoi perepisi*. St. Petersburg: Izdanie statisticheskago otdela tsentral'nago statisticheskago komiteta, 1861.

Troitskii, N. A. "Protsess 14-ti." *Sovetskoe gosudarstvo i pravo* 9 (1984): 119–26.

———. "Vospominaniia Very Figner, zapisannye akademikom N. M. Druzhinym." *Sovetskie arkhivy* 2 (1987): 64–66.

Turgenev, Ivan. *Fathers and Sons*. Translated by Rosemary Edmonds. New York: Penguin, 1975.

Turton, Katy. "Keeping It in the Family: Surviving Political Exile, 1870–1917." *Canadian Slavonic Papers* 52 (September-December 2010): 396–407.

Tyrkov, A. V. *K sobytiiu 1 marta 1881 goda*. Rostov-on-Don, Russia: Tipografiia donskaia rech, 1906.

Ulam, Adam B. *Prophets and Conspirators in Prerevolutionary Russia*. New Brunswick, N.J.: Transaction, 1998.

Valenze, Deborah. *The First Industrial Woman*. New York: Oxford University Press, 1995.

Valk, S. N., ed. *Arkhiv "Zemli i Voli" i "Narodnoi Voli."* Moscow: Izdatel'stvo politkatorzhan, 1932.

———. "Pobeg Sergeia Degaeva." *Krasnyi arkhiv* 6 (1929): 219–22.

Venturi, Franco. *Roots of Revolution: A History of the Populist and Socialist Movements in Nineteenth-Century Russia*. Translated by Francis Haskell. New York: Knopf, 1960.

Verhoeven, Claudia. *The Odd Man Karakozov: Imperial Russia, Modernity, and the Birth of Modern Terrorism*. Ithaca, N.Y.: Cornell University Press, 2009.

Vodovozova, E. N. *Na zare zhizni*. Moscow: Izdatel'stvo Khudozhestvennaia literatura, 1964.

Volk, S. S. *Narodnaia Volia, 1879–1882*. Moscow: Izdatel'stvo Nauka, 1966.

———, ed. *"Narodnaia Volia" i "Chernyi Peredel": Vospominaniia uchastnikov revoliutsionnogo dvizheniia v Peterburge v 1879–1882gg*. Leningrad: Lenizdat, 1989.

Voronikhin, Andrei Vladimirovich. "V. N. Figner v russkom osvoboditel'nom dvizhenii 1873–1884gg." PhD diss., Saratov University, 1992.

Wachtel, Andrew. *The Battle for Childhood: Creation of a Russian Myth*. Stanford, Calif.: Stanford University Press, 1990.

Wade, Rex A., and Scott J. Seregny, eds. *Politics and Society in Provincial Russia: Saratov, 1590–1917*. Columbus: Ohio State University Press, 1989.

"Women Students at Zurich," *Women's Journal* 4, no. 29 (1873): 231.

Wood, Elizabeth. *The Baba and the Comrade: Gender and Politics in Revolutionary Russia*. Bloomington: Indiana University Press, 1997.

Wortman, Richard S. *Scenarios of Power: Myth and Ceremony in Russian Monarchy, From Peter the Great to the Abdication of Nicholas II*. Princeton, N.J.: Princeton University Press, 2006.

Yarmolinsky, Avraham. *Road to Revolution: A Century of Russian Radicalism*. New York: Collier Books, 1968.

Zaionchkovskii, P. A. *The Russian Autocracy in Crisis, 1878–1882*. Translated and edited by Gary M. Hamburg. Gulf Breeze, Fla.: Academic International Press, 1979.

Zuckerman, Frederic S. *The Tsarist Secret Police Abroad: Policing Europe in a Modernizing World*. New York: Palgrave Macmillan, 2003.

INDEX

Tetiushi: Alexei Filippov's move to, 31; description of, 3–5; Figner life in, 3; VNF's move from, 63; VNF's philanthropic work in, 187, 246, 252; VNF's return after Switzerland, 68; VNF's return after Revolution, 249
thick journals, 25–26, 266n67
Tikhanovich, A. P., 144
Tikhomirov, Lev, 128, 132
Tolstoi, Count Dmitrii, 138
Trepov, General Fyodor, 79, 92
Trial of the Fifty, 73–75
Trial of the Fourteen, 136–37, 142–44, 148–49, 285n39
Trial of the 193, 78–79, 275n87
Trial of the Sixteen, 110
Trigoni, Mikhail, 109
Trotsky, Lev, 214
tsaricide, 97, 134–35
Tsemirov, General, V. M., 143, 145
Turgenev, Ivan, 39, 268n22
Turton, Katy, 182

Ulam, Adam, 76
underground mines, 99, 102, 108, 110–11; on Malaia Sadovaia Street, 111–13, 119
Union of Equal Rights for Women, 191
University of Kazan, 31, 35–36
University of Zurich, 29–30, 34, 36–40, 51–55, 59, 68
Uspensky, Gleb, 115–16, 129, 169

Vania, 182–83
Velikie Luki, 221, 223
Verhoeven, Claudia, 97
Viazmin, 81–83, 94
Vodovozova, Elizaveta, 17
Volkenstein, Ludmila: correspondence with VNF, 184; death, 186; friendship with VNF, 159; idolization of, 167–70; incarceration, 154, 165; protests, 160–61; release from Shlisselburg, 171; Trial of the Fourteen, 144; VNF's biography of, 186, 199

Voronezh meeting, 94–96
Vpered!, 47
Vyborg, VNF's move to, 192

Wachtel, Andrew, 32, 263n1
What Is to Be Done?, 16–17, 26, 47, 266n68
women: debate about in Zurich, 51–53; liberation, 106; limited education options, 12; limited public opportunities for, 27; maligning of character of women in Zurich, 49–51; oppression, 41; in People's Will, 100; quest of autonomy, 41; in revolutionary movements, 129; subordinate position, 11
Women's Medical Courses, 53
women's suffrage: 206–207
World War I: Bolshevik policy, 216; effect on VNF's condition, 201; Lenin's position on, 201; Provisional Government stance on, 212; Russian withdrawal, 222; start of hostilities, 201; VNF's position on, 201

Zaionchkovskii, Peter, 135
Zapechatlennyi trud: influence, 243; publication, 242
Zasulich, Vera: acquittal, 136, 275n91; Culture and Liberty, 219; funeral for victims of the February Revolution, 207; representative of Political Red Cross, 126; shooting of Trepov, 79, 92, 100; stature, 189, 211, 240
Zavalishin, F. I., 123
Zemlia i volia. See Land and Freedom
Zheliabov, Andrei: arrest, 112, 114; creation of People's Will, 94; execution, 122; irrelevance for Stalin, 257; irritation with VNF, 109; leadership, 118, 125, 144; legendary status, 243; terrorist plots, 103, 112
Zhelvakov, Nikolai, 126–27
Zurich: center of learning and science, 38; description of, 37–41; radical activity in, 39–40; Russian colony in, 40–56, 59, 61–62, 68; VNF's in exile in, 196

LYNNE ANN HARTNETT is an assistant professor of history at Villanova University. She is the director of Villanova's Russian Area Studies program and of Villanova's Center for the Study of Violence and Conflict. She lives in Bucks County, Pennsylvania, with her husband, three children, and miniature schnauzer.